STUDIES IN IMPERIALISM

general editor John M. MacKenzie

When the 'Studies in Imperialism' series was founded more than twenty years ago, emphasis was laid upon the conviction that 'imperialism as a cultural phenomenon had as significant an effect on the dominant as on the subordinate societies'. With more than fifty books published, this remains the prime concern of the series. Cross-disciplinary work has indeed appeared covering the full spectrum of cultural phenomena, as well as examining aspects of gender and sex, frontiers and law, science and the environment, language and literature, migration and patriotic societies, and much else. Moreover, the series has always wished to present comparative work on European and American imperialism, and particularly welcomes the submission of books in these areas. The fascination with imperialism, in all its aspects, shows no sign of abating, and this series will continue to lead the way in encouraging the widest possible range of studies in the field. 'Studies in Imperialism' is fully organic in its development, always seeking to be at the cutting edge, responding to the latest interests of scholars and the needs of this ever-expanding area of scholarship.

Rethinking settler colonialism

Manchester University Press

Rethinking settler colonialism

HISTORY AND MEMORY IN AUSTRALIA, CANADA, AOTEAROA NEW ZEALAND AND SOUTH AFRICA

edited by Annie E. Coombes

MANCHESTER UNIVERSITY PRESS
Manchester and New York

distributed exclusively in the USA by Palgrave

Published by Manchester University Press
Oxford Road, Manchester M13 9NR, UK
and Room 400, 175 Fifth Avenue, New York, NY 10010, USA
www.manchesteruniversitypress.co.uk

Distributed in the United States exclusively by
Palgrave Macmillan, 175 Fifth Avenue,
New York, NY 10010, USA

Distributed in Canada exclusively by
UBC Press, University of British Columbia, 2029 West Mall,
Vancouver, BC, Canada V6T 1Z2

British Library Cataloguing-in-Publication Data is available

Library of Congress Cataloging-in-Publication Data is available

ISBN 978 0 7190 7169 0 paperback

First published by Manchester University Press in hardback 2006

This paperback edition first published 2011

Printed by Lightning Source

CONTENTS

[v]

CONTENTS

FIGURES

NOTES ON CONTRIBUTORS

Brook Andrew is an interdisciplinary conceptual artist whose work is based around photo-media, installation and neon. He is known for his comments on cultural and international perspectives on race, celebrity and politics, from a Wiradjuri (Aboriginal Australian) position. His work has been exhibited widely both in Australia and internationally (www.brookandrew.com).

Leonard Bell is Associate Professor of Art History at the University of Auckland. His books include *Colonial Constructs* (1992) and *The Maori in European Art* (1980); and he has contributed essays to *Orientalism Transformed: The Impact of the Colonies on British Culture* (1998) and *Double Vision: Art Histories and Colonial Histories in the Pacific* (1999).

Deborah Bird Rose is Senior Fellow at the Centre for Research and Environmental Studies, Institute of Advanced Studies, the Australian National University. She is the author of *Country of the Heart: An Indigenous Australian Homeland* (2002), *Nourishing Terrains, Australian Aboriginal Views of Landscape and Wilderness*, *Dingo Makes Us Human* (winner of the 1992–93 Stanner Prize), and *Hidden Histories* (winner of the 1991 Jessie Litchfield Award). Her work in both scholarly and practical arenas is focused on social and ecological justice.

Christine Boyanoski is an independent art historian, curator and lecturer. Her doctoral thesis was 'Decolonising Visual Culture: Canada, Australia, New Zealand and South Africa and the Imperial Exhibitions 1919–1939', and her research interests include the legacy of Empire in Great Britain and the former colonies. She has curated many exhibitions and published extensively on Canadian art in scholarly journals, including the *Oxford Art Journal*.

Annie E. Coombes teaches at Birkbeck College, University of London, in the School of History of Art, Film and Visual Media, where she is Professor of Material and Visual Culture. She is the author of *Reinventing Africa: Museums, Material Culture and Popular Imagination* (1994); *History After Apartheid: Visual Culture and Public Memory in a Democratic South Africa* (2003); *Berni Searle: Memories are Made of This* (2003), and co-editor (with Avtar Brah) of *Hybridity and its Discontents: Politics, Science, Culture* (2000). She is a member of the editorial collective of *Feminist Review* and the editorial board of *Third Text*.

Elizabeth Furniss is an Assistant Professor of anthropology at the University of Calgary. Her scholarly interests include the anthropology of colonialism and contemporary Aboriginal–settler relations in Canada, Australia and New Zealand. She has carried out long-term ethnographic research among Secwepemc Aboriginal communities in central British Columbia, and her recent publications include: *Victims of Benevolence: The Dark Legacy of the Williams*

NOTES ON CONTRIBUTORS

Lake Residential School (1995) and *The Burden of History: Colonialism and the Frontier Myth in a Rural Canadian Community* (1999).

Martin Legassick is Professor of History at the University of the Western Cape. He has taught at the universities of California, Sussex, London and Warwick, and has written widely on periods in the history of South Africa. Following his 1991 return from exile to South Africa, he undertook considerable research on the Gordonia area of the Northern Cape, of which his contribution to this collection is one product.

Sarah Nuttall is Senior Researcher at Wits Institute for Social and Economic Research, University of Witwatersrand, Johannesburg. Her areas of interest are African, South African and postcolonial literatures and cultures, and her publications have a particular interest in autobiography and other self-narratives. She is co-editor (with Kate Darian-Smith and Liz Gunner) of *Text, Theory, Space: Land, Literature and History in South Africa and Australia* (1996) and *Negotiating the Past: The Making of Memory in South Africa* (1998).

Fiona Paisley teaches history in the School of Arts, Media and Culture at Griffith University, Queensland. Her book *Loving Protection: Australian Feminism and Aboriginal Women's Rights, 1919–1939* was published in 2000. She has written widely on Aboriginal and women's history in Australia, and her account of Aboriginal and British childhood in Australia is forthcoming in the *Gender and Empire* volume of the *Oxford History of the British Empire*. She is currently completing a project on representations of race and culture and pan-Pacific women's conferences, from 1920 to the 1950s.

Ruth B. Phillips is Canada Research Chair and Professor of Art History at Carleton University in Ottawa, having recently completed a term as director of the University of British Columbia's Museum of Anthropology. She is the author of *Trading Identities: The Souvenir in Native American Art from the Northeast, 1700–1900* and co-editor (with Christopher Steiner) of *Unpacking Culture: Art and Commodity in Colonial and Postcolonial Worlds*.

Parvathi Raman is Lecturer in the School of Oriental and African Studies, University of London. Her research and teaching interests include Indian political and social identity in South Africa, historical perspectives on transnationalism and diaspora, migration and modernity, African and Asian communities in Britain, and philosophical issues in history and anthropology.

Lisa Reihana lives in Auckland, New Zealand, where she was born in 1964. She has Maori affiliation to Ngaa Puhi, mixed with English and Welsh ancestry. As a leading artist in film and multimedia, Reihana has received many awards and grants, and has exhibited extensively in New Zealand and internationally since 1990. The images she contributes to this collection are derived from the video installation *Native Portraits n. 19897* (www.lisareihana.com).

Berni Searle was born in Cape Town in 1964, where she currently lives and works. Best known for producing digital video and lens-based media installations, her work references ongoing explorations around issues of

[ix]

self-representation, personal and collective identity. Searle was short-listed for the international Artes Mundi award in 2004, and in 2003 she was presented with the prestigious Standard Bank Young Artist award. She exhibits widely in South Africa and internationally.

Paul Tapsell is of Te Arawa and Tainui descent. A former curator of the Rotorua Museum, an Oxford scholar and a post-doctoral fellow at the Australia National University, he is now Director (Maori) of the Auckland Museum and Senior Lecturer at Auckland University.

Nicholas Thomas was born in Sydney in 1960. He has conducted wide-ranging research on art, culture and history in the Pacific and is now Professor of Anthropology at Goldsmiths College, University of London. His books include *Entangled Objects* (1991), *Colonialism's Culture* (1994), *Possessions* (1999) and, most recently, *Discoveries: The Voyages of Captain Cook* (2003).

Gillian Whitlock is director of postgraduate studies in English, media and art history at the University of Queensland. Her most recent publication is *The Intimate Empire: Reading Women's Autobiography* (2000), and she is currently working on a book about memoir in recent Australian writing.

Leslie Witz is Associate Professor in the Department of History at the University of the Western Cape, Cape Town. His main areas of research are public history, labour history and teaching methodologies. He is the author of *Apartheid's Festival* (2003) and *Write Your Own History* (1988), and the co-author of *How to Write Essays* (1990).

ACKNOWLEDGEMENTS

My thanks to the contributors for their extraordinary patience and tolerance in the face of the various setbacks which delayed the publication of this collection. Thanks also to Ann Curthoys, Gillian Whitlock and Nicholas Thomas for discussions about the nature of national histories and settler colonialism.

Many thanks to Sadhana Sutar for her careful editorial assistance in preparing the final manuscript for delivery to Manchester University Press, for being such good company in stressful circumstances and for the wonderful Indian food she managed, despite the time constraints, to prepare for our mutual consumption.

GENERAL EDITOR'S INTRODUCTION

From its inception, the 'Studies in Imperialism' series has been concerned in various ways with notions of dispossession and repossession, with the effects of dismembering and remembering the past upon perceptions in the present. It has also addressed the multiple layers of ambiguity and ambivalence, shrouded in both noise and silence, associated with violence in colonial and imperial settings, as well as the effects of the related cultural phenomena on the so-called metropolitan societies (English, Welsh, Scottish and Irish) within the British Isles. But it would of course be quite wrong to see only a series of lines of cultural force running backwards from the settler territories once known as 'Dominions' to a European centre. Such lines operate within each contested nation, as well as among all of them, not least between the neighbours Australia and Aotearoa New Zealand, Canada and the USA, South Africa and other African colonies of settlement, and also South Africa as a central pivot between Atlantic and South Pacific worlds. And the central conditioning factor of such disputed representations and commemorations is the relationship of settlers and their descendants with indigenous peoples.

All such relationships are subject to process and dynamic, to expressions of dominance and the re-voicing of the dominated, to the struggles that are inherent in the politics and ideologies of monuments, myths and museum displays. Moreover, dispossession takes many different and cumulative forms. It can be of land and landscape, of distinctive ways of seeing and using the environment and animals, of language, culture, family, lifestyles, identities, as well as gender and generational relationships. Often these are achieved not just by conquest and seizure, by military and economic means, but also by religion, education, and supposed social improvement, all perpetrated in the name of 'civilisation' and 'progress'. All of these are treated or touched upon in the striking group of essays that make up this book. Their authors analyze many examples of grappling with the past through a variety of media and disciplines. Many of them consider the significance of art in all its forms, and it is therefore appropriate – and strikingly innovative – that the work also incorporates contemporary artistic invocations of the complex association of past and present, white and indigenous.

These essays remind us again of the need to escape the nationalist pre-occupations which used to dominate the history of these various lands. In recent times, we have had a number of publications taking a strongly comparative approach, including several in this series. But this book moves forward in a significant way. It forcefully points out that we must escape a purely 'British World' perspective, viewing so many phenomena as the transplanting of a European model into exotic space. These essays deal in differences as well as similarities and collectively assert the notion that the distinctive character of the several territories examined comes from the nature of their indigenous peoples, and the character of their relationships with the white settlers who established themselves so violently among them. And in further comparisons, we should also link all this to the experience of Spanish, Portuguese, Dutch, Russian, American, and French colonies of settlement (and perhaps, over shorter time-spans, German, Italian, and Japanese).

But the collection should also make us mindful of the ways in which these acts of violence, destruction and dispossession are still with us. The overweeningly powerful still flaunt and justify their power. Sometimes, the dispossessed and persecuted of the past become persecutors in the present. It is not necessary to give examples, for they are before us every day. And earlier inhabitants of the land simply will not go away. Perhaps I may be forgiven a very personal and local reflection. I currently live in the region of the Picts, that mysterious and dispossessed people who have left us only highly suggestive and beautiful stone carvings, with merely the barest hint of their language in a few place names. Yet a culture destroyed by waves of settlement in the fairly distant past has sometimes contributed to a strangely emblematic myth of Scotland, embattled and often newly assertive.

In this same area of north-eastern Scotland, a travelling people who happily accepted the name of 'tinker folk', moved around the landscape, living close to nature often in temporary homes, hunting and gathering, enjoying their own musical and oral culture (including a distinctive version of English, often conveniently impenetrable to outsiders), offering essential services like occasional labour, carefully crafted artefacts, fishing for river pearls, sewing, acts of clairvoyance, and much else. Their lifestyle, which survived until at least the 1930s, has been eloquently described in the works of Betsy White. But the post-Second World War period produced an economic, social and political world in which their marginal existence was no longer acceptable. Soon the hand of authority was against them. Persecuted by the police, chased off land, pursued by school attendance officers, their children removed from them into the tragically euphemistic 'care', they were forced to settle and, to a certain extent, assimilate. The parallels should be noted. From a European point of view, as well as from the standpoint of the urban dweller in North America, southern Africa, Australia and New Zealand, we are not dealing with some geographically remote and chronologically distant phenomenon. These violent acts of pressure into conformity are all around us, calling for our alertness and involvement.

John M. MacKenzie

INTRODUCTION

Memory and history in settler colonialism

Annie E. Coombes

This collection focuses on the different ways in which the long history of contact between indigenous peoples and the heterogeneous white colonial communities which settled in Australia, Aotearoa New Zealand, Canada and South Africa has been obscured, narrated and embodied in public culture in the twentieth century, and the various contests over historical memory which have more recently emerged.

I have limited the scope of the collection to these geographical instances, because these countries have a number of features in common in terms of their colonial histories. Their common status initially as colonies and subsequently as 'Dominions' in the early twentieth century, when they had a greater degree of autonomy within the wider British Empire as ostensibly *self-governing* colonies, meant that they also developed an ambivalent relationship to the imperial metropolitan centre. In all these nations, while the French (in the case of Canada) and the Dutch (in the case of South Africa) were early colonisers, a preponderance of colonial communities which made their homes there on a permanent basis in the early twentieth century – whether out of choice, necessity or by force – were Irish, Scottish and English. Consequently we might expect certain similarities in the kinds of administrative structures and civic institutions imposed during the colonial period. One of the contentions of this collection is, however, that despite a shared familiarity with cultural and political institutions, practices and policies among the white settler communities – notwithstanding the ways in which class and gender might mediate their experiences – the distinctiveness which could be said to mark out the various white constituencies as 'Australian', 'South African', 'Canadian' or 'New Zealander' is fundamentally contingent on their relationship to and with the various indigenous communities they necessarily encountered. In other words, the colonisers' dealings with indigenous peoples – through resistance, containment, appropriation,

[1]

assimilation, miscegenation or attempted destruction – is the historical factor which has ultimately shaped the cultural and political character of the new nations, mediating in highly significant ways their shared colonial roots/routes.

The term 'settler' has about it a deceptively benign and domesti- cated ring which masks the violence of colonial encounters that produced and perpetrated consistently discriminatory and genocidal regimes against the indigenous peoples of these regions. In each of these countries the communities which were transformed, displaced and marginalised and the peoples who were subjected to attempted genocide through the colonial process have more recently renewed their claims for greater political representation and autonomy. Their voices have been crucial in shifting the assumed political authority of earlier and predominantly white British settler communities. One of the main aims of this collection is to insist that an understanding of the political and cultural institutions and practices which shaped these colonial societies in the past can provide important insights into the available means for contesting its legacy of unequal rights by historically marginalised peoples in the present.

The notion of 'settler society' has been the subject of some scrutiny in a number of recent collections, which have provided significant contributions to our understanding of metropolitan colonial relations. Indeed, many of the authors in this volume have long been concerned to develop an adequate model for the comparative study of colonial–indigenous relations. Much of this research shares a desire to historicise and analyse the idea of 'the frontier' in settler colonialism.[1] Other collections similarly preoccupied with another central myth associ- ated with settler colonialism have focused on the significance of the land and the landscape as a determinant in the formation of white settler identities,[2] and this has led to research critically assessing the history of land management and ecology in colonial societies.[3] These more recent studies have concentrated primarily on Australian case studies and comparative analysis has been limited to one other national context, usually South Africa or Aotearoa New Zealand. However, even in these collections few of the fascinating case studies engage with comparative material within the same case study. One of the earliest monographs to lead the way in such an intellectual enterprise can be found in the analysis of the political economy of the development of capitalism in settler societies in Donald Denoon's work of 1983.[4]

Rethinking Settler Colonialism expands on the project of compara- tive research begun in these studies. It is also a response to Denoon's earlier plea, and Ann Curthoys's later reiteration, for a greater integra- tion of parallel scholarship treating settler colonialism in Australia,

Aotearoa New Zealand, Canada and South Africa, which Denoon rightly lamented for its frequently exclusive nationalist bias.[5] A number of the contributions to this collection attempt cross-cultural and intra-national comparison. In addition the overall structure of the collection encourages a dialogical relation between contributions within each thematic section which acts to highlight both the shared and the distinctive features of the national contexts under consideration.

This collection addresses another critical absence in the body of scholarship devoted to colonial settler–indigenous relations, through a consideration of the historical significance of cultural practices and institutions as integral to the analysis of settler–indigenous relations. Where this is tackled in other collections on settler colonialism, it has been largely confined to a discussion of colonial literature and travelogues in terms of the representation of settler colonial or indigenous peoples or versions of these in the British metropolitan imagination.[6] With a few notable exceptions, any analysis of visual culture's contribution in this context, has usually been accomplished through a national frame.[7]

The broader premiss for the comparative research represented in this collection is that while there are certain features common to white settler societies emerging as a direct result of British colonisation, there are many other aspects which were determined by the different material and social realities encountered. I believe that a comparative analysis is crucial as a means of fully comprehending the complexities of colonial–indigenous relations. In particular we need to acknowledge that ideas of 'self' and 'nation' were forged not only in response to the heterogeneous nature of the aspirations of the migrant and largely European communities which first colonised and settled in what were often perceived as outposts of empire, but that they *also* derived in response to the challenges presented by the reality of encountering indigenous peoples with highly differentiated political, cultural and social structures. In addition, it is clear that one of the features of settler colonialism in the national contexts dealt with here has been the ambivalent relationship of the white settler communities with the British metropolitan imperial centre. Davia Stasiulis and Nira Yuval-Davis have pointed out in an exemplary analysis of the political and economic conditions pertaining to the formation of settler communities:

> Colonial settlers, the offspring of European imperialism, refused to integrate with the indigenous population. Moreover, they kept Europe as their myth of origin and as a signifier of superiority even when formal political ties and/or dependency with European colonial powers had been abandoned. This sense of identification with the 'mother country'

has not, however, mitigated the unevenness and the fragility of settler identities, which were often forged in defence against metropolitan contempt.[8]

Consequently attentiveness to the particularities of encounter should enable the reader to understand the nature of the colonial institutions which were erected to contain the threat to European political and cultural supremacy, on the one hand, *and* the distinctions which were to mark them out as, for example, peculiarly Australian or South African, on the other.

An important feature of the contributions to *Rethinking Settler Colonialism* is that analysis of historical material is framed by a concern to engage with tensions and contradictions which have become increasingly unsustainable but which have always been at the heart of the former colonies of European settlement. In other words, much of the research in these pages has been prompted by recent political developments and is an attempt to reinstate the fundamental importance of a study of the past for an understanding of the present.[9] Consequently a number of the essays move between an analysis of historical and contemporary events, and most are concerned with ways and means of adequately representing *national* histories in the present which are not monolithic accounts.

The book is organised through four themes that together provide a means of exploring some of the characteristics distinctive to the colonial encounter and indigenous and migrant challenges to colonial rule in Australia, Aotearoa New Zealand, Canada and South Africa. These are developed in a series of interdisciplinary case studies which analyse various strategies for self-fashioning across the boundaries of public and private, individual and collective, national and imperial, indigenous and colonial domains.

The essays in Part I, 'Colonial culture: institutions and practices', focus on colonial administrative structures and their intersection with the emergence of settler civil society in terms of welfare policy, regional colonial administration, the development of labour unions and their relationship with and part in the creation of foundational national myths. Gillian Whitlock considers how assimilation policies, in particular those concerned with child welfare involving child removal, were structural to settler colonialism in both Australia and Canada. She argues that although these policies should be framed in the light of particular and local contingencies, there are also many similarities which further our understanding of the conditions reproducing particular relations between indigenous communities and immigrants under settler colonialism. Her chapter focuses on the impact of the testimony of stolen and removed children in Australia and Canada in the past two decades and the possibility such testimony offers for a re-evaluation by non-indigenous intellectuals of the privilege of their position as settler subjects, which has productively complicated their sense of belonging and offers a challenge to conventional histories of settler colonialism.

Leslie Witz compares two occasions in South Africa which were used to cement an *official* history for the Dutch settlers: the 1938 centenary festival of the 'Great Trek' commemorating the founding of the Boer Republics in 1838 and the 1952 tercentenary festival which commemorated the landing of Jan van Riebeeck at the Cape in 1652 as the originating moment of European settlement. The chapter focuses in particular on how the Garment Workers' Union under the leadership of Solly Sachs attempted to stem the tide of support for these official histories by many of their members who were targeted by the promotional propaganda associated with the celebrations. Witz consequently demonstrates the contested nature of these official versions of history which were to become so central to apartheid ideology. He shows how different versions of settler pasts have always been part of a highly contested view of history.

Martin Legassick's chapter is a close analysis of the role of the colonial magistrate in the subjugation of indigenous peoples under settler colonialism. He focuses on John Scott, magistrate on the Northern Border of the Cape Colony from 1880 in order to demonstrate how the role of magistrate is transformed from that of legal custodian concerned with the imprisonment, punishment and control of the 'Bushmen', or San, for 'stock theft' and 'vagrancy' to that of entrepreneur and amateur anthropologist whose primary activity involved despatching the same San to Cape Town for scrutiny either in relation to 'research' or as a living spectacle in private and public exhibitions in Europe. Legassick argues that this transformation coincided with their disappearance as a 'threat' to colonisation.

In Part II, 'The ordering of culture: new nations for old', contributors focus on the struggles over the representation of *national* histories through analyses of key cultural institutions and monuments, both historically and in terms of contemporary strategies. Paul Tapsell Te Arawa's chapter analyses the potential roles allocated to the exhibition and display of Maori artifacts and heritage in a museum celebrating the national identity of Aotearoa New Zealand. The proposals for Te Papa Tongarewal: The Museum of New Zealand were devised in the wake of the 1980s' Waitangi Tribunal instigated by Aotearoa New Zealand's third Labour Government to investigate abuses of the original treaty – a moment that seemed to provide Maori, finally, with an opportunity to voice their grievances and seek compensation. The new museum became a symbol of the success of the bicultural policy of the State. Tapsell complicates the euphoria of the moment by analysing the problems arising from the presentation of Maori as a unified group and the distortions which inevitably follow in the representation of history in the museum.

Leonard Bell's chapter looks at the conflict of interests represented by the events and monuments erected to his own memory by the self-styled 'Father of Auckland', John Logan Campbell (1817–1912), the Scottish merchant, speculator and landowner. Having erected his own commemorative statue, Campbell proposed another to the 'great Maori race' on an adjacent hill. While such actions may represent the apparently predictable constructions of a nationalist settler identity, Bell's chapter makes it clear that such commemorative practices are rarely uncontested and often result in surprising afterlives which ultimately transform their original meanings.

Ruth B. Phillips's chapter also explores the relationship between moments of national commemoration or celebration, political contestation and, in this case, major museum exhibitions. She argues that, with increasing historical distance, the twenty-five-year period from 1967 to 1992 is emerging as a critical moment for the postcolonial reform of Canadian museology with four major exhibitions featuring the arts of the First Nations of Canada organised during this period. Her research provides an opportunity to explore a more general pattern of relationships between the staging of exhibitions and the broader formulation of national policies. As with Tapsell's chapter in the context of Aotearoa New Zealand, Phillips's contribution, focusing on the Canadian context, challenges any simplistic understanding of the moral rectitude of a politics of pluralism. Taken together,

> the four shows comprise a mini-history of change that is historically significant and irreversible, though also uneven and incomplete. It illustrates not an uninterrupted vector of progress towards decolonisation but rather an uneven line whose dips and rises mirror swings from liberalism to reaction in Canadian politics.

Nicholas Thomas's chapter explores the comparative construction of Captain James Cook as a foundational figure in the national histories of both Aotearoa New Zealand and Australia. While initially uncritically produced by settler communities in both countries as an heroic adventurer, more critical revisionist accounts have emerged over the last thirty years. Thomas explores the contrasts between the historical accounts produced in Australia and Aotearoa New Zealand, arguing that these exemplify fundamentally distinct approaches to settler–indigenous histories and relationships in the two countries. In particular, recent Australian assessments are quite different from their counterparts in Aotearoa New Zealand which, Thomas argues, are shaped by a national commitment to *biculturalism* which construes Cook and Maori as founding partners in the shaping of a joint history.

Christine Boyanoski's contribution focuses comparatively on the ways in which new national identities were projected through the fine art pavilions and exhibitions organised by representatives from Aotearoa New Zealand, Australia, South Africa and Canada at the 1924 *British Empire Exhibition* at Wembley. She shows that these new histories, which attempted to provide alternatives to the British imperial narratives of settlement and discovery, inevitably ended up reproducing similarly selective memories which have had a lasting impact on our understanding of settler colonialism.

Part III, 'Engagement and resistance', provides comparative instances of historical and contemporary challenges to the colonial legacy from indigenous and migrant communities. Elizabeth Furniss analyses two foundational settler narratives from rural Australia (Queensland) and rural Canada (British Columbia), both of which are being publicly challenged by indigenous peoples in the process of land rights' activism. Both narratives focus on the central theme of 'a romantic yet fateful last stand of the local indigenous people ultimately overwhelmed by European settlers and militia'. Furniss argues that the similarity of these historical narratives is, in part, a means of legitimising the colonial presence on indigenous land common to all settler colonialism, while the differences between the two narratives, and their modification over time, reveal the distinctiveness of the historical, political, economic and social contexts of Australian and Canadian colonialism.

Parvathi Ramen analyses the way in which Indians came to define themselves as Indian South Africans in Durban in the 1940s, tracing how a displaced and divided community came to reconfigure its identity and struggle for reassertion of social and political space under segregation and apartheid. Through an examination of the cultural and political practices that helped shape the language of being 'Indian' in South Africa, she demonstrates the ways in which notions of 'community' were developed and performed. *Indianness* was articulated through acts of translation which drew from the discourse of imperial brotherhood, the developing dialogue of Indian nationalism and an idealised sense of Indian *tradition* that was integrated with a sense of belonging in South Africa. The language of 'Indianness' was transformed from one that voiced a temporary settlers' struggle for rights to one demanding permanent citizenship in the South African State. This narrative has continuing relevance today as Indian South Africans continue to negotiate with the State and to debate among themselves about their place in the *new* South Africa.

Fiona Paisley argues that British justice was invoked by both settler philanthropists and indigenous activists as an effective means of dealing with various kinds of settler violence in the 1920s and 1930s. She investigates the notion of *Britishness* and its importance for Aboriginal activism as well as for contemporary white women's campaigns for Aboriginal women's rights, and considers the ways in which the forms and modes of opposition to government assimilationism mobilised by indigenous and non-indigenous individuals and groups complicated colonial–postcolonial binarisms of 'us' and 'them'.

Part IV, 'New subjectivities and the politics of reconciliation', the final section of the book, explores some of the different voices and strategies for articulating the complexities of lived experience in transforming societies with a history of settler colonialism. Autobiography and testimony are explored in literature, visual art and the embodied narratives of museum display. Deborah Bird Rose analyses the role of landscape themes, presented in national heritage centres, which seek to provide a historical account of settler colonialism. She argues that in some ways these might open up the possibility of a new moral accountability in terms of indigenous/settler and immigrant relations. Her chapter is a comparative analysis of the place of such foundational myths in the USA in interpretive centres concerned with pioneer narratives and the Oregon Trail, and the use of similar foundational rhetoric in Australian national histories. She explores the nature of the stories people invent in order to re-inscribe places they have come – through violence – to 'own' and 'know' with a new, morally acceptable, presence. By so doing she hopes to discover a new kind of restorative knowledge.

Sarah Nuttall's chapter focuses on the importance of autobiography in post-apartheid South Africa. She argues that transformations in the genre are indicative of broader changes taking place in South Africa and that they demonstrate a more complex set of personal and political identifications: for example, attempts to write narratives which reach beyond the binary of apartheid or resistance and which might produce a more complicated understanding of the history of settlement. Nuttall considers in what ways the term 'settler' still has currency in this context or how it has been rendered richer or possibly redundant by a more complicated understanding of the exchanges which have always formed an integral part of this category.

In addition to the essays in the collection, contributors from Australia, Aotearoa New Zealand and South Africa have been commissioned to provide artists' pages which intersect with the central themes of the collection. The work of Brook Andrew, Lisa Reihana and Berni Searle is characterised by an engagement with the dialectical relationship between past colonial and settler histories and its legacy for lived experience in the present. As multimedia artists and film-makers their work interrogates the difficulties of inhabiting subject positions which are riven with conflictual inherited histories – colonial, migrant, and indigenous – and which are also marked by sexuality, class and ethnicity. Their work provides another analytical dimension to the collection which complements that of the historical case studies, providing a dialogue with some of the major themes represented in the book. For example, dilemmas which might arise from multiple forms of hybridisation and creolisation, resulting, on the one hand, from cross-cultural interactions and exchanges (from the transaction or appropriation of *things* and ideas) and, on the other hand, from sexual unions among peoples of different cultural and social standing in the colonial hierarchy and who in subsequent generations may inhabit a more ambiguous status. The layering of both *found* and constructed images through the photographic medium also has the advantage of unmasking the technologies and procedures involved in cultural representations and in images which have subsequently taken on an iconic character in the formation of a national identity in Australia, South Africa and Aotearoa New Zealand (Andrew's *kookaburru*, Reihana's colonial postcards and Searle's souvenir teaspoon of the sort associated with colonial exhibitions). All three artists' work is characterised by a search for an effective way of embodying the complex and contradictory heterogeneous nature of what it might mean to be Maori, Aboriginal or 'coloured' in contemporary cultures with a history of long-standing settled colonial communities.

Brook Andrew's own description of himself as 'Blak, Kweer, Gay, with Fair Skin' immediately produces a riposte to the ways in which many identities are so often attributed through visible markings such as skin colour. Not only ethnicities but sexual, cultural and social choices are similarly conflated through this discriminatory logic. His text is a reflection on how such assumptions affect his own life and relationships, and the dilemma of being cast in a marginal role in terms of both sexuality and ethnicity, while himself being fully appreciative of the positive pleasures of both. The *kookaburru* of Brook Andrew's pages, a version of *ignoratia (kookaburru)*, is an iconic figure in Australian lore and, like the kangaroo, is designed to call up a quintessential *Australianness*, less threatening than other indigenous cultural manifestations involving human agency, as well as troubled colonial pasts and the vexed question of restitution and compensation. But this cute and raucous feathered friend has been given a malevolent aspect in Andrew's work, and, partnered with the intimate and frank ruminations of his text, they effectively cast a shadow over the authority of an image of Australia and Australians as an outdoor wonderland for the hale and hearty – the preserve primarily of the white heterosexual male.

Lisa Reihana's work is developed from a photo and video installation commissioned for the opening of Te Papa Tongarewal: *Native Portraits n. 19897*. For this commission Reihana trawled the museum's extensive collection of early ethnographic photographs and postcards of Maori and re-animated them in ways which deliberately draw attention to the silences and imposed constraints of the ethnographic photographic studio. The colonial photographs were effectively re-staged using contemporary Maori, ambiguously sporting both period-specific and contemporary clothing, a strategy which effectively disrupted the temporal distance (and 'safety') of the ethnographic document. Through the use of video, the action of posing (now visible and usually withheld from the viewer) invokes a kind of agency which remains illusive in the early photographs. This is colonialism as masquerade, and masquerade has always contained the possibility of enacting a strategic appropriation. In a very fundamental sense, then, this work is about how identities are made and re-made in a colonial context and how agency is wrested from the jaws of colonial erasure. Her artists' pages for the collection develop this theme. This time our attention is drawn to the 'traffic' in images of Maori promoted through the postcard. Foregrounding the supposed neutrality of the postal service's directives – 'this space may be used for correspondence' or 'for inland postage only' – and staging contemporary Maori, on the one hand, in an androgenous contemporary suit and hat and, on the other, as a professional nurse. Both representations challenge the kinds of uniform colonial ethnographic subjects that produced a more homogeneous notion of Maori identity. The photographs are overwritten in cursive scripts which often recount the banalities of daily life for the folks 'back home' in Belfast or London, and which creates a disjuncture reinforcing the impression of the parallel universes that have historically often been the lived experiences of Maori and Pakeha.

Berni Searle's pages are a version of an installation entitled *Profile*. In this collection the artist's face is reproduced as four profiles turning towards one another. On her cheeks are the physical traces left by pressing various iconic objects associated with South Africa's colonial pasts: a souvenir spoon with the heraldic lion and unicorn; the calligraphy of an Arabic prayer; cloves and the crucifix from a rosary. Sometimes the remains of previous pressings are still visible beneath the surface of the next. For Searle, these objects conjure up a series of pasts which have literally impressed themselves on some of South Africa's communities. They are remnants of a series of encounters and transactions, the traces of which remain in her own family and have taken root in various forms of cultural expression: cooking, praying, linguistic facility. They are also objects which speak of 'a degree of domesticity' through the nature of their associations with the portability of souvenir – the collectability of memory. These then have also become objects associated with choices rather than with the grand design of an imposed colonial agenda.

The artists, historians, art historians, anthropologists and literary historians who have contributed to this volume are, in one way or another, exercised by the question of how to adequately represent the impact of the legacy of settler colonialism on the present in Aotearoa New Zealand, South Africa, Canada and Australia. They are also concerned to explore the complexities of the historical encounters between indigenous, migrant and settler communities rather than to reproduce a set of essentialising positions which take no account of the painful but nonetheless transformative nature of such encounters. It is my hope that the willingness of the contributors to think comparatively and historically across different colonial contexts will lead to a better understanding of why it is that, despite so many similarities at the outset of these various colonial projects, their violent and damaging legacy has resulted in such different quandaries, the resolution of which will necessarily demand attentiveness to the continuing experience of unequal rights by those cast in minority roles.

Notes

1 H. C. Allen, *Bush and Backwoods: A Comparison of the Frontier in Australia and the United States* (Ann Arbor: Michigan State University Press, 1959); F. Alexander, *Moving Frontiers: An American Theme and its Application to Australian History* (New York: Kennikat Press, 1969 [1947]); R. Dixon, *Writing the Colonial Frontier: Race, Gender and Nation in Anglo-Australian Popular Fiction, 1875–1914* (Cambridge: Cambridge University Press, 1995); H. Lamar and L. Thompson (eds), *The Frontier as History: North America and South Africa Compared* (New Haven, CT: Yale University Press, 1981); M. Legassick, 'The Frontier Tradition', in S. Marks and A. Atmore (eds), *Economy and Society in Pre-Industrial South Africa* (London: Longman, 1980); N. Mostert, *Frontiers: The Epic of South Africa's Creation and the Tragedy of the Xhosa People* (New York: Knopf, 1992); L. Russell (ed.), *Colonial Frontiers: Indigenous–European Encounters in Settler Societies* (Manchester: Manchester University Press, 2001).

2 K. Darian-Smith, L. Gunner and S. Nuttall (eds), *Text, Theory, Space: Land, Literature and History in South Africa and Australia* (London: Routledge, 1996).

3 W. Beinart and P. Coates, *Environment and History: The Taming of Nature in the United States of America and South Africa* (London: Routledge, 1995); T. Griffiths and L. Robin, *Ecology and Empire: Environmental History in Settler Societies* (Melbourne: Melbourne University Press, 1997).

4 D. Denoon, *Settler Colonialism: The Dynamics of Dependent Development in the Southern Hemisphere* (Oxford and New York: Oxford University Press, 1983).
5 D. Denoon, 'The Isolation of Australian History', *Historical Studies*, 22:87 (1986); A. Curthoys, 'Cultural History and the Nation', unpublished paper (2002).
6 A. Blunt and G. Rose (eds), *Writing Women and Space: Colonial and Postcolonial Geographies* (New York and London: Guilford Press, 1994); Darian-Smith *et al.*, *Text, Theory, Space*; Dixon, *Writing the Colonial Frontier*; T. Goldie, *Fear and Temptation: The Image of the Indigene in Canadian, Australian, and New Zealand Literatures* (Kingston, ON: McGill–Queen's University Press, 1989).
7 For some notable exceptions see N. Thomas, *Possessions: Indigenous Art/Colonial Culture* (London: Thames & Hudson, 1999); N. Thomas and D. Losche (eds), *Double Vision: Art Histories and Colonial Histories in the Pacific* (Cambridge: Cambridge University Press, 1999); see also Christine Boyanoski, 'Decolonising Visual Culture: Canada, Australia, New Zealand and South Africa and the Imperial Exhibitions, 1919–1939', unpublished PhD thesis, Birkbeck College, University of London (2002).
8 D. Stasiulis and N. Yuval-Davis (eds), *Unsettling Settler Societies: Articulations of Gender, Race, Ethnicity and Class* (London, Thousand Oaks, CA, and New Delhi: Sage, 1995), p. 20.
9 See for example, A. E. Coombes, *History After Apartheid: Visual Culture and Public Memory in a Democratic South Africa* (Durham, London: Duke University Press, 2003 and Johannesburg: Wits University Press, 2004).

ARTISTS' PAGES

Facing history
Lisa Reihana, Berni Searle
and Brook Andrew

Maori Beauties   Photo by Dento

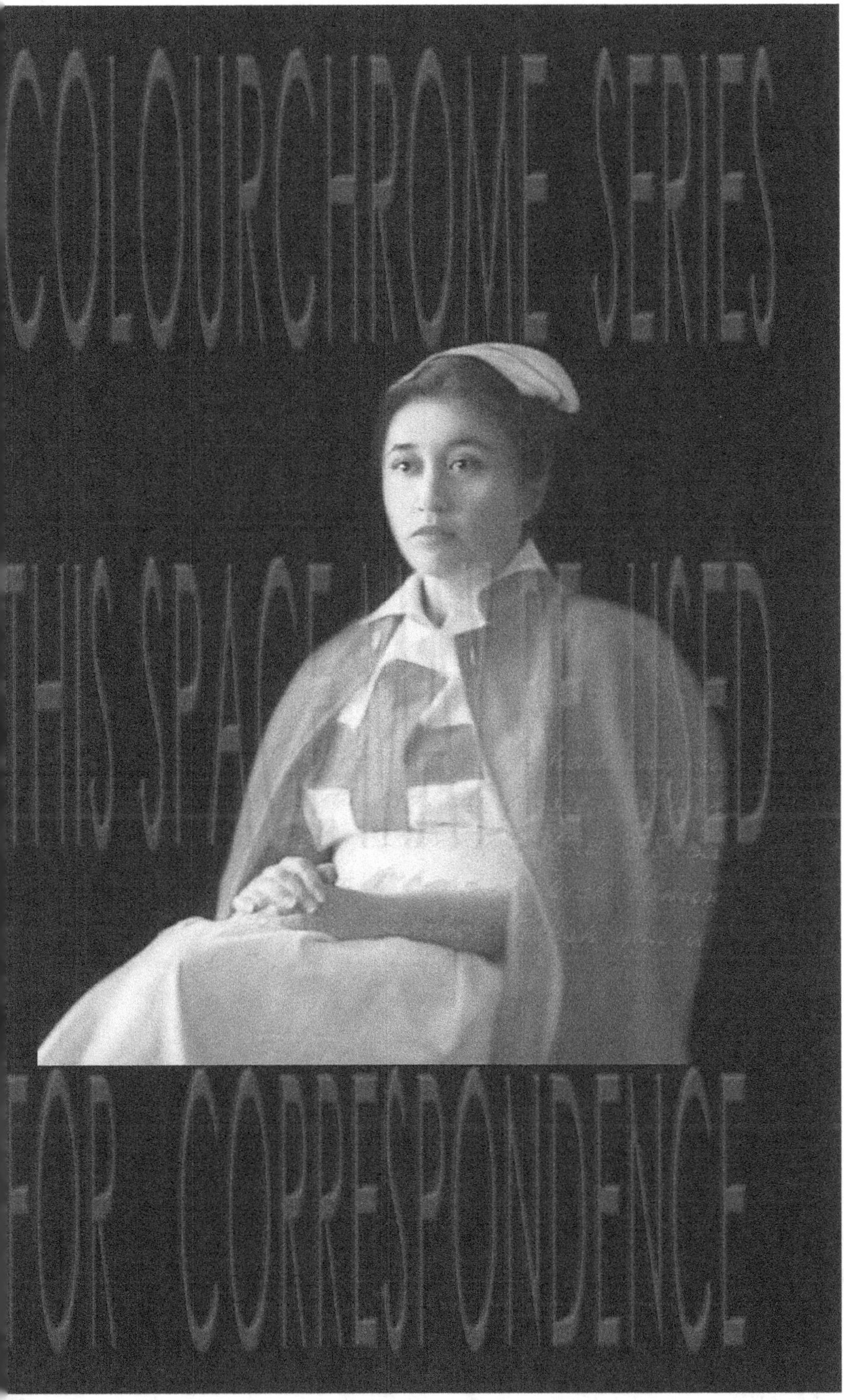
COLOURCHROME SERIES
FOR CORRESPONDENCE

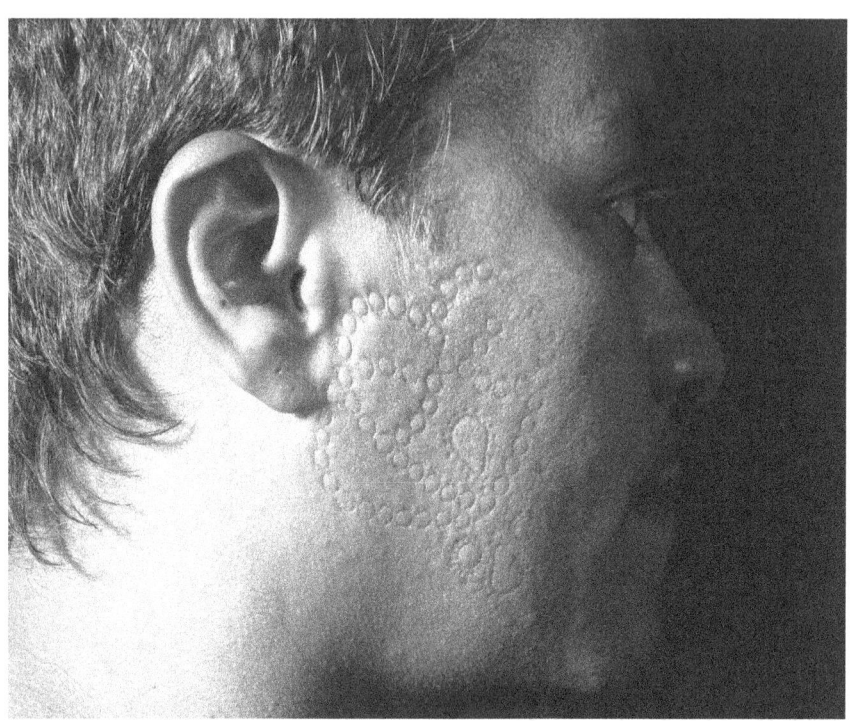

british coat of arms spoon

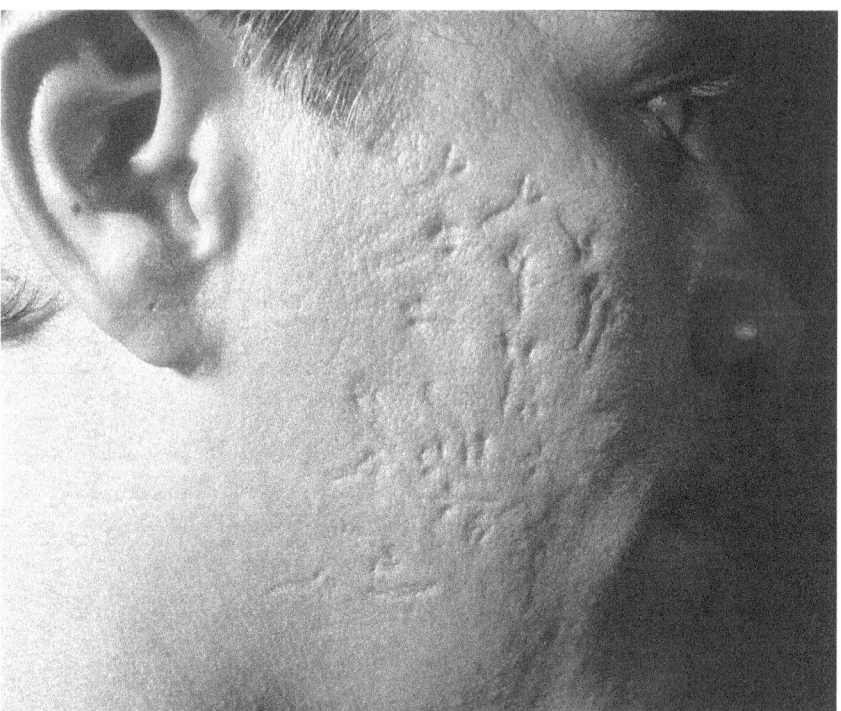

whole cloves

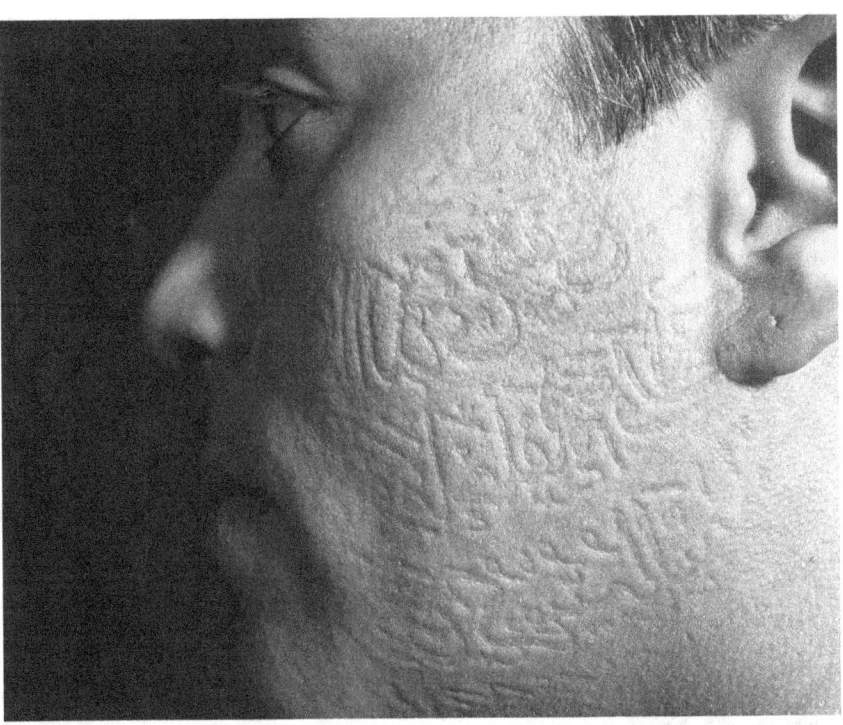

arabic prayer/rakan

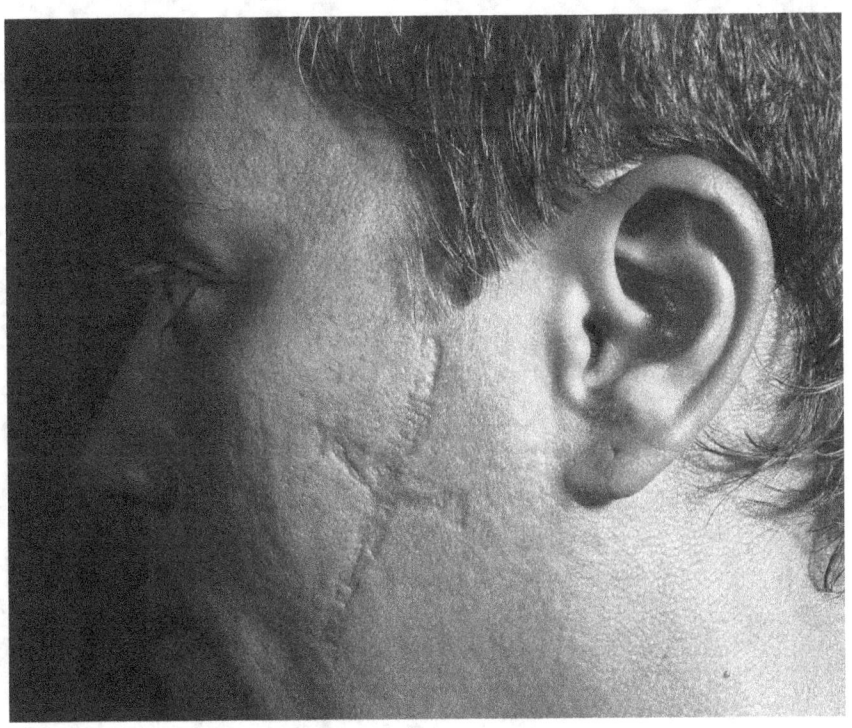

rosary/cross

I didn't realise how different I was, until I said, 'Blak people hate Asians too'. I have come to find myself in a dilema. A dilema about colour. Skin colour. Eye colour. The way I brush my hair, th far away from myself then I do now. 'Fuck off!' he said after I said '...don't point at me', as he waved his folk at my blakness. Or maybe to whiteness too? Who knows. I don't know. I thought I did...until now. I remember times meeting other blakfellas, glaring at each other, all school politics aside, thinking 'You don't look Aboriginal'. Now I talks to me about writing a documentary on racism in Australia. Great, i think in bizarre self torture. This has got t Reminded as a no-body in a white world with blak people staring at me like a gubbu. Pulling down my darras as caught between worlds, how they like to see us. Torture trap, caught between worlds. The drama of it. Both of the each other, we are their whip, their punching bag, their slave, their misplaced and denied, the cut between bloo viewing platforms, reminding us of our position for their own loathing, their own frustration and hatred for each o sticks of their fires, we, their flesh and blood, we the lands that connect them. Burn both their camps down. The we have the black soul; they both look twice. How discusting. To cut at ropes which bind them, to let loose and k gather the tears so plentiful, to rip out the soul of racism in both eyes. To heal the pain of the black souls, of all b anguish diseased by hatred and racism. And finish this - A culture of denial, a culture of illusion. Th

en smirked. Kept eating his take away. 'I don't want to talk about it anymore'. The anthropology of my up-bringing. The total control of who I am – right down to a person I love. I've never felt so race, about his detest of white people. I know an aspect of them is naraga, an aspect of me is naraga, but only to nd slander, slander about muligee-ness, not necessarily anything else. Then, getting looks at high school when s glare. Because I don't look it, we don't look it. Never looked it. But what is it. Up and down. Is love like this? He walk away and leave me here with all this abuse that never stops coming. Being the white shield of a black soul. e lie of entrapment or perverse secret about identity, kinship, culture, belonging...Walking, wondering; we are not corner and the opposite corner too, both of them in their ceremonial standing grounds/fighting grounds, backs to both complain to me; I hear them; whispering, shouting, screaming. They both have no trouble, up high in their ith others like me, splitting as the wave of us rip each other. The two opposites clap, yell abuse, loathe. We, the have a fair skinned brother, sista, uncle...', whatever their suspicion, it is skin deep. We have the milky white skin, r. To free jealousy, hatred, stupidity and lust. To love this land together. To slice the flesh thinly and sparingly, to e pain of the white soul, of all white souls. To see who side who is on, to remember who we are in a world full of ility of visibility. The blood chain. IMAGE: Brook Andrew. Ignoratia, 2003. Cibachrome, 1240x2000mm.

Ignoratia

I didn't realise how different I was, until I said, 'Blak people hate Asians
too.'
He frowned then smirked. Kept eating his take-away.
'I don't want to talk about it anymore.'
I have come to find myself in a dilemma. A dilemma about colour. Skin
colour. Eye colour. The way I brush my hair, the way I notice things. The
anthropology of my up-bringing. The total control of who I am – right
down to the person I love. I've never felt so far away from myself then as
I do now.
'Fuck off!' he said after I said, '. . . Don't point at me,' as he waved his
fork at my face, chatting about race, about his detest of white people.
I know an aspect of them is naraga, an aspect of me is naraga, but only
to blackness. Or maybe to whiteness too? Who knows. I don't know.
I thought I did . . . until now.
I remember times of dodging punches and slander, slander about
muligee-ness, not necessarily anything else. Then, getting looks
at high school when meeting other blakfellas, glaring at each other,
all school politics aside, thinking, 'You don't look Aboriginal.'
Now I know why both camps glare. Because I don't look it, we don't
look it. Never looked it. But what is it?
Up and down. Is love like this?
He talks to me about writing a documentary on racism in Australia.
'Great,' I think in bizarre self-torture. 'This has got to stop.'
Close the door. Walk away and leave me here with all this abuse that
never stops coming. Being the white shield of a black soul. Reminded
as a no-body in a white world with blak people staring at me like a gubbu.
Pulling down my darras as if they concealed some lie of entrapment or
perverse secret about identity, kinship, culture, belonging . . .
Walking, wondering; we are not caught between worlds, how they like
to see us. Torture trap, caught between worlds. The drama of it. Both of
them. Over there, in that corner and the opposite corner too, both of them
in their ceremonial standing grounds/fighting grounds, backs to each other,
we are their whip, their punching bag, their slave, their misplaced and
denied, the cut between blood and flesh.
They both complain to me; I hear them whispering, shouting, screaming.
They both have no trouble, up high in their viewing platforms, reminding
us of our position for their own loathing, their own frustration and hatred
for each other. I stand linked with others like me, splitting as the waves of
us rip each other. The two opposites clap, yell abuse, loathe. We, the sticks
of their fires. We, their flesh and blood. We, the lands that connect them.
Burn both their camps down.
The sarcasm. 'Oh, but I have a fair-skinned brother, sista, uncle . . .',
whatever their suspicion, it is skin deep.
We have the milky white skin, we have the black soul; they both look
twice. How disgusting.

To cut at ropes which bind them, to let loose and be many, be whatever. To free jealousy, hatred, stupidity and lust. To love this land together. To slice the flesh thinly and sparingly, to gather the tears so plentiful, to rip out the soul of racism in both eyes. To heal the pain of the black souls, of all black souls. To heal the pain of the white soul, of all white souls. To see whose side who is on, to remember who we are in a world full of anguish diseased by hatred and racism.
And finish this – A culture of denial, a culture of illusion.
The children of invisibility of visibility. The blood chain.

Brook Andrew

PART I

Colonial culture: institutions and practices

CHAPTER ONE

Active remembrance: testimony, memoir and the work of reconciliation
Gillian Whitlock

In Australia and Canada over the past decade reconciliation has become a pre-eminent framework for promoting the rights of indigenous peoples. In the last two decades of the twentieth century more that 30 Truth and Reconciliation Commissions were set up around the world as reconciliation became a powerful discourse in the pursuit of human rights. Although it has always been the case that '[i]ndigenous peoples continue to experience "the frontier" everywhere',[1] their experiences of dispossession, assimilation and dispersal are to be understood in specific historical, social and cultural contexts, and it follows that reconciliation emerged in distinctive ways in the settler colonies. In this chapter my interest is in how indigenous and First Nations' testimonies about child removal, a practice fundamental to policies of assimilation in Canada and Australia until relatively recently, have brought the burden of history home to non-indigenous citizens with particular force. Testimony about child removal has become a powerful resource in the construction of indigenous cultural memory. It is apparent also, however, that these testimonies impact on non-indigenous cultural and individual memory in ways that are deeply troubling, producing 'glimpses of a past that no longer seems to be ours'.[2]

Reconciliation places emphasis on individual experiences and expressions of apology and responsibility for the past, and it includes symbolic gestures such as memorials and walks, extending to broader social and community processes that pursue reparation and restitution in the courts and legislatures (such as land rights and financial payments for damages and restitution). This chapter is concerned with the personal dimensions of the reconciliation movement and has a specific interest in the ways that testimony and memoir have become vehicles for the individual and personal experiences of reconciliation in a process of interracial dialogue. These autobiographical engagements have been one of the most visible engagements with the legacies of settler colonialism in Canada and Australia in the recent past. The question of whether reconciliation addresses or merely manages this turbulence is, of course, a critical issue.

As a framework for producing cross-cultural dialogues and expressions of atonement and forgiveness, reconciliation *brings together* victims and witnesses in a reckoning with the past. Reconciliation has been institutionalised in, for example, the Truth and Reconciliation Commission (TRC) in South Africa, Reconciliation Australia (formerly the Council for Aboriginal Reconciliation) and the Statement of Reconciliation of the Indian Residential Schools Resolution Canada (IRSRC). Although my interest here is in the autobiographical acts that, in part, constitute the work of reconciliation, the question of the effectiveness of reconciliation in producing political and social change, as well as appropriate material compensation, justice and restitution, needs to be kept in mind. In the second edition of his authoritative study of the human rights movement, *Crimes Against Humanity: The Struggle for Social Justice*, Geoffrey Robertson argues forcefully for prosecution as opposed to benevolent strategies or pardon, amnesty and national reconciliation.[3] Similarly Gayatri Spivak, among others, expresses concerns about testimony as a vehicle of containment,[4] and it needs to be kept in mind that *testimony* in this discussion is presented to effect healing, and is engaged in processes of *discursive justice*.[5] It is not evidence offered for prosecution.

The material and lived experiences of First Nations and indigenous peoples in Canada and Australia continue to be shaped by extraordinarily high rates of poverty, death, unemployment, youth suicide, substance and sexual abuse, domestic violence and family breakdown. There is little evidence to date that the vast difference in the material circumstances of indigenous and non-indigenous peoples in Australia and Canada has not been lessened by the symbolic aspects of reconciliation. There remains much for which to apologise. It must be asked whether a preoccupation with apology and symbolic acts of reconciliation has diverted attention from the need to radically reform the conditions in indigenous and First Nations' communities and to address the situation of urban indigenous peoples.

During the 1990s similar reckonings with the legacies of settler colonialism were triggered by testimonies of child removal in Australia and Canada. Canadians were faced with extensive evidence of abuses in an institution that was visibly present and well known in western Canadian communities – the Indian residential school. These schools, in which a large proportion of the First Nations' population in western Canada was educated from 1879 to 1986, have become the focus of

[25]

claims that in Canada the education of First Nations' peoples must be recognised as a programme of institutionalised cultural genocide. In Australia, too, the phenomenon of the 'stolen generations' has led to claims that education policies under settler colonialism resulted in the cultural genocide of indigenous Australians – 'stolen generations' refers to the children who were taken from their birth families and raised in institutions and foster homes, a process of removal that began in the nineteenth century and came to an end in recent decades. Australia had no residential schools as such; instead, there were various state and private institutions which pursued assimilation through the dispersal of indigenous families and the education of indigenous children. In both Australia and Canada over the late 1990s and early years of the twenty-first century an outpouring of testimony, elicited in part by semi-judicial processes, has produced evidence that cannot be ignored. The removal of children (both voluntary and forced) from Aboriginal communities in those colonies and nations was a feature of the consistent and vigorous policy of assimilation through the dispersal of indigenous families.

In Canada the Federal Government and representatives of the Churches and missionary societies involved have formally apologised in a 'Statement of Reconciliation' as a response to the revelations of abuse in residential schools, and legal processes of reparation are under way.[6] In Australia the response has been very different. The refusal of the Federal Government to make formal apology on behalf of the nation and the delayed reparation are policies that appear to have the support of the majority of the population since the release of the *Bringing Them Home* report. Yet, the failure to respond adequately has produced a deep sense of personal shame in a large minority of the Australian population, and many in the intelligentsia, in particular, have used memoir to express their feelings of estrangement. Shame is not evident in recent Canadian memoir, perhaps because the State has openly taken up processes of reconciliation and apology, in both word and through reparation. There is now, in both Australia and Canada, a repeated insistence that child removal is a non-Aboriginal story also, 'a site of introspection, discovery and extirpation – a site of self-knowledge from which we can understand not only who we have been as Canadians but who we must become if we are to deal justly with the Aboriginal people of this land'.[7]

Testimony by indigenous and First Nations' peoples in both countries during the 1990s chronicled the effects of child removal with renewed force. Their testimony registered: it was heard by and acknowledged within the dominant culture, though with differing effects. It was called into question, it is true, by arguments that testimony given

[26]

outside of a court of law and without cross-examination lacked legitimacy. This criticism fails to recognise the long-established practices of *natural testimony*, the tradition of recognising the legitimacy of first-person accounts given by witnesses outside of a formal legal context;[8] it is, however, a reminder that those testimonies have been taken up most actively in networks seeking an outcome of discursive justice rather than prosecution and legal judgment. The testimony of those who have been affected by child removal has been powerfully effective in eliciting an open and active response since the 1990s. In Australia a series of memoirs perform acts of witnessing in response to this testimony, characteristically reflecting subjectively on how white-settler colonialism has located non-indigenous Australians as complicit in policies of assimilation and dispossession. In this way, memoir has become a vehicle for witnessing and recognition. In Canada the question of how to respond to the testimony about residential schools and dispersal is a recurrent issue. The active response of church and state institutions in making apology and, in some cases, reparation seems to have alleviated to some extent the sense of moral taint and the desire for personal reconciliation that lingers among a significant minority of non-indigenous Australians. They and non-indigenous Canadians have come to understand themselves as placed in history in ways they had not previously recognised: 'I struggled with an amorphous sense of guilt that I sensed many other people in North America shared, but which was never talked about.'[9] As a result there is a turn towards *talking* in various forms of memoir, for example in more self-reflexive forms of historical narrative, in expressions of concern about how indigenous stories are dealt with in the dominant culture – what Helen Hoy calls the commodification of indigenous texts for the white palate[10] – and in considering which kinds of intellectual work can best pursue inter-racial dialogue.

The emergence of child removal as a site of memory in these geographically remote yet historically proximate settler states gives rise to a number of issues. Firstly, it alerts us to the connections between memory and identity politics, and the ways in which acts of memory in the present construct changing relationships to the past. Here acts of remembering take on performative meaning within a charged field of contested moral and political claims: 'memories are acts of commemoration, of testimony, of confession, of accusation. Memories do not merely describe the speaker's relation to the past but place her quite specifically in reference to it. As assertions and performances, they carry moral entailments of various sorts.'[11] Secondly, the similarities in play here are a reminder of the wider circuits in the politics of race and reconciliation, and of the importance of separation narratives in

the dynamics of trauma, memory and healing which drive reconciliation. Thirdly, the similarities between these contemporary narratives
of trauma in Canada and Australia alert us to the racial dynamics of
settler colonialism, an organising grammar that was at the heart of a
civilising mission that repeatedly represented invasion in terms of
benevolence.

The racial politics of child removal

Several studies point to the importance of a comparative perspective
in examining settler politics of race and assimilation.[12] Armitage argues
that Australia and Canada, as developed welfare states, have similar
principal assumptions with regard to social policy. In both countries
child welfare policy has been and remains a part of the general framework of social policy established by Britain and the settler governments; and child removal has been integral to the two countries'
policies of assimilation, policies pursued from the 1860s to the 1960s,
intensifying in the 1920s and 1930s when it became evident Australian and Canadian Aboriginal peoples were neither disappearing nor
merging with the general population, as anticipated.[13] In both contexts
indigenous/First Nations' vigorous and increasingly public campaigns
of resistance have emerged in recent years. Armitage's comparative
study of social welfare policies in Australia, Canada and New Zealand
indicates a similarity of objectives and major policy periods: 'in each
of these countries, policy has been consistent for up to a hundred
years and then has changed within ten years'.[14] Why?

Armitage argues that the common framework for race relations in
these settler societies was established by the 1837 House of Commons Select Committee on Aborigines, prior to which there had been
no unified set of social policies for colonial administration; *Bringing
Them Home* similarly identifies the committee as a seminal influence
on policy-making in the Australian colonies. The formulation recommended in 1837 drew heavily on the Royal Commission report on the
Poor Law, tabled to the House of Commons in 1834. Both reports dealt
with policies concerning the 'correct' way to deal with a population
which operated outside of the accepted economic structure and was
a potential source of disorder. Armitage indicates a series of shared
assumptions: the purpose of policy was to bring

> outsiders, whether poor or aboriginals, within the established institu-
> tions of British society – particularly the wage economy; a commitment
> to legal and regulatory process anchored in a separate law for those
> outside the mainstream of society, pending their full citizenship; the
> appointment of 'protectors' and 'overseers' to establish and maintain

discipline; a recognised place for organized Christianity as an essential element in the process of producing citizens and, finally, a special recognition for the situation of children, who were considered particularly open to change, education and salvation.[15]

These paternalistic policies were established to maintain settler dominance and administered by teachers, missionaries and public servants. There was of course a fundamental difference between the application of these policies to the poor and to Aboriginal and First Nations' populations. In the case of the latter these policies were instrumental in the dispossession and dispersal of indigenous peoples and the establishment of white settler societies in which these peoples were accommodated as a labouring and servant class rather than as an independent 'first' nation. On the other hand, the phenomenon of the 'home children' – the white child-removal operation whereby English orphans or children taken from their parents by 'benevolent' organisations were shipped to Canada, Rhodesia, South Africa, Australia and New Zealand and assigned as labourers and domestics – is an example of how the poor and the indigenous peoples were similarly classified and 'protected'.[16] This, too, is a reminder of the permeable boundaries between different social groups.

To establish a point of origin in a particular inquiry is risky; after all, the 1837 committee did not make specific recommendations about the management of British colonies in North America; furthermore, the way that these policies were implemented in Australia and Canada in the 100 years which followed varied significantly among the colonial and, later, the national and sub-national, or state and provincial, jurisdictions. In Australia until 1967 Aboriginal affairs were a state responsibility; in Canada federal government was responsible for the welfare of First Nations' peoples. The institutional means of child removal were quite different in each case, although the outcome was the same. In Australia the institutionalisation of indigenous childhood was organised through the establishment of Aboriginal reserves, where children were separated from their parents and raised in dormitories, half-caste homes and in placements with non-indigenous families. Protectors and protection boards, welfare boards and the police were variously the agents of welfare policy in different state jurisdictions, but they were directed with the same intent. In Canada the church-operated Indian residential school was the central institution in the policy of social engineering, the concentration of residential schools being greatest in the Prairie Provinces and British Columbia and day-schools more common in Ontario and eastern Canada. As Armitage suggests, because of continuing federal control, Canadian policy towards First Nations' peoples has been more unified than Australian policy toward Aboriginal peoples.[17]

Nevertheless by identifying the work of the 1837 House of Commons Select Committee as a genesis for policies of assimilation through education in settler colonies, Armitage begins to establish a framework that subtends the policies of protection, integration and assimilation through residential schools, reserves, foster homes and adoption agencies over a long period of time and in very difference constituencies. Using the 1837 Act as a starting point also indicates the implications of paternalism, domination and benevolence in the institutions of settler societies. This combination of coercion, control and consent has been notoriously resilient and impervious to indigenous resistance; it has also been seductive to settler subjects and flexibly translated into very different policy frameworks. As indigenous and First Nations' testimonies about child removal and child abuse have been circulating since the early 1990s it was inevitable that their effects would be profoundly disturbing to both those who give testimony and those who bear witness.

Testimonial

Testimonial evidence about the effects and abuses of child removal is not a recent phenomenon. Historians of the Indian residential schools in Canada and of 'stolen generations' in Australia emphasise what Anna Haebich calls a 'twilight of knowing'.[18] In federal and provincial archives in Canada there are numerous First Nations' petitions protesting about the schools. In Australia signs of indigenous resistance almost coincide with proposals for the institutionalised separation of Aboriginal children from their families. Yet it is only recently that the histories of these institutional processes of child removal have emerged. Recent histories, by Anna Haebich, John Milloy and J. A. Miller, of child removal practices in Canada and Australia stress the ongoing indigenous resistance to these policies. There was between First Nations' peoples and settlers a subtle and shifting interplay of forces rather than simple authority and submission. Residential-school narratives frequently emphasise that the children domiciled there were not entirely powerless; nor were they passive bystanders. First Nations' peoples insist on the agency of their forebears in the Indian residential schools: 'they belonged to a world which was of their own making'.[19] There is plentiful archival evidence of this agency and resistance. Isabelle Knockwood recalls how children at Shubenacadie Residential School used Mi'kmaw to make up obscene word plays and nicknames for the nuns or to alter Latin words in hymns to ribald alternatives.[20]

The strict rules governing everything from the consumption of food to relations between the sexes were flouted, although the most commonly reported form of student resistance was desertion. Doris Pilkington-Garimara's *Follow the Rabbit-Proof Fence* tells the story of her mother Molly, who with two other girls had escaped from the Moore River Native Settlement in 1931.[21] The three girls walked 1,600 km to reach their community of Jigalong, following the rabbit-proof fence that runs from the northern to the southern coast of Western Australia. During winter, runaways from Indian residential schools in Canada were particularly at risk due to the harsh climate. Art Collison recalls three days of hardship while running away from Edmonton's Indian residential school during the autumn: 'it was so cold we huddled together to keep warm'.[22] Nine boys ran away from Williams Lake residential school in February 1902, and 8-year-old Duncan Sticks was found dead the next day, 13 km from the school and *en route* to his village.[23] Residential school narratives in Canada present very clear instances of First Nations' parents exercising choice strategically by supporting the schools economically and using them in accord with their own need of support in hard times. For example, Alice French links her annual sojourn in the residential school to her father's fortunes in hunting and his need of assistance following the death of her mother from tuberculosis.[24] In Australia, on the other hand, 'stolen generation' narratives focus on the traumatic effects of forced removals. Voluntary acceptance and the strategic use of institutional care by indigenous Australians do not figure in the cases documented in *Bringing Them Home*, for example, and more positive memories of removal have not been well received.[25] Prominent Aboriginal activist Lowitja O'Donoghue recalled that she and her 4 siblings were placed voluntarily in Colebrook Home by her white father when she was 2 years of age.[26] Following the publication of her story her right to identify herself as belonging to the 'stolen generations' was questioned, for removal *against* parental wishes is at the heart of Australian separation narratives during the 1990s, suggesting that traumatic memory is seen as a more legitimate or appropriate formulation for these narratives. In both Canada and Australia, narratives of child removal which are not cast in terms of traumatic memory – and there are only a few, for example, Basil H. Johnston's *Indian School Days* (1998) and Nancy Barnes's self-published *Munyi's Daughter*[27] – are likely to be seen as deviant and misguided (see, e.g., Hosking's comparison of different memory practices in narratives about Colebrook Home).

Telling in this context, then, is not new, though the public acknowledgement of this history of struggle *is* a recent development. It is the

harnessing of traumatic memories of separation to a politics of reconciliation that produced in the 1990s the threshold for speaking and
hearing about child removal. And it is in this discursive framework
that child removal has become such a powerful genre of memory and
part of public discourse in the 1990s. This constitutes the threshold
whereby a 'twilight of knowing' was displaced by open and public
acts of telling and hearing. Contemporary separation narratives circulate in a variety of textual forms: drama, popular music, film, autobiographical writing, fiction and poetry. Child removal testimony has
been elicited most vigorously by the semi-judicial commissions
established in Australia and Canada in the 1990s, wherein individual
and often anonymous testimonies were threaded together to produce
a consistent, coherent and damning historical narrative of child removal
as an agent of assimilation policy. It is evident in Carmel Bird's selection of narratives from *Bringing Them Home*, for example, that some
who had not previously recognised any part of their own history
as 'indigenous' came to recognise and lay claim to an indigenous
identity through a powerful and emergent narrative for indigenous
cultural memory: the stolen generations.[28]

One critical development has been the idea that to speak of trauma
is a means of both healing the individual and producing collective
catharsis, and it has become increasingly powerful as a framing narrative for separation stories. Framing devices and iconic moments are
especially apparent as testimonies of separation often circulate in
edited fragments, with victims located out of time and space. Iconic
moments in separation discourse recur in these collective narratives:
the ritualistic stripping away of all that they had known; removal as
a violent ejection from a pre-lapsarian state of innocence; the silen-
cing by authoritarian figures in alien institutional or domestic space;
and the long and often violent process of re-socialisation. Framing
devices include statements by editors, commissioners, collaborators
and indigenous collectives. In the recent past this framework characteristically draws on the therapeutic paradigm of reconciliation, a
powerful discourse for acts of engagement between indigenous and
non-indigenous subjects in settler societies.

This was evident in Canada, in 1994, when the Assembly of First
Nations published *Breaking the Silence*, a collection of testimonial
fragments linked to suggest that 'through the stories of those who
attended residential school, a healing process is seen to have developed over time that includes four aspects: recognizing, remembering,
resolving, and reconnecting'.[29] In Linda Jaine's *Residential Schools:
The Stolen Years*, individual stories are similarly gathered in an act of
resistance and healing: 'The stories in this book are the voices of our

community. Each story given, as a gift, is an act of resistance. An act of healing.'[30] Suzanne Fournier describes the preparation of *Stolen from Our Embrace* as a 'healing journey': 'I received gifts of wisdom and acceptance, I felt a profound responsibility to relate to the world the stories and secrets that people had entrusted to me.'[31] The production of testimony through the gathering together of fragmentary narratives was encouraged by the work of the Royal Commission on Aboriginal Peoples in Canada and the Human Rights and Equal Opportunity Commission (HREOC) in Australia. The introduction to the HREOC report argues that the devastation wrought by child removal 'cannot be addressed unless the whole community listens with an open heart and mind to the stories of what has happened in the past and, having listened and understood, commits itself to reconciliation'.[32] In the edited version of some stolen generations' narratives Commissioner Ronald Wilson describes the process of storytelling as the beginning of an individual and collective healing process. A sequence similar to the aspects defined in *Breaking the Silence* is used as a shaping device here too:

> Reparation can only begin when there is an understanding that comes through listening, followed by an acknowledgement of the shameful deeds of the past and a genuine expression of regret. Reparation can then be followed through with practical measures designed to facilitate reunions . . . [and] the provision of appropriate compensation and finally to a fresh approach to current laws, practices and policies dealing with the welfare of Indigenous children.[33]

Testimony always needs to be understood as a constrained auto-biographical performance rather than a moment of *free* speech.[34] Testimony cannot be discussed without attention to the conditions that allow it to circulate and be witnessed in the dominant culture. In postcolonial contexts in particular, testimony is characteristically the genre of the subaltern witnessing to oppression to a less oppressed other, and in a form which the other can recognise as culturally and socially appropriate. Editorial control varies in degree but is never absent. Spivak has written of her uneasiness over the current preoccupation with testimony. Most particularly, she suggests that the traumatic legacies of settler colonialism (which is most acutely evident in the situation of First Nations' peoples) is currently *managed* through the production of testimony.[35] This forces us to question how child removal testimonies are both released and contained/constrained by their current circulation in conduits of healing and reconciliation. How do discourses of reconciliation *manage* these testimonies of child removal? What are the opportunities presented and the constraints

[33]

imposed by current discourses of separation? There is risk in the act of giving testimony, often coming in the form of a transaction to which the subaltern cannot accede. Thus, for example, Tomson Highway (1998) chose fiction rather than autobiography as the vehicle for his own experiences of child removal in writing *The Kiss of the Fur Queen;*[36] while in *My Place* Sally Morgan's grandmother refuses to disclose 'the whole truth'.[37] It is evident that indigenous writers make strategic use of their opportunities to document traumatic personal histories, and it is by no means the case that they choose to tell all. There are various reasons for this. For example, Ruth Hegarty speaks of her primary responsibilities as being to her community in the process of writing her testimony of a childhood in the Cherbourg mission *Is That You Ruthie?*[38] Indigenous writers and speakers are canny in their assessment of the risks they take when releasing indigenous testimony into the wider community, for what they have to say frequently calls the settler community to account.

For indigenous peoples the fact that individual and collective memory have become major idioms in the construction of identity now means that quite different interpretive reconstructions of the past can be produced and legitimised. As Antze and Lambek point out, not only has memory assumed new importance in contemporary culture but it attends particularly to the role that trauma and victimisation have come to play within a politics of memory.[39] Child removal narratives, then, have become instances of active remembrance, a performance of remembering and reconstruction that recalls and commemorates the past variously. They have become recognised as a genre of memory that both constitutes and shapes indigenous selfhood. Separation narratives are one of the most powerful ways of imagining the self in terms of indigenous/First Nations' identity: 'who people are is closely linked to what they think about memory, what they remember, and what they can claim to remember'.[40] As we have seen, this function is frequently presented as therapeutic for the individual and for the indigenous and First Nations' community more generally. More than this, as a memory practice it constitutes First Nations' communities in new and powerful ways, emphasising a history of struggle and the persistence of indigenous histories and identities in the face of policies of cultural genocide. For these reasons the arguments have been made in both Australia and Canada that such testimonies are to be held in a specific archive modelled on the Shoah collection of Holocaust testimony, and that the process of gathering testimony is to be ongoing. These demands are made in the First Nations' study of residential school impact and healing *Breaking the Silence*, for example, are they are reiterated in *Bringing Them Home*, which led to the establishment of the 'Bringing Them Home' archive at the National Library in Canberra.

Discourses of reconciliation privilege the therapeutic paradigm in pursuit of individual rehabilitation and meeting the collective needs of First Nations' peoples; that paradigm also carries the burden of initiating healing within the national community. Stories of child removal now circulate not just as counter-discourse in the specialist communities of Aboriginal history and child welfare but as part of mainstream knowledge and debate about national histories and good citizenship. It is at this level that we can begin to consider Spivak's concern for the management of crises of postcoloniality through testimony. For the idea that individual healing occurs through revelation of suffering is extended in reconciliation discourses to suggest that the truth of suffering can be a source of regeneration, a collective catharsis and a means of creating a moral community which has come to terms with the violence of its national history.[41] The trauma and mourning of First Nations' peoples becomes the crucible for a reconstructed national narrative and identity.

The idea that the legacies of a violent history can be addressed in the present in the form of a dialogic process which addresses guilt and restitution is not particular to settler colonies. It can be linked to more *global* processes of reconciliation and truth-telling. Elazar Barkan connects a new era of morality, beginning in the 1990s, with self-examination, national self-reflexivity and a willingness to embrace guilt in the interests of building an interpretation of the past that all parties can share. He suggests that two subjective identities have developed, those of the victim and the perpetrator, and are linked in a discourse of restitution that is

> a discussion between the perpetrators and the victims. This interaction between the perpetrator and the victim is a new form of political negotiation that enables the rewriting of memory and historical identity in ways that both can share ... The discourse of restitution underscores the opportunities and the ambivalence embedded in this novel form of politics.[42]

Barkan's comparative framework is quite vast and ambitious, drawing together discussions of very different processes of restitution, and is unlike the more precise formula based on the settler colony framework which is the basis of Armitage's study. It raises the question whether the desire to redress some of the injustices and 'unfinished business' of settler colonialism could be induced without this larger international movement for social justice. Of course this international movement was itself fuelled by the reconciliation processes established in South Africa, most notably the TRC which elicited an outpouring of testimony and confession which dominated South Africa's print, radio and television journalism once hearings began in April 1996. The processes of the HREOC inquiry into stolen generations in Australia, the Royal Commission on Aboriginal Peoples in Canada, and the TRC in South Africa produced a contemporaneous outpouring of testimony to trauma from these settler colonies. In each, the past was told through the personal recollections of those who suffered, and these accounts of trauma played a dramatic and very public role in the reconciliation process.

Barkan's work indicates the larger discursive context of guilt and retribution which has contributed to the particular conditions whereby separation narratives could assume unprecedented valency and importance in Australia and Canada in the 1990s and also, to return to Spivak, the terms under which they might be contained and managed. Generically testimony is a form of autobiography which involves two subjects, two texts of self-fashioning, with a fundamental power differential between them. The outcomes of testimony can be uncertain, and yet as a speech act it is designed to engender a new awareness in the witness.[43] In discourses of reconciliation these two acts of self-fashioning are understood dialogically, and so collective and historical conflicts are reframed into a personal and individual process of negotiation and recognition. Testimony is heard and acknowledged, initiating an often painful re-membering and acknowledgement in the witness. This painful re-membering by the perpetrator has given a new impetus to the work of memoir in settler cultures.

Memoir

Leigh Gilmore has suggested that memoir became *the* genre of choice in the skittish period around the turn of the millenium.[44] In settler cultures we can observe particular socio-historical determinants for this turn to memoir in the 1990s. Memoir and testimony read together indicated the deeply subjective and personal ways that discourses of reconciliation and reparation shape connections between settler subjects and indigenous and First Nations' peoples. These two autobiographical forms of narrating a life in history might be understood as diametrically opposed, one to the other. The memoir is traditionally the prerogative of the literate élite, and the testimony is conventionally a means by which the experiences of the disempowered and dispossessed are acknowledged and circulated. Quite different histories are brought into the public record by these genres. Reading them together, it is evident that they can be linked in a network of exchange which elicits interrelated subjective encounters with history. Black testimony triggers white memoir – memoir, that is, which reflects actively on history and responsibility, on race and reconciliation. This intertextuality is important in grasping the interrelationships between indigenous and non-indigenous subjects under settler (post)colonialism.

Arguably the failure of any kind of formal apology or move to reparation in Australia following *Bringing Them Home* places more pressure on the work of subjective performances in recognition of indigenous testimony. In Australia in the 1990s there was a turn to what Chris Healy calls 'performative history', a mapping of how we experience our historicality.[45] The historian who coined 'stolen generations', Peter Read, whose work was instrumental in bringing child removal to light, suggests that a millenial angst divides some contemporary Australians from previous generations. He questions whether indigenous and non-indigenous forms of belonging can be reconciled: 'I belong but I do not belong; I seek a solemn union with my country and my land but not through aboriginality; I understand our history but it brings me no relief.'[46] With some insight Read recognises that what he is describing here, a sense of dispossession induced by the burden of racial guilt, may be limited to people like him: university-educated, urban, middle-class and Anglo-Celtic.

The memoir has become the genre of choice for intellectuals who write about their profound sense of anxiety and implication in the dispossession of Aboriginal Australians. A number of public intellectuals – Drusilla Modjeska, Stephen Muecke, Henry Reynolds, Robert Manne, Inga Clendinnen, as well as Peter Read – describe themselves as, one way or another, displaced persons, profoundly shaken by the copious testimony to trauma by indigenous Australians in the recent past. Memoir, understood as a reflection of the self in history, is personal and often conversational; it is well suited to examine critically the resources, responsibilities and strategies available to the public intellectual at this particular historical conjuncture. It is a form of self-reflective history which emerges in, among others, Inga Clendinnen's *True Stories* and *Tiger's Eye*, Henry Reynolds's *Why Weren't We Told?*, Read's *Belonging* and Robert Manne's *The Culture of Forgetting*.[47] In each case the memoir is used to figure a more critical and personally accountable relation to the past, one produced by a sense of crisis in the wake of heard testimony which convinces the author that historical narrative must change into different, more self-reflexive and morally engaged, forms.

These memoirs are a sign of the struggle to write about the past in ways which might respond to the delicate transactions of apology and reconciliation. As I have indicated elsewhere,[48] we might understand this as part of a more wide-ranging crisis in legitimating intellectual work. Zygmunt Bauman has argued that one way we can recognise the fundamental changes produced by globalisation and modernity is by examining the impact on a crucial social category: the intellectual.[49] Bauman talks about the implosion of intellectual vision, a 'falling upon oneself'. In postmodernity, Bauman suggests, intellectuals have been called on to reassess their own position in society, to reorient their own collectively performed function and develop new strategies. It is clear that in settler cultures this crisis is fuelled by quite specific and urgent demands that intellectual works contribute to social justice and reconciliation.

As this eloquent and copious testimony is in the process of remaking First Nations' people's collective memory, it is of urgent necessity that we attend to how the nation is situated for the intellectual work of rewriting memory and historical identity. A sense of anxiety on this point infuses, in particular, the work of historians of child removal. Milloy for example, presents his study (originally a submission to the Commission on Aboriginal Peoples in Canada) as an act of reconciliation, maintaining that

> it is critical that non-Aboriginal people study and write about the schools, for not to do so on the premise that it is not our story, too, is to marginalize it as we did Aboriginal people themselves, to reserve it for them as a site of suffering and grievance and to refuse to make it a site of introspection, discovery and extirpation – a site of self-knowledge from which we can understand not only who we have been as Canadians but who we must become . . .[50]

Anna Haebich, from whose work the HREOC drew extensively in compiling its report, similarly presents her history of stolen generations as a shared history of Aboriginal and non-Aboriginal Australians, a history which 'speaks to us of a past that lies at the very core of our nationhood, a past that we can no longer ignore . . . [which] will continue to haunt our consciousness until we begin, as a nation, to grapple with it "through our hearts" '.[51] There is a moral anxiety here that non-indigenous Canadians and Australians will either fail to hear these stories of trauma and loss or that they will fail to recognise the shameful implications for their own culture. Discourses of reconciliation require ethical performances of civic virtue by witnesses who accept their own complicity.[52]

Autobiographical work that explores complicity and intersubjectivity is inevitably controversial. Collaborative interracial work which witnesses to testimony of indigenous trauma and explores interracial conversation is proving unexpectedly difficult to produce. Conventions whereby indigenous telling of trauma is mediated by a non-indigenous witness who exerts control are endemic and hard to change into dialogic ways of telling. The problems of devising intersubjective and interactive styles of personal history are evident in some recent memoirs which circulate as 'stolen' lives. In Canada Rudy Wiebe and Yvonne Johnson's *Stolen Life* is the story of a young Cree woman currently serving a life sentence for murder.[53] The story is told collaboratively, Wiebe witnessing to Johnson's story of trauma and, in turn, presenting it to persuade the wider public that justice has not been done. The collaboration, potentially problematical in itself, between a white man and an Aboriginal woman has created concern about the ways in which Wiebe creates meaning from Johnson's trauma, 'producing' the discursive assemblage through which her story can be understood.[54] Johnson's life story reaches the market which currently exists for 'stolen' narratives through Wiebe, who positions it for this white readership. In her discussion of *Stolen Life* Susanna Egan laments that this collaboration has not produced a 'limit-case narrative', an exploration of trauma that 'pushes the boundaries for modes of telling and enables me to read and understand in new ways'.[55] The question might be whether child removal narratives can function in this way for the non-indigenous reader and, furthermore, what different investments might be required of indigenous and non-indigenous readers of testimony? For subaltern subjects, the collaborator–intermediary is notoriously difficult to displace, and this is one of the risks subjects take when choosing to testify: it may be that child removal testimony is unable to deliver 'limit-case narrative' and innovations in intersubjective autobiographical performance.

Peter Read's recent memoir *Belonging* raises similar issues. Read was instrumental in shaping stolen generations' narratives in Australia, and as a result he feels the need to imagine new ways of belonging for non-indigenous Australians like himself. In *Belonging*, Read's own history is told amid other autobiographical narratives and records of other types of enquiry, knowledge and writing about attachment and dispossession – for example, a series of interviews, poetry, and country music. Read's own reflections on belonging are impelled in a critical and self-conscious way by these alternative autobiographical narratives. Ultimately Read models what he calls a kind of belonging-in-parallel, a model of coexistence between the majority cultures and the Aboriginal, which he dramatises in an exploration of the country that has had a deep significance for him since his childhood, and through rites of passage as a husband and parent. Alongside Read is Dennis Foley, an indigenous man, for whom Australia is *Gai-mariagal* country. Through Read, Foley tells the dramatic story of the dispossession and survival of his people. Unlike Paddy Roe, the indigenous co-traveller in Stephen Muecke's *Reading the Country*,[56] Foley does not become a first-person narrator in this memoir, although he and Read are pictured together on the cover, each symbolically touching the earth of Gai-mariagal country. What does Foley bestow on Read as they enact this belonging-in-parallel in the spirit of reconciliation? Foley enriches Read's knowledge of the land, and so intensifies Read's ethical belonging. These are the processes of reconciliation at work: truth is heard and acknowledged; indigene and settler move on together to the 'deep future' that awaits them. Reconciliation discourses generate a desire for ritual and social closure that will separate the past from the present, and this can allow a new social amnesia about race to surface: a belief that race is no longer the basis of privilege.[57] In *Belonging* Read forgets much of what he has learned through stolen generations.

These are problems of the heart, and they strike to the core of the unfinished business of settler colonialism in Australia and Canada. Child removal narrative has the capacity to trigger a profound sense of intersubjectivity in communities that, for a long time, understood indigeneity in binary terms; as an identity on the other side of a frontier, or a dying race. This narrative has been able to convey to those who have not heard it before a sense of how pervasively racism has functioned in the project of settler colonialism. Benevolent social welfarism has been shown to be complicit in the dispersal of Aboriginal families, to devastating effect. Yet these lessons about benevolence and good intentions are hard to learn.

Peter Read, who understands perfectly the problematical workings of benevolence and good-hearted whiteness in his book about the stolen generations, *A Rape of the Soul So Profound*,[58] nevertheless invokes 'good-hearted Whites' as a gesture of hope in *Belonging*. Margery Fee, in her discussion of Wiebe's part in *Stolen Life*, points out that, for all of his good intentions, for all that he hopes that his work with Johnson represents a careful listening, it may be yet another example of power disguising itself as benevolence.[59] Performances of reconciliation through memoir become deeply problematical when they promote performances of 'doing history' which forget what we have learned from other styles of historical enquiry. It is both the strength and weakness of reconciliation discourses that they appeal to emotion and, specifically, to that most unreliable site of remembrance, the heart.

For First Nations' peoples in Australia and Canada child removal narrative is a site of memory which has produced a powerful sense of liberation: trauma can be spoken of and recognised at a time when collective responsibility for this suffering has been established. The question of whether individuals can be psychologically healed through public testimony is an important one and, as may be seen from the case of those who tell different stories about experiences of child removal, such as Basil Johnston, Nancy Barnes or Molly Lennon.[60] Similarly, the suggestion that individual speaking of pain and trauma can produce social healing brings together individual and collective processes in ways that have been critically questioned. These are foundational tenets of reconciliation, and while testimony offers First Nations' peoples a powerful way of shaping their history, individually and collectively, it is not clear that reparation will follow. Indigenous peoples themselves are aware of the risks of testimony, and acutely so of the ways that their stories can be *managed*. They have argued, for example, that to identify as 'victims of benevolence' is to invite a therapeutic model of individual and collective healing, a 'talking cure' which does not benefit Aboriginal peoples. For example the case was made at the Canadian Royal Commission that calls for reconciliation, healing and therapy which shape the terms of witnessing are in the interest of the Churches and state institutions which are to be held to account for child removal rather than the interest of indigenous peoples.[61] In Australia Bain Attwood has drawn attention to weaknesses in stolen generations' narrative, suggesting that the grounding in memory work through oral testimony and autobiography rather than verifiable forms of evidence leaves indigenous accounts open to question in legal proceedings that pursue reparation.[62] Nevertheless, despite the risks involved in the production, evaluation and transmission of First Nations' peoples' stories as 'tactical histories' in cultural territories beyond their control,[63] indigenous organisations and collectives (such as the Council for Aboriginal Reconciliation and the Assembly of First Nations) continue to be committed to offering their stories as gifts which can initiate interracial communication.

Has there been an epistemic and discursive break in race relations in the past ten years, as Armitage suggests? Failed attempts to produce more dialogic forms of life writing which encompass indigenous and non-indigenous histories, the example yet again of the troubling outcomes of benevolence and the impotence of good intentions, the reminder that First Nations' peoples must contend with the fact that they frequently gain access to power and knowledge in ways which are carefully managed by non-indigenous interests: all these are entirely congruent with the ongoing dynamics of settler colonialism. Descriptions of what it might be that characterises the identity politics of settler colonialism emphasise *multiple relationality, negotiation, exchange* and *ambivalence*: 'the keystone of settler analysis is its insistence on the fraught and antagonistic relationality that is an inescapable vector of all institutions and subjectivities within the settler culture'.[64] The processes of exchange occurring around testimony of child removal in Australia and Canada now confirm some of what we already know about the ongoing dynamics of colonisation and resistance in nations founded in settler colonialism. They also give rise to as yet unanswerable questions. Can acts of remembrance initiate a new ethics for living in the contact zone of settler colonialism? Are we witnessing a process of cleansing and healing through apology which will forgive us our trespasses and produce a meaningful reconciliation? Evidence of memoir suggests that reconciliation discourses are themselves freighted with anxiety, desire and longing in settler cultures. Indigenous child removal narratives and nonindigenous memoirs which seek to bear witness play out yet again that fraught relationality and desire for the closure of belonging which is the irreconcilable legacy of invasion and settlement.

Notes

1 P. Havemann (ed.), *Indigenous Peoples' Rights in Australia, Canada and New Zealand* (Auckland: Oxford University Press, 1999), p. 1.
2 P. Antze and M. Lambek (eds), *Tense Past: Cultural Essays in Trauma and Memory* (New York: Routledge, 1996), p. xvi.
3 G. Robertson, *Crimes Against Humanity: The Struggle for Global Justice* (London: Penguin, 2002), p. 284.
4 G. Spivak, 'Three Women's Texts and Circumfession', in A. Hornung, E. Ruhe, M. Cliff, D. Dabydeen and O. P. Adisa (eds), *Postcolonial Autobiography* (Amsterdam: Rodopi, 1998).
5 J. Frow, 'The Politics of Stolen Time', *Meanjin*, 57:2 (1998), 351–67.
6 The following is from the 'Statement of Reconciliation', published by the Indian Residential Schools Resolution Canada (available online: www.irsr-pi.gc.ca/english/reconciliation.html): 'One aspect of our relationship with Aboriginal people over this period that requires particular attention is the Residential School system. This system separated many children from their families and communities and prevented them from speaking their own languages and from learning about their heritage and cultures. In the worst cases, it left legacies of personal pain and distress that continue to reverberate in Aboriginal communities to this day. Tragically, some children were the victims of physical and sexual abuse.
    The Government of Canada acknowledges the role it played in the development and administration of these schools. Particularly to those individuals who experienced the tragedy of sexual and physical abuse at residential schools, and who have carried this burden believing that in some way they must be responsible, we wish to emphasize that what you experienced was not your fault and should never have happened. To those of you who suffered this tragedy at residential schools, we are deeply sorry.'
7 J. S. Milloy, *A National Crime: The Canadian Government and the Residential School System 1879 to 1986* (Winnipeg: University of Manitoba Press, 1999), p. xviii.
8 C. A. J. Coady, *Testimony: A Philosophical Study* (Oxford: Clarendon Press, 1992), p. 26.

9   V. Freeman, *Distant Relations: How My Ancestors Colonised North America* (Toronto: McClelland & Stuart, 2000), p. xiv.

10 H. Hoy, *How Should I Read These? Native Women Writers in Canada* (Toronto: University of Toronto Press, 2001).

11 Antze and Lambek, *Tense Past*, p. xxv.

12 A. Armitage, *Comparing the Policy of Aboriginal Assimilation: Australia, Canada and New Zealand* (Vancouver: University of British Columbia Press, 1995); Havemann, *Indigenous Peoples' Rights in Australia, Canada and New Zealand*; T. Goldie, *Fear and Temptation: The Image of the Indigene in Canadian, Australian, and New Zealand Literatures* (Kingston: McGill–Queens University Press, 1989).

13 Armitage, *Comparing the Policy of Aboriginal Assimilation*, p. 106.

14 Ibid., p. 185.

15 Ibid., p. 4.

16 K. Bagnell, *The Little Immigrants: The Orphans Who Came to Canada* (Toronto: Macmillan, 1980); P. Bean and J. Melville, *Lost Children of the Empire: The Untold Story of Britain's Child Migrants* (London: Unwin Hyman, 1989).

17 Armitage *Comparing the Policy of Aboriginal Assimilation*, p. 101.

18 A. Haebich, *Broken Circles: Fragmenting Indigenous Families 1800–2000* (Fremantle: Fremantle Arts Centre Press, 2000), p. 563.

19 *Breaking the Silence: An Interpretive Study of Residential School Impact and Healing as Illustrated by the Stories of First Nation Individuals* (Ottawa: First Nations' Health Secretariat, 1994), p. 27.

20 I. Knockwood and G. Thomas, *Out of the Depths: The Experiences of Mi'kmaw Children at the Indian Residential School at Shubenacadie, Nova Scotia* (Lockeport, Nova Scotia: Roseway Publishing, 1992).

21 D. Pilkington-Garimara, *Follow the Rabbit-Proof Fence* (St Lucia, Queensland: University of Queensland Press, 1996).

22 L. Jaine (ed.), *Residential Schools: The Stolen Years* (Saskatoon: University of Sakatchewan Press, 1995), p. 37.

23 E. Furniss, *Victims of Benevolence: The Dark Legacy of the Williams Lake Residential School* (Vancouver: Arsenal Pulp Press, 1995), p. 63.

24 A. French, *My Name Is Masak* (Winnipeg: Peguis Publishers, 1992).

25 S. Hosking, *Homeless at Home, Stolen and Saved: 3 Stories from Colebrook Home* (Canberra: Association for Commonwealth Literature and Language Studies Conference, Australia, 2001).

26 L. O'Donoghue, 'Media Release', *Australian Humanities Review Online*: www.lib .latrobe.edu.au/AHR/archive/Issue-March-2001/odonoghue.html 2001 (accessed 20 August 2003).

27 B. H. Johnston, *Indian School Days* (Norman: University of Oklahoma Press, 1998); N. Barnes (2000), *Munyi's Daughter: A Spirited Brumby* (Henley Beach: South Australia, Seaview Press, 2000).

28 C. Bird (ed.), *The Stolen Children: Their Stories* (Sydney: Random House, 1998).

29 *Breaking the Silence*, p. 123.

30 Jaine, *Residential Schools*, p. x.

31 S. Fournier and E. Crey, *Stolen from Our Embrace: The Abduction of First Nations Children and the Restoration of Aboriginal Communities* (Vancouver: Douglas & McIntyre, 1997–98), p. 14.

32 *Bringing Them Home: Report of the National Inquiry into the Separation of Aboriginal and Torres Strait Islander Children from their Families* (Sydney: HREOC, 1997), p. 4.

33 Quoted in Bird, *The Stolen Children*, p. xv.

34 See, e.g., G. Whitlock, *The Intimate Empire: Reading Women's Autobiography* (London and New York: Cassell, 2000), and, G. Whitlock, 'In the Second Person: Narrative Transactions in Stolen Generations Testimony', *Biography*, 24:1 (2001), 197–214.

35 Spivak, 'Three Women's Texts and Circumfession', p. 7.

36 T. Highway, *Kiss of the Fur Queen* (Toronto: Doubleday, 1998).
37 S. Morgan, *My Place* (Fremantle: Fremantle Arts Centre Press, 1987).
38 R. Hegarty, *Is That You Ruthie?* (St Lucia: University of Queensland Press, 1999).
39 Antze and Lambek, *Tense Past*, p. viii.
40 Ibid., p. xxi.
41 M. Humphrey, 'From Terror to Trauma: Commissioning Truth for National Reconciliation', *Social Identities*, 6:1 (2000), 7–27, at 9.
42 E. Barkan, *The Guilt of Nations: Restitution and Negotiating Historical Injustices* (New York: W. W. Norton, 2000), p. xviii.
43 S. Felman and D. Laub, *Testimony: Crises of Witnessing in Literature, Psychoanalysis, and History* (New York: Routledge, 1992).
44 L. Gilmore, *The Limits of Autobiography: Trauma and Testimony* (London: Cornell University Press, 2001), p. 1.
45 C. Healy, *From the Ruins of Colonialism: History as Social Memory* (Cambridge: Cambridge University Press, 1997).
46 P. Read, *Belonging: Australians, Place and Aboriginal Ownership* (Cambridge: Cambridge University Press, 2000), p. 21.
47 I. Clendinnen, *True Stories* (Sydney: ABC Books, 1997); I. Clendinnen, *Tiger's Eye: A Memoir* (Melbourne: Text Publishing, 2000); R. Manne, *The Culture of Forgetting: Helen Demidenko and the Holocaust* (Melbourne: Text Publishing Company, 1996); H. Reynolds, *Why Weren't We Told? A Personal Search for the Truth about Our History* (Ringwood, Vic.: Viking, 1999).
48 G. Whitlock, 'Why Then a Writer of Memoirs Is a Better Thing Than an Historian?', in R. Dalziell (ed.), *Selves Crossing Cultures* (Sydney: ASC, 2000).
49 Z. Bauman, 'Is There a Postmodern Turn?' in S. Seidman (ed.), *The Postmodern Turn: New Perspectives on Social Theory* (Cambridge: Cambridge University Press, 1994).
50 Milloy, *A National Crime*, p. xviii.
51 Haebich, *Broken Circles*, p. 16.
52 Whitlock, 'In the Second Person', p. 211.
53 R. Wiebe and Y. Johnson, *Stolen Life: The Journey of a Cree Woman* (Toronto: Alfred A. Knopf, 1998).
54 S. Egan, 'Telling Trauma: Generic Dissonance in the Production of *Stolen Life*', *Canadian Literature*, 167 (2000), 10–29, at 18.
55 Ibid., p. 26.
56 K. Benterrak, S. Muecke and P. Roe, *Reading the Country: Introduction to Nomadology* (Fremantle: Fremantle Arts Centre Press, 1996).
57 M. Humphrey, 'From Terror to Trauma', p. 21.
58 P. Read, *A Rape of the Soul So Profound: The Return of the Stolen Generations* (St Leonards, NSW: Allen & Unwin, 1999).
59 M. Fee, 'Reading Aboriginal Lives', *Canadian Literature*, 165 (2000), 5–7, at 7.
60 R. McKenzie and J. Gibson, *Molly Lennon's Story: 'That's How it Was'* (Adelaide: Aboriginal Heritage Branch, South Australian Department of Environment and Planning, 1989).
61 R. Chrisjohn, Sherri Young and Michael Maraun, *The Circle Game: Shadows and Substance in the Indian Residential School Experience in Canada* (Penticton, BC: Theytus Books, 1997), p. 16.
62 B. Attwood, '"Learning About the Truth": The Stolen Generations Narrative', in B. Attwood and F. Magowan, *Telling Stories: Indigenous History and Memory in Australia and New Zealand* (Crow's Nest, NSW: Allen & Unwin, 2001), p. 211.
63 P. van Toorn, 'Tactical History Business', *Southerly*, 59 (1999), 252–66, at 255.
64 A. Johnston and A. Lawson, 'Settler Colonies', in H. Schwarz and S. Ray (eds), *A Companion to Postcolonial Studies* (London: Blackwell, 2001), p. 365.

CHAPTER TWO

Solly Sachs, the Great Trek and Jan van Riebeeck: settler pasts and racial identities in the Garment Workers' Union, 1938–52[1]

Leslie Witz

In 1951, a journalist for the *New Statesman and Nation*, who was also secretary to the League for Colonial Freedom, visited what he described as the 'region of permanent white settlement' in Africa, 'from the southern border of the Congo to the Cape of Good Hope'. On his travels he reported that European settlers had established their own imperial systems of control in the area, in effect colonising 'the Bantu, the non-European'. The result, he noted, was that all aspects of society, particularly in South Africa, were dominated by racial oppression to the extent that it 'penetrates the most intimate relations between man and man and man and woman, invades the lives of everyone, tempts and besieges even the most unwilling heart'. Industrial developments that had taken place in Central and Southern Africa since the 1940s were not easing this racial oppression: on the contrary, the settler – or, as he termed it, 'the white man' – was finding new ways to extend forms of segregation, 'binding the African to pre-conditions of helotry' under the terms of either apartheid or white dominion.[2]

Yet, in South Africa, the picture painted by that journalist was not entirely bleak. Where the 'white man ... [had] ... settled as a native',[3] it was to a group of Afrikaans-speaking white women that he pointed as presenting a chance for racial integration to take place. These women were members of the Garment Workers' Union (GWU), a trade union based largely in the South African industrial heartland of the Witwatersrand. The majority of its 6,000 (in 1940) to 13,000 (in 1951) members were Afrikaans-speaking women, racially designated by the Board of Trade and Industry as 'European', who worked as machinists in clothing factories.[4] Coming from very conservative rural backgrounds, they regarded 'the natives as being pretty well sub-human',[5] though by the 1950s, the writer noted, something of this attitude had disappeared, and members of the union were beginning to shed their racial prejudices. Much of this change in attitude he ascribed largely to Solly Sachs, the general secretary of the GWU between 1928 and 1952, who had breached this 'solid wall of prejudice' by emphasising the need for unity in the workers' struggle for better living and working conditions. For the journalist, members of the GWU thus represented a 'Hope for White and Black' in South Africa, as they helped create 'a climate of opinion where the issues of a multi-racial society' were 'no longer acute, frightening or insoluble'.[6] The writer issued a word of caution, however: even among these workers there were still 'deep-set feelings of contempt and dislike for their non-white fellow members',[7] feelings which he ascribed to the social and economic pressures of a racially structured society.

What were those pressures and how did they operate? How did they play themselves out at specific times in the world of the GWU and its members? I address these questions by examining in some detail two commemorative festivals in which GWU members were invited to participate, even if only in a limited way: the 1938 centenary festival which commemorated the movement of farmers from the coastal plains to the highveld, cast as an odyssey of the pre-ordained founding of the 'Afrikaner nation' and labelled the 'Great Trek'; and the 1952 tercentenary festival which transformed the 1652 arrival at the Cape of Jan van Riebeeck, a commander of the Dutch East India Company with the task of setting up a revictualling station, into the originating moment of European settlement and South African history. The focus is primarily on this latter occasion, in which the 'white race' was conceived of as the exclusive and inclusive South African nation and Van Riebeeck proclaimed as the initiator of the policy of apartheid.[8]

GWU members were encouraged to participate in and become part of the communities of memory that these two festivals constructed. In 1938 their participation in the events of the festival of Afrikaner nationhood was directly encouraged; there is, however, no evidence of a concerted attempt in 1952 to include the garment workers in the proceedings, and it appears from the GWU records that the union paid little attention to the festival. Instead workers' allegiance to the 'European nation' of Jan van Riebeeck and his wife Maria was sought more indirectly through the pages of two magazines, *Sarie Marais* and the short-lived *Klerewerkersnuus* (Clothing Workers' News). The former magazine, established in 1949, was designed for young, working, modern, Afrikaans-speaking women, while the latter publication, which began in 1950, specifically targeted what it referred to as 'white women and girls'[9] working in clothing factories. In both instances – 1938 and 1952 – the primary purpose was to wean clothing industry workers away from the sway of Sachs and the largely class-based ideology of the union and into the Afrikaner Nationalist fold in its various forms. A key element in the strategic offensive of the Afrikaner Nationalists was to emphasise issues of race, paying particular attention to what they termed the 'dangers' of economic and social integration. The leaders of the GWU spent much time devising strategies to rebuff this offensive, offering alternative historical visions and memories in the process. To focus on these commemorative events and their relationship to the GWU thus provides a means by which to examine these contests and the struggles to designate and define historical constituencies in racialised pasts.

The 1938 centenary festival

The *voortrekker* centenary was arranged by the Afrikaans Language and Cultural Association (ATKV) and was concerned primarily with inculcating the sense of a classless, unified, white Afrikaner *volk*. Central to this identity was a history that was structured by an anti-imperial framework, the spatial movement of the trek signifying a struggle against colonial domination emanating from the Cape towards the 'freedom' of the Boer Republics on the highveld. The progression of ox-driven wagons from various centres was used to create local and national identities in expression of which individuals embarked on their own travels, associating the space of the trek with personal journeys of identification with an Afrikaner past. From different parts of the country these wagons traversed the 'Road of South Africa' to Pretoria where the foundation stone of a voortrekker monument was laid.[10] Travelling through different towns, the festival drew together the white Afrikaans-speaking population, 'stretching from the Cape to Pretoria', in 'a massive cultural orgy'.[11]

The voortrekkers of 1938 bore the Afrikaner nation on their journeys to Pretoria and simultaneously covered the route of racial conquest. As the nine wagons passed through 500 towns, covering the route of South Africa – which, it was proclaimed, the voortrekkers had made 'inhabitable for a white race' – streets were renamed after voortrekker leaders, new-born babies were given names commemorating the trek and, in speech after speech, the 'virtues of the Voortrekkers' and the 'impregnable frontier for western civilisation' established by them were extolled.[12] The history which was conveyed on these journeys of conquest began with Van Riebeeck's arrival at the Cape and his founding of 'the cradle of our South African civilisation' at the foot of Table Mountain; and it reached its turning point when Sarel Cilliers made a prayer to God prior to the battle with a section of the Zulu army at Blood River in 1838.[13] The voortrekkers were named as the 'true founders' of white South Africa, outstripping all potential claimants, with the trek of 1938 seen as bringing that history to its destination in an Afrikaner-led 'glorious Blood River victory' and the emergence of 'white South Africa'.[14]

Central to this discourse of an anti-imperial, racially triumphant, Afrikaner nationalism which was borne on the trek of 1938 was the image of the maternal duty of Afrikaner women in the service of the volk, embodied in the term *volksmoeder* (volks mother), enlisting the private domain of mothering in the service of the volk. In the 1920s, with large numbers of white Afrikaans-speaking women moving to urban areas, taking up employment in factories, and, with the enfranchisement of white women imminent, patriarchal domination within *white* households had come under increasing threat. Within Afrikaner Nationalist circles it became politically necessary to actively encourage women to enter the public sphere, while continuing to define that participation through the home and the mother.[15] Coupling ethnic and gender identities through the idealised 'mother in the house' as a universal category provided the bonding to shore up the imagined community of white Afrikaners.

The construction of the volksmoeder was dependent both on establishing a sense of internal coherence and on situating its discourse in antagonism to an external identity depicted as a threat – in this instance, black men and women. This 'peril' was located within both the domestic and the public sphere, where the importance both of the household in maintaining Afrikaner purity and of measures to protect jobs was articulated, in magazines like *Die Boerevrou*, by asserting racial exclusivity and superiority. The message was reinforced in the trek of 1938, where images of Africaner women in immaculate white bonnets and dresses served as 'boundary markers visibly upholding the fetish signs of national difference and visibly embodying the iconography of race and gender purity'.[16]

The Kappie Kommado *and the union guard*

In the late 1930s such images of white Afrikaner women protecting and maintaining the racial purity of the volk were directly threatened by the growing strength of the GWU. Its women members were becoming increasingly assertive within the household, in which they were often the primary wage-earner, and on the factory floor, showing increasing allegiance to the union which had almost consistently secured higher wages for them; and they were being attracted to an ideology which used symbols of an Afrikaner past but cast them in terms of class, rather than nationalist, struggle. The general secretary of the GWU, Solly Sachs, was concerned to show to members that the 'Afrikaner people are not the only ones who suffer bitterly from Imperialist exploitation' and that Afrikaners, like all nationalities, would not achieve independence until the imperialism associated with monopoly capitalism was destroyed.[17] This found resonance in the plays written by GWU members in which the poverty of the Afrikaner was depicted as the outcome of class oppression, with wealthy Afrikaners sometimes portrayed as the oppressors. Such an approach was anathema to the emergent Afrikaner Nationalist movement, which, through its newspapers, like *Die Vaderland*, accused Sachs of 'spreading poisonous teaching among our workers, destroying our spiritual values and uprooting the South African worker from his association with relation and nation'.[18]

When the GWU leadership decided that its members would participate in the 1938 festival it evoked a similar response from the Afrikaner Nationalist movement. The GWU formed a 400-strong Kappie Kommando to take part, and its members, in voortrekker dress, attended specially arranged song-and-dance classes to prepare themselves for the various ceremonies, with the intention of paying homage to the men they proclaimed as their ancestors. Voortrekker leaders Piet Retief, Dirkie Uys and Sarel Cilliers were constructed by the GWU leadership as having 'a deep love for freedom', and workers were encouraged to follow in their assumed tradition and fight for liberation against the forces of capitalism.[19] The entire aim of the centenary festival, to promote unity of the volk, was being subverted by the GWU. The Nasionale Raad van Trustees (NRT), a body established by the Afrikaner *Broederbond* in 1936 to establish trade unions that would be consistent with the cause of Afrikaner nationalism, and cast itself as the rescuer of factory workers from the jaws of both capitalism and communism, accused the GWU of making 'a mockery of our national traditions'. The NRT agent who concerned himself with the GWU, D. B. H. Grobbelaar, demanded that the garment workers participate in the festival not as a class, 'but all together with us as Boers – the factory girl together with the professor's wife'.[20] Only the 'new-born nation' of Afrikaners, maintained Grobbelaar, would be able to put the capitalists 'in their place'.[21]

Grobbelaar consistently constructed and saturated categories with racial meanings in order to designate the GWU as un-nationalist. He accused Solly Sachs of being a communist, who, in collaboration with a clique of Jewish capitalists, was subtly and surreptitiously attempting to achieve Jewish domination of the world. The means by which to achieve that domination, according to Grobbelaar, was to accentuate class categories, not racial markers. From 1937 the NRT had attempted to show that the GWU leadership was transgressing the imagined boundaries of race by organising parties at which the garment workers apparently danced with 'natives'.[22] When the GWU stated its intention to participate in the 1938 festival Grobbelaar again relied on racial associations to designate the activities of the union as foreign to the national citizenry of white Afrikaners. 'You and Johanna Cornelius [GWU national organiser] who all day organise and address kaffers', he wrote to Solly Sachs, 'will you dare to bring them along to the celebrations? They are all your fellow workers and "comrades".'[23]

The showdown between the NRT and the GWU leadership took place three months after the commemorative events of December 1938. In the interim a union guard of loyal members was formed to defend the GWU from the Afrikaner Nationalists. The guard, its members wearing a uniform of black skirt, white blouse cut in a waistcoat style, trimmed with red buttons and cords, and small Glengarry cap, would hold marching and singing exercises while keeping a look out for Nationalist infiltrators.[24] On 9 March 1939 a debate between Sachs and Grobbelaar took place in the Selborne Hall, Johannesburg, with the union guard present. Sachs and Grobbelaar outlined their positions, although the latter was barely audible above the jeering that accompanied his presentation. The vote expressed almost unanimous approval for Sachs, only 15 of the 2,000-strong audience indicating support for Grobbelaar.[25] This was a clear indication that the Nationalists were not making inroads into the union, and they admitted as much at the Ekonomiese Volkskongres in October 1939 during which no mention was made of an attempt to take over the GWU.[26]

Afrikaner Nationalists regarded their failure to take over the union as due to the military-style tactics of the dictatorial Sachs and the presence of the union guard. This might indicate that the running of the union was less democratic than Sachs was given to suggest, and, in a agitated environment, with the guard ever present, that it was difficult for members to express dissent with the leader. Yet, there does seem to have been much more of a spontaneous allegiance to the GWU and its leaders than the Nationalists would credit. The strong organisational structure of the union, the formation of a workers' cadre that was totally loyal to the leadership, together with the visible attainment of material benefits, all contributed to the warding off of the Nationalist assault. Moreover much the same symbols of an Afrikaner national past were utilised by the GWU as by the Nationalists to define *loyalty*. While not cast in the same terms, the union's use of those symbols did not entirely upset an Afrikaner past that was littered with male heroes and stoic volksmoeders on a journey away from colonial and capitalist oppression. The pervasive anti-imperial framework of the centenary trek of 1938 enabled the union to identify its membership and their activities with an Afrikaner nationalist past.

Crucially, the union leadership self-consciously demarcated racial boundaries. In 1938, 82 per cent of the clothing industry's workforce in the Transvaal and the Free State was designated 'European' by the Board of Trade and Industry, 14 per cent as 'native' (most of them men), with 'coloureds' and 'indians' comprising the remainder.[27] The 'native' workers were separated from the GWU both on the shopfloor – they were mainly pressers – and in their organisation, belonging to the South African Clothing Workers' Union, members of which received little assistance from fellow-workers in their struggles. 'Coloured' workers, mainly female machinists, were later accepted into the GWU, but in a parallel branch. The GWU leadership maintained that the only way it could keep the union in place was by establishing these racially separate structures.[28] Indeed, when in its publicity material the GWU referred to race it was with the sense that all workers were naturally white and that 'racial hatred' was about Afrikaners hating non-Afrikaners, and 'Britishers', in turn, expressing enmity against Afrikaners. By categorising 'workers and citizens' in terms of *European* races the GWU kept itself carefully within the racial demarcations that Grobbelaar and the NRT accused it of violating.[29]

On the beach with the Van Riebeecks at Granger Bay

It was the cross-class alliance among whites with an identity determined as Afrikaans and a past written as a struggle for freedom that provided the basis for the election success of the National Party (NP) in 1948. The hold that the NP had on state power, however, was fragile, not only because of the narrowness of its election victory, but because of the pressure it was under to come up with a policy that would deal with the growth in African urbanisation and the accompanying upsurge in political militancy in the 1940s, perceived by most whites as an imminent threat to the supremacy that they had taken for granted. In this tenuous position the 'quest for legitimacy across [white] class lines' became a crucial component of NP's political strategy, playing a major role in formulating apartheid policy and a history and identity for whites *as* whites that reinforced and authenticated their notions of supremacy.[30] The voortrekker past that had been produced since the 1870s was not ideal for these purposes, as it set itself against other white identities. Many of those whom the NP sought to incorporate within a settler nation could not associate themselves with a history that was, at its core, based on a struggle against those who they identified as ancestors. The coincidence in 1952 of the tercentenary of Jan van Riebeeck's landing provided the ideal moment at which to claim another set of historical events as the basis of a white identity.

The NP government gave its wholehearted support and financial backing to an initiative from the Federation of Afrikaans Cultural Associations (FAK) for a proposed Van Riebeeck festival to assume a national character by drawing together the races, where 'race' referred to what was deemed to be an ancestry based on language and culture, the one related to an Afrikaans-speaking world, the other to an English-speaking one. The festival was designed to commemorate a commonality of all whites as a distinct nation with their joint past deriving from Europe and Van Riebeeck. With the need to show beginning, progress and achievement of a self-proclaimed nationhood, the festival's central committee decided to focus on producing the past via a series of historical exhibitions. Among other items, these involved a reconstruction of the landing of Van Riebeeck at Granger Bay and a pageant in Adderley Street, Cape Town, depicting highlights of 300 years of South African history. Presenting a history for Van Riebeeck was no easy matter, as there was no single *European* narrative which could be easily drawn on. Rather, there were different histories which at times were complementary, but equally stood in contradistinction to each other. The past which was eventually scripted by the festival's pageant committee, with the help of Professor H. B. Thom of Stellenbosch University, stressed a consensual history of the 'white nation', commencing in 'Africa: Dark and Unknown', followed by seventy floats emphasising European settlement and co-operation, and ending with 'Africa Liberated'.[31] Even this history created problems, as depictions of the South African War showing Boer women in mourning dress were criticised by representatives of the Chamber of Mines, the Anglo-American Corporation and sections of the English-language press for 'putting white against white' instead of advocating a 'united race' to face the 'danger' of being 'overwhelmed by the Bantu'.[32] Threatened with a pull-out from the Anglo-American Corporation and the Chamber of Mines, the scripted past for Van Riebeeck was hastily revised to tone down the South African War depictions and to place more emphasis on the coming of union in 1910.

This shifting of the direction for the Van Riebeeck festival was not received with great enthusiasm within Afrikaner Nationalist circles, particularly in the north of the country where the Afrikaner Broederbond dominated the Nationalist movement. More than the watering down of the South African War scenes, it was the exclusion of Afrikaner women from Van Riebeeck's history that was a major issue. Van Riebeeck, the lone man on the coastal plains, could not be the founder of white South Africa in the voortrekker past without his family to accompany him. It was white women, asserted a FAK delegation, who had provided the men with white companions, held the family together and were 'absolutely essential' in ensuring 'the whiteness of the developing volk'.[33]

The ATKV went out of its way to devise schemes that would highlight the role of Afrikaner women in the portrayals of South African history for the Van Riebeeck festival. Other than in the float processions, the image of woman as wife and mother of the nation was promoted by popularising the icon of Maria de la Quellerie (van Riebeeck) as the 'housewife' who devoted her life to Jan and these other 'womanly' tasks.[34] The Afrikaans women's magazine *Sarie Marais* began a 'Search for Jan van Riebeeck's Wife' for the pageant of the landing at Granger Bay. The essential criteria for the part were that she had to be of small stature, about 23 years of age, with dark eyes and light-brown hair so as to match the seventeenth-century portrait of her by Dick Craey. The winner would receive £75, travel to Cape Town, be dressed in an appropriate costume, and stand silently, on the beach at Granger Bay, alongside the eminent South African actor Andre Huguenet as he played the part of Jan van Riebeeck. Her only duty was to serve wine to Jan and the accompanying soldiers, and then to present him with the cask containing the 'Treasury of the Nation'.[35]

This 1952 emphasis on white women in the iconisation of Maria was not solely an extension of *volksmoeder* discourse: there was also the popularisation of her image as the Cape's first lady and someone who combined tolerance with an appropriate application of know-ledge. Maria de la Quellerie became a 'woman of breeding', who, after being welcomed by 'a group of savages' at the Cape, lived a 'lonely, isolated life' because she had no one from 'her own social sphere' with whom to communicate and she feared the 'little, brown Hottentot men'. Yet, it was this isolation that made Maria, more than Jan – who sometimes dirtied his hands in the employ of the Dutch East India Company – the bearer of a European racial essence that was constituted in social terms as innately aristocratic, her blue blood bestowing on the Company fort the title of 'THE FIRST HOME' at the Cape.[36]

Maria's colonial imagery coalesced with a shift that was starting to occur in Afrikaner Nationalist discourse about women in the 1950s.

The narrative of Afrikaner women as housewives and mothers of the community of the volk began to incorporate a greater sense of modernity in place of a reliance on the *pastness* of tradition. This was no more evident than in the magazine that had launched the search for Maria de la Quellerie, *Sarie Marais*. Although there were items of historical interest, its areas of concentration were stories of romance and how Afrikaner women had achieved success. In 1951–52 *Sarie Marais* also ran a controversial column entitled '*Sê my Dokter*' (Tell Me Doctor), in which a doctor gave advice to 'mothers, young women, daughters' on 'specific ailments and dangers to which they are exposed as women'. Letters flooded in to the magazine, some offering support for the supposed informative function of the column, others condemning it for showing no respect for the privacy of the body. The editor defended the column on the basis that medical knowledge was an absolute necessity for the modern woman.[37] This modern woman, as characterised on the front cover of *Sarie Marais*, wore the latest fashions, smoked cigarettes – which were manufactured by the Rembrandt Tobacco Corporation in factories where the employment of 'white girls' was preferred – and drank tea. The latter image represented a marked shift away from *Die Boerevrou* where the drinking of coffee had been the metaphor used to draw the women into a bounded community around the imagined ceremony of imbibing the *volksdrank* (people's drink). The drinking of tea was regarded as the preserve of those who were 'uppity' and would not associate with the 'real' *boerevrou* around the coffee table;[38] by 1952 tea drinking had established an association with a knowledge of the modern world and the 'women of South Africa' became 'ladies' who were now to be found seated 'Round the Tea Table' discussing matters of topicality rather than communality.[39]

Although white women were still identified with the home and Maria was given the appellation of 'THE FIRST HOME MAKER',[40] the person who won the competition to 'Act Van Riebeeck's Wife at [the] Festival'[41] was more than merely a face to match that of Craey's portrait. Frances Holland from Durban was an actress who had appeared on stage, in movies and on radio. Apparently quite fortuitously, she was also a descendant of both the 1820 settlers from England and the voortrekker leader Andries Pretorious, thus embodying (and reproducing) the drawing together of the European 'races' towards which Maria de la Quellerie had earlier worked and which Jan van Riebeeck/Andre Huguenet was ritualising in 1952. Frances's husband, Douglas Fuchs, was the regional director of the South African Broadcasting Corporation in Natal, a good friend of Andre Huguenet and the chair of the Durban Van Riebeeck festival committee. Yet, it was as Frances Holland that

Maria took her place on the beach alongside Andre Huguenet in 1952.[42] In a ceremony from which she had previously been excluded by both the daily diarist of the Dutch East India Company at the Cape in the seventeenth century and the artistic imagination of Charles Davidson Bell, who had painted his depiction of the landing in 1850, she now 'stood at Jan's side in the presence of the men [and 20,000 spectators] who formed his small band of pioneers and . . . listened to the simple service when he planted the flag' at Granger Bay on Saturday 5 April 1952.[43]

The professional factory worker from Europe

The imagery of the modern European women associated with Maria de la Quellerie in the pages of *Sarie Marais* was paralleled by its depictions of white Afrikaner women at work. No longer were these women portrayed as defenceless beings needing to be saved by the proponents of Afrikaner nationalism, but were individuals who could make choices about whether and where to work. Articles told about Afrikaner women as wine-makers, filling-station attendants and factory workers with a sense of self-respect, the women being lauded for showing economic self-sufficiency.[44] Soon after it was established the magazine ran a feature, in the form of a debate, on whether married women should work. Although *Sarie Marais* asserted that it was presenting both sides of the argument, there was a clear sense throughout its early editions that it favoured the working women who became 'economically independent' and so could lead a 'fuller and more satisfactory life'.[45] Importantly, in addition to being workers, women were cast by the magazine as consumers who purchased products rather than making them at home; and its advertisements of clothing, shoes, forms of medication and cigarettes were supplemented by weekly articles on the latest fashions, including a pictorial account of a visit to the House of Christian Dior, and on new styles of blouse, short dresses for evening wear and clothes designed specially for the South African woman. The front cover of the first edition of *Sarie Marais* contained a background pencil sketch of a *voortrekkernooi* (young voortrekker woman) wearing a kappie; in the foreground was a *moderne nooientjie* (modern young women) in an 'attractive' striped shirt. Claiming descent from the former, the editor maintained that the montage showed how modern fashions borrowed from the old;[46] yet, the voortrekkernooi on the cover was fading into the background shadows, to be replaced by the foregrounded Afrikaner working woman who was 'civilized' and belonged to the modern world out of Europe and Maria de la Quellerie.

The modern working woman of *Sarie Marais* was not entirely welcomed by those who expected the magazine to carry the stamp of what they termed the 'ideal Afrikaner woman'. Letters appeared describing *Sarie Marais* as a mere translation of the kind of women's magazine readily acquired in Britain, one which targeted not the 'ordinary girl', like an 'Anna' or a 'Sarie', but the 'foreign form', a 'Grace' or a 'Joyce'. It was criticised for concentrating heavily on fashion and ignoring church matters, and the volk's moral and spiritual values. For a magazine that was supposed to develop the volk's character, all it was doing, claimed one writer, was feeding on images of woman's bodies, particularly on the front cover and other pictorial representations, but also the stories, nearly all of which contained descriptions of the female body. What these letter-writers presented as most disturbing was that the depictions of the bodies of white women would inadvertently transgress the constructed boundaries of race, for 'native men', it was claimed, could now buy these bodies from magazine vendors for a mere sixpence and then use them to decorate their houses. These racial imaginings were unacceptable, and it was suggested that the front cover depict instead 'natural scenes'; meanwhile, these letter-writers recommended, those who purchased the magazine should destroy the front cover in case the 'natives' managed to get hold of them.[47]

Yet, such letters disapproving the depictions in *Sarie Marais* were not, in terms of those published in the magazine, the overwhelming response: there were many more whom defended its contents, claiming that the diversity of topics it covered both entertained and gave invaluable information to the modern woman. The writers of the condemnatory letters were accused of remaining tied to the past and not moving forward into the modern world. The 'ideal Afrikaner woman' was not one who never changed her hairstyle, who did not wear lipstick and who sacrificed her life to the kitchen, wrote Mrs Visser of Durbanville, but was instead constantly searching to enrich herself and develop her position by investigating opportunities beyond the home. As far as the front cover was concerned, Mrs Coetzer of De Doorns wrote, anyone – white or coloured – could acquire far more sensational pictures from other available magazines: there was nothing in the pictures to specifically entice the imagined racial transgressions constructed by the defenders of the 'real and traditional' Afrikaner woman.[48]

These contested shifts in the definition of the Afrikaner woman, particularly in the work context, were evident when another attempt was made by Nationalist groups to take control of the GWU in the late 1940s and early 1950s. There were two spheres from which these offensives were mounted, the one being from within state structures

– very soon after it came to power in 1948 the National Party Government appointed a commission of inquiry into the affairs of the GWU – the other from the clothing factories in Germiston, where many of the Afrikaans-speaking white workers were employed. The latter, on which I here focus, labelled itself the 'Action Committee', maintaining that it was concerned to preserve for white women workers both skilled and semi-skilled jobs in the clothing industry. At the time many black women workers were becoming machinists in factories on the Witwatersrand, and white women were voluntarily moving out of the industry into higher paid office jobs.[49] The 'White Workers' Protection Society', as the 'Action Committee' styled itself, asserted that white women had been pressured into leaving the industry by employers intent on low rates of pay for long hours of work. The GWU, according to the Action Committee, had not afforded any protection to these white workers because the union, being run by a 'little Russian Jew', did not have the interest of the Afrikaner at heart.[50] This was reminiscent of the discourse the NRT had used in the 1930s to project the 'Afrikaner's inborn sense of freedom . . . the most characteristic attribute of the Afrikaner nation', the opposite of the racial characterisation of Sachs. After struggling through a 'stormy three centuries of . . . history', representatives of the Action Committee asserted, the Afrikaner had emerged 'triumphant' and lit the fires of political liberation in 1949 at the opening of the Voortrekker Monument in Pretoria. Now the time had come to achieve economic freedom as well, by replacing the current leadership of the GWU with Afrikaners, 'flesh of your flesh and blood of your blood'.[51]

At the same time as an Afrikaner past was being produced in *Klerewerkersnuus*, the magazine – launched as an organ of 'national opposition' to 'racial equality'[52] – was also drafting the white workers in the clothing industry into a European past that was more consistent with the emergent trend in *Sarie Marais*. White workers in the industry were labelled as naturally skilled and European, while black workers were considered naturally unskilled and non-European. A European heritage was marked as the essential element to acquiring proficiency: 'Efficient men and women were imported from overseas. They were all from the Western countries and they trained local men and women workers. Men and women workers were also sent from here to Europe to receive training there.' European heritage gave the white worker an 'inbred skilfulness', making her 'more intelligent than the non-European'. Inexorably, this led to the appearance of the image of the professional European worker, 'hard-working, skilful and intelligent', 'capable of a regular and high production', thereby contributing to the 'prosperity of the industry'. Unlike Solly Sachs, these workers, in the words of *Klerewerkersnuus*, were clearly not 'descendants of imported products of doubtful origin'.[53]

The union's attempts to keep the Nationalists at bay were less successful in this period than they had been in 1938. Although there was still a firm commitment on the part of members to the leadership, the Germiston branch of the union was shut down because of the 'confusion' and 'disorder' which the GWU's central executive claimed had arisen there.[54] Clearly the circumstances that confronted the union in 1938 were markedly different from those of the late 1940s and early 1950s: the Nationalists had acquired state power and the racial basis by which the workforce had been defined had altered. Even more than this, however, the historical constituency on which the GWU had built and sustained its powerful position, in relation both to the employers and to the Nationalists, had begun to be modified. No longer were the white members of the GWU the same *volksmoeders*, or 'rebel's daughters', whom Sachs had idealised.[55] Their identities were shifting towards a modern past that was derived no longer from the voortrekkers but from Jan and Maria van Riebeeck and 'Western civilisation'.

In order to encourage participation in May Day processions in the early 1950s, Sachs tried to arouse sentiments similar to those he had elicited in 1938. In line with its policies of parallel unionism, the GWU ensured that the route taken by the 'non-European demonstration' would 'avoid contact' with that taken by 'garment workers'. Despite Sachs's protestations, the response from both the leaders and the members of the union was one of apathy and lack of interest.[56] Indeed, the history that the GWU was beginning to promote was not one that fitted in with Sachs's image of an anti-imperialist past. In the *Garment Worker*, the union's official organ, articles began to appear about clothing factories and their histories, stories which told of a 'picturesque' past that had been devoid of conflict, a past where 'ox-wagons' (the symbol of the 1938 centenary trek) and mail coaches (a key symbol of the Van Riebeeck festival) traversed an 'uninhabited' land that, without history, had become transformed into modern cities with 'motor cars, trains . . . aeroplanes', and H. J. Henochsberg (Pty), Ltd.[57] Although Sachs maintained much of his union support base, until he was banned in 1952 and left South Africa the following year, and despite the union's running battle with the Nationalists, there were the beginnings of a much greater consensus between this historical record of modern South Africa and that which the Nationalists were deriving from the Van Riebeecks. It was little wonder, then, that shortly before his banning order was served Sachs bemoaned what the union had become – 'a cold-blooded, cheque book organisation'.[58]

'Hope for white and black'

A little over a year later Solly Sachs was banned under the Suppression of Communism Act and decided to leave South Africa. He spent the remaining twenty-three years of his life in Britain and was quickly forgotten by the membership of the GWU in which he, along with the writer from the *New Statesman*, had placed great faith. Even prior to Sachs's departure there had been signs that members were associating themselves with a broad white identity, rather than a narrow Afrikaner one. Constructing 'racial solidarity amongst its beneficiaries'[59] had been one of the central elements of apartheid policy, and the Van Riebeeck festival of 1952 was a key moment in the production of this racially exclusive national identity. Selected events and associated icons from various pasts were used to specify the founding moment of a settler nation that defined itself as the South African nation. The white workers, whom Sachs did not want to write off 'as a bunch of white overlords',[60] were no longer drinking coffee and struggling against the forces of imperialism, but now were sipping tea, which had been elevated to the status of 'the national drink',[61] at the table of Jan and Maria van Riebeeck at the Castle in Cape Town.

The Nationalists did not so easily forget Sachs, against whom they had battled, largely unsuccessfully, for many years. In 1963, the Afrikaans magazine *Die Huisgenoot*, identified him as one of the greatest enemies of South Africa.[62] And what of the journalist who had pinned so much hope on the garment workers? Well, his deepest fears came to fruition as an even stronger sense of a racialised white identity developed in South Africa over the next thirty years: successive NP governments, totally averse to any negative criticism of the racially constituted South African nation they had constructed and promoted, refused to allow him back into the country. In the interim he had become one of the most prominent and prolific historians of Africa, writing books on ancient African kingdoms, the beginnings of the Atlantic slave trade and African nationalist movements. He was finally invited back to South Africa some seven years after Nelson Mandela had been released, an event that he celebrated as 'a moment of affirmation in the record of Africa's history...[an] entirely convincing denial of the mythologies of modern racism'.[63] By 1997, however, he was too frail to travel and, on 21 April, in a small ceremony at the University of Bristol, Basil Davidson, who had 'been expelled from the old South Africa at the beginning of his career', was awarded an honorary doctorate by the University of the Western Cape in recognition of his work in 'combating the racist presumption that Africa has no history of note' and 'bringing the contours of that previously hidden history to public knowledge'.[64]

Notes

1   This chapter is based on research conducted for 'The Project on Public Pasts', funded by the National Research Foundation (NRF), based in the history department at the University of the Western Cape. The financial support of the NRF towards this research is hereby acknowledged. Opinions expressed in this paper and conclusions arrived at are those of the author and are not necessarily to be attributed to the NRF. I wish to thank also my colleagues Ciraj Rassool and Gary Minkley, with whom I have worked in close collaboration over the years on areas of public history. In this chapter I draw on that work.
2   B. Davidson, *Report on Southern Africa* (London: Jonathan Cape, 1952), pp. 11–25, 270.
3   Ibid., p. 11.
4   South African Board of Trade and Industry Report no. 303, k285/2.
5   Davidson, *Report on Southern Africa*, p. 179.
6   Ibid., p. 187; B. Davidson, 'The Hope for White and Black', *The New Statesman and Nation*, 4 August 1951.
7   Davidson, *Report on Southern Africa*, p. 186.
8   *Die Transvaler*, 'Van Riebeeck Supplement', 4 April 1952; for an extensive account of the Van Riebeeck festival see L. Witz, *Apartheid's Festival* (Bloomington: Indiana University Press, 2003).
9   *Klerewerkersnuus*, 24 February 1950.
10 D. Mostert (comp.), *Gedenkboek Van Die Ossewaens Op Die Pad Van Suid-Afrika* (Cape Town: Nasionale Pers, 1940), p. 110.
11 *Cape Argus*, 8 August 1938; D. O'Meara, *Volkskapitalisme: Class, Capital and Ideology in the Development of Afrikaner Nationalism 1934–1948* (Johannesburg: Ravan Press, 1983), p. 76; see also A. Grundlingh and H. Sapire, 'From Feverish Festival to Repetitive Ritual? The Changing Fortunes of Great Trek Mythology in an Industrializing South Africa, 1938–1988', *South African Historical Journal*, 21 (1989), 19–37.
12 Grundlingh and Sapire, 'From Feverish Festival to Repetitive Ritual?', pp. 19–20; Mostert, *Gedenkboek*, p. 59.
13 Mostert, *Gedenkboek*, pp. 116, 112.
14 Ibid., p. 117.
15 J. Hyslop, 'White Working-Class Women and the Invention of Apartheid: "Purified" Afrikaner Nationalist Agitation for Legislation Against "Mixed" Marriages, 1934–1939', *Journal of African History*, 36 (1995), 60–5; M. du Toit, 'Women, Welfare and the Nurturing of Afrikaner Nationalism: A Social History of the Afrikaanse Christelike Vroue Vereniging, c.1870–1939', PhD thesis, University of Cape Town (1996), pp. 201–3.
16 A. McClintock, *Imperial Leather* (New York: Routledge, 1995), pp. 377–8.
17 E. S. Sachs to D. B. H. Grobbelaar, 17 December 1938, Garment Workers' Union Records, Historical Papers, University of the Witwatersrand (hereafter GWU), Bcc1.10.
18 *Die Vaderland*, 16 July 1936; for an account of the plays written by members of the GWU, see E. Brink, 'Plays, Poetry and Production: The Literature of the Garment Workers', *South African Labour Bulletin*, 9:8 (July 1984).
19 *Garment Worker*, October 1938.
20 Grobbelaar to Sachs, 27 October 1938, GWU, Bcc1.10.
21 Grobbelaar to Sachs, 11 January 1938, GWU, Bcc1.10.
22 'Klerewerkers en die Voortrekker-Eeufees', pamphlet issued by the GWU, 1938, GWU, Bcc1.10.

23 Grobbelaar to Sachs, 27 October 1938, GWU, Bcc1.10.
24 Minutes of meeting of GWU union guard, 9 February 1939, GWU, Bch 9.
25 For differing accounts of the meeting, see *Garment Worker*, March (1939) and *Die Transvaler*, 10 March 1939.
26 Speech by Dr A. Hertzog at Ekonomiese Volkskongress, October 1939, in L. Naude, *Dr A. Hertzog, Die Nasionale Party en die Mynwerkers* (Potchefstroom: Potchefstroom Herald, 1969), pp. 259–72.
27 South African Board of Trade and Industry Report no. 303, k285/2.
28 For accounts of parallel unionism in the clothing industry see L. Witz, 'Separation for Unity: The Garment Workers' Union and the South African Clothing Workers' Union 1928 to 1936', *Social Dynamics*, 14:1 (June 1988), 34–45, and 'Support or Control? The Children of the Garment Workers' Union', in A. Mabin (ed.), *Organisation and Economic Change* (Johannesburg: Ravan Press, 1989), pp. 120–45.
29 'An Appeal to All Garment Workers and to All Other Workers and Citizens', c.1939, GWU, Bch1.
30 D. Posel, *The Making of Apartheid, 1948–1961: Conflict and Compromise* (Oxford: Oxford University Press 1991), p. 270.
31 See Witz, *Apartheid's Festival*, chapter 2, for an extensive account of these negotiations over the presented past of the Van Riebeeck festival; see also C. Rassool and L. Witz, 'The 1952 Jan van Riebeeck Tercentenary Festival: Constructing and Contesting Public National History in South Africa', *Journal of African History*, 34 (1993), 447–68.
32 'Report for the Festival Fair Committee on the Political Aspect in the Transvaal, 1951', Cape Archives, Donges Collection, A1646, vol. 339; *Benoni City Times*, 13 July 1951.
33 'Bedenkinge in verband met die historiese volksoptog', 4 August 1951, Institute for Contemporary History, University of the Free State (INCH), PV 379, A11/13.
34 The Government's Department of Agriculture, which since 1949 had published the 'first Official Journal for the Housewife', *The Woman and Her Home*, produced a special edition for the Van Riebeeck festival with a front cover showing the wife of Kommandeur Jan van Riebeeck. Penny stamps depicting the portrait of Maria by Dick Craey were issued for the tercentenary, forming part of a commemorative set. The Cape Town City Council decided to name a street after her and the Dutch royal family signalled its intention, on behalf of the people of Holland, to present Cape Town with a statue of Maria de la Quellerie. Under the auspices of Zuid-Afrikaansche Stichting Moederland (South African Foundation Motherland), a biography entitled *Huisvrouw van Jan van Riebeeck* (Housewife of Jan van Riebeeck), written by W. C. Mees, was published in Holland.
35 *Sarie Marais*, 26 September 1951; *Die Volksblad*, 20 September 1951.
36 G. Mills, *First Ladies of the Cape* (Cape Town: Maskew Miller, 1952), pp. 1, 9; I. Wilson, *They Founded for the Future* (Cape Town: Maskew Miller, 1952), p. 16.
37 *Sarie Marais*, 26 December 1951.
38 L. Kruger, 'Gender, Community and Identity: Women and Afrikaner Nationalism in the Volksmoeder Discourse of Die Boerevrou (1919–1931)', M.Soc.Sci. dissertation, University of Cape Town (1991), pp. 244–7; O'Meara, *Volkskapitalisme*, p. 204.
39 'Round the Tea-Table', *The Woman and Her Home*, March (1952), 51.
40 Wilson, *They Founded for the Future*, p. 14.
41 *Cape Times*, 18 August 1951.
42 *Sarie Marais*, 20 February 1952.
43 Mills, *First Ladies of the Cape*, p. 6.
44 *Sarie Marais*, 6 and 27 July 1949; 3 August 1949; 26 October 1949.
45 Ibid., 3 August 1949.
46 Ibid., 6 July 1949.
47 Ibid., letters pages for 17 May, and 7, 14, 21 and 28 June 1950.
48 Ibid., 7, 14, 21 and 28 June 1950.

49 Board of Trade and Industry Report no. 303, k285/2; H. A. F. Barker, 'The Economics of the Wholesale Clothing Industry in South Africa (1907–1957)', D.Comm. thesis, UNISA (1961), p. 366.
50 *Klerewerkersnuus*, 1, 16, 22 September 1950.
51 Ibid., 22 September 1950.
52 *Die Vaderland*, 9 February 1950.
53 *Klerewerkersnuus*, 24 February and 24 March 1950.
54 Minutes of the CEC, GWU, 12 June 1951, GWU Baal.
55 'Heil Die Afrikanerwerkster: n Brief van E. S. Sachs', GWU, Bce2.1; E. S. Sachs, 'Heil Volksmoeder, Werkster!', Garment Worker, May–June (1952), and Sach's, *Rebel's Daughter* (London: MacGibbon & Key, 1957).
56 Minutes of the CEC, GWU, 21 February 1950, 24 April 1950, 12 February 1951, 14 January 1952 and 5 May 1952, GWU, Baal.
57 *Garment Worker*, January–February 1950.
58 Minutes of the CEC, GWU, 14 January 1952, GWU, Baal.
59 M. Mamdani, 'Reconciliation Without Justice', *Southern African Review of Books*, November–December (1996), 4.
60 E. S. Sachs to W. H. Andrews, 26 March 1947, GWU, Bce2.1
61 E. Rosenthal, *Tee: Drie Eeue Lank in Ons Land* (Johannesburg: Tee Buro, 1952), p. 10.
62 *Die Huisgenoot*, 4 October 1963.
63 B. Davidson, *Africa in History* (London: Phoenix, 1992), p. xv.
64 Citation for the award of the degree of Doctor Litterarum (honoris causa) to Basil Davidson by the University of the Western Cape, 21 April 1997.

CHAPTER THREE

From prisoners to exhibits: representations of 'Bushmen' of the northern Cape, 1880–1900

Martin Legassick

In my opinion it would be useless to attempt to get a conviction against these [Bush]men for the crimes they have committed or been accessory to. The Evidence necessary if ever existed has now disappeared . . . To place them in service even far from here in the Colony would be of little avail as even if they stayed quietly for a time when the wild fit came over them they would make for the [Orange River] Islands again. The only suitable place for them is Robben Island . . . It is probable that feeling they could not get over the sea they would settle down contentedly and I think would earn their keep and wages. They would also be available for Bushman lore researches.[1]

The author of these words, John Scott, was appointed special magistrate on the Northern Border of the Cape Colony in 1880, at the end of the second resistance war fought by the 'Kora' of the Orange River. He served there, his base first in Kenhardt and then in Upington, on the Orange River, until 1887. He presided over the Baster settlement established in Gordonia (formerly Koranaland), north of the Orange, to defend the frontier and act as a buffer for the Cape Colony against further attacks from the interior. Among his duties was dealing with the 'Bushmen', inhabitants of the area.[2] Through an examination of his relations with 'Bushmen' it is possible to see the transformation of Scott's Cape liberal ideology into one approximating turn-of-the-century racism. Imprisoning them for breaches of colonial law, essentially because the 'Bushmen' refused to become a part of the cheap black labour force required by the colony, Scott also became involved in organising them as subjects of ethnographic research and objects of exhibit and display.

In his book *The Birth of the Museum*, Tony Bennett takes issue with Douglas Crimp for describing the *museum* as another Foucaultian 'institution of confinement'. While the museum and the prison are both articulations of power and knowledge relations, the museum, he insists, is an institution not of *confinement* but of *exhibition*. In contrast to the withdrawal of objects and bodies from the public gaze as punishment took the form of incarceration, the

> institutions comprising the 'exhibitionary complex' . . . were involved in the transfer of objects and bodies from the enclosed and private domains in which they had previously been displayed . . . into progressively more open and public arenas where, through the representations to which they were subjected, they formed vehicles for inscribing and broadcasting the messages of power . . . throughout society.

Institutions of confinement and exhibition moreover solved the problem of order in different ways. Both were attempts to transform an 'ungovernable populace to a multiply differentiated population': the new forms of discipline and punishment did this through techniques of surveillance, whereas the exhibitionary complex sought to

> transform [the problem] into one of culture . . . winning hearts and minds as well as the disciplining and training of bodies . . . [Its institutions] through the provision of object lessons in power – the power to command and arrange things and bodies for public display – . . . sought to allow the people . . . to know rather than be known, to become the subjects rather than the objects of knowledge.

There was a difference between displays of power which sought to terrorize and those, as in the exhibitionary complex, which sought

> rather to place the people – conceived as a nationalized citizenry – on this side of power, both its subject and its beneficiary . . . And this power marked out the distinction between the subjects and the objects of power not within the national body, but, as organized by the many rhetorics of imperialism, between that body and other, 'non-civilised' peoples upon whose bodies the effects of power were unleashed with as much force and theatricality as had been manifest on the scaffold. This was, in other words, a power which aimed at a rhetorical effect through its representation of otherness.[3]

Or, as Annie Coombes explains, by the last part of the century the exhibitionary complex had become a vehicle for social imperialism, welding together the classes in the metropolis at the expense of 'othering' the periphery.[4]

The focus of Bennett's and Coombes's writing is the effects of the exhibitionary complex on the population of the metropolis. At the colonial periphery, however, the 'Bushmen' became inducted in the nineteenth century into both facets of the power relations of the metropolis – the institutions of confinement and those of exhibition. Indeed, they passed from being colonial prisoners to being metropolitan exhibits: from standing in the dock of a real court and being condemned by a magistrate, they came to stand in the dock of public display, condemned by science as inferior beings.

Representations of the San

'Bushman' is a category constructed historically from outside the people to whom it refers, and 'San' probably no less so.[5] Originally, according to Robert Gordon, both terms designated 'lumpen-categories' – for example, 'Bushman' originally embraced all the dispossessed, the non-owners, and only towards the end of the nineteenth century was there an attempt to give the category an ethnographic content;[6] nevertheless both have become invested with historical and corporeal reality.

Originally the 'Bushmen' were constructed in the discourse of South African colonists as inveterate stock-thieves, vermin deserving only to be hunted down and exterminated. In the late nineteenth century they became, in evolutionist terms, the quintessential *primitive*, our savage ancestor. In the twentieth century this savagery has become ennobled:[7] their image has become transmuted into that of a 'harmless people', the human past living in the human present, for whose way of life one is supposed to feel a vague nostalgia.[8]

An important cusp in their representation was reached when the 'Bushmen' were viewed as a scientific curiosity to be *researched*, a shift that coincided, more or less, with their disappearance as a *threat* to colonisation. Historically, this transformation was associated above all with the work of Wilhlem Bleek and Lucy Lloyd who, in 1866, began interviewing 'Bushmen' in an attempt to scientifically investigate their language, folklore, etc.[9] This venture was undertaken at a time when there was a growth of interest in the preservation and classification of their rock art, George W. Stow, author of *The Native Races of South Africa*, having been among the first involved in such work.[10]

Much of the scholarship has presented a rather romantic view of Bleek, one of a liberal universalist. An important recent article by Andrew Bank, however, highlights Bleek's racial theories. Bleek argued in social evolutionist terms that the language of the 'Bushmen' was 'primitive' and compared it with the communication of primates. He was also among the first to classify the indigenous peoples of South Africa as *Hottentot*, 'Bushmen' and 'Bantu', primarily in terms of language, but also within an evolutionary framework. He was, moreover, sympathetic towards the biological racial science that was

[65]

beginning to develop. As such he was a precursor of biological racist thinking, though the heritage of his work has been to present the 'Bushmen' as benevolent and creative. He, like John Scott, as we shall see, is an example of the Janus face of nineteenth-century Cape liberalism.[11]

Bleek's subjects had, ironically, been prisoners in the Breakwater prison, convicted of sundry crimes, including stock theft and murder. The incarceration of 'Bushmen' was a new development in their treatment. In the eighteenth century, white (and probably also brown) colonisers had waged a war of physical extermination, rather than of capturing and imprisoning them, and in many areas this continued into the nineteenth century, being practised in the northern Cape when Scott took up his post there in 1880. From the start of the nineteenth century, however, along the Northern Border a different approach began to develop:

> Formerly the Bushman tribe committed frequent depredations on the frontier Inhabitants, but since the last years they have become more peaceable, and the Inhabitants have found it in their interest to supply occasionally their wants, as their depredations were mostly committed, when all the resources of nature, on which they subsisted, failed, and the fear of perishing by hunger induced them to take refuge to marauding.[12]

It was also during this period that what Penn calls the 'subtle infiltration' of missionaries, merchants and government finally broke the back of San resistance south of the Orange and brought them within the framework of colonial law.[13]

When they penetrated 'Bushmanland' most Basters and whites appear at first to have continued the practice of hunting down the San and killing them. Louis Anthing, magistrate in Namaqualand, investigated the situation in the early 1860s and concluded that 'during the last ten years a wholesale system of extermination of the Bushman people had been practised' – in many cases their murder being utterly without pretext. Anthing implicated Kora and Xhosa in this as well as white settlers and Basters. Theft, he said, was the provocation; but questions remained:

> Are not the thefts perhaps acts of retaliation, part of a system of retaliation, for wrongs inflicted? For kinsmen murdered? Which were the first, the thefts or the murders? Suppose the thefts were first, have not the murders aggravated the original cause? And if the thefts were first, under what circumstances were they committed? Are not the Colonists intruders, usurpers of the Natives' lands? The Bushmen lived upon game and the seed of grass which grows in their country – Is not the game driven away by the ingress of the strongest, who have horses and

guns with which they chase it far and wide? Is not the grass eaten by the numerous flocks and herds of the farmers? Are not even some of the water places taken from the original inhabitants? These causes have stimulated, perhaps almost driven the Bushmen, from necessity, to rob the intruders. And what alternative had they? To go into the service of the farmers? A life which I doubt little is in most instances such as to offer little inducement. Tales of harshness, cruelty, deception, have reached me before now.[14]

The subjection of the 'Bushmen' to the system of colonial law by the later 1860s, reflected in their imprisonment, therefore already represented some transition in their treatment.

The passage quoted at the start of the chapter illustrates how, in the mind of colonial officials like Scott, this new form of social control of the 'Bushmen' through subjection to colonial law and imprisonment was bound up with viewing them as subjects of scientific investigation. With them being seen by the emergent 'science' of anthropology as members of a 'vanishing race', imprisoned 'Bushmen' provided conveniently captive subjects for research. The archives of the colonisation of the Northern Border provide rich material for tracing the representation of 'Bushmen', as well as of their treatment of a transformatory cusp.

Magistrate John Scott and punishment of the 'Bushmen'

Scott was almost 36 years of age when he took up his position as special magistrate for the Northern Border in May 1879, in the middle of the Kora war. He had begun his career in 'native affairs' as a provisional magistrate with Bacala, in Tembuland, from August 1876 to October 1878. While in this position he had acted as captain of Tembu levies under Major Elliott during the war against the Gcaleka, September 1877–April 1878.[15] As Elliott put it, Scott

> induced wavering clans to join their Chief Gangalizwe, who had crossed the Bashee with me into Gcalekaland. He then joined a Native Division under my command and undertook the dual duties of Ordnance and Commissariat Officer which he discharged with marked zeal and ability ... with that marked resourcefulness for which he is noted, [he] requisitioned arms, ammunition and supplies of groceries from the few scattered trading stations in the Territories.[16]

Thereafter Scott became acting chief magistrate of Tembuland, between April and July 1878, and then was appointed chief clerk of the Native Affairs Department in Cape Town in October 1878.

While on the Northern Border, Scott was a conscientious corres-
pondent with the colonial authorities in Cape Town. His comments
on the 'Bushman' to these authorities indeed serve as an index of
'progressive' colonial opinion on the subject. The colonial authorities
took note of his achievements in the northern Cape. On Scott's retire-
ment in June 1902 Walter Stanford, chief secretary of the Native
Affairs Department, wrote to him: 'Your able administration as Spec
Comm of a large area of country on the Northern Border met with the
high approval of Government at the time, leading to your appoint-
ment to the other important posts in the service which you have
since so honourably filled.'[17] And, significantly, among his achievements, Scott later listed: 'Succeeded in almost entirely clearing the
Northern Border Districts of Marauding Bushmen.'[18]

When he arrived he had a relatively benevolent attitude to the
'Bushmen'. Almost his first comments were:

> There are still a great many Bushmen scattered up and down the country
> in small bodies. They are quite wild, very few speak Dutch, they build
> not even the rudest hut, just putting a few bushes together as a shelter
> from the wind. They do not attempt to keep stock. Some members of a
> family will work for a time, and on the goats thus earned the rest will
> live, using the milk as long as game can be got, but slaughtering the
> milk-giver if game fails. They go almost naked, spend their time in
> hunting game, searching for roots, and in sleeping; have an invincible
> repugnance to settled work, alleging that the farmers ill-treat them and
> cheat them out of their wages. In spite of the hardships they undergo,
> they are a merry light-hearted people. *They do not systematically prey
> on the farmers' flocks and herds as Kafirs do; indeed they pride them-
> selves on not stealing, but when hunger drives them they do not scru-
> ple to take a sheep, goat, horse, or mule to satisfy their hunger. It is a
> matter of surprise that so little stock is lost by their depredations. The
> loss by theft, as far as I can learn from patient enquiry among the
> farmers, is trifling compared to what our eastern farmers suffer.* These
> Bushmen seem doomed to die out, and that before very long. As far as
> I can learn, many of their women are barren and the rest have but small
> families.[19]

Apparently 'Bushmen' engaged as shepherds would earn about 10s a
month, or else a goat ewe, together with cast-off clothes 'and in most
cases a not illiberal ration of meat with a little bread and coffee'; they
might also earn a gun.[20] Wives and children would work at a farmer's
homestead, although Scott also reported in 1883 that

> at present the only demand for labour is for herds unencumbered with
> families. Such form but a small proportion of the native population.
> I know of many cases of men with a wife, 3 or 4 children, and an old

mother or father who cannot get employment because it does not pay to feed the lot for the sake of the man's services.[21]

After a year or two on the Northern Border his views began to change. He continued to try to root out the the farmers' practice of arbitrarily shooting 'Bushmen': 'The going out of the farmers in Bushmen hunts should be discouraged as much as possible and I endeavour to do this.'[22] Cases did, however, occur. During 1883, for example, a 'Bushman', two women and a child were shot, 'presumably by white farmers, under circumstances – with regard to the child especially – of peculiar atrocity ... when the unfortunate results of this shooting were discovered a horrible crime was committed to hush up the whole affair'. Scott believed the shooting took place when the farmer tried to arrest the 'Bushman'.[23] Commenting on some farmers' attempt to arrest a 'Bushman' believed to have killed a farmer named Claasen in 1885, Scott wrote:

> There being no warrant and the Claasens having no personal knowledge of any crime having been committed it is a question whether they were legally justified in attempting by force of arms to arrest Jacob Basterd. And it might even be held that the latter was to some extent legally justified in resisting by force of arms an illegal arrested [sic] attempted to be effected by farmers armed with rifles.

'Bushmen', he added, 'very rarely attempt to resist the Police, but they do not look upon the farmers as having the right to arrest them. Then the police never resort to the use of firearms but as a last resource, while I am afraid from what I know of the farmers that they are inclined to resort to it if they fancy themselves at all justified.'[24]

Over his years at the Northern Border, enforcement of the law apparently changed the situation regarding 'Bushmen hunts':

> I notice a considerable improvement since coming to the border. At first farmers hardly ever reported to the police that Bushmen were about but seemed to consider it was their own work to hunt them up. Now reports are very generally sent in and often on very slender grounds so that at times the police officers are tempted to pay little attention to them.[25]

At the same time, perhaps through having to enforce the law in the court, Scott became less sanguine about the 'trifling' nature of 'Bushman' theft:

> Ample experience of the past forbids the hope that they will ever be civilised or rendered innoxious neighbours by any means which can be applied to them locally. The farmers are a long suffering people but exasperated by the losses inflicted on them by these wretched wanderers

[69]

there is little doubt that the latter will be eventually shot down as wild beasts ... What makes the Bushmen thefts so exasperating is that to obtain a couple of days [sic] food for a single family they think nothing of killing a valuable horse eating very little of the carcass and wasting the rest.[26]

Here it is 'farmers', according to Scott, who viewed the 'Bushmen' as 'wild beasts', but two months later Scott himself labelled them not only 'wild animals' but 'irreclaimable savages' – in South Africa a phrase notoriously associated with Governor Benjamin D'Urban's ill-fated annexation of Xhosa territory in 1835.[27]

> The Bushmen consider the whole country to be theirs, and that they have a perfect right to supply their wants from the flocks and herds that have caused their game to disappear. By preference they would live on game, but failing that, farmers' stock will do. With few exceptions, they are *irreclaimable savages*, and will be exterminated. Brought much into contact with them, it is hard to make one self believe that they are anything better than *noxious wild animals, who should be treated as wolves and jackals are.* They cannot organise, so that they can hardly become a serious danger. Meanwhile they make themselves an intolerable nuisance ... It is exasperating almost beyond endurance for a farmer to see all these people enjoying themselves in utter idleness, while he can often not get a servant of any sort to help him in his work, and knows that it is his stock which enables these squatters to live in idleness. I often wonder that the farmers have not taken the law into their own hands [against?] these cumberers of the ground, especially as it might be done with little chance of detection.[28]

Scott here accused the 'Bushmen' of failure to take service with farmers – which he identified with 'idleness', ignoring of course the labour involved in providing for one's subsistence. He had earlier described the 'idleness' of the 'state of nature' in which they lived:

> If the Bushman and Hottentot does [sic] not take service ... he can squat about the country, keeping the few goats he may have earned before as a protection against the operation of some clauses of the Vagrant Act, living upon game, roots, and honey, and amusing himself to his hearts content, dancing and merrymaking with his women and companions. Were there no stock-owners in the country there is no reason why those natives should be interfered with in their method of enjoying themselves, but game and roots often fail, and honey beer produces a craving for flesh, and the farmer's flocks must supply the want.[29]

Moreover, many of them had guns, which helped them 'to live a sort of independent life'.

He subsequently qualified such sentiments: 'On the other hand little inducement to work is held out. The man in service is not much better off than the man who lives free.'[30] Yet, once again, he slipped from describing the farmer's exasperation to internalising that exasperation:

[S]quatting and wandering Bushmen have to a greater extent than usual plagued the farmers by stock-stealing. Some of these thefts have been of a nature so exasperating that average humanity feels itself almost justified in adopting any means of redress or prevention ... Meanwhile unless some steps can be successfully taken to compel Bushmen and Hottentots to work for their living here or elsewhere, the problem remains, and will be solved in the way of 'natural results' which is anything but a pleasant outlook.[31]

Taking service with farmers was, then, for Scott, their only alternative to extermination.

By 1884 he had located the character of the 'Bushman': 'the history of the last 200 years forbids one to hope that Bushmen will ever live in the neighbourhood of people who have stock to be stolen and where the Bushmen have a tract to fall back on that suits their wild mode of life without so conducting themselves that "atrocities" are the natural outcome'.[32] And, in the following year, Scott made explicit his conclusion: the 'native question' is a 'police question'.

The great majority ... of the native population consists of Hottentots and Bushmen, and those who are the offspring of a mixture of these, in my opinion, quite distinct races. Of these a few, naturally good and well brought up by judicious Dutch masters, are invaluable servants, especially as shepherds, for which occupation in this part of the country very special qualifications are required. The rest with hardly an exception are incorrigibly lazy, filthy, and disgusting in their habits, habitual stock thieves, preferring to live a half-starved, miserable, hunted existence to working for an honest living ... The whole native question in this District is then one of Police.[33]

He added:

Those who do enter service only do so on compulsion, and while in my opinion no native in farm service is treated with more consideration than the trustworthy servant of a Dutch Boer, I must admit that a bad servant has a bad time of it with a Dutch master. If this latter is convicted of assaulting or ill-treating his servant, it is only reasonable that in awarding punishment the provocation received should be considered, and no one who does not know the average Hottentots of this part of the country can form any just idea of how exasperatingly provoking they can be.[34]

[71]

On his arrival in 1880 Scott had explained the reluctance of the 'Bushmen' to enter service on the basis of allegations that farmers ill-treated them and cheated them out of wages; by 1885 he was, however, justifying the farmers' assaults on the grounds of the 'provocation' offered by the 'Bushmen'!

Over the same period his appreciation grew as to what was involved in the 'police question' – the capture of 'Bushmen':

> No person unacquainted with this part of the country can form any adequate idea of the almost superhuman powers required to conduct an efficient pursuit of Bushmen here . . . the country is almost uninhabited, water places are few and far between. Spoor can only be followed in the day-time under an almost tropical sun. Bushmen when fleeing pursue such devious paths that the direct distance between places is about trebled in following their spoor and to follow this latter at all requires a practical skill which seems almost miraculous to the uninitiated. Travelling in the cool of the night the Bushman can cover almost as much ground as a mounted man can by day.[35]

Scott's patience with the penalties available for theft was lessening:

> During the year many petty thefts of stock have taken place, and there have been a few convictions. Great efforts have been made to combat the evils complained of by the application of the Vagrant Law but with very little success. The punishment provided is not felt, the expense of feeding prisoners has been great, and the vagrants have been kept moving about so that the loss of stock attributable to them has been to some extent fairly distributed . . . Most of these thefts are committed with impunity, and when a conviction is obtained no punishment which is felt by the culprit seems available. Hard labour is amusement compared with farm service, rice water is better than roots, prison rations are a continual feast, the gaol is a comfortable shelter, prison clothes and blankets are luxuries only enjoyed in gaol, and flogging is hardly felt. Prison life is a little dull, there are no women and no tobacco, and that is all the punishment there is in it.[36]

Again and again he returned to this theme:

> For short terms of imprisonment under the Vagrant Act, the squatters care nothing. To have any good effect the Act will have to be applied in such a way as to scatter the heads of families, this leaving the children destitute to be apprenticed 'according to law'. To do this will cost a large sum of money, to say nothing of the moral bearing of so applying the law.[37]

Again, in a detailed explanation: 'The punishments the law provides are not deterrents to the sort of evildoers we have here. At first I thought the lash would deter but although well laid on it has proved quite useless. One man took three floggings of 36 lashes each in less than three months and then stole again and that not from necessity.'[38]

One solution he favoured was the settlement of the country by white farmers, rather than their presence on short-term leases with no compensation for making improvements (e.g. erecting buildings) on the land they occupied. This was because farmers with short leases, on generally unsurveyed farms, found it difficult to get convictions under the Vagrancy Act.[39] The solution he increasingly pressed for to induce the 'Bushmen' to engage in productive labour was a 'modern' one, involving what today would be termed *social engineering*: the forcible removal of the 'Bushmen' to a more *settled* part of the Cape:

> It would be just as cheap, not so exasperating to the natives, and, if that has any bearing on the matter, more in accordance with the code of morality which modern ideas fancy should influence Governments, to remove these people at the public expense to a part of the Colony where experience shows that they have not the same scope for, nor temptation to, lawless living, and where under a more constant supervision than can possibly be exercised in these wilds they make not altogether bad servants.[40]

One should note Scott's reasoning. On the Northern Border, where they still had access to some land on which to roam, the 'Bushmen' were useless servants; but, if moved to the western Cape, where there was no vacant land on which to subsist that would tempt them away from service, then they could become usefully employed. Moreover, it was 'moral' to forcibly relocate them, when by remaining in the north they would risk extermination by white farmers. Commenting on these ideas, an official in Cape Town noted: 'It is difficult to know what to do under the circumstances.' He did not think it would be right to despatch 'Bushmen' to Cape Town, though he hoped a regime of strict repression in the north would induce them to come southward.[41]

Eventually Scott did begin despatching 'Bushmen' to Cape Town, as in 1884 when he sent 14 men, 12 women and 16 children, all of 'one clan':

> The men have all been roaming wild on the Bult for a long time. Some of them have been to the Breakwater for cattle theft. They were arrested on suspicion of theft recently. It was very doubtful if a conviction would have been laid and the prosecutor not appearing there seemed no alternative but to send them away to manual labour and eventually to be destroyed. They were told that they could not any longer be allowed to roam wild over the Bult and were offered a free passage to Cape Town provided that when there they would take service at such places and on such terms as Government might direct, wives not to be separated

from their husbands nor children under 14 years of age from their parents. This offer was accepted with apparent alacrity by all the men provided they might collect and take with them their women and children . . . I would recommend that these people should not be asked if they will take service at such and such a place at such and such wages, but that after a suitable situation has been found for a family they should be told 'You are to go to so and so and each of you is to do such and such work and you are to stay such a length of time and to receive so much wages.'[42]

'They seldom get on with a master selected by themselves but when a master is given to them and they are at all fairly treated they make useful and contented servants.'[43] The experiment was, however, not a success.

Scott also appears to have used his magistrate's powers to supply child 'apprentices' to farmers farther south. In 1886 he received the following letter from a farmer in Calvinia, south of 'Bushmanland':

I have been told that you give away youngsters to the farmers round about to be cared for and trained. If any should again come before you please let me have a few for my own use and also for my children still I will be the father of all seeing that they are well fed and clothed our Magistrate's wife would also like to have a little boy. I would like to have about 6 (4 boys and 2 girls). You may enquire how I have trained those I had but mine are mostly of age now so I should like to have a new stock.[44]

Whether or not Scott supplied this farmer and, if he did, whether the 'Bushmen' remained with the farmer is not known.

Magistrate John Scott, science, and the exhibition of 'Bushmen'

Selecting the children of Bushmen as apprentices was only a little short of selecting 'Bushmen' for the purposes of scientific investigation or popular exhibition. Contemplating the 'moral' approach of forcibly removing 'Bushmen' to Cape Town, it was no step whatsoever to collaborating with their removal to be exhibited. As the epigraph to this chapter indicates, in 1881 Scott was keen to send 'Bushmen' to assist in the Bleeks' researches. The response from J. Rose Innes of the Department of Native Affairs in Cape Town stated that the Government had no objection, provided the 'Bushmen' were 'willing to enter into the engagement proposed'.

From 1883 Scott became directly involved in selecting 'Bushmen' for exhibition in Europe. The nineteenth century in Europe was 'quite unprecedented in the social effort . . . devoted to the organization of spectacles'[45] – following on from the eighteenth-century tradition of street and fairground entertainment involving displays of human and animal 'freaks'. Living South Africans were marketed in a range of popular shows in nineteenth-century Britain: 'Bushman' children in 1845–47; 'Bushmen' again in 1847; 'native tribesmen' in 1850–52; so-called 'Earthmen' in 1851–55; 'Zulu Kafirs' in 1853, and again in 1865 and 1879–80.[46]

In parallel there had developed – modelled on the 1851 *Great Exhibition* at the Crystal Palace – the tradition of government-sponsored exhibitions. These were in the first place great hymns of praise to European industry, progress and 'civilisation' which

> sought to make the whole world, past and present, metonymically available in the assemblages of objects and peoples they brought together and, from their towers, to lay it before a controlling vision ... transforming displays of machinery and industrial processes, of finished products and *objets d'art*, into material signifiers of progress – but of progress as a collective national achievement, with capital as the great co-ordinator.[47]

In 1883 or 1884 W. A. Healey, an employee of the impresario Gilarma Farini of the Westminster Aquarium in London, visited the northern Cape. With the assistance of Scott, he obtained the services of one Gert Louw, the Baster who had captured the Korana leader Klaas Lukas at the end of the 1879–80 war. Gert Louw procured six 'Bushmen' in the Kalahari, and with Healey returned with them to England. There the husband and wife, two young men, and a boy and girl were taken over by the 'monster-monger' Farini,[48] who exhibited them in 1884 as 'Earthmen'. 'A small bit of desert had been improvished [*sic*] at the Aquarium with the aid of a thick layer of rich sand, and on this they went through a number of illustrations of life in their native home'. The constructed term 'Earthmen' (who supposedly differed from 'Bushmen' because they dug holes in which to live in the earth) was redolent of the 1851–55 display. They were displayed in the USA from December 1884 through 1885.[49]

Gert Louw's family was supposed to receive monthly remittances through Scott from Britain, but these were not sent.[50] Instead, in 1885, Farini himself travelled to the northern Cape, bringing back with him Gert Louw as guide. This was 'the pinnacle of his fascination with Africa', claims his biographer. It was 'unparalleled adventure ... he searched for diamonds, scouted ranch lands, explored rocky falls, hunted wild animals, ate everything the natives offered him, examined and carefully pressed flora and fauna, and nearly killed himself and his companions at least once or twice'.[51] Farini claimed to have discovered in the course of his travels a 'lost city of the Kalahari', and on his return to Europe he took with him one or more 'pygmies' (not found for him by Scott).[52] The *Cape Argus* reported on one of these:

Altogether Mr Farini has quite a travelling museum of specimens from the country, including one pygmy, smaller than a Bushman. It is anticipating the journey a little to mention this lad, as he was obtained from a tract to the west of Lake Ngami – the furthest point in Mr Farini's journey: but he will be included in the curiosities of the expedition ... There were five or six of them but they ran away, or rather were 'induced' to go by some traders or trekkers of some kind who came across them and the man who went for them.[53]

Farini commented on 'the poor Bushman' that he

is hardly dealt with. The big game is driven from the country by the Boers and their flocks, the small game he cannot hunt, as his poisoned arrow and bows are always taken from him; so he is obliged to steal some of the flocks to exist, for which he is punished by depriving him of his liberty which he loves so well. Is it a wonder he resists capture so desperately? But the march of civilisation has no ears for the cries of these poor wretches whom it crushes if they stand in its way.[54]

In Upington, on his return journey, Farini met Scott, of whom he subsequently wrote as having been 'the right man in the right place, always tempering justice with kindness' – the stereotype of the paternalistic colonial. He remarked that Scott was a 'jack-of-all-trades. With his official duties he mixes up doctoring, blacksmithing, carpentering, tinsmithing, waggon-making etc. etc. His newly-built, brick residence, with stables, out-houses, and garden, would compare favourably with those of any African town.' He made no reference to Scott's assistance to Healy in procuring the 'Bushmen' in 1883–84.[55]

In 1886 Scott once again sent a 'Bushman', Klaas Tilletjies, his wife and their child for display in England – this time to the government-sponsored *Colonial and Indian Exhibition*. This man was 'a stock thief under security to come up for sentence if [called] on within six months'.[56] In a revealing letter on his approach to 'Bushmen', Scott wrote:

The man is a very good specimen indeed. The woman is larger but pure bred and possessed of the peculiar female Bushman physical characteristics in a well marked degree. They are dressed in European rags. Their proper full dress is a sort of collar and pair of [spriers?] business and I am afraid would shock the British Nation. However I have asked Colonel Eustace [magistrate in Namaqualand] to provide them with skins. If he has not done so, you can give them a few Cape sheep skins and springbok skins (easily to be got in Cape Town) and a little fat and they will soon make themselves dress suits. The man . . . is a good Bushman . . . I [do] not apprehend any trouble. Anyhow a Bushman is [no?] sort of an animal. If anyone in authority, say Mr Shaw in full rig, were to tell him . . . such and such a place, for such and such . . . quietly acquiesces . . . but if ask him 'please to do so' . . . would altogether refuse.[57]

Elizabeth Dell has claimed that in the displays of 'Bushmen' earlier in the nineteenth century there had not necessarily been an emphasis on physical grotesqueness (as had been the case, for example, with Saartjie Baartman).[58] Whether or not that had been the case, certainly Scott regarded the physical features of the 'Bushmen' he despatched as worthy of note.

Scott collected and sent what was described as 'the interesting collection of "Bushmen" weapons and utensils now on exhibition in the Cape Court'. In Cape Town he was thanked by the royal astronomer, as chairman of a sub-committee assisting the *Colonial and Indian Exhibition*, for 'selecting the Bushman family and . . . numerous other matters when your local knowledge and experience were requisite'.[59] Later he received a letter of thanks from the Cape Prime Minister enclosing a diploma and medal from the President of the Royal Commission 'for the valuable assistance you rendered in connection with the representation of this Colony at the Colonial and Indian Exhibition'.[60]

The catalogue of the 1886 *Colonial and Indian Exhibition* described a 'Kafir Kraal and Bushman Hut . . . They are occupied by four Kafirs, and by a Bushman and his wife, who will carry on their respective native industries, including the manufacture of weapons, sticks, baskets, wickerwork mats, sieves, beadwork and wire ornaments',[61] though none of the male 'natives', at any rate, would have had much time for carrying on 'industry' in their huts. The main Cape exhibit was a diamond mine. Dell wrote:

> In tune with the Cape's serious, business-minded approach to its representation at Exhibitions, the catalogue entry describes the demonstration of an important mining process . . . diamonds were setting the Cape apart as a viable territory, for active imperialism. For the first time in 1886, the colony's self-representation could demonstrate real prosperity.[62]

F. Cundall, author of an 1886 reminiscence of the *Colonial and Indian Exhibition*, commented that the 'diamond exhibit has proved to be the chief feature in the African court, and indeed one of the most popular in the whole exhibition'.[63] Apart from the Malays, all the other men were employed in working on the diamond mine exhibit. Klaas Jaar, the 'Bushman', can be seen in the photo of this display in Cundall's book.[64] With a shortage of labour, all hands were no doubt required. Dell places emphasis on the presentation of ethnic difference

[77]

and exoticism in this display.[65] My own reading of it is to emphasise that South African males were portrayed, during the country's mineral revolution, as migrant labourers – if 'migrating' only from their hut in the exhibition's compound to the diamond display! But it was very ironic that the 'Bushman' in London was involved in a display of productive labour, when the main complaint of Scott and colonial thinking generally about the South African 'Bushmen' was that they were unwilling to become servants of the colonists!

Scott's successors in the northern Cape and the 'Bushmen': the 1890s

Scott spent nearly ten years on the northern border of the Colony. He later wrote: 'I do not think any other official has been able to endure the life there for half that period.'[66] It affected his personal life, since he did not think it fair for his wife to live with him, and so kept up two establishments, which led him into debt.[67]

By the end of Scott's service in the northern Cape the 'Bushman problem' was, in his eyes, beginning to vanish:

> Fortunately the number of Bushmen who will insist on trying to live by hunting, which really means living on stolen stock, is rapidly diminishing. They are continually worried about [sic] by the Police so that many take service and long sentences of imprisonment have been obtained against the most notorious of them. Comparatively few who go to the Breakwater ever return.[68]

The situation was confirmed by a visiting commissioner: 'I have been credibly informed that the whole of the Northern Border is entirely free from Bushmen, Korannas, and other wandering natives',[69] and Scott again commented, in early 1888, on the diminution of crime, with half the previous stock thefts, only two master-and-servant cases and very few vagrancy charges, and the near-disappearance of marauding 'Bushmen'.[70]

Later that year Scott left Gordonia, where he was succeeded as special magistrate by C. Bam. With the decline of the 'Bushman' as a 'menace' the attitude of officialdom turned towards paternalism.[71] The more effective occupation of land (by whites and Basters), together with the disappearance of game, in fact meant that 'Bushmen' struggled to survive. Indeed, by the 1890s, what was happening was the *de facto* establishment of a 'location' for 'Bushmen' being fed by the State.

In his 1896 annual report the magistrate wrote:

> There are no native locations in my district but one big location, viz, the Kalahari desert, in which there are usually wandering about three or

four hundred Bushmen, several of whom have already died of starvation. I do not know if you are aware of the fact that I have been feeding a lot of Bushmen women for some time at Government expense, whose husbands are in gaol for stock theft. Now, I may just mention that in good seasons the farmers' stock are left to roam unprotected in the desert, and no Bushman will steal any, but, on account of the drought, they have had no alternative, as they possess nothing, and merely live by the chase and on roots. One difficulty now is what to do with them. Even the women I am feeding will clear away with the first rains that fall. They are dying out fast, and I believe in a few years time not many will be left.

I do not know if the Government would be prepared to do anything for them (but it is almost a pity to let them die out like this); if so, I would suggest that someone be appointed to merely supervise them. They might be registered, and allowed to make huts in the desert, and roam at will; only in scarce times might they go to the Inspector, who will supply them with food at Government expense. It is a matter for serious consideration, and perhaps you may be able to suggest something better.

Again echoing Scott, he suggested a plan: 'arrest the lot as vagrants, and send them to the Western Province as servants to farmers. The Bushman, as a rule, makes a splendid herd. Of course it would be a great expense to Government, but it is, perhaps, the only way to civilise them.'[72]

During this period the Village Management Board in Upington employed prison labour, almost all of them 'Bushmen'. The succeeding magistrate claimed that the removal of 'Bushman' prisoners to the Breakwater in Cape Town or to the prison in Kimberley meant that Gordonia was 'gradually becoming thinned of them'[73] – but his successor argued that on release the prisoners returned to the area, 'being assisted on their way by free railway passes and rations'.[74] Certainly, by the turn of the century, the 'Bushmen' had been driven out of 'Bushmanland' and southern Gordonia, and taken refuge in the Kalahari. Thus in 1899 the magistrate could write:

The Hottentot race is fast dying out. The Bushmen and Korannas are a nomadic people and live for the greater part of the year in the Kalahari, existing upon the tsamma and wild potatoes of the desert. When this natural food fails them, they come into the more inhabited parts of the district, and eventually generally find their way to the gaol, being arrested either for vagrancy or theft of stock. These people are useless as servants, never having been under a roof, and knowing nothing about work, nor the use of spade or shovel. The only employment which is suitable for them is that of herds ... The great decimation of royal game which goes on year by year in this district is due to a large extent to the Bushmen, who destroy the big game for the sake of food.[75]

An editorial in the Kimberley *Diamond Fields Advertiser* in 1907 summed up the new colonial approach to the 'Bushmen', who were

> disappearing from the face of the land that once was theirs, and in a few years will be as extinct as the dodo. In consequence of a fate that is inevitable, we have it on the best authority that more than one European museum would only be too glad of a 'specimen' or two. If, therefore, any reader should know of a docile Bushman who has no particular use for himself, the scientific world would be truly grateful if that same Bushmen could be induced to pack himself in formalin, or something of the sort, and ship himself to Europe for the purpose of ornamenting a dust-proof show case, side by side with the mummies of Egypt. And we can promise him this distinction, that many an honest white man will have to be satisfied with a much less honourable use for his mortal coil.[76]

Preservation in a museum as a 'primitive species' was now the substitute for living display.

From 1906 on Gordonia became a part of an area scoured by grave-robbers, both local and from Europe, for the remains of 'Bushmen' – collected and deposited in museums for use in physical anthropological research into 'racial types'.[77] Along with this, L. Peringuey, director of the South African Museum, began to organise the production of plaster casts of living 'Bushmen' from the prisons and villages of the northern Cape, searching for 'pure specimens' among the remnants of farm labourers, herders, etc.[78]

By 1924 the situation had worsened for the San, who did not figure in the racial division of Gordonia which took place in the 1920s.[79] A government surveyor with knowledge of Gordonia wrote of the 'Mier country' – he was referring essentially to the present-day Kalahari Gemsbok Park: 'The only natives up there at present are a few nomadic "Bushmen" and a tract of land about 60,000 morgen in extent (four farms) with a borehole should be reserved for them at Rooibrak or Matamata on the Oup River, and they should also be allowed to hunt for food but not calves or cows in calf.'[80] That reserve was not established; instead the Kalahari Gemsbok Park was established in 1931. One Donald Bain assembled various 'Bushmen' from this area and displayed them at the *Johannesburg Empire Exhibition* of 1936. This led to renewed agitation for the conversion of the Gemsbok Park into a 'Bushman reserve', though that was not realised. However, after various adventures and escapades also involving a showman, Conraad Macdonald, 'Bushmen' were 'permitted' to establish themselves in the Kalahari Gemsbok Park, from where they were evicted by the Nationalist Government only in the 1970s, and moved to the nearby Mier 'coloured reserve'.[81] These were the ancestors of the San, who, in 1999, were finally granted territory in the area by the present Government: ownership of 40,000 hectares outside the Kalahari Gemsbok Park and partial control over 50,000 hectares within it.[82]

Notes

1   J. H. Scott, Special Magistrate, Kenhardt, and Special Commissioner on the Northern Border to Secretary for Native Affairs, Cape Town, 13 January 1881, Cape Archives Repository (CAR), Cape Town NBC13.
2   I have used the term 'Bushmen' in this chapter to emphasise the 'othering' and the dehumanisation characteristic of the period about which I write: according to Wilmsen, 'the terms "Bushman" and "forager" lump together more than a dozen living southern African peoples – plus several others who have disappeared under colonial pressures and introduced disease – who have distinct languages and traditions and whose economies cover the entire spectrum of indigenous forms from extensive foraging to intensive agropastoralism. They are imposed category terms that mark persons as belonging to social entities that nowhere exist . . . the term, and category, "Bushman" . . . is a colonial construct . . . created to control subjugated peoples in manageable, depoliticised, arbitrarily bounded enclaves of homogeneity in a previously flourishing landscape of political-social diversity': Edwin Wilmsen, 'Decolonising the Mind: Steps towards Cleansing the Bushman Stain from Southern African History', in P. Skotnes (ed.), *Miscast: Negotiating the Presence of the Bushmen* (Cape Town: University of Cape Town Press, 1996), p. 188.
3   T. Bennett, *The Birth of the Museum* (London: Routledge, 1995), pp. 59–67, 92–3.
4   Annie E. Coombes, *Reinventing Africa: Museums, Material Culture and Popular Imagination in Late Victorian and Edwardian England* (New Haven, CT: Yale University Press, 1994), pp. 111ff.
5   On this section see also S. Dubow, *Scientific Racism in Modern South Africa* (Cambridge: Cambridge University Press, 1995), pp. 20–5.
6   R. Gordon, *The Bushman Myth: The Making of a Namibian Underclass* (Boulder, CO: Westview Press, 1992), p. 179.
7   Though Jan Smuts, in an address to the South African Association for the Advancement of Science in 1932, could still refer to them as occupying 'the lowest scale in human existence': see 'Climate and Man in Africa', *South African Journal of Science*, 29 (1932), 129, quoted in Dubow, *Scientific Racism in Modern South Africa*, p. 51
8   For Wilmsen, both stereotypes are equally harmful: 'Canonizing peoples in a reified category "Bushmen" as personifying ontologically authentic humanity is as damaging – to us and to them – as demonising them: the dehumanising effect is identical': 'Decolonising the Mind', p. 190; see also Gordon, *The Bushman Myth*, p. 217.
9   See, *inter alia*, W. Bleek, 'Report on Progress in Study of Bushman Language and Literature', 15 April 1973, CAR NA 448.
10 See R. A. Young, *The Life and Work of George William Stow* (1907), especially pp. 116ff.; A. E. Voss, 'The Hero of the Native Races: The Making of a Myth', in M. van Wyk Smith and D. McLennan (eds), *Olive Schreiner and After: Essays on SA Literature in Honour of Guy Butler* (Cape Town: Philip, 1983). Compare Bleek Papers, Manuscripts and Archives, University of Cape Town, C15, R. Truman to Miss Lloyd, 1 June 1882, with Theal, as quoted in J. Marais, *The Cape Coloured People 1652–1937* (Johannesburg: Witwatersrand University Press, 1957), p. 14, that Bushman paintings 'were seldom superior to the drawings on slates made by European children eight or nine years of age'. Stow, though today regarded as a racist, was seen as a 'Bushmanophile' at the turn of the twentieth century. The *Diamond Fields Advertiser* for 18 February 1907, for example, spoke of his 'partiality for the Bushmen', and that according to Stow 'there would seem to be

very little that a Bushman does not know. And besides being so clever he is also so superior; something in fact between one of Fenimore Cooper's noble Red Indians and an archangel, and owing to the degraded position he now occupies solely to his sweet disposition.' This, however, the paper added, 'need not blind us to the enormous amount of research he has accumulated towards the solution of the problem of the origin of the primitive inhabitants of South Africa'.

11 Andrew Bank, 'Evolution and Racial Theory: The Hidden Side of Wilhelm Bleek', *South African Historical Journal*, 43 (November 2000), 163ff.; see also M. Legassick, 'The State, Racism and the Rise of Capitalism in the Nineteenth-Century Cape Colony', *South African Historical Journal*, 28 (1993), 336–9

12 Civil Commissioner, Worcester, to Acting Sec to Government, 7 February 1834, CAR GH19/4. The former Tulbagh District became the Worcester District, embracing the whole Northwestern Frontier, in 1822.

13 See Nigel Penn, ' "Fated to Perish": The Destruction of the Cape San', in Skotnes, *Miscast*, in which he revises the usual idea that the back of San resistance was broken in the eighteenth century: see, for example, Marais, *The Cape Coloured People*, p. 15. Mission stations among the San tended to be short-lived. For this eastern area see also P. van der Merwe, *Die Noordwaartse Beweging van die Boere voor die Groot Trek, 1770–1842* (The Hague: Van Stockum & Zoom, 1937), pp. 136–75, 241–62; A. Stockenstrom, *The Autobiography of the Late Sir Andries Stockenstrom, Bart*, ed. C. W. Hutton (Cape Town, 1887), vol. I, chs 11, 17 and 21; J. L. Dracopoli, *Sir Andries Stockenstrom 1792–1864: The Origins of the Racial Conflict in South Africa* (Cape Town, 1967), pp. 63–5, 78–9, 114.

14 Anthing, 21 April 1863, CAR A39–1863, p. 3; see also Marais, *The Cape Coloured People*, pp. 27–9.

15 See Memorandum, Native Affairs Office, 8 September 1907, CAR NA 504, A148.

16 H. G. Elliott, Testimonial to Scott, 12 June 1902 NAD, CAR NA 504, A148.

17 W. E. Stanford to Scott, 30 June 1902, CAR NA 504 A148.

18 Scott, Memorandum, n.d., CAR NA 504, A148.

19 Scott, 8 January 1880, CAR G13–1880, p. 169; emphasis added.

20 Scott, 7 January 1881, CAR G20–1881, pp. 81–2.

21 Scott to SNA, 28 September 1885, CAR NBC15.

22 Scott to Under Colonial Secretary, 3 November 1885, CAR NBC17.

23 Scott, 11 January 1884, CAR G3–1884, p. 45.

24 Scott to Under Colonial Secretary, 3 November 1885, CAR NBC17.

25 Ibid.; see also Scott (January 1888), CAR G6–1888, p. 21: farmers were 'getting out of the habit of being their own judges and executioners'.

26 Scott to SNA, 24 November 1882, CAR NBC15.

27 See, for example, W. M. Macmillan, *Bantu, Boer and Briton*, rev. edn (Oxford: Clarendon Press, 1963), p. 135.

28 Scott (early January 1883), CAR G3–1883, p. 123; emphasis added (months given in parentheses for archival materials are inferred; these documents are undated).

29 Scott, 7 January 1881, CAR G20–1881, pp. 81–2.

30 Scott to SNA, 28 September 1883, CAR NBC15.

31 Scott, 11 January1884, CAR G3–1884, p. 45.

32 Scott to SNA, 6 February 1884, CAR NBC15.

33 Scott, 15 January 1885, CAR G2–1885, pp. 43–4.

34 Ibid.

35 Scott to Under Colonial Secretary, 3 November1885, CAR NBC17.

36 Scott, 7 January 1881, CAR G20–1881, pp. 81–2.

37 Scott (early January 1883), CAR G3–1883, p. 123.

38 Scott to SNA, 28 September 1883, CAR NBC15: 'the farmers with hardly an exception live in tents and wagons'.

39 See, e.g., ibid.; Scott, 15 January 1885, CAR G2–1885, pp. 43–4; Scott to Under Colonial Secretary, 3 November 1885, CAR NBC17.

40 Scott (early January 1883), CAR G3–1883, p. 123.

41 Minute on Scott, 24 November 1882, CAR NA167.

42   Scott to SNA, 2 February 1884; also Scott to RM, Springbokfontein, 1 February 1884, CAR NBC15.
43   Ibid.
44   J. van der Merwe, Drift, Calvinia, to Civil Commissioner, Kenhardt, 6 June 1886, CAR NBC 10.
45   T. Bennett, *The Birth of the Museum*, p. 65, quoting R. D. Altick, *The Shows of London* (Cambridge, MA: Harvard University Press, 1978).
46   E. Dell, 'Museums and the Re-Presentation of "Savage South Africa" to 1910', Ph.D thesis, University of London (1994), pp. 51–95, 294–323. The Cape Archives Repository photograph collections also contain two advertisements for the exhibition of 'Bushmen' 'under the direction of Mr S. Tyler' at the Portico, Newington, in 1841, in connection with a lecture at Exeter Hall by Dr R. Knox., CAR Elliott Collection, E9328; Morrison Collection, M1045. See also James Steele, 7 Dalrymple Place, Edinburgh, to Governor Harry Smith, 30 December 1848, CAR CO4041, mentioning the exhibition of a 'Bosjesman's child' with its parents in Edinburgh in 1848: the parents were stereotyped by the writer as 'sunk intellectually into the lowest situation of which humanity is capable – rising little above the beasts which perish and apparently incapable of moral and religious training', though he believed that the child could become an 'intelligent christian under a suitable education'.
47   Bennett, *The Birth of the Museum*, pp. 66–7.
48   Dell, 'Museums', p. 265.
49   *Morning Post*, 15 September 1884, quoted in Dell, 'Museums', p. 321; see also p. 320
50   S. Peacock, *The Great Farini: The High-Wire Life of William Hunt* (Toronto: Penguin, 1995), pp. 305–8: while Peacock describes Healey as Farini's 'right hand man', Dell does not make this connection; Scott to SNA, 26 February 1885, CAR NBC16; see also S. Peacock, 'Africa Meets the Great Farini', in B. Lindfors (ed.), *Africans on Stage: Studies in Ethnological Show Business* (Bloomington: Indiana University Press, 1999), pp. 94–6.
51   S. Peacock, 'Africa Meets the Great Farini', pp. 97–100.
52   See G. Farini, *Through the Kalahari Desert: A Narrative of a Journey with Gun, Camera, and Notebook to Lake N'Gami and Back* (London: Sampson Low, 1886); Scott to Colonial Secretary (c.22 July 1885), CAR NBC17.
53   *Cape Argus*, 22 July 1885, p. 3; interestingly, this article, an interview with Farini on his return to Cape Town, makes no mention of the so-called 'lost city'!
54   Farini, *Through the Kalahari*, p. 442.
55   Ibid., pp. 434–5.
56   Scott to Mr Tooke, 29 January 1886, CAR NBC17; see Private Secretary to Premier to Scott, 20 January 1886 (telegram), CAR NBC9: 'Please wire name of Bushman prisoner and where tried so that Government may have the papers. It would not be legal to make his release conditional on his going to England but you might privately arrange with him that when he was released he should go to England . . . '. Scott claimed that 'there is nothing approaching the illegal about the matter': Scott to Tooke, 29 January 1886, CAR NBC17.
57   Scott to Mr Tooke, 29 January 1886, CAR NBC17: 'They are to receive for six months service ten goats (say £5) between them.'
58   The 1851 'Earthmen' were described in the press, for example, as 'exquisitely proportioned, each movement being instinct with natural grace, and might form perfect models for the sculptor': *Sunday Times*, May 1853, quoted by Dell, 'Museums', p. 51.
59   D. Gill, Royal Observatory, to Scott, June 1886, CAR NBC10.
60   Sydney Cowper, Treasury, to Scott, 31 January 1887, CAR NBC 11. There returned from London one Klaas Jager – another name for Klaas Tilletjies – with his wife and child. RM, Namaqualand, to Scott, 12 January 1887, CAR NBC10.
61   *Catalogue of the Exhibits of the Colony of the Cape of Good Hope, Colonial and Indian Exhibition of 1886*, quoted by Dell, 'Museums', p. 341; the catalogue also

mentions 'Native implements, collected for the Commission by Mr Scott, Northern Border Commissioner'.

62 Dell, 'Museums', pp. 158–9. The *Colonial and Indian Exhibition* was preceded in South Africa by the 1885 *South African Exhibition* in Port Elizabeth, which served as a dress rehearsal. There were no living exhibits in the latter, and the book describing it places a heavy emphasis on colonial industry and, even where 'natives' were concerned, on the products of 'civilisation' rather than of tribalism. It refers, almost as a footnote, to 'a representation of what has become known as native curios': C. Cowen (ed.), *The South African Exhibition, Port Elizabeth, 1885* (Cape Town: Argus, 1886), p. 45; see also Dell, 'Museums', pp. 127–8.
63 Quoted in Dell, 'Museums', p. 159
64 F. Cundall (ed.), *Reminiscences of the Colonial and Indian Exhibition* (London: Clowes, 1886), facing p. 86, shown in Dell, 'Museums', p. 158.
65 Dell, 'Museums', pp. 159–60.
66 Scott to Secretary NAD, 16 June 1902, CAR NA504 A148.
67 Stanford to J. Frost, Minister of Native Affairs, 20 June 1902, CAR NA504 A148.
68 Scott to Under Colonial Secretary, 3 November 1885, CAR NBC17.
69 Nightingale, 8 July 1887, CAR G60–1888, p. 4.
70 Scott (January 1888), CAR G6–1888, p. 21: he attributed this also, admittedly, to good rains and the opening up of employment opportunities at Van Wyk's Vlei.
71 C. Bam, 4 November 1890, CAR British Bechuanaland: Report of the Administrator for 1889–1890, C6269, 1891, p. 50, confirmed that stock thefts had become of rare occurrence; compare Bam 27 April 1894, CAR C7629, 1895, p. 42.
72 C. B. Scholtz, 12 December 1896, CAR G19–1897, p. 68.
73 J. Smellekamp, 28 January 1898, CAR G42–1898, p. 66.
74 O'Connell, 15 February 1899, CAR G31–1899, p. 59.
75 Ibid.: 'During the past year 100 Bushmen had been convicted of stock theft', he wrote; see also O'Connell to W. Napier, Bulawayo, 1 June 1898, CAR 1/UPT 5/3/2.
76 *Diamond Fields Advertiser*, 18 February 1907.
77 See M. Legassick and C. Rassool, *Skeletons in the Cupboard: South African Museums and the Trade in Human Remains* (Cape Town: South African Museum, 2000).
78 P. Davison, 'Material culture', Ph.D, University of Cape Town (1991), pp. 145–58; Dell, 'Museums', pp. 245–8.
79 See M. Legassick, 'The Racial Division of Gordonia, 1921–1930', *Kronos*, 25 (1998).
80 Jackson to Cornish-Bowden, 12 January 1924, CAR Pretoria Archives, LDE 3953, 11106.
81 R. J. Gordon, '"Bain's Bushmen": Scenes at the Empire Exhibition, 1936', in B. Lindfors, 'Saving the Last South African Bushman: A Spectacular Failure', *Critical Arts*, 9:2 (1995), 28–48; C. Rassool and P. Hayes, 'Science and the Spectacle: Khanako's South Africa, 1936–1937', in W. Woodward, G. Minkley and P. Hayes (eds), *Deep Histories: Gender and Colonialism in Southern Africa* (Amsterdam: Rodopi, 2002); see also South Africa Archives, Pretoria, CAR NTS 9587 382/400, Parts I–IV.
82 See, e.g., *Cape Times*, 22 March 1999.

PART II

The ordering of culture:
new nations for old

CHAPTER FOUR

Taonga, marae, whenua – negotiating custodianship: a Maori tribal response to Te Papa: the Museum of New Zealand

Paul Tapsell, Te Arawa

I am a descendant of the Arawa people of Rotorua in Aotearoa – New Zealand. My knowledge, my understandings, my sense of accountability to my people, were instilled in me by my elders, all of whom have now passed on. I'm privileged to have gone through university, to work in museums and to be involved in the interpretation and performance of *taonga* – the cultural treasures of our people – and the elucidation of taonga to those who perhaps do not understand them the way our people do.

I wish to start my discussion by recalling one particular elder and mentor, Tomairangi Kameta, who is a very recent ancestor of Ngati Whakaue, Te Arawa (figure 4.1). He died nine years ago. He supported my move to museum work when I was a young graduate looking to make a career out of my anthropology training. Tomairangi was the first elder to realise that my museum interests could serve our tribe. In 1990 he and other elders assisted me in gaining the position of curator at the local government-run Rotorua Museum, a museum rich in Te Arawa taonga. This museum is located in the heart of Te Arawa on the sub-tribal lands of Ngati Whakaue and surrounded by the geothermal city of Rotorua. It was a sink or swim situation, as I had neither formal nor tribal training in caring for taonga. My elders realised my difficulty and took me under their wing. During the day I learned how to care professionally for the thousands of items in the museum's fine arts, photography, social history, archival, natural history and ethnology collections. Then, in the evenings, I would visit the elders with whom I spent many hours learning the deeper customary meanings represented by our tribal treasures scattered throughout these collections. On occasion a lesson would end with the sun rising – just time enough to go home, shower and head back

4.1 Tomairangi Kameta, late Te
Arawa elder, retelling the story
of Houmaitawhiti

to work! Of all my elders Tomairangi remained my closest guide and
mentor, someone I could always turn to for advice concerning all
things Maori, someone who could demonstrate the spiritual and
practical differences between *lore* and *law*, someone who continually
reminded me to see our world as a matrix of genealogical connections
ultimately joined under one universe.

Before Tomairangi passed away, he advised me to view issues of
concern as a carved central post, a *poutokomanawa*, taking on different appearances according to the vantage point from which one gazes
upon it. In practice this is the central supporting post of a *whare
tupuna*, or ancestral meeting-house, which embodies all of a kin group's
ancestry. The poutokomanawa represents both the eponymous ancestor
of a kin group and the epoch in which an important historical event
took place. Depending on your genealogical connection to that ancestor
you will have a particular view of the event.

If we look at the poutokomanawa named Houmaitawhiti, each of
us sitting around this taonga will see something slightly different
(figure 4.2). You may see him as a stylistic expression in wood, a post-
contact example of Maori utilisation of European resources, or perhaps
an exciting work of nineteenth-century primitive art. Today, however,
I invite you to look from my genealogical perspective at Houmaitawhiti
– as a person who lived over twenty generations ago, an important
figure in Te Arawa's history, someone admired by all of Te Arawa as
the father who motivated us, his children, to leave the relative comfort of Rangiatea (Ra'iatea in the Tahitian Islands) to seek out a new

4.2 Houmaitawhiti, poutokomanawa (central support post of a meeting-house) figure in Rotorua Museum

life in Aotearoa. That voyage in our doubled-hulled canoe *Te Arawa* was full of drama, and many stories about the voyage are told by elders today, utilising the deeper meanings embedded in such taonga as Houmaitawhiti. Eventually our people arrived at Maketu in the Bay of Plenty around 700 years ago and we have since populated the lands, lakes and geothermal regions of inland Rotorua. As for Houmaitawhiti, he was an old man by the time we set sail for Aotearoa, so instead of coming with us, he chose his son Tama te Kapua to take the lead, and remained in Rangiatea from where he still acts as our genealogical anchor in life, before spiritually embracing us back home in death.

Taonga such as Houmaitawhiti allow our histories to be re-lived. So long as their power – *mana, tapu* and *korero* – are maintained and the *marae* context (ritual meeting space–place between host and visitor) in which they are performed continues to flourish, then the genealogical narratives each taonga represents will continue to be vital to their descendants through the generations. Mana is the ancestral power of the gods, tapu is the spiritual order that protects them so that they can travel through the generations, and korero is the knowledge – the oral traditions, the prayers and the words – embodied in taonga that nourishes the *mauri*, or life-force, of each such item. Taonga are not limited to carved or weaved items: they can also take the form of a song, a geothermal hot-pool or a photograph. What is important is the ancestor–descendant connection, the relationship between kin group, their lands and resources (represented by taonga) and the customary context in which it all makes sense: the marae.

The marae is the paramount focus of tribal identity – the ultimate expression of a kin group and its *mana o te whenua*, or customary authority over surrounding estates. Most marae today are located in front of a kin group's whare tupuna, and through the marae these taonga, or ancestors, are empowered, brought back to life. The marae context allows descendant elders to perform the taonga so that they may bring forward ancestors from the past to spiritually interact with their present-day descendants. Taonga also assist elders in guiding the recently departed back to our Maori spiritual homeland while, at the same time, reminding the living of our kin group connections with each other and with our surrounding ancestral landscape.

The taonga on display in the Rotorua Museum are no different from the taonga you find on marae, in elders' homes or exhibited in the many museums around the world, including Te Papa – the Museum of New Zealand. All taonga have come from a tribal background via an ancestral pathway. Some of our ancestors date back to a time before we arrived in Aotearoa, while others are very recent; some of them can be presented in very stylised, artistic forms, others in more simple ones. It is about recognition of our past and of the political, social and economic significations that each taonga once had in relation to particular tribal lands across all of Aotearoa. Every tribe was, and still is, dependent on its relationship with the land, in terms not of ownership but of belonging. Over the generations, through occupation and conquest, the lands of Aotearoa became an genealogical cloak of entwined relationships, of the myriad ancestral interactions by which taonga continue to provide us descendants with the keys to unlock the lessons of the past. When we walk across our tribal lands we are walking beside our ancestors and using the precedents they have set over the past twenty generations to guide us into the future. We do not turn our backs on our ancestors; rather, we look at how they dealt with situations in their time so that we ourselves might be able to find a way in ours, a pathway forward for all the people of our tribe. Such is the power of taonga – an image, a textbook, a spiritual guide, a signpost and a genealogical roadmap all in one.

Although Maori and Pakeha (European settlers) have lived alongside each other for over 150 years, our Pakeha neighbours remain mostly ignorant of the inherent complexity of Maori tribal society and its marae rituals. Urbanisation has only confounded the situation by isolating tribal marae – socially, politically and economically – from their now city-raised descendants. Today's urbanised Maori are more likely to seek access to perceived Pakeha-controlled opportunities via a pan-Maori identity rather than by empowering ancestral kin relationships through the home tribes' marae, around which New Zealand's cities have been built. Out of this ethnic identity contest has arisen a new phenomenon known as the urban, or pan-Maori, marae, thus perpetuating the media's propensity to put all Maori into one racially biased basket. In reality, there remain over fifty major tribal groups in Aotearoa, of which Te Arawa is but one. Te Arawa comprises around 16 autonomous kin groupings, including Ngati Whakaue, and within Ngati Whakaue there are 20 major families. At the last count, my family alone accounts for around 3,500 living descendants and has affiliations to over 20 marae – and it is on marae that we speak our concerns, not through the media.

When speaking to non-Maori audiences I have found it helpful to present Maori tribal society as a conglomerate of fiercely independent nations and the marae as our seats of parliament – our debating chambers. In the early 1800s, prior to the Treaty of Waitangi, leaders of these 'nations' were competing for access to European trade goods and the social, political and economic power that such access represented. Marae flourished in the rapidly shifting power contexts of nineteenth-century New Zealand, as the nations at first battled one another, before unifying forces to fight the Pakeha tide of colonisation. The 1840 Treaty of Waitangi, which I expand upon later, provided relief and protection for those nations struggling politically for access to European trade goods. Article 2 was crucial to the eventual acceptance of the treaty by all the tribal leaders of New Zealand, for that article expressed the Crown's promise to protect the chiefly authority of all tribes in their customary trusteeship over their resources.[1] The chiefly focus of that trusteeship is the marae.

To expand further, the marae is more than the precinct that extends out in front of a meeting-house: it is also portable. The marae concept is something that goes way back into our Polynesian homelands and has been part of our culture for probably 3,000–4,000 years. Ancient in origin, the tribal marae continues to be a place for dynamic inter-action of ritualised conversation and ideas, and is contained by rules that effectively ameliorate differences and misunderstandings. Those who decide such rules of engagement are the people who belong to the marae: the *tangata whenua*, or descendants of the surrounding ancestral lands.[2] So, for example, were you to come to our marae and stand before us, we would be welcoming you but we woud also be prescribing how that welcome is to proceed from beginning to end. We'd weep for our dead, exchange talk, exchange gifts and exchange breath by pressing noses with the *hongi*. Completing the hongi signifies that the ancestral tensions we each bring to our encounter have been ameliorated. The *wairua*, or spirits, of our ancestors have now departed to their respective homelands and we, the living, can proceed to the reason for your presence in the first place at our marae.

As marae are portable they can be evoked by the tangata whenua wherever they may wish on their homelands. This is normally in front of the tribe's chiefly meeting-house but it can also be in a park, hotel lobby or the foyer of the local museum, as would often occur when I was working at the Rotorua Museum. And on all such occasions the tangata whenua (my Ngati Whakaue elders), not the museum or any other tribe represented by taonga in the collections, would take the host role, and greet not only the distinguished visitors into that space (the museum foyer) but all the attending tribes (wider Te Arawa kin groups and beyond). The marae is who we are.

Twenty years ago the New Zealand Maori exhibition *Te Maori* toured the USA.[3] In my opinion the early success of *Te Maori* owed much to the home elders agreeing to create outside each venue entrance a marae space through which visitors had to pass to gain access; thereafter they were guided around the taonga and invited to experience them ancestrally through the guides' eyes. It seems that all who visited *Te Maori* were moved by the experience: it was a coming of age in Maori–Pakeha relations – the 'holy grail' of Maori exhibitions – and gave rise to today's bicultural nationhood ideology.[4] The Crown's Museum of New Zealand Project, which evolved directly out of *Te Maori*, sought to recapture the exhibition's Maori essence and combine this with emerging Pakeha ideas of *nationhood*. The marae, as observed during *Te Maori*, became central to the bicultural approach and over the ensuing decade transformed from tribal space into 'Our Place'. New bicultural (crown) concepts, like *taonga Maori* and *mana taonga*, displaced customary marae (tribal) protocols – law defining lore. In 1998 the Museum of New Zealand's crown-appointed trustees welcomed the world across its marae threshold and into *Te Papa* – Our Place. But whose place is it really?

To make sense of how Te Papa arrived at its mana taonga and marae concepts we need to revisit the final venue of *Te Maori*, the Auckland Art Gallery, back in 1987. Busloads of elders journeyed from all over Aotearoa to Auckland to welcome visitors into *Te Maori* and meet their carved ancestors. Whereas local tribes had maintained the marae at earlier venues, for example Te Ati Awa-Ngati Toa in Wellington, by the time *Te Maori* arrived in Auckland the crown-appointed organisers had decided to run the marae themselves. They chose, for whatever reason, not to seek guidance from Ngati Whatua o Orakei – tangata whenua of Auckland – regarding the performance of Maori protocols at the Auckland Art Gallery, the organizers inviting instead elders from elsewhere in the country to maintain a marae based not on land but on the incoming tribe's genealogical association with the exhibited taonga, thereby upsetting the tangata whenua. Furthermore the incoming elders were requested to rotate with other tribes on a weekly basis *taking turns* as tangata whenua. Many of the attending elders became very uncomfortable when they arrived at the Art Gallery and discovered they were expected to play such a role on another tribe's ancestral land. From a tribal perspective this *rotating* marae concept based upon taonga rather than ancestral lands was unprecedented. It was especially unusual because the tangata whenua were nowhere to be seen. So how did the incoming elders deal with the situation, given that the Crown had funded their trip to the city and provided accommodation and refreshments? In the case of Te Arawa, my elders avoided compromise by, first and foremost, insisting on acknowledging the tangata whenua, even though they were absent. In so doing, Ngati Whatua o Orakei's ancestral presence was seen to settle over proceedings. Thus the crown-imposed marae paradox, based on connection to taonga rather than land, was instantly transformed into a non-marae space of Maori interaction between two kin groups operating under the ancestral governance – mana o te whenua – of Auckland's paramount tribe, Ngati Whatua o Orakei.[5]

Perhaps because all of the dialogue during these ceremonies was conducted in the Maori language, the Crown and its museums missed the subtlety of what was really occurring. Missed were the ritual deconstruction of the marae paradox and the reconfirmation by visiting tribes of tangata whenua's paramount status. Nevertheless, the Museum of New Zealand Project was not to be deterred: in the years that followed it ignored warnings from esteemed elders of Wellington and wider tribes (for example Pateriki Te Rei and Kuru-o-te-Marama Waaka), and continued developing the marae paradox of *Te Maori* under the invented label of *mana taonga*. On their own each of these words, mana and taonga, expresses deep and very traditional concepts, yet putting them together has created an entirely novel understanding. What does mana taonga mean? According to Te Papa, it means that anyone who enters its museum doors and is represented by taonga Maori (treasures of Maori origin) or taonga Pakeha (treasures of non-Maori origin) may exercise the right to stand upon its marae as tangata whenua: in reality, a sophisticated re-run of *Te Maori* at its final Auckland venue. There is no escaping the fact, however, that Te Papa's nation-space agenda must also take account of the Treaty of Waitangi. In 1987 when *Te Maori* was in Auckland the Crown was still four years from admitting its failure to protect the rangatiratanga of Ngati Whatua o Orakei.[6] Since then numerous settlements have been made and hundreds more claims await hearings. New Zealand's Treaty relations have moved well beyond the dictatorial days of *Te Maori*; yet for all the Crown's rhetoric of honouring the Treaty, it has still to fulfil its trustee responsibility to the local kin group on whose land Te Papa stands. And therein lies the contradiction.

For now my focus is the Treaty: it is important to appreciate Te Papa's on-the-ground reality. Whereas Article 1 of the 1840 Treaty acknowledges the Crown's right to govern (*kawanatanga*), the second article states the Crown's agreement to protect the chiefs (*rangatira*) and sub-tribes (*hapu*) in the unqualified exercise of their chieftainship (*rangatiratanga*) over their lands (*whenua*), villages (*kainga*) and all their treasures (*taonga*). In simple terms, the Crown promised to protect tribal leaders' trusteeship (rangatiratanga) over their kin groups' resources – land, people and taonga. In return Maori signed over sovereign rule (kawanatanga) of the islands of New Zealand to the Crown of England. History, however, demonstrates that the Crown's Treaty promise of this double trusteeship was ignored from as early as 1843 (the Wairau incident). Since then tribes throughout Aotearoa have battled the Crown through their generations seeking redress. In the 1980s, around the same time *Te Maori* came home from the USA, New Zealand's third Labour Government provided the Waitangi Tribunal with retrospective powers. For the first time Maori had a forum in which they could voice their Treaty grievances and seek return of resources and compensation. This process generated new hope of a Crown–Maori partnership regarding the future social, political and economic development of the nation. Not surprisingly, the Museum of New Zealand Project sought to symbolise the Treaty partnership aspirations of our country, and Te Papa's bicultural ideology

– two people, one nation – was born. But casting Maori as one unified group detracts from the on-the-ground complexity of Maori tribal society. And by creating its own Maori rules – mana taonga and non-tribal marae – it appears that Te Papa, as an arm of the Crown, continues to disregard its ongoing Treaty responsibility to the local kin group on whose land it stands.[7] It may come as no surprise, therefore, that one of the four main tribes of Wellington, Ngati Toa, has an outstanding Treaty claim against the Crown over the reclaimed foreshore on which Te Papa rests.

Essentially, the Crown (kawanatanga) has assigned itself rangatiratanga status within the walls of Te Papa from within which it now dictates to the nation what it means to be Maori but without respect for its Treaty partners, namely the local tribes of Te Ati Awa, Ngati Tama, Ngati Mutunga and Ngati Toa (Te Ati Awa-Ngati Toa). Imagine how it feels for members of my tribe, Te Arawa, travelling eight hours to Te Papa to commune with their ancestral treasures resting under the mana of Te Ati Awa-Ngati Toa, and on arrival find instead of being ritually greeted by home elders, they are not only welcomed in by employees but then invited to assume tangata whenua status on the museum's marae? Not surprisingly, my elders were very unhappy. How would you feel if you were invited by a stranger into someone else's home and told to help yourself?

Te Arawa has experienced this quandary on a number of occasions since the mid-1990s: time and again the Crown has attempted to prescribe mana taonga in place of customary marae rituals of encounter.[8] Fortunately, these encounters mysteriously transformed into mana o te whenua situations at which Te Papa could do little but watch. How did this happen? Quite simply really: all Maori are related – that's the magic of knowing your *whakapapa* (genealogy). So, before my elders journeyed they would telephone their Wellington relations to ensure that Te Ati Awa-Ngati Toa elders were aware of their trip to Te Papa, thus enabling tangata whenua to properly greet Te Arawa and our interaction with taonga to proceed according to the ancestral reality of being Maori: whakapapa. There was one time in particular when we phoned Te Ati Awa-Ngati Toa: 'We're turning up to the museum at such-and-such a time, anyone told you? No? OK we'll meet you on the steps.' Next day, we arrived at the museum, and when the doors opened the staff discovered who it was up in front – the tribal leaders of Wellington. Well, this caused a stir, but it was too late: ritual had begun, chants filled the air and Te Arawa followed the tangata whenua into the museum's designated marae space. While the tangata whenua crossed over the court to take up their home-people role, Te Arawa maintained a position opposite. A customary marae had now formed, complete with the genealogical tension generated by one visiting tribe standing on another's ancestral land. We, the guests, now felt comfortable and the people of the land, the tangata whenua, felt comfortable too. The ritual of encounter continued, as refined by our ancestors over countless generations, until all is completed with the hongi, or pressing of noses. Museum management looked on in bewilderment, confused by the loss of control over proceedings, and declared: 'We have done it all wrong! My elders just smiled: 'Then we've been doing this marae thing wrong for over 100 generations . . .'.

Now to tie these thoughts together. The marae provides the ideal forum for taonga interactions to proceed so that everyone can celebrate our grand ancestral past. Tangata whenua right of occupation – mana o te whenua – is expressed through oratory and song, then later balanced by the provision of hospitality – manaakitanga – to visitors. It was their ancestors' blood that was spilt on the land, which has become infused into the land. Consequently, any taonga, no matter their origin, resting on a tribe's land must first be ameliorated with the spirituality of the land before further access can be allowed. So, if Te Arawa arrive in Wellington to see an ancestral treasure such as Te Takinga, our expectation is first and foremost to be provided with an opportunity to acknowledge Te Ati Awa-Ngati Toa, the *hunga tiaki* (customary guardians) of our taonga, the people of the land, for spiritually watching over our ancestor while he dwells in Te Papa. When that is completed we can proceed to our taonga, after which partaking in food and hospitality completes the cycle.

Essentially, what I am saying is that even though our taonga exist in national museums they remain under the mana, the authority of those who belong to the land on which those buildings stand. It matters little who may have placed our taonga in those museums – what does matter is how they are spiritually protected. Only the tangata whenua are qualified to fulfil that role, and this becomes truly acute when we are talking about ancestral remains. It is expected by Maori that our ancestral remains resting in museums be accorded spiritual protection of a status equivalent to that one would find associated with an *urupa*, or cemetery. Yet in Wellington Maori staff are expected to maintain spiritual protection of taonga and ancestral remains without the formal assistance of the tangata whenua elders. Is that fair? Imagine that you had to work with nuclear material but were denied protective clothing! For all Maori working in museums, the protection required to fulfil hunga tiaki duties is the mana of the tangata whenua. No other protection will suffice (figure 4.3).[9]

To conclude, the solutions are, I think, simple. All we need to do is to start thinking about how to involve local indigenous people at

[95]

4.3 Pukaki on Te Papa-i-Ouru Marae in front of Tama te Kapua (meeting-house) surrounded by his Te Arawa descendants

governance level in our national museums. Ensuring their involvement provides opportunities for interactive relationships and the exchange of ideas, be these local, national or global in dimension. There is no escaping the ancestral domains layered in the foundations of museums. If museums are serious about forming partnerships with indigenous peoples, then I suggest they start with those closest to home. Let those people guide you. Let them demonstrate the complementarities of land and people, earth and sky, modernity and aboriginality. There is no denying the tensions inherent to such pairings, but surely we can work through them? Is that not what our mothers and fathers did when they came together? They worked through their tensions and we are the result. Recently the Auckland Museum chose to explore its relationship with the tangata whenua, and today that museum has a complementary and effective Maori governance system which leads the world on issues of indigenous partnerships. Its gifting home of the Ngati Whakaue's ancestral treasure, *Pukaki*, set a world-wide precedent for museums.[10] Without going into detail, this celebrated event released the magic contained in taonga – the illusive magic that museums have been attempting to reinvent since *Te Maori*. For whatever reason, museums became preoccupied with recreating the physical marae place rather than seeking local elder assistance on how best to evoke a marae space. As Pukaki's return demonstrated, the alchemy of the taonga is still accessible if and when they are performed on marae under the ancestral authority of the people who belong to the land: the tangata whenua. For koro Tomairangi it was all so simple. He saw the universe we live in as a map of genealogical interconnections, and no matter where he stood in our world he was interrelated with the land, the sky and all beings dwelling between them. To his mind, the Museum of New Zealand could no more separate itself from the land than could separate the stars from the sky. But then he would crack one of his wry smiles: '*Kei te pai e tama*, that is but my view of the *poutokomanawa*.'

Glossary

hunga tiaki	(Te Arawa dialect for *kaitiaki – kaitiakitanga*) guardian – spiritual and/or physical – who must be *tangata whenua*; trustee; manager of *taonga* (and estates) on behalf of wider kin group; protector; custodian (male or female); a customary role fulfilled by or delegated to members of the *tangata whenua* tribe's senior family, i.e. elders (*rangatira*) and their spiritual advisors (*tohunga*); the term may be applied to wider kin group
korero	oratory; to speak knowledge; speech; talk; verbal discourse; orally transmitted knowledge; true account of the past; historical utterance; narratives associated with ancestors.
koro	old man, elder; term of endearment
mana	authority; power; prestige; status; integrity; self-esteem; source of energy from the gods transmitted through ancestors; ancestral power embracing people and their estates
mana o te whenua	(Te Arawa dialect for *mana whenua*) mantle; customary authority associated with specific ancestral lands performed by *rangatira* on behalf of kin group; may also be descriptively applied to the *rangatira*, the kin group or the *marae*; exclusively associated with *tangata whenua*; similar to *turangawaewae* – ancestral home: 'a place to stand'
marae	meeting ground; central courtyard; plaza; communal meeting-place in front of an ancestral

[97]

	house; three-dimensional space extending beyond a tribal meeting-house or a war canoe prow; political, social and economic focus of tribal lands (*whenua*); a place where kin group elders receive visitors, perform ritual and conduct oratory
rangatira	kin group leader, esteemed elder who carries the authority of the kin group; servant of the kin group; trustee, guardian of the kin group's resources
tangata whenua	people of the land; home tribe; local people; descendants of a specific Maori kin group organised according to a common ancestor; kin group which holds exclusive customary authority over specifically defined estates
taonga	any tangible or intangible item, object or thing that represents a kin group's genealogical identity in relation to its estates and resources and is passed down through generations
tapu	protect; sacred; prohibition; set apart; indication of presence of ancestors which, if transgressed, can inflict ill-fortune – its balancing state is *noa*, meaning profane, common, everyday, free from ancestral influence
tikanga	discipline of the ancestors; lore and customs carefully maintained and passed down through the generations by elders (*rangatira, tohunga*); ancestral correctness associated with all tapu ceremonies, hui and taonga, especially in a marae context; principles
tohunga	spiritual advisor to the rangatira and his or her kin group; specialist in oratory and ritual
whenua	land – ancestral estate which nourishes a kin group; afterbirth, placenta

Notes

1   Sir I. H. Kawharu, 'Mana and the Crown: A Marae at Orakei', in I. H. Kawharu (ed.), *Waitangi: Maori and Pakeha Perspectives of the Treaty of Waitangi* (Auckland: Oxford University Press, 1989).
2   M. Marsden, 'God, Man and Universe: A Maori View', in M. King (ed.), *Te Ao Hurihuri: Aspects of Maoritanga* (Auckland: Longman Paul, 1975).
3   S. M. Mead (ed.), *Te Maori: Maori Art from New Zealand Collections* (New York: Abrams, 1984); see also Mead, *Magnificent Te Maori: Te Maori Whakahirahira* (Auckland: Heinemann, 1986).

4 B. Dibley, 'Museum, Native, Nation: Museological Narrative and Postcolonial Nation Identity Formation', MA dissertation, University of Auckland (1994).

5 P. Tapsell, 'Taonga: A Tribal Response to Museums', D.Phil thesis, Oxford University (1998).

6 *Waitangi Tribunal Report: Orakei. Wai 9* (Wellington: Government Printer, 1987).

7 Tapsell, 'Taonga'.

8 Ibid.

9 M. W. Kawharu (ed.), *Whenua: Managing Our Resources* (Auckland: Reed Publishing, 2002).

10 P. Tapsell, *Pukaki: A Comet Returns* (Auckland: Reed Publishing, 2000).

CHAPTER FIVE

Auckland's centrepiece: unsettled identities, unstable monuments

Leonard Bell

If you need a memorial look about you. (Epitaph on the graves of Christopher Wren, St Paul's Cathedral, London, and John Logan Campbell, Maungakiekie/One Tree Hill, Auckland)

From 1901 to 1912 the Scottish-born John Logan Campbell (1817–1912), a pioneer European settler of Auckland (in 1840), merchant, speculator and landowner, then popularly known as the 'Father of Auckland',[1] orchestrated or initiated a series of events and constructions that amounted to the staging of a self on a huge scale, with a denouement that was posthumous, and not what he would have anticipated. In 1901 he had gifted to the young city a 230-acre site, to be made into a public park, on the lower slopes of the 602-foot volcanic cone called One Tree Hill, or Maungakiekie, which for 300 years until the 1790s had been a Maori *pa* (fortified settlement).[2] The erection of a larger-than-life statue of the still-very-much-alive Campbell – for which he provided the land and the finance – at the entrance of the so-named Cornwall Park followed in 1906. At its unveiling Campbell proposed that a monument, a 'towering obelisk dedicated to the great Maori race', be set on the summit of the adjacent One Tree Hill,[3] also a public domain, where Campbell was to be buried and which was regarded as *wahi tapu* (sacred) by former Maori occupants, in particular Ngati Whatua of the Auckland region and Tainui of Waikato. Campbell's will provided for this monument. A 100-foot obelisk, with a bronze statue of a full-standing Maori 'warrior chief' at its base, was eventually unveiled by the Maori King Koroki in 1948.

The park and monument complex, initiated during the period in which New Zealand shifted from *mature* colony to *independent* dominion (1907) in the British Empire, constitutes an aesthetic shaping that can be related to notions about putative national(ist) and regional(ist) settler-colonial identity, though not in straightforward or

[100]

settled ways. It can be risky to take the behaviour and representations of an individual as an index of wider social phenomena, to conflate person and collective. Campbell, however, was a *celebrity*, an iconic figure, in his society. His presented self had become public property and that self and his 'good works' were identified with, and assisted in their formulation, by many people in Auckland. A nexus, then, between individual and collective can be postulated. Campbell's self-staging and its afterlife can be considered, though, not simply as a validation or embodiment of stereotypical characterisations of settler-colonial identity, but as a cultural phenomenon close examination of which reveals that settler-colonial identifications[4] have been much more complicated and unresolved than the standard picture in New Zealand has generally allowed. Even if Campbell was a consummate actor on the public stage, calculating in his attempt to fix a place for himself in the historical record, the park and monument complex constructed in his name has been a problematical combination of elements that have not co-existed comfortably. The complex has been subject to conflicting evaluations and responses, a condition that may well have its source in the ambivalences and splits within both Campbell himself and the society whose members identified so strongly with his public persona.

The standard picture of settler-colonial identity in New Zealand has had a confidently asserted distinctiveness and a spirit of inde-pendence emerging clearly among European New Zealanders in the 1890s and early 1900s, even while attachment to Britain and things British remained strong.[5] This reputed sense of difference, of a New Zealand society that was *new* and distinct from the 'Old World', has routinely been linked to the nationalism of the socially progressive Liberal governments of the period.[6] At the level of culture (popular, fine arts, musical, literary and design) this was frequently articulated in the cooption or appropriation of Maori myths, legends, landscapes and artefacts, motifs and subjects generally, which were held to be unique to New Zealand and thus unambivalent markers of *New Zealandness*.[7] This characterisation of identity now appears simplistic, partial, even clichéd. Particularly wanting has been the implication that this sense of distinct identity was unified and unproblematically subscribed to by the European New Zealand (Pakeha) population – in a *settled* condition.[8]

There has been a general tendency among historians of late colonial New Zealand to treat the cultural as if it simply reflected extant conditions and states of consciousness, as if it were peripheral to the *main* show. There has been little recognition of the cultural as constitu-tive, that cultural activities and products – images and objects, music, plays, monuments, museums, parks, the use of food, for example – can be fundamental to the making or negotiation of social identities.[9] Yet settler colonials themselves could be well attuned to how visual representations and objects can play primary roles in shaping senses of the past and the relationship of people to place; in attempted constructions of the *shared memories* and narratives that societies, in particular *new* societies, need.

There has been an apparent lack of realisation, too, that cultural products can, irrespective of their makers' intentions, manifest in their material forms and the responses they generate, and, in the changing circumstances of their ongoing use, the complexities of purported identities and relations. They are not just static things, fixed in their functions, but are mutable, offering an interplay of elements that can take on new and conflicting roles and meanings according to the relationships of those with interests in them. A cultural artefact's *identity*, the sets of values and meanings with which it is endowed, can be as contradictory as those of both its maker and its viewers, 'friends and foes'.[10] Following the 'careers' of artefacts can suggest how difficult it is to isolate any internally coherent identity – national, regional, late colonial, postcolonial, whatever.

Campbell himself was a complex man, one demonstrably pulled in several directions: his personality and behaviour were marked by inconsistency, ambivalence and restlessness. Insofar as Cornwall Park and its crowning section, the One Tree Hill summit monument complex – obelisk with the statue of a Maori warrior, grave and tree, an attempt to shape a place in a man's image – has been subject to radically different evaluations, it can now be seen as a monument to the complexities of what the man represented, and of Maori–Pakeha and Maori inter-tribal relationships through to the present. Landscape art and artefacts emerge as a site of interacting forces and tensions that disallows any singularity of meaning and effect.

A summary sketch of the broader parameters of Maori–settler-colonial relationships might be useful. New Zealand, unlike most colonies, had a foundational agreement between the indigenous people, Maori, and the Crown: the 1840 Treaty of Waitangi, in which Maori were guaranteed sovereignty over their lands and resources. That Treaty took back seat to the actualities of colonial expansion from the mid-nineteenth century and into the twentieth century. It was largely ignored in this period in which Maori, as well as becoming a minority, experienced major loss of land through post-land war confiscations and both legitimate and dubious purchases by colonists and their descendants. It has been only since the mid-1980s that the history, nature and legitimacy of these transactions have been seriously reassessed and substantial efforts made by both Labour and National governments to redress historical wrongs. Fundamental to these processes has been the assertion of the Treaty of Waitangi and its sustaining principles as the bases for negotiation. Easier said than done, however, since the meaning of the Treaty and what those sustaining principles actually were or are have been subject to differing interpretation and ongoing disagreement.

The lands that became Auckland were sold by Maori, principally Ngati Whatua, even if the validity of some of those sales has been questioned recently. While the Auckland region had been densely populated by Maori in the seventeenth and eighteenth centuries, from the early 1800s to the late 1830s it was largely abandoned; the consequence of devastating inter-tribal warfare. However, by 1840 Ngati Whatua, the major tribe since the mid-eighteenth century, were returning, and Maori from other tribes, particularly from the Waikato to the south, also were settling there. Ngati Whatua invited Governor Hobson, the first governor of the colony, to make Auckland his capital for a complex of reasons – their own security and greater ease of access to European technology and economic–social advantages among them. The first European settlers in Auckland in the 1840s–50s needed Maori support and goodwill – for provisions, for labour, as a market for its merchants in a period when the European population was small. The balance quickly changed: from the mid nineteenth century settler numbers grew rapidly, so that by 1900 Maori had become a small and relatively powerless minority in a city of c.100,000. How crucial that early Maori support had been for the development of the city was forgotten by most Pakeha. The Maori population of Auckland remained small and marginal until the 1950s and 1960s. With major migration of rural Maori to the cities beginning after the Second World War, the demographics of Auckland have radically altered: it is now the largest Polynesian city in the world, with Maori again an assertive and vital presence.[11]

In 1906 Campbell had advocated that obelisk 'dedicated to the great Maori race' when Maori presence in Auckland was peripheral, and the fortunes of Maori in New Zealand, in terms of institutional power, social and economic well-being and population size, at a low ebb. Obelisks may immediately imply fixity, permanence, the imposition of a *view* and a set of values, the conquest of a place. Obelisks, parks and public statues may function as landmarks that organise people's experiences, physical, emotional, ideological, of the surrounding space – *devices* by which people are directed to a particular view. Yet the One Tree Hill summit monument has embodied sharply divergent roles and values, at different times and for diverse groups, its mutability perhaps exemplifying that 'the relativity of historical relationships [is] not simply one of shifting values but also of the varying circumstances of the beholder, whose perceptions [are] themselves contingent with history'.[12]

Alois Riegl distinguished between 'intentional' and 'unintentional' monuments: intentional monuments are intended by their makers to memorialise their subjects, whether great individuals or events, and fix their greatness for all time; unintentional monuments are either artefacts not originally intended as monuments, but which effectively come to be so regarded by later viewers, or actual monuments, the original intended meanings and values of which have changed,[13] whether calculatedly so on the part of later viewers, through changed socio-political circumstances and different perceptions of the past, or as the effect of the passage of time on people's memory of the original subject. That immortalised individual might simply have been forgotten. An intentional can become an unintentional monument – to some thing or idea very different from, even in conflict with, that which was originally intended for it.

Metamorphoses unintended by Campbell characterise the One Tree Hill–Maungakiekie obelisk and summit complex. That this monument can now be seen to stand for instability might be apt in that Campbell's sense of being in New Zealand was marked by a profoundly unsettled consciousness. The actual manifestations of this – frequent sojourns in Europe until the 1880s, with his final settlement in New Zealand resulting more from financial necessity than any over-riding loyalty to the colony, fragilities in his personal relationships, swings of fortune – have been documented in meticulous detail by Russell Stone.[14] Campbell was one of the first Europeans to settle and buy land – most notably 1,000 acres of One Tree Hill and surrounds in 1853 – in what became Auckland; by 1900 the largest city in New Zealand. Trained as a doctor in Edinburgh, Campbell emigrated primarily in the hope of making his fortune. In Auckland he set up as a merchant and over the next seventy years, despite those lengthy periods in Europe, to which his children were sent for their education, played prominent roles in the development of the city from 'wilderness' to 'civilisation'.[15]

He regarded art as central to this progress; a belief to which his close involvement with, and patronage of, art and a succession of artists attest. He financed Auckland's first art school, the Free School of Art (1878–90),[16] envisaged 'a magnificent art gallery' (never built) in Cornwall Park 'for the exhibition of pictures by New Zealand artists',[17] and was himself the subject of numerous portraits by painters, sculptors, photographers, illustrators and cartoonists.[18] His was the best-known public face in Auckland, *becoming* effectively the face of settler-colonial Auckland. His career in Auckland and the growth of that city were routinely equated: '[h]e has been identified from the beginning with the city he loves;[19] and '[t]he history of his life is the history of the city'.[20] He figured as *the* foundational individual in a city without an actual founder, but whose citizens demonstrably needed one for a narrative of settlement and indigenisation. Campbell himself played a primary part in the formulation of his public persona and the mythologising of his life – he was the author of his public self. His story of his early years in Auckland, *Poenamo. Sketches of the Early Days of New Zealand: Romance and Reality of Antipodean Life in the Infancy of a New Colony* (1881 and 1898), has been described as 'an attempt at creating history', in which Campbell presented a 'fictitious image of his self in order to justify his interpretation of history',[21] and featured as the father figure seminal to the birth and growth of the city. And Campbell's 'My Autobiography: A Short Sketch of a Long Life', completed in 1907 though not published, has been characterised as 'a carefully filtered version of the past composed by an old man conscious of his Father of Auckland image, anxious . . . to keep the good opinion of a community that was bent on venerating him'.[22]

The numerous visual representations of Campbell contributed to this mythologisation, notably the 9.5-foot bronze statue by the British sculptor Henry Pegram, ARA, on a granite pedestal atop a massive pile of rocks – the whole standing 35 feet high at Cornwall Park's entrance, unveiled on Empire Day 1906. This statue – authoritative, far-seeing, judicious in pose and look – combining in one figure a portrait of an individual and the celebration of that favourite Victorian and Edwardian social type the 'great man' was the largest public sculpture in Australasia, much larger than the local statues of Queen Victoria. Clearly, France's Third Republic ruling that no monument could be made to a living person[23] would have meant little to Auckland's settler colonials. Martin Warnke has argued that 'giantism seeks to relate the great individual to the landscape in grandiose monumental form, so that he appears superhuman and overpowering'.[24] The excess of Pegram's statue suggests both a nationalistic assertiveness and a settler-colonial insecurity – an instance of histrionic over-determination. Nowadays adjacent to a busy arterial traffic route the giant Campbell seems oddly lost, displaced by historical changes. The association of Campbell and One Tree Hill was integral to his mythologisation as the originator and patriarch of Auckland. The synonymity of person and place was articulated visually in Wilhelm Dittmer's 1902 portrait of Campbell in the *New Zealand Graphic* (see figure 5.1), in which

5.1 John Logan Campbell

the face and body of 'Auckland's leading citizen'[25] are framed by, and elided with, Cornwall Park and One Tree Hill – prior to his burial at the summit, in 1912, his physical incorporation within the mountain, and the administrative incorporation of One Tree Hill's summit into Cornwall Park. Campbell's gift to Auckland of Cornwall Park, the opening of which he described as 'the grandest incident of my life and its crowning happiness',[26] secured the identification of place and person. Such was its strength that there were popular moves to rename the park Campbell Park and One Tree Hill Mount Campbell, moves which Campbell opposed as disrespectful of the Duke of Cornwall and derogatory to Maori.[27]

Nevertheless, the subsequent shaping of the park and the summit, in which Campbell had a controlling hand even after his death, became for many Pakeha a monument to him and to the origins of Auckland.

It might also seem a monument to colonial domination with Campbell's burial on the summit, a sacred place for Maori, cementing that occupation in place. Indeed the represented power of Campbell and what he embodied might seem overwhelming, almost a caricature of settler-colonial attempts to dominate. Yet what the mountain meant for Maori and the nature of Campbell's relationships with Maori particularly as inflected in the later, posthumous summit development, and responses to it, complicate and problematise any singular typification of the monument as an emblem of colonial conquest and confident settler-colonial self-assertion.[28]

Auckland city, on an isthmus between the Pacific and the Tasman Sea, has numerous volcanic cones, the most imposing and most visible from all directions of which is One Tree Hill/Maungakiekie. From its summit there are stunning vistas over the surrounding land, harbours and oceans. It holds a commanding position in the region. Thus, it had been a long valued and contested site among Maori: a vitally strategic site, a locus of power. Settled by Maori in the early sixteenth century, and called Te-totara-a-ahua (*totara*: which stands alone) before it was renamed Maungakiekie, it became one of the largest fortified pa, with extensive plantations and terracing – a sculpted mountain, a cultural product as much as a natural land formation. It was abandoned as a habitation by Maori as a result of epidemics and inter-tribal warfare in the pre-colonial period,[29] and was sold in a large parcel of land by the Ngati Whatua chief, Kawau, to an Irish immigrant, Thomas Henry, in 1845. Its post-European settlement denomination One Tree Hill was inspired by the presence of a single giant tree on the summit, firstly, according to Ngati Whatua legend, a totara, planted c.1600 to mark the burial place of the whenua, the afterbirth and umbilical cord of Chief Koroki – a signifier of the oneness of land and people – and later a *pohutukawa* tree. This pohutukawa was cut down prior to Campbell's acquisition by 'some Goth . . . for firewood's sake'[30] in 1852, and in the early 1870s was replaced by (at least) two pine trees (figure 5.2). In 1962 only one remained, and that was finally felled at the beginning of 2001 (figure 5.3), by which time many Aucklanders, it appeared, had come to believe that 'One Tree Hill' denoted that single pine tree – a misfounded belief that had become central to community memory or imagining.

Campbell was always acutely aware of the significance the mountain, its summit and the legendary totara tree had for various Maori *iwi* (tribes). As a first European settler in Auckland he acknowledged his need of Maori help in getting established, for which he was always grateful. Campbell had a deeply felt respect for Maori people and culture, and deplored the ignorance and insensitivity with which they

5.2 One Tree Hill/Maungakiekie with the obelisk and trees on the summit

5.3 The summit with the obelisk alone, after the removal of the tree

were treated by many later nineteenth-century European settlers in the city.[31] Yet, as a landowner and speculator he did not appear to really understand how crucial to Maori was their continued possession of land.[32] More specifically, he had opposed the replacement of the pine tree with another totara,[33] which would have functioned as a symbolic restitution after the summit had been incorporated into Cornwall Park. Nevertheless, the 1906 obelisk proposal and the 1912 bequest for its construction could be regarded as an acknowledgement of the debt he owed to Maori, a recognition of their position as *tangata whenua* (people of the land), and all that implied in colonial relations, and an idealistic attempt both to mediate the difference in significance that the mountain had for Maori and Pakeha and to establish that settler-colonial and indigenous peoples could have mutual interests, despite the differences between them.

Given the actualities of settler-colonial dominance in Auckland, such an orientation might have come across as merely tokenistic, masking the very real thrusts of colonial vision and land consumption. Certainly, during Campbell's life and through to the mid-1930s, the actual shaping and control of the public meaning of Cornwall Park and the summit remained firmly in Pakeha hands. Yet, the very facts of the proposal and provision of an obelisk to honour Maori on a most revered site allowed several possibilities – for example, that monocultural domination could be brought into question; that the prior and rightful place of Maori could be reasserted. Indeed, these possibilities were to be forcibly articulated in direct relation to the obelisk project and the summit complex, to which a tree was integral. So while Pegram's huge statue of Campbell and its accompanying rock base is now not really *seen*, the obelisk and summit complex have a compelling ongoing presence.

Campbell was both grandiosely self-serving and genuinely altruistic. He mused that 'things do take such funny turns in our varied lives',[34] and the same could be said of the obelisk project and the summit complex – an exercise in both individual and – given settler-colonial identification with Campbell's public persona – collective self-aggrandizement. Many great cities have obelisks – London, Rome, Paris, New York, Washington, DC, for example.[35] Auckland's obelisk could have marked the *arrival* of the city and the colony, acknowledging Auckland as part of *civilisation* – a modern city, for the obelisks of those American and European cities functioned as imperial monuments and as elements integral to their modernisation.[36] Yet those obelisks also pointed to the past, positing a continuity between that past and the present society.[37] In Auckland's case, the reference to a past took on a different and local inflection specific to relations between coloniser

[109]

and colonised. For the concomitant homage to Maori that the obelisk was intended to monumentalise suggests recognition that the very nature of settler occupation of what had been Maori land was contestable, *unsettled*. Whatever its other functions, the very physical presence of the obelisk dedicated to Maori has functioned as a pointed reminder, restoring to visibility and awareness[38] that Maori had historical precedence in the land. Insofar as obelisks connote immortality, this one could signal that Maori presence was ongoing, not erased.[39] The proposed obelisk, then, embodied contradictory forces. Certainly, the subsequent career of the obelisk and its surrounds has brought sharply into question whether, or how, those forces could occupy the same space simultaneously. The summit complex can be seen to have generated tensions between itself and the space it inhabits, to have unintentionally created a location in which the hurts of Maori–Pakeha interactions, past and present, have been focused and acted out.[40]

In 1902 a report on Cornwall Park's desirable design was commissioned from the young American landscape architect Austin Strong, the step-grandson of Robert Louis Stevenson.[41] In a utopian manner, Strong wrote of Cornwall Park as a 'perfect place', its 'wonderful and commanding situation' unequalled 'in the whole world'. He stressed that the main feature of Cornwall Park was the mountain: 'All my design has been worked with the view of throwing the hill itself into bold relief', with 'no trees . . . where Maori fortifications are to be seen'.[42] Overall, the plan Strong drew up, in consultation with Campbell, envisaged not just the co-existence of Maori and European, indigenous and imported landscape, architectural and botanical elements, but their fusion: a merging of the European 'picturesque' and the 'native'. Fundamental to the hoped-for result – something unique, place-distinctive – was not the effacement of things Maori but their co-presence and centrality in this identity. While that could be seen as an aspect of a more comprehensive cooption of things Maori by Pakeha seeking a socio-cultural distinctiveness, nevertheless the landscape garden to be created represented a desire for union – with Maori and with the land to which European settlers had come: the park, as the location in which differences could be resolved and harmony achieved.[43]

Very little was actually done towards the development of the land as a park until the mid-1920s; likewise steps to activate the proposed obelisk were not taken until the mid-1930s. While the main reason for this may have been financial – the likely costs exceeding Campbell's bequest – there was some resistance to the very idea of an obelisk on the summit.[44] It has been claimed that 'Major monuments owe their siting to a desire to take over beautiful or striking stretches of landscape for political purposes and to impose a political message on a whole region.'[45] Undoubtedly Campbell and Auckland's citizens had their political agendas, yet it is clear from the documents relating to the planning, construction and unveiling of Campbell's obelisk that there were crucial Maori involvements in the realisation of the project once it got underway. While Campbell and Pakeha had taken over this historic Maori site for their varied purposes, it was not simply a one-sided appropriation. The obelisk was not imposed on Maori. Nor were those Maori involved in the project merely token or silent partners. They were people of stature and authority. At the same time, there was little consensus among Maori about Campbell's gift and its meaning; indeed, the monument has had radically differing messages for different groups of people.

In 1938 the trustees of Campbell's estate advised the attorney-general, H. G. R. Mason, that 'the plans of the monument have been discussed with the Maori race, and . . . [have] the whole-hearted approval of Maori leaders throughout a very extensive area'.[46] In January 1937 Geo. Graham, of the Akarana Maori Association, who liased between concerned Maori and the trustees of Campbell's estate, reported, with a corroborating list of 153 signatures attached, that 'the leading chiefs and chieftainesses of the Maori people throughout the Auckland Provincial District' supported 'the appropriateness of the obelisk', given 'the significance of the historic site selected'.[47] Graham stressed that R. Atkinson Abbott and Richard Gross, the architect and the sculptor responsible for the design of the obelisk and the accompanying statue, should consult with Maori over the 'detail of the design',[48] particularly in relation to the Maori motifs used and the style, pose and gesture of the bronze Maori warrior. That this figure stands 'in a bold attitude grasping a mere'[49] rather than reaching skywards, weaponless, resulted from such consultation. Pose, gesture and look were intended to represent Maori guardianship over place and people, in contrast to the architect's conception, the figure of a grateful Maori, unarmed, his 'old-time weapons' discarded, reaching up to grasp 'the opportunities for a new and fuller life made possible by the advent of European civilisation'.[50] From the Maori perspective the statue was to represent autonomy not subordination; and the strength of Maori voice extended to the sculptor, Gross, chosen in preference to H. W. Feldon, nominated for the job by the trustees.[51]

Sir Apirana Ngata (1874–1950), Ngati Porou, a leader of Maori cultural revival,[52] one of the most powerful and respected men in Maoridom, spoke for those Maori opposed to the obelisk project, in particular the proposal to make the monument's unveiling the focus of the centennial celebrations of the settlement of Auckland and New Zealand. Auckland city itself was a negative entity for Ngata because of its close involvement with the 'confiscation of Maori land [and] the pressures of European settlement at the expense of Maori communities'.[53] For Ngata no obelisk could symbolically compensate for that confiscation; nor could it restore to collective consciousness Maori rights and historical precedence in ways beneficial to contemporary Maori.

Still, the support for the obelisk project of Ngati Whatua and Tainui leaders, in particular people of such renown and mana as Princess Te Puea Herangi (1883–1952) and King Koroki (1908/9–66),[54] was decisive, though what the obelisk meant to them would have differed from what it meant to most Pakeha Aucklanders. The obelisk, though completed in time, was not the focus of the centennial celebrations; indeed, it was not unveiled until 1948, in accord with Maori insistence that the ceremony be delayed until the Second World War, in which many Maori served, was over.[55] At the ceremony itself, on 24 April 1948, primarily Maori leaders officiated – in the speeches, prayers of dedication and accompanying chants, and the actual unveiling (by King Koroki). Both Pakeha and Maori speakers characterised the summit monument as a symbol of, and a force for, unity between Pakeha and Maori. Lou Parore, Ngati Whatua, spoke of Campbell's 'foresight, goodwill and affection for Maori', and described Gross's statue as 'looking towards the sun to bring light, warmth and love into our hearts' (figure 5.4).[56] M. H. Wynyard, chairman of the One Tree Hill Trust, offered to Maori the planting of another totara on the summit to compensate for the loss of the historic and sacred tree.[57] At that time it was hoped that the monument would provide a space, both literal and symbolic, which Maori and Pakeha could share, and in which their different histories and experiences would come together in harmonious resolution.

By 1948, however, there were suggestions that for most Pakeha in Auckland the monument did not carry such a portentous load. Although the unveiling was reported in the two Auckland daily newspapers the attention it received was cursory. In the *New Zealand Herald*, with the largest circulation in the country, 'Obelisk Unveiled: Tribute to the Maori People', occupied fifty-three easy-to-miss short lines on page 8, a page otherwise given over to a random assortment of small items.[58] Could the report's location and its apparent low interest in this event, so important to Maori, have been an index of a general Pakeha lack of recognition both of the unveiling and of the displacement of Maori during the colonial period? Moreover, the proffered totara was not planted.

The *Auckland Star* described the unveiling ceremony as the 'culminating act in an historical drama which began in the early days

5.4 Richard Gross's sculpture of the Maori warrior on the base of the obelisk

of the colony'.[59] For all the rhetoric and goodwill professed in 1948, however, the monument complex remains unsettled, its changing cultural roles correlating with the shifting nature of the relationships between the various players in the 'historical drama'. This came into sharp focus in October 1994, when the radical Maori activist Mike Smith took a chainsaw to the summit's lone pine tree, calling it 'a shrine of our oppression'.[60] The tree had become an integral component of the summit as monument, as cultural and aesthetic artifact. Smith's attempted destruction of it gained him a prosecution for vandalism and provoked angry responses from many Aucklanders, for whom the tree had assumed an iconic status, standing for civic pride and a worthy local history, something to be celebrated, not an object of shame. Dario Gamboni has observed that, 'far from being only an expression or symptom of reception, the often elaborately staged destructions of works of art must be considered as means of communication in their own right'.[61] The prime aim of Smith's iconoclastic action was communicative – to concentrate public attention on the New Zealand National Government's proposal to make final settlements, within ten years, of all outstanding claims by Maori iwi, in redress for colonial injustices under the Treaty of Waitingi, to a maximum of $1 billion – a 'fiscal envelope' viewed by many Maori as inequitable and precipitate. Given the omnivisibility and sheer physical presence of One Tree Hill and its obelisk, which constitute a scenographically spectacular site and sight, the stage Smith chose for his performance guaranteed him and the 'historical drama' a place in the public eye.[62] For Smith the obelisk was 'a very potent symbol of the colonization of this country and how our [Maori] values have been replaced'.[63] Ranginui Walker, then professor of Maori studies at the University of Auckland, characterised the obelisk, and the accompanying grave and pine tree, a 'symbol of European domination'.[64]

It is not difficult to appreciate how the summit complex could be seen to bury historical actualities under local and national myth-making,[65] nor why the obelisk, in its commanding position, could be equated with panoptic colonial power. However rather than marking a fully achieved power, this huge object, excessive, 'out of place' in its environment, could be a signifier of the unrealisable: the place and what it represented for other Maori could not be fitted comfortably into some colonial master-plan. The obelisk is conspicuously inscribed as 'a permanent record of the achievement and character of the great Maori people', and the gaze of the attendant bronze Maori warrior, sanctioned by Maori leaders of the 1930s and 1940s, had been envisioned as conveying a protective guardianship over place and peoples. This figure could be seen both to challenge any assertion of mono-cultural power and to thwart any quest for panoptic mastery. That the obelisk and summit complex attract conflicting readings does not vitiate any one of them: rather they co-exist uneasily.

There is still no consensus among Maori about the summit complex. Some Maori leaders continue to regard it as a 'symbol of . . . unity between Maori and Pakeha'.[66] In 1994 the spokesperson for Ngati Whatua, the summit's guardians, viewed Smith, who was from another iwi, as a trespasser with no right to do what he did: 'Our ancestors allowed the Pakeha to go there and put up a monument. I'd never go against what they did.'[67] Sir Hugh Kawharu, a Ngati Whatua *kaumatua* (elder and leader), later noted that for his tribe all of Maungakiekie was *tapu* and that in attacking the tree the protesters (Smith and others after him) had attacked the mountain: 'If anyone wants to make a political statement involving the mana of Ngati Whatua there is a clear protocol. Take it to Orakei, the marae . . . to take unilateral action . . . without discussing it with Ngati Whatua is an insult.'[68]

Smith observed: 'I'm perceived as either public enemy No. 1 or a national hero, depending on who you talk to.'[69] Ironically, that could apply to Campbell also. Ranginui Walker noted that the 'aura of permanence' of the tree, grave and obelisk 'belies the swirl of history round them'.[70] Campbell, acutely conscious of the 'swirl of history', attempted to give aesthetic form to history's complexities and confusions through narratives and material artefacts; yet his awareness that 'things do take such funny turns' might well have extended to these aestheticisings, that they could become part of that fluid 'swirl', resisting resolution, rather than monologically concluding the drama. Walker submitted that the beginning of an equitable and genuinely postcolonial relationship between 'tangata whenua and city fathers' could be achieved by replacing the pine tree with another totara.[71] From 1994 to early 2001 the pine tree, necessarily supported by steel trusses and a protective iron grill, became as much a material artefact as a natural organism – a public sculpture and an inadvertent metaphor for the still unsettled state of Maori–Pakeha relations over the legacy of colonial occupation.

This came into fraught relief in September 1999 when the beleaguered tree was again attacked by Maori activists, for whom it represented the negative legacies of colonialism; continuing social and economic inequities for many Maori, as well as an alleged ongoing Pakeha failure to comprehensively realise the provisions of the Treaty of Waitangi *vis-à-vis* Maori sovereignty over land and resources. There have been further twists and turns to the 'drama', focusing specifically on the tree and its fate. The attacks in 1999 and June 2000, resulting in prosecutions for wilful damage, hastened the terminal decline and the eventual necessary Auckland City Council removal of the tree in January 2001. This generated a further diversity of responses among both Maori and Pakeha, both the changing perceptions of the monument and the complexities of identifications among New Zealand's peoples clearly demonstrating that any putative singular national or local identity would be mythical, not real.

Ngati Whatua condemned the attacks, while in the same period lodging a claim before the Office of Treaty Settlements alleging that the 1845 sale of Maungakiekie was invalid, since land regulations then excluded the sale of sacred sites.[72] In contrast, Richard Prebble, MP, leader of the economically right-wing Act Party, launched his party's Treaty policy for the 1999 election at the foot of the dangerously unstable pine tree.[73] This was regarded as an appropriate 'launching pad' for Act's pledge to 'close off all new Treaty of Waitangi claims by the end of [2000], and abolish the Waitangi Tribunal five years after that'.[74] For Act the assault on part of the monument complex represented a threat to civic order, social equilibrium and the economic health of the country. With the tree's final demise the news media and a significant number of local citizens responded as if the city's virtue and history, even the legitimacy of the State, had been threatened by the attack on the tree, as if the loss of the tree was a tragedy to be collectively mourned – striking evidence of how a monument can become the locus for assertions of a local or national identity, however much that identity might require historical amnesia and the disregard of the different histories, perceptions and senses of identity of others in the same society.

The parklands surrounding Maungakiekie/One Tree Hill continue to be used and enjoyed by large numbers of people in what is now a multi-ethnic and cosmopolitan city. With the support of Ngati Whatua, a grove of indigenous replacement trees, including totara and pohotukawa, has been planned for the summit.

It has been dramatically highlighted how intensely the summit complex has constituted a site where various identifications and allegiances have been made or implied. It may have represented an attempt by Campbell and his Pakeha constituency to demonstrate their roots in New Zealand soil; to show that they, too, like Maori, belonged to the place. That there is an *overdone* quality to the summit complex may suggest that for some Pakeha it had a compensatory dimension, even if unconsciously so; that it embodied uncertainties about whether in fact they, like Maori, did belong. The aim of this exploration of the events surrounding the summit of One Tree Hill/Maungakiekie has been to suggest how complicated and riven with contradiction could be colonial settler (and their descendants') self-stagings and identifications, even when their protagonists may immediately have appeared to be in control. And Maori views of, and involvements in, the monument or its component parts have been similarly complex and multiple. To see the obelisk and summit complex as just a sign of colonial conquest or as a cynical appropriation of a Maori sacred site would be simplistic. What was initially an attempt to stabilise the past and the present in terms of Maori–Pakeha relationships has been a drama of misconnections. While a monument remains, it can now be seen as a monument to ongoing and unresolved socio-political processes. It is apt that the Latin *monere*, from which the word 'monument' derives, means to warn as well as to remind. This monument, very much 'alive', re-invigorated by present socio-political urgencies, continues to play a significant role in generating argument about those urgencies. Rather than a site of shared values and meanings, it has become unstable terrain of conflicting meanings and viewpoints.

Notes

1 For Campbells's biography, see R. C. J. Stone, *The Young Logan Campbell* (Auckland: Auckland University Press, 1982), and *The Father and His Gift: John Logan Campbell's Later Years* (Auckland: Auckland University Press, 1987).

2 For the history of One Tree Hill/Maungakiekie and its surrounds, and Campbell's ownership and gift, see: ibid.; M. H. Wynyard, *The Story of Maungakiekie: The Ancient Maori Fortress and Now One Tree Hill, a Favourite Lung of Auckland* (Auckland: Wilson & Horton, 1958); various publications of the Cornwall Park Trust Board Incorporated, such as *Cornwall Park: A Handbook* (Auckland: Cornwall Park Trustees, 1985), and *Cornwall Park: The Story of One Man's Vision* (Auckland: Cornwall Park Trustees, 1994).

3 Campbell, quoted in the *New Zealand Herald*, 25 June 1906.

4 Balibar has argued that 'in reality there are no identities, only identifications, either with institutions or other subjects': E. Balibar, 'Culture and Identity (Working Notes)', in John Rajchman (ed.), *The Identity in Question* (London and New York: Routledge, 1995), p. 187.

5 See, e.g., R. Jebb, *Studies in Colonial Nationalism* (1905), cited in J. Eddy and D. Schreuder (eds), *The Rise of Colonial Nationalism* (Sydney: Allen & Unwin, 1988); A. Siegfried, *Democracy in New Zealand* (London: Bell, 1914); K. Sinclair, *A Destiny Apart: New Zealand's Search for National Identity* (Wellington: Allen & Unwin, 1986), David Hamer, Introduction to the 1982 edition of A. Siegfried, *Democracy in New Zealand* (Wellington: Victoria University Press–Price Milburn).

6 See, for example, Siegfried, Sinclair and David Hamer, *The New Zealand Liberals: The Years of Power 1891–1912* (Auckland: Auckland University Press, 1988), P. Gibbons and L. Richardson, 'Parties and Political Change', and E. Olssen, 'Towards a New Society', in W. H. Oliver (ed.), *The Oxford History of New Zealand* (Wellington: Oxford University Press, 1981), pp. 197–225, and pp. 250–78 respectively.

7 See, e.g., J. O. C. Phillips, 'Musings in Maoriland – or Was There a *Bulletin* in New Zealand?', *Historical Studies*, 20:81 (1983), 520–35; L. Bell, *Colonial Constructs: European Images of Maori 1840–1914* (Auckland: Auckland University Press, 1992); R. Wolfe, *Well-Made New Zealand: A Century of Trademarks* (Auckland: Reed Methuen, 1987); J. Belich, 'Myth, Place, and Identity', *New Zealand Journal of History*, 31:1 (1997), 9–29.

8 More recently, Belich has argued a more subtle picture of late colonial New Zealand as a society characterised by a dualism: the emergence of a sense of a distinctive national identity and difference of the 'new' from the 'old' (or, rather, an assertion of this), coupled with what were in fact closer economic and cultural ties with Britain than in the mid-colonial period – what he calls 're-colonisation': J. Belich, *Making Peoples: A History of New Zealanders from Polynesian Settlement to the End of the Nineteenth Century* (Auckland: Penguin Books, 1996), and 'Re-Colonization in New Zealand, 1880s to 1960s', Inaugural Professorial Lecture, University of Auckland, 1997. Belich has pursued his notion of re-colonisation more vigorously in his recent *Paradise Re-Forged: A History of the New Zealanders from the 1880s to 2000* (Auckland: Penguin Books, 2001).

9 What Wolff (1992) observed of 'mainstream sociology' could equally apply to mainstream historical studies in New Zealand: 'The problem is that mainstream sociology, confidently indifferent, if not hostile, to developments in theory, is unable to acknowledge the constitutive role of culture and representation *in* social relations': J. Wolff, 'Interdisciplinarity in the Study of Art', in L. Grossberg, C. Nelson, P. A. Treichler (eds), *Cultural Studies* (New York: Routledge, 1992), p. 710.

10 D. Gamboni, *The Destruction of Art: Iconoclasm and Vandalism since the French Revolution* (New Haven, CT, and London: Yale University Press, 1997), p. 11.

11 For the Treaty of Waitangi and the precolonial and early colonial history of the Auckland region, see respectively: C. Orange, *The Treaty of Waitangi* (Wellington: Allen & Unwin, 1987), and R. C. J. Stone, *From Tamaki-Makau-Rau to Auckland* (Auckland: Auckland University Press, 2001).

12 K. Forster, 'Monument/Memory and the Mortality of Architecture', *Oppositions: A Journal for Ideas and Criticism in Architecture*, 25 (fall, 1982), 7.
13 Alois Riegl, 'The Modern Cult of Monuments: Its Character and Origins' (trans. Kurt Forster and Diane Ghirardo), *Oppositions*, 25 (fall, 1982), 21–51; Riegl's essay was originally published in his *Gesammelte Aufsatze* (Augsburg-Vienna: Dr Benno Filser, 1928).
14 Stone, *The Young Logan Campbell*; and *The Father and His Gift*.
15 John Logan Campbell, *Poenamo. Sketches of the Early Days of New Zealand: Romance and Reality of Antipodean Life in the Infancy of a New Colony* (London and Edinburgh: Williams & Norgate, 1881), pp. 98–9.
16 R. C. J. Stone, 'A Victorian Friendship and Auckland's First School of Art', *Art New Zealand*, 30 (1984), 52–5.
17 'Rata', *Cornwall Park (Maungakiekie). A Princely Gift to the People of New Zealand by Sir John Logan Campbell: A Retrospect and Glimpse into the Future* (Auckland: Brett Publishing Co., 1904–5), p. 25.
18 See L. Bell, 'John Logan Campbell (1817–1912): A Career in Images', *Art New Zealand*, 67 (1993), 88–92, 106.
19 *New Zealand Herald* (11 June 1901).
20 *Weekly Graphic*, 26 June 1912.
21 J. Fitzgerald, 'Images of Self: Early New Zealand Autobiography by John Logan Campbell and Frederick Edward Maning', *Journal of Commonwealth Literature*, 23:1 (1988), 16–47.
22 Stone, *The Father and His Gift*, p. 249.
23 S. Michalski, *Public Monuments: Art in Political Bondage 1870–1997* (London: Reaktion Books, 1998), p. 43.
24 M. Warnke, *Political Landscape: The Art History of Nature* (London: Reaktion Books, 1994), p. 145.
25 *New Zealand Graphic*, 14 June 1902.
26 Auckland Institute and Museum, Campbell, 'My Autobiography: A Short Sketch of a Long Life, 1817–1907', unpublished manuscript, p. 76.
27 Stone, *The Father and His Gift*, p. 245, quoting Campbell's 'My Autobiography', p. 422; *New Zealand Graphic*, 16 May 1903; and Campbell to the editor, *Auckland Weekly News*, 10 September 1903.
28 Jacobs explores 'how imaginative spatialities of desire and cultural politics of territory are fundamental parts of colonial and post colonial formations' in all their variabilities and complexities: J. Jacobs, *Edge of Empire: Post Colonialism and the City* (London and New York: Routledge, 1996), p. x.
29 For a Maori view of the historical meaning and importance of Maungakiekie, see R. Walker, 'Trees Company', *Metro* (January 1995), 139–40.
30 *Daily Southern Cross*, 14 August 1875.
31 Stone, *The Young Logan Campbell*, pp. 56–73, in particular.
32 Ibid., p. 73.
33 Campbell refused to plant a totara 'lest it should prejudice the siting of the obelisk he had planned': *Cornwall Park: A Handbook*, p. 6.
34 Campbell, 'My Autobiography', p. 89.
35 Regarding obelisks, specifically the Washington Monument, Washington, DC, and 'great cities', see C. L. Griswold, 'The Vietnam Veterans' Memorial and the Washington Mall: Philosophical Thoughts on Political Iconography', in W. J. T. Mitchell (ed.), *Art and the Public Sphere* (Chicago, IL, and London: University of Chicago Press, 1992), pp. 84–9.
36 As noted by A. Hassam, 'Antiquity, History and Modernity: Australian Perceptions of Imperial London', paper presented at 'The Colonial Eye' conference, University of Tasmania, Hobart, 3–6 February 1999.
37 Ibid.
38 'The purpose of all these monuments, these mnemonic schemes, these words – even the word monument itself – is to return an idea to consciousness, to re-mind,

and hence to restore, a thought to life': W. Gass, 'Monumentality/Mentality', *Oppositions*, 25 (fall, 1982), 129.

39 In 1906 Campbell had proposed the obelisk 'in memoriam' to the 'great Maori race'. While Campbell believed that the best future for Maori lay in assimilation, there was some concern in the later 1930s lest the words 'in memoriam' should imply that the 'Maori race' was finished, whereas it was held that the obelisk should represent both their 'past greatness' and 'faith in the future': see Memorandum from the Attorney-General, H. G. R. Mason, to A. G. Osborne, MP, Folder 313, Correspondence 1938, John Logan Campbell Papers, MS 51, Auckland Institute and Museum. The words, 'in memoriam' were not inscribed on the obelisk.

40 Regarding the contention that 'only when art confronts the public space as such can it become effective within it', Young wrote: 'This might be construed in two ways: art confronting a space with its own invisible past, or an artwork that creates a tension between itself and the space it inhabits. The successful monument might be regarded as the one that does both': J. Young, *The Texture of Memory: Holocaust Memorials and Meanings* (New Haven, CT, and London: Yale University Press, 1993), p. 104. In Young's scheme, which does not account for unintended consequences, these qualities would be intentional.

41 Austin Strong was the son of the American artists Joseph and Isobel Strong (née Osbourne), the daughter of Robert Louis Stevenson's wife Fanny; he spent his childhood in Samoa and New Zealand, where he was sent to school.

42 Report of Austin Strong, Landscape Architect, New York, to the Trustees of Cornwall Park (with a covering letter to John Logan Campbell), 2 February 1902, pp. 23, 17, Folder 271, John Logan Campbell Papers.

43 See, e.g., R. Harbison, *The Built, the Unbuilt and the Unbuildable: In Pursuit of Architectural Meaning* (London: Thames & Hudson, 1991), p. 27.

44 Note, for instance, P. W. Burbidge to the editor, *New Zealand Herald*, 14 September 1938, in which he claimed that there was a 'lack of interest of the Maori race on the whole towards the proposed obelisk' and that an obelisk would spoil the summit.

45 Warnke, *Political Landscape*, p. 18.

46 Folder 313, Correspondence 1938, John Logan Campbell Papers.

47 G. Graham to A. E. Bollard, Chairman, Trustees of the John Logan Campbell Estate, 19 January 1937, Folder 312, John Logan Campbell Papers.

48 Ibid.

49 As reported by R. Atkinson Abbott to the Trustees of the John Logan Campbell Estate, 8 July 1937, Folder 312, John Logan Campbell Papers.

50 R. Atkinson Abbott to the Trustees of the John Logan Campbell Estate, 12 August 1933, Folder 311, John Logan Campbell Papers.

51 A. E. Bollard, Chairman, Trustees of the John Logan Campbell Estate, to H. W. Feldon, 16 September 1938, Folder 313, John Logan Campbell Papers.

52 For Ngata see: *The Dictionary of New Zealand Biography*, vol. 3 *1901–1920* (Auckland and Wellington: Auckland University Press–Department of Internal Affairs, 1996), pp. 359–62; and Ranginui Walker, *He Tipua: The Life and Times of Sir Apirana Ngata* (Auckland: Viking, 2001).

53 Sir Apirana Ngata to Sir Ernest Davis, Mayor of Auckland, 20 September 1938, Folder 313, John Logan Campbell Papers.

54 For Te Puea, see M. King, *Te Puea* (Auckland: Sceptre, 1987); and for King Koroki, see *The Dictionary of New Zealand Biography*, vol. 4: *1921–1940* (1998), pp. 275–7.

55 G. Graham, Akarana Maori Association, to the Trustees of the John Logan Campbell Estate, 26 October 1940, Folder 315, John Logan Campbell Papers; and A. E. Bollard to the Governor-General, 30 October 1939, Folder 314, ibid.

56 *Auckland Star*, 24 April 1948.

57 Ibid.

58 *New Zealand Herald*, 26 April 1948.

59 *Auckland Star*, 24 April 1948.
60 Quoted by F. MacDonald, 'Cutting Rights', *New Zealand Listener*, 14–20 January 1995, p. 34.
61 Gamboni, *The Destruction of Art*, p. 22.
62 Gamboni, Ibid., p. 67, has argued that 'monuments have been privileged targets for attack because [they] may be deformed and thus transformed into monuments of their own degradation'. There have been other attacks on colonial monuments in New Zealand in recent years: for instance, the statues of both Sir George Grey, colonial governor and sometime prime minister, in Albert Park, Auckland, and Sir John Balance, Liberal prime minister in the 1890s, in Wanganui, lost their heads (even if, in the case of Grey, only temporarily).
63 Quoted by MacDonald, 'Cutting Rights', p. 34.
64 Walker, 'Trees Company', p. 140.
65 In this respect, regarding post-Second World War monuments in Germany that refer to the Nazi era, see M. Broszat (and S. Friedlander), 'A Controversy about the Historicisation of National Socialism', in P. Baldwin (ed.), *Reworking the Past: Hitler and the Holocaust and the Historians' Controversy* (Boston, MA: Beacon Press, 1990).
66 Graham Latimer, Chairman, Maori Council, quoted by MacDonald, 'Cutting Rights', p. 35.
67 Ruby Grey, Orakei Maori Trust Board, quoted by MacDonald, 'Cutting Rights', p. 36; he further quoted Grey saying: 'We are only kaitiake [guardians]'.
68 Quoted by P. English, 'Grove Option to Replace Lone Pine on Summit', *New Zealand Herald*, 25 September 1999.
69 Smith, quoted by MacDonald, 'Cutting Rights', p. 36.
70 Walker, 'Trees Company', p. 140.
71 Ibid.
72 Kawharu, quoted by B. Orsman, 'Ax Taken to One Tree Hill Myth: Three Historical References Cast Doubt on the Totara-Axing Legend', *New Zealand Herald*, 18–19 November 2000.
73 *New Zealand Herald*, 1 November 1999.
74 R. Laugesen (political editor), 'Act Will End Treaty Claims', *Sunday Star–Times*, 30 October 1999.

CHAPTER SIX

Show times: de-celebrating the Canadian nation, de-colonising the Canadian museum, 1967–92

Ruth B. Phillips

Show times, as I intend the term, are moments when museums organise comprehensive and *definitive* exhibitions in connection with a major event in the life of the community.[1] Such exhibitions are a sub-category of the super-show genre, and they have become a standard element in the commemoration and celebration of important national anniversaries, world's fairs, the staging of international athletics' competitions or the 'year' of some group or country – the wave of millennium shows having been the most recent example.[2] Museums welcome major anniversaries and events as opportunities for mounting projects that would normally be beyond their scope. A simple formula usually applies: the bigger the event, the greater the budget and the more ambitious the exhibition. Shows staged at such times are thus by definition larger than life, conceived from the start on a scale far beyond normal levels of institutional and governmental funding. They are also predicated on the availability of corporate sponsorship and/or special allocations of public money. At show times, then, a museum's ties to the business and political establishments are unusually close and transparent. The glare of publicity picks out the sponsors' logos on posters, advertising and exhibition signage, laying open to public scrutiny relationships of dependence that normally are at least partly masked.

Given this phenomenon of heightened visibility, it is not surprising that in post-1960s' Canada, as in other settler nations engaged in processes of decolonisation, show times that foreground the heritages of internally colonised indigenous peoples have become also protest times.[3] In this chapter I look at four exhibitions of indigenous art, between 1967 and 1992, organised by or in close collaboration with Canada's national museums. The series begins with The Indians of Canada Pavilion organised for Montreal's *Expo '67* in Canada's centennial year. The second show, *The Spirit Sings*, was organised for the Calgary Winter Olympics in 1988. The final two, *Indigena* and *Land, Spirit, Power*, were mounted in 1992, the 500th anniversary of Columbus's first voyage to the Americas. Each of the shows marked an event that drew national and international attention; and each became a site of indigenous intervention into standard narratives of Canadian history, while being exploited by indigenous artists and activists to focus public attention on contemporary issues such as land claims, sovereignty and social problems. With growing historical distance, the twenty-five year period from 1967 to 1992 is emerging as critical for the postcolonial reform of Canadian museology. I argue that, taken together, the four shows comprise a mini-history of change that is historically significant and irreversible, though also uneven and incomplete. It illustrates not an uninterrupted vector of progress towards decolonisation but rather an uneven line whose dips and rises mirror swings from liberalism to reaction in Canadian politics. The analysis of this period, then, provides an opportunity to explore more general patterns of relationship between the staging of exhibitions, the broader formulation of national policies and the politics of pluralism.

One final prefatory note: the politics and the people involved in the four exhibitions were closely interrelated. Canada's communities of museum professionals and Aboriginal activists are relatively small, and many individuals were involved as advisors, curators or critics in more than one of the exhibitions. The controversy surrounding *The Spirit Sings*, for example, was the immediate stimulus for the creation, in 1989, of a national Task Force on Museums and First Nations (TFMFN) by the Assembly of First Nations and the Canadian Museums' Association that was co-chaired by one of the artists who worked on the *Expo '67* project. One member of the TFMFN was curating the 1992 *Indigena* exhibition even as the TFMFN was meeting. As a curator of *The Spirit Sings* and a member of the TFMFN I speak as both insider and outsider, and also as one whose practices as a scholar and museum professional have been profoundly influenced by the history I recount.

The un-birthday: The Indians of Canada Pavilion at Expo '67

Expo '67 was the most dazzling of the many commemorative projects organised to celebrate Canada's centenary, and The Indians of Canada Pavilion emerged as a surprise highlight of the event. It was the first major exhibition in Canadian history in which indigenous people attained full control over the representation of their histories and cultures.[4] Perhaps typically for the decade, the pavilion's popularity arose not because it participated in the general mood of celebration but because it mounted a radical critique of the standard progressivist representations of Aboriginal history. The details of how the pavilion came about are intimately connected to broader political and historical currents. In 1962, when planning for *Expo '67* began, status Indians in Canada – those legally recognised under the Indian Act – had been able to vote in federal elections for only two years. Enfranchisement was the culmination of a new era of opposition to official assimilationist policies that had begun in the years following the Second World War, strengthened by models provided by the US civil rights movement and global movements of national liberation. The decision to establish a separate Indian pavilion at *Expo '67* was one product of this activist climate, and its specific realisation was the result of a campaign for self-empowerment waged by Aboriginal people working within the federal bureaucracy in Ottawa.

The initial plans for the 1967 *World's Fair* folded the histories of Aboriginal peoples, like those of other 'ethnic groups' within Canada, into the master narrative of a single Canada Pavilion.[5] The installations would have located the *contributions* of Aboriginal peoples in the pre-confederation period, thus effectively excluding them from the main story – the century since confederation – that was the focus of the celebration. As one bureaucrat envisioned it, 'some Indian artifacts [would] be dimly spotlighted amidst a dreamworld forest'.[6] The pavilion would thus have reinscribed the standard settler narrative of Canadian history in which indigenous peoples are subsumed as *contributors* to a linear and progressivist historical trajectory of the nation. In 1965, however, First Nations' people brought in by the Department of Indian and Northern Affairs (DIAND) to serve on advisory committees for *Expo '67* forced the Government's agreement to the creation of a separate Indians of Canada Pavilion and gained control over its design and storyline.[7] This design, created by a government architect, was based on the traditional conical birch-bark wigwam or hide teepee and was juxtaposed with a new totem pole commissioned of Kwakwaka'wakw carvers Tony and Henry Hunt – a design that 'gigantized', in Susan Stewart's terminology,[8] two of the most widely disseminated popular-culture icons of *Indianness*. Although the artefacts displayed within the pavilion were chosen, with the help and advice of museum staff, from the collections of the National Museum of Canada, they were inserted into a narrative radically different from that originally envisioned by pavilion planners or museum ethnologists. I give here only a brief summary of the research on its development and installations that Sherry Brydon and I have discussed elsewhere in greater detail.[9]

One of the most dramatic features of the pavilion was its programme of specially commissioned contemporary art.[10] A number of First Nations' artists from across Canada, at that time unacquainted, who had begun to gain regional recognition during the preceding few years were brought together to create an ambitious programme of murals, paintings and sculptures for the pavilion's exterior. One of these young artists was Tom Hill. Now a museum director and a prominent figure in the Canadian art world, he has said that the project 'brought a sense of the power of the artists, people all of a sudden realized what they could do, as artists, to communicate ideas'.[11] The use of modernist abstract styles demonstrated a number of the artists' facility with the formal vocabulary of mainstream fine art, while the new works in traditional stylistic and conceptual idioms countered the still-widespread impression that traditional Indian art and culture had disappeared. The more recent exhibitions of contemporary art I discuss later in the chapter are, in a very real sense, a direct result of this initial coming together of native artists from across Canada at *Expo '67*. It established a powerful precedent for future national native artists' organisations like SCANA, the Society of Canadian Artists of Native Ancestry, which have, among other things, lobbied effectively for the loosening of the exclusive hold of ethnographic museums on contemporary Aboriginal art, which they wish to have inserted into Canada's art galleries.

If the overall effect of the exterior visual ensemble of the pavilion was to attract visitors through references to the familiar, the interior presented them with something they had not seen before. In March and April of 1966 members of the pavilion's advisory committee together with a hired public relations agent had travelled across Canada to test their draft storyline at meetings with native people.[12] This tour, though hurried and informal, represents one of the first attempts at a broadly conceived national sampling of Aboriginal opinion, and it prefigured initiatives and strategies of collaborative exhibition development that have now become general practice.[13] The organisers were careful to make clear in the exhibition's text and publication that their authority to speak was grounded in the consultative process. As the exhibition brochure told the visitor, the installations presented the answers given by native people across Canada to the question: 'What do you want to tell the people of Canada and the world when they come to Expo in 1967?'[14] The artists were instrumental in ensuring that the consultants' voices were heard, and they resisted censorship by Indian Affairs' officials. The pioneering abstract painter Alex Janvier told a journalist at the time that when the Government had asked the artists to paint a positive, cheery picture, he and the other native artists bristled: 'How come our people are dying in the jails and rotting in the mental hospitals and here we're going to tell the world we're doing great?' they asked. 'Let's tell it as it is.'[15]

The critique of historical and contemporary relations between natives and non-natives in Canada contained in the pavilion was by far the most comprehensive that had ever been presented in so public a forum. Mid-twentieth century museum representations of Aboriginal culture had changed little from those of the preceding half-century, continuing to locate a *pure* and *authentic* era of Aboriginal culture in the remote past and to accept both the inevitability and the benefits of assimilation. In contrast, The Indians of Canada Pavilion stressed the negative aspects of contact, on the one hand, and the currency and value of traditional practices, on the other. As an internal report to the Indian Advisory Council noted, the guiding principle was that 'the Past should not dominate the Present and the Future; the Present is the crucial part which should be projected'.[16] This shift in emphasis was highly significant. It overturned a century of museum representations of native life in which exhibits focused almost exclusively on the pre-contact and early contact periods as the locus of authentic Aboriginal life. The new approach was evidenced first of all by the allocation of space within the pavilion. The representation of the pre-contact period was contained in two ante-rooms, while the focus in the main exhibition area was squarely on the present and the recent past.

The main area, inside the tepee proper, was a large circular space called 'The Drum'. In the six bays that opened out of it the impacts of settlement on Aboriginal people were examined from a native perspective. The bay that addressed the activities of missionaries was particularly dramatic, displaying Iroquoian false face masks and a sculpture of a bear, one of the most important spiritual beings for many native peoples. A shaft of light in the form of a Christian cross projected on the bear both expressed the imposition of foreign belief systems on indigenous belief systems and positioned Aboriginal spirituality as the object of a repression so violent that it could be figured as a crucifixion. Text panels stated: 'The early missionaries thought us pagans. They imposed upon us their own stories of god, of heaven and hell, of sin and salvation', and also that 'we spoke with God the Great Spirit in our own way. We lived with each other in love, and honoured the holy spirit in all living things.' The extent of native control over the pavilion was nowhere so evident as in this installation, which was mounted despite the fears (which proved unfounded) of

Indian Affairs' officials that it would occasion strong protest from Catholic French Canadians.

The display entitled 'The Government and the Indians' was illustrated by a large geo-political map of Canada showing Indian reserves and asserting their importance to Aboriginal peoples – one of the strongest messages that had emerged from the 1966 national consultations. As one text panel stated 'the reserve is our last grip on the land, many of our people fear that, if the reserve should disappear, the Indian would disappear with it'.[17] The brochure further detailed the special historical responsibility of government to Indians, the contemporary needs of Aboriginal people for 'the retention of an Indian identity, a sense of independence, the right to manage their own affairs, and to determine their own destiny'.[18] In an adjacent display, a barrel-vaulted bay entitled 'Work Life' was covered with photos portraying Indians engaged in a wide range of traditional and modern industrial activities. The text pointed out the 'abnormally high number living on government relief'. At the exit the visitor was confronted with the image of an unsmiling and poorly dressed woman standing with her four small children at the door of their log cabin. The final bay addressed education and the alien forms imposed on native children through assimilationist policies:

> Dick and Jane in the storybook are strangers to an Indian boy. An Indian child begins school by learning a foreign tongue. The sun and the moon mark passing time in the Indian home. At school, minutes are important and we jump to the bell. Many precious hours are spent in a bus going to a distant school and coming home again.[19]

Adjacent to these texts were 'large blown-up photographs of tattered, unhappy-looking Indian children placed beside pictures of white Canadian children playing in the comfort of suburbia'.[20]

From 'The Drum' a staircase led visitors down into the final exhibition space, 'The Future', where they could pick up headphones and hear a final message that refuted the trope of the vanishing Indian and articulated an alternative vision of the future emphasising mutual respect and affirmed difference:

> Some of my people see in the dark coals a world where the Indian is a half-remembered thing and the ways of the old men are forgotten.
>
> But I see another vision, I see an Indian, tall and strong in the pride of his heritage. He stands with your sons, a man among men.
>
> He is different, as you and I are different, and perhaps it will always be so. But, in the Indian way, we have many gifts to share.

The rejection of paternalism was clear: 'The trail we walk is our own, and we bear our own burdens. That is our right.'

The Indians of Canada Pavilion constituted a moment of dramatic rupture with many key conventions of colonialist representation. This break was not – and could not have been – total, and in several important ways the pavilion's installations continued to employ the discourse of the dominant society. Throughout the pavilion the masculine pronoun, for example, was used exclusively – 'the Indian' was always 'he', despite the presence of many female images.[21] Despite the availability of qualified women, all the commissioned artists were men and there were no women on the Indian advisory committee. The privileging of the male voice evidences the success with which patriarchal norms had, during the centuries of colonial rule, come to overlay Aboriginal practices based on very different notions of gender and power. In retrospect the exclusion of the female voice seems an omen of the degree to which gender would, in the near future, become a site of increasing difficulty in Aboriginal politics.

The doubleness and the divided subjectivity imposed on native people by a still-colonial bureaucracy was revealed also by the alternation of first- and third-person narration in the texts associated with the pavilion. While the text panels addressed the visitors in the first person, speaking directly as 'we' to 'you', the brochure spoke in the third person – of how 'the Indian' had fared in the past and of 'his' goals for the future. Although the substance of the brochure seems to have been a remarkably faithful summary of the community consultations and advisory committee discussions, its messages are distanced by the reportorial, ethnographic voice of the public relations consultant hired to compose it. It thus continued to mediate the Aboriginal voice according to a paternalistic ethos that had not yet given way to a fully empowered Aboriginal community.

The critique of historical and anthropological discourse initiated by The Indians of Canada Pavilion would become more profound in the years that followed, but in 1967 there was still an acceptance of the dominant society's categories. Although the use of quotation marks in the text panels and brochure ironised and distanced words like 'Indian', the terms continued to be employed. Similarly, the use of the standard anthropological culture–area concept as an organising principle limited the degree to which totalising representations could be deconstructed. Perhaps the most enduring of the Western literary and anthropological conventions invoked in the pavilion was the romanticised construction of the pre-contact past as an Edenic paradise free from conflict and want – a convention that remains intact today in the rhetoric of many environmentalists, adherents of New Age religions, and Hollywood Indians – and not a few First Nations' activists and leaders. The opening lines of 'The Beginning' in the

Pavilion brochure – 'All the creatures of the world lived, one with another, in harmony and order. All owed each other respect and reverence' – read very much like an animist version of the Book of Genesis. At other moments the use of a Longfellowian English to evoke an ideal future – 'Sit now by the fire and rest, my brother. We will talk of the time to come' – seemed to reference a related millenarian tradition.

From today's vantage point the evocation by Aboriginal people of a Judeo-Christian trope of original harmony, like the patriarchal language, is problematical. Many native creation stories, with their Great Trickster figures and dualities of constructive and destructive force, structure chaos, order and morality differently, and against these narratives the overlay of doctrines of the noble savage and the lost Eden seem alien. Yet those tropes were deployed at *Expo '67* in a carefully calculated manner to invert progressivist and evolutionist doctrines associated with assimilationist policies. Their rhetorical power derives from their resonance both for non-natives and for Christianised Aboriginal people, reflecting historical processes not only of hybridisation but of mimicry. As Homi Bhabha has observed, 'mimicry can be subversive; you use the language of the master in an alloyed form, in order to deflect the dominating ideologies being imposed on you'.[22] The combination of mimicry and subversion inside the pavilion was analogous to that found on the outside: the installations, like the architecture, exploited popular and touristic images of *Indianness* while simultaneously resisting them.

Museums and other institutions were slow to pick up the challenges raised by The Indians of Canada Pavilion, although important exceptions can be cited. In British Columbia, for example, a number of important and pioneering collaborations with First Nations' communities and artists were developed during the 1980s by the British Columbia Provincial Museum (now the Royal British Columbia Museum) and the University of British Columbia's Museum of Anthropology. Several exhibits at Vancouver's *Expo '86* reflected the impact of those institutions' innovative approaches. But it would take two more decades *and* the crisis provoked by the native boycott of *The Spirit Sings* exhibition mounted for the Calgary Winter Olympics in 1988 for the issue of museum representation to be addressed seriously on a national scale. By and large, between 1967 and 1988 the representation of Aboriginal culture in major expositions and cultural events continued to inscribe pre-*Expo* narratives. This was paralleled by a stalemate in active governmental attempts to address the reform of the Indian Act and problems of sovereignty and Aboriginal rights.[23]

Olympic contestations: The Spirit Sings

The 1988 Calgary Winter Olympics was, after Vancouver's *Expo '86*, the next international event to be held in Canada on a scale comparable to that of the Montreal *World's Fair*. The decision to focus the major art exhibition of the Calgary cultural festival on Aboriginal art was in part the result of circumstance – Calgary's largest and most active museum, the Glenbow Museum, has particular strength in the areas of ethnology and Western history – and in part a reflection of longstanding patterns of *borrowed identity* in North American settler societies in which indigenous imagery is appropriated to the identity of the nation, especially before an international audience.[24]

The Glenbow's decision to focus the exhibition on the early contact period resulted also from a desire to make use of the special opportunity afforded by the Olympics to bring back to Canada objects collected by missionaries, soldiers and curio-collectors during the early contact period that had not since returned to North America. While the project of gathering them together in order to further historical and aesthetic understandings of Aboriginal material culture and art had always been dear to the hearts of scholars, only the kind of super-budget available for a show connected to an event like the Olympics could support such a project. The rarity of the objects also appealed to the popular 'treasures' model that often lay behind the super-shows of the 1970s and 1980s. The project began in an era of relatively generous public funding and centralised museum organisation. It was supported by the National Museum of Canada (now the Canadian Museum of Civilisation, or CMC), which provided the show's only other venue and seconded two of its curators to work on the exhibition, and by the now-disbanded National Museums' Corporation.[25]

The Spirit Sings, with a budget of $2.6 million, was the most costly exhibition that had ever been produced in Canada. It was also the most controversial.[26] Two years before the opening date, when Shell Oil was announced as the corporate sponsor, the Lubicon Cree, a band of Alberta Indians, called for a boycott of the exhibition in support of their unresolved land claim. Shell was one of several oil companies drilling on land to which the Lubicon laid claim and from which they had recently been evicted, resulting in great suffering and social destabilisation. The announcement that Shell Oil was to sponsor an exhibition celebrating the past glories of Aboriginal art and culture appeared to Lubicon leaders the ultimate hypocrisy. They organised an energetic campaign to persuade the approximately 100 museums of which loans had been requested to join the boycott. Although an earlier Lubicon call for a general boycott of the Winter

Olympics had not been heeded, the boycott of the exhibition met with some success, attracting a great deal of publicity and widespread support among the academic world. It also generated fierce debates within many of the museums that were contacted, particularly in Europe, especially after the boycott gained the support of the Assembly of First Nations, Canada's largest Aboriginal political organisation. In the end, although the boycott attracted considerable sympathy and support, most museums *did* lend to the exhibition, in some cases because of pressure exerted by the Canadian Government through diplomatic channels. *The Spirit Sings* presented more than 600 objects, a great many of which were unpublished and almost totally unknown, had never before been returned to North America, and had rarely or never been publicly displayed by the museums that owned them. The exhibition drew almost a quarter of a million visitors in Calgary and Ottawa.

Although the boycott of *The Spirit Sings* began as a strategy for drawing attention to a land claim, it soon stimulated a much more wide-ranging critique of museum practice. The issue of corporate sponsorship quickly broadened to encompass a critique of the exhibition's exclusive focus on the early contact period. While many Aboriginal viewers welcomed the opportunity to see early pieces, objections were raised about the exhibition's failure to address more fully the negative effects of colonialism and to include a section on contemporary problems and life-styles. As I have said, these were precisely the issues Aboriginal activists had fought hard to foreground in the 1967 Indians of Canada Pavilion. For many First Nations' viewers the sight of the beautiful old objects, many ordinarily hidden away in distant museums and made with techniques and skills long forgotten, was a painful reminder of loss, producing an emotional excess that could not be accommodated by the exhibition's discursive frames of historical ethnography and aesthetic appreciation. Further debates developed around repatriation and the display of sacred objects. After the exhibition opened in Calgary representatives of the Kahnawake Mohawk of Quebec went to court to force the removal of an Iroquois mask they regard as a ritually active object that should not be publicly displayed. That similar false face masks had been chosen by the Aboriginal curators of the *Expo '67* and displayed without controversy in The Indians of Canada Pavilion, located only a few miles from the Kahnawake reserve, indicates the growth of active opposition to the display of spiritually active objects during the intervening twenty years.[27]

As the boycott gained momentum and the debates heated up during the winter and spring of 1988 the country was preparing for a fall federal election. Native leaders were quick to exploit the connections between the issues the exhibition had raised and the larger questions of sovereignty on their political agenda. It was against this background that the director of the CMC, George MacDonald, committed his institution to help organise a national forum that would provide the occasion for a full airing of the concerns of the native community. The conference, held in November 1988 during the last days of *The Spirit Sings* Ottawa showing, led directly to the commissioning of the TFMFN to study the longstanding problems in the relationships between Canadian museums and First Nations revealed by the controversy and to develop mutually acceptable guidelines for the future.

The TFMFN and its regional working groups met between 1989 and 1992. In the course of these meetings Canadian museum professionals were brought to reassess their most basic premises about scholarly research and to confront the inherently political nature of all processes of representation. Ultimately, it forced most museum practitioners to accept that exhibitions are never pure or disinterested scientific inquiries, being rather complex events that give voice to the interests of particular communities. The logical conclusion – that the interests of First Nations should be taken into account when their communities are being represented – began to acquire normative force. The TFMFN report *Turning the Page: Forging New Partnerships Between Museums and First Peoples*, issued in 1992, articulated a new ethics of museum practice. It modelled relationships of partnership and collaboration between museum professionals and Aboriginal communities on the basis of principles of sharing and mutual respect, and sought to ensure that those principles would inform all future projects of research and representation.[28] More specifically, the report acknowledged the rights of Aboriginal people to have access to all objects of native heritage and to repossess human remains and objects held illegally.[29]

De-celebrating discovery: Indigena *and* Land, Spirit, Power

At the time when the TFMFN was carrying out its work, two major exhibitions of contemporary Aboriginal art were being developed at the two national museums. Each responded in its own way to the issues of voice and representation raised by The Indians of Canada Pavilion and *The Spirit Sings*, and to the challenge of native empowerment within the museum. *Indigena: Contemporary Native Perspectives* was organised for the CMC by its curator of contemporary

Indian art, Gerald McMaster, and his associate Lee-Ann Martin.[30] It brought together paintings, sculptures, installations and new media pieces, many specially commissioned, that addressed the meaning of the 500 years since Columbus's arrival from the perspective of the indigenous peoples of the Americas. The exhibition was the first show to be mounted by a large Canadian museum in which all the key participants – curators, artists and writers for the publication – were members of the Aboriginal community.[31] *Land, Spirit, Power: First Nations at the National Gallery of Canada* was organised by one native and two non-native curators.[32] The exhibition was the National Gallery's response to the sustained lobbying of Aboriginal artists for inclusion in the NGC's permanent collections and exhibition spaces. It also acknowledged the maturing of a continent-wide contemporary native art movement whose opening salvo in Canada had been the art commissioned for the outside of the *Expo '67* pavilion.

Despite the commonalities of style and conceptual approach among the artists represented in these shows, the two exhibition projects complemented rather than paralleled each other. Because the artists who contributed to *Indigena* were asked to comment directly on the meaning of the 500 years since Columbus's arrival, the project was, by intent, a profoundly didactic exhibition whose goal was to *de-celebrate* the 500 years of European intervention in Aboriginal life. The paintings, sculptures and installations all confronted the visitor with the retelling of history from a native point of view, chronicling and mourning a tragic history of repression and death, but also affirming the strengths that had allowed Aboriginal people to resist annihilation and to survive. So comprehensive and revisionist a critique had not been mounted in a major Canadian museum since the didactic installations of the *Expo '67* exhibition. And, like The Indians of Canada Pavilion, the contestations of Aboriginal people served to challenge the triumphant celebratory gestures grounded in uncritical settler narratives that were being proclaimed by other institutions during the quincentennial year. (Unlike the US, Canada does not identify Columbus's voyages as foundational to its national history, and that may have made it easier for Canada's national museums to support two such dissenting exhibitions.) In contrast to *Indigena*, the NGC's *Land, Spirit, Power* was the less overtly political: it took up the challenge of accommodating alternative artistic modernisms and postmodernisms, relying not so much on a rhetoric of confrontation as on one of aesthetic seduction. Although many of the works of art were lightened by a wit and humour that avoided the darker and more sombre emotional tone of those included in *Indigena*, it was in its own way no less radical.

Two large and complex installations illustrate particularly well the contrasting intentions and atmospheres of the two shows. They are Joane Cardinal-Schubert's *Preservation of the Species: DECON-STRUCTIVISTS (This is the House that Joe Built)*, in *Indigena*, and Rebecca Belmore's *Mawu-che-hitoowin: A Gathering of People for Any Purpose*, in *Land, Spirit, Power*. Each installation occupied a central position within its exhibition, not only spatially but, I would argue, conceptually. *DECONSTRUCTIVISTS* brought together themes which Cardinal-Schubert had been pursuing for many years. On the claustrophobic black-painted walls of the gallery Cardinal-Schubert wrote out a series of history lessons for strangers constructed as cultural other. Haunting landscapes recalled from childhood, the suicide of an Aboriginal boy, the petroglyphs that mark the prairies with ancient histories, family photographs, an altar to lost souls – all were brought together with a fenced-in reservation peopled by stick figures in babushkas that recalled both sacred offerings and rural poverty, and a peep-show that positioned the viewer as voyeur. Belmore's work was very different. It was spare, quiet and minimalist. On a plywood platform painted with flowers that suggested both old linoleum and flitting shadows on a forest floor, Belmore arranged a circle of chairs taken from her own kitchen and the living spaces of the women who were closest to her. The work issued a tacit invitation to sit down, to put on the earphones dangling over each chair back, and to listen to the voices of Belmore's female community talking about their lives as native women in Canada, their struggles, their joys and the sources of their strength.

Both of these works were at once broadly conceived and intensely personal. Both spoke of stereotyping, racism and the toll paid by the victims of those evils. Although both installations had interactive components, and relied on text and speech as much as on visual images, in other respects they adopted very different strategies. Cardinal-Schubert stated clearly her intention to disrupt the equilibrium of her viewers and to discomfort them. A text placed next to a Duchampian peep-show included in her installation read: 'It is uncomfortable to peek through the little holes of this site. You miss some of the picture. What's more, it is an uncomfortable and unsettling experience. Good! Now you know how I have felt for most of my life.' Belmore, in contrast, made use of the testimony of the human voice, of the oral tradition, of common discourse. She welcomed viewers into the circle of the native community, and used the traditional Aboriginal tactics for resolving conflict and reaching understanding through talking circles and the counsel of elders.

[133]

Both exhibitions stimulated mixed responses. The overt expressions of anger in *Indigena* upset many people, including some strong supporters of Aboriginal empowerment in the museum community who believed the TFMFN was already addressing many of the issues the exhibition raised. The political messages and stylistic eclecticism of *Land, Spirit, Power*, on the other hand, led the art critic of Canada's major national newspaper to accuse the NGC of opportunism.[33] Despite these reactions and the internal contrasts of the two shows, both were important therapeutic moments for the artists and their audiences. Taken together, they illustrated that art can be both sword and balm. The public acknowledgment of injury that occurred through the staging of these exhibitions in Canada's national museums was an essential step in the healing necessary to a process of reconciliation and change. The public expression of anger and the inscription of alternative historical narratives also are integral to this process. As Jimmie Durham wrote in one of his works in *Land, Spirit, Power*:

> If we do not let our memories fail us
> The dead can sing and be with us.
> They want us to remember them,
> And they can make festivals in our struggles.

In *Land, Spirit, Power* the dead were feasted at the same time as their pain was remembered. In *Indigena* they were mourned with an angry grief too long pent up and denied the dignity of public commemoration.

Museums and the performance of postcolonial politics

Mieke Bal has written that museum professionals have come to accept 'the idea that a museum is a discourse, and an exhibition an utterance within that discourse'.[34] I have focused here on four exhibitions that, because of their commemorative functions and super-show scale, were particularly loud utterances that have continued to resonate in the Canadian museum world. Some of that resonance has come from the innovative and influential models of process they introduced; some has come from the presentation of installations and works of art whose critical discursive power has been similarly influential; and some has come from the super-show's inherent capacity to attract debate, contestation and publicity. John Miller has put it thus: 'Blockbuster exhibitions, by engendering surplus frustration as a ritual in [their] own right, tend to recuperate dissent as part of the totality of the overall event.'[35]

This mini-history also suggests that the interrelationship between super-shows that focus on indigenous peoples and the performance of postcolonial politics in settler societies is tighter than has been generally recognised. The ritual dramas of exhibition and protest that were played out, through and around the four exhibitions discussed here stand in significant relationship to reformist political initiatives that took place outside of the museum. In March 1994 – in the aftermath, one could argue, of the Columbus quincentennial – the Canadian Government announced plans to dismantle the federal Department of Indian and Northern Affairs (DIAND), a paternalistic agency set up to administer policies of directed assimilation imposed on the First Nations since the nineteenth century that were premissed on the belief that indigenous peoples were incapable of running their own affairs. This decision, taken even as *Indigena* and *Land, Spirit, Power* were continuing their national tours, repeated, with a precision that is almost uncanny, the time interval between The Indians of Canada Pavilion of 1967 and the issuance two years later of a government White Paper proposing to repeal the federal Indian Act – the other pillar that supports Canada's management of its indigenous peoples. In both of these cases, strong protest by Aboriginal people fearful of losing the vital financial subsidies historically associated with the Indian Act and its administration by DIAND prevented the Government from following through on its intended initiatives. The parallels between these two pairings of radically revisionist exhibitions and dramatic shifts in government policy are striking. I am not proposing a direct and mechanistic cause-and-effect relationship between major museum exhibitions and political actions. In both cases the confrontational exhibitions that preceded momentous governmental announcements seem, rather, to have done two things: first, to draw widespread attention to historical problems in the relationship between Canada and the First Nations; and, second, to serve as rehearsals for the effective Aboriginal campaigns of protest that followed.

For most of the long history of Canada's internal colonisation of its Aboriginal peoples the power to determine how that history is recounted has been vested in a narrow stratum of the non-native population. The four exhibitions discussed here facilitated a process by which a new cultural intelligentsia comprised of Aboriginal artists and intellectuals re-appropriated the right to publicly remember the past and to represent the present according to its own measures of value and importance. They were the products of a particular combination of ingredients that marked the second half of the twentieth century in Canada: the liberalisation of race politics; the Liberal governments that were in power through most of that period,[36] and the increasingly effective Aboriginal activism that put pressure on *both* museums *and* federal policy-making. This potent mixture has led

[135]

Canadian museums to take important steps toward the institution-alisation of multivocality. At times, as in the case of *Expo '67* and *Indigena*, it has led also to a kind of reversed univocality, in which Aboriginal voices have been privileged or exclusively empowered to represent their histories and cultures within national institutions.

The four exhibitions here discussed were temporary. The best evidence of effective change in museums comes, however, with the creation of long-term or *permanent* installations. That evidence was provided in the fall of 2002 and the winter of 2003 when the two national museums that have figured in this discussion, the NGC and the CMC, opened major new long-term exhibitions. The NGC began to unveil the latest of its periodic reinstallations of its galleries of Canadian historical art, which for the first time integrates indigenous arts, ranging from pre-contact archaeological objects to twentieth-century paintings and sculptures, within its narrative of Canadian art history. The CMC opened its long-awaited First People's Hall which presents the histories and cultures of Aboriginal people.[37] The conceptual plan and themes of the hall were developed by an Aboriginal advisory committee whose members included a number of museum professionals. Its themes stress the diversity of the First Nations, their active engagement with and contributions to Canadian society throughout the contact period, and the ancient and intimate relationship that Aboriginal people have with the land – a relationship based on knowledge that is, in turn, expressed through oral tradition.

These recent developments are recognisably and lineally connected to the history of contestation briefly chronicled here. The messages of First Nations' people, articulated through and in relation to this series of public exhibitions, have displayed a remarkable consistency and strength that have been further tempered only by the heat of contestation. At the beginning of the new millennium both land claims and self-government negotiations and Aboriginal activism in the museum have moved into a new register, one that has shifted from an anti-colonial rhetoric to one of sovereignty. In 1998 the landmark Nisga'a Land Claims Treaty both established new forms of Aboriginal political autonomy and created new models for repatriation and shared responsibility for cultural property in public museums. The stories of the four exhibitions that, arguably, prepared the way for such contemporary developments strongly suggest that the ritual performances that take place at show times are interrelated in complex ways with larger political dynamics. They suggest that the rehearsals of memory and desire that museums foster are both reflective and generative, influencing institutional–legal enactments and reifications that take place beyond their walls.

Notes

1   An earlier version of this paper was published in D. McIntyre and K. Wehner (eds), *National Museums, Negotiating Histories: Conference Proceedings* (Canberra: National Museum of Australia, 2001).
2   On the notion of the super show see J. Alsop, *The Rare Art Traditions: The History of Art Collecting and Its Linked Phenomena* (New York: Harper & Row, 1982); and see J. Miller for the closely related notion of the 'mega-exhibition' in, 'Shows You Love to Hate: A Psychology of the Mega-Exhibition', in R. Greenberg, B. W. Ferguson and S. Nairne (eds), *Thinking About Exhibitions* (New York: Routledge, 1996).
3   Exhibitions displaying indigenous objects organised in connection with the Australian bicentennial, the Seville Olympics and the USA's Columbus quincentennial celebrations are examples of this phenomenon. Associated exhibitions were targeted by indigenous peoples as occasions on which to contest colonial representations of their histories. See T. Bennett, '1988: History and the Bicentenary', *Australian–Canadian Studies*, 7:1–2 (1989), 154–62; J. Quick-to-See-Smith, *The Submuloc Show/Columbus Wohs: A Visual Commentary on the Columbus Quincentennial from the Perspective of America's First People* (Phoenix, AZ: Atlatl, 1992); and W. Jackson Rushing, 'Contrary Iconography: The Submuloc Show's Quincentenary De-Celebration', *New Art Examiner*, 21:10 (1994), 30–5.
4   I use the terms 'indigenous', 'native', 'Aboriginal' and 'First Peoples' interchangeably in this chapter, as all are commonly used currently in Canada.
5   One bureaucrat considered, for example, that 'Indian paintings should be a part of the general Art Exhibit . . . [and] the contribution of the Indian, of maize, potatoes, and tobacco might be part of a general display of agricultural achievements, as his use and design of sleds, birch-bark canoes, toboggans and snowshoes might be part of a general story of the development of transportation': Department of Indian Affairs and Northern Development (hereafter DIAND) Archives 1/43–3 V. 1, Letter from H. M. Jones, Acting Deputy Minister, Indian Affairs, to J. A. Roberts, Deputy Minister, Department of Trade and Commerce, June 1963.
6   DIAND 1/43–3 V.1, 'Storyline, Government of Canada Pavilion, Montreal 1967', December 1963.
7   See G. Manuel and M. Posluns, *The Fourth World: An Indian Reality* (New York: Free Press, 1974), p. 172. Officials worried that their department's sorry history as the agent of repression and racism would occasion 'negative' statements Memos from the period show that officials knew that 'the traditional image of the federal Indian Affairs Branch is not a good one among Indians', who had been guilty 'until very recently' of 'a blind attitude of cultural superiority from which Indians were viewed by other Canadian groups': NAC RG 10/8575 1/1–2–2–18, part 2, 'Participation in Canada's Centennial by People of Indian Ancestry – Some Policy Considerations' (unsigned), 24 September 1964, p. 2.
8   See Susan Stewart, *On Longing: Narratives of the Miniature, the Gigantic, the Souvenir, the Collection* (Baltimore, MD: Johns Hopkins University Press, 1984).
9   Sherry Brydon's superb research on the pavilion is fundamental to this discussion. See her honours thesis, 'The Indians of Canada Pavilion at Expo '67: The First National and International Forum for Native Nations', Carleton University, Ottawa, 1991; and R. B. Phillips and S. Brydon, 'Arrow of Truth: The Indians of Canada Pavilion at Expo '67', *Journal of Canadian Studies*, forthcoming.
10 See S. Brydon, 'The Indians of Canada Pavilion at Expo '67', *American Indian Art Magazine*, 22:3 (1997), 54–7.
11 Personal communication to Sherry Brydon, Ottawa, 18 March 1991, quoted in Brydon, ibid.
12 Meetings were held with 'groups of Indian leaders, craftsmen, artists and others' in Vancouver, Edmonton, Montreal and Amherst, Nova Scotia.
13 See R. B. Phillips, 'Introduction: Collaboration in Exhibitions – Towards a Dialogic Paradigm', in L. Peers and A. Brown (eds), *Museums and Source Communities*

(London: Routledge, 2003), and other essays in that volume; see also the special issue *of Museum*, 'Museums and Native Americans: Renegotiating the Contract' (January–February 1991).

14   *The Indians of Canada Pavilion – Expo 67* (Ottowa: Controller of Stationery, 1967); the brochure contained an expanded version of the exhibition text.

15   D. Staples, 'Artist Alex Janvier', *Edmonton Journal*, 31 January 1988.

16   Kanien'kehaka Raotitioakwa Cultural Centre Files, Minutes of the Second Meeting of the Indian Advisory Council, held in Montreal, April 20–3, 1966, p. 6,

17   Quoted in 'Canadian Indians at EXPO '67', *Sanity* (July–August 1967).

18   *The Indians of Canada Pavilion*, p. 9.

19   The brochure was even more explicit: 'School curricula and text books are usually designed for children of a European background and have very little relationship to the Indian child's home experience.'

20   Rosemary Speirs, 'Indian Pavilion Shocks Complacent Non-Indians', *Leader–Post* (Regina, Sask., and syndicated to newspapers in Ottawa, Toronto and Montreal), 1 May 1967, p. 6.

21   The privileging of the masculine in the pavilion echoes that of *Expo '67*, the general theme of which was 'Man and His World': individual pavilions were entitled 'Man the Creator', 'Man the Explorer', 'Man the Producer', 'Man the Provider' and 'Man and the Community'.

22   'Art and National Identity: A Critics' Symposium', *Art in America*, 9 (September 1991), 80–4.

23   At the closing ceremonies of the 1976 Montreal Olympics white performers paraded in stereotypical Indian costumes, despite protests from local Mohawk and Seneca. A plan to include an Indian war party attacking a stagecoach in the opening ceremonies of the 1988 Calgary Olympics was cancelled after protest from members of the organising committee, but in the official logo a war-bonneted Indian bust was juxtaposed with the emblems of Olympic sports. At Vancouver's *Expo '86* the representation of the Aboriginal place in Canadian history as an opening chapter was a throwback to pre Expo '67 conventions: see M. Ames, *Cannibal Tours and Glass Boxes: The Anthropology of Museums*, 2nd edn (Vancouver: University of British Columbia Press, 1992), pp. 117–24.

24   See N. H. H. Graburn, 'Natives and Hi-Tech: Canadian National Symbols at World's Fairs, 1951–1986', paper presented at the Kroeber Anthropology Society, Berkeley, California, 1987.

25   *The Spirit Sings* was to have been the opening show at the new CMC, but the building was not completed in time.

26   For the content of the exhibition see its two publications: Glenbow Museum, *The Spirit Sings: Artistic Traditions of Canada's First Peoples*, and *The Spirit Sings: Artistic Traditions of Canada's First Peoples, A Catalogue of the Exhibition* (both Toronto: McClelland & Stewart, 1987). Useful overviews of the controversy are J. Harrison, 'Completing a Circle: "The Spirit Sings"', in N. Dyck and J. B. Waldram (eds), *Anthropology, Public Policy and Native Peoples in Canada* (Montreal: McGill–Queen's University Press, 1993); and L. Stainforth, 'Did the Spirit Sing? An Historical Perspective on Canadian Exhibitions of the Other', MA disseration, Carleton University, Ottawa (1990).

27   See R. B. Phillips, 'Disappearing Acts: Iroquois "Art" and Regimes of Visibility and Invisibility', in M. S. Phillips and G. Schochet (eds), *Questions of Tradition* (Toronto: University of Toronto Press, 2004).

28   See T. Nicks, 'Partnerships in Developing Cultural Resources: Lessons from the Task Force on Museums and First Peoples', *Culture*, 12:1 (1992), 87–94; and T. Wilson, G. Erasmus and D. W. Penney, 'Museums and First Peoples in Canada', *Museum Anthropology*, 16:2 (1992), 6–11.

29   The report also recommends that the treatment, display and disposition of sacred objects and objects of cultural patrimony be based on extra-legal moral and ethical considerations.

30   See G. McMaster and L.-A. Martin, *Indigena: Contemporary Native Perspectives* (Vancouver: Douglas & McIntyre, 1991).
31   Important precedents for indigenous curatorship and control in exhibitions were established by smaller native-run institutions such as the Woodlands Indian Cultural Centre at Brantford, Ontario, and the Ojibwa Cultural Foundation in West Bay, Ontario.
32   They were NGC curator Diana Nemiroff, anthropologist Charlotte Townshend-Gault and Saulteaux-Ojibwa artist and curator Robert Houle. See their catalogue *Land/Spirit/Power: First Nations at the National Gallery of Canada* (Ottawa: National Gallery of Canada, 1992); and W. J. Rushing, 'Contingent Histories, Aesthetic Politics', *New Art Examiner*, 20 (1993), 14–20.
33   J. B. Mays, 'Breaking Traditions', *Globe & Mail*, 10 October 1992.
34   Mieke Bal, 'The Discourse of the Museum', in Reesa Greenberg, Bruce W. Ferguson and Sandy Nairne (eds), *Thinking About Exhibitions* (London and New York: Routledge, 1996), p. 214.
35   Miller, 'Shows You Love to Hate', p. 269.
36   Jean Chretien was minister of Indian affairs in 1968 and became prime minister in 1993.
37   Both new installations build on previous ones. During the 1990s the NGC devoted one of the contemporary art galleries to examples of contemporary Aboriginal art. Since its opening in 1989 the CMC has devoted its Grand Hall to north-west coast house fronts, monumental sculpture and displays of material culture and art.

CHAPTER SEVEN

The uses of Captain Cook: early exploration in the public history of Aotearoa New Zealand and Australia

Nicholas Thomas

In both Australia and Aotearoa New Zealand, Captain Cook has loomed large in public history: his visits have been understood as foundational moments, as marking the true beginnings of the histories of each nation. His voyages are extensively marked through monuments and place names; they are celebrated in a plethora of popular historical works, poems, plays, films, texts for children and souvenir objects; his landings have been, and continue to be, frequently re-enacted. Their commemoration has sometimes been subject to protest and criticism of Cook has occasionally been aired. Yet, despite the discredited imperial ideologies with which exploration has been so intimately associated, Cook's popularity has been surprisingly resilient. This chapter does not attempt to review the whole range of representations and reinterpretations of Cook's voyages to the two antipodean colonies of white settlement, or elsewhere; instead, my interest is more specifically in how key aspects of Cook's encounters with Maori and indigenous Australians have been imagined and re-imagined.

The process began with the reworking of the journals of James Cook and Joseph Banks into the official published narrative of the voyages, 'for making discoveries in the southern hemisphere', as the rather cumbersome title put it. The individual responsible was John Hawkesworth, a literary gentleman and sometime collaborator of Samuel Johnson, who appeared to the Admiralty's lords to be a respectable choice, but whose treatment of the primary materials involved, in many readers' eyes, 'improvement' that amounted to mutilation. His controversial book suppressed an aspect of Cook's and Banks's response to indigenous Australians that has become crucially important since. It conversely drew attention to an intractable and profoundly troubling aspect of the encounter with Maori that since has been imagined differently, perhaps neutralised. Here I begin with the encounters of 1769 and 1770, and proceed to explore how they have been remade, first in late nineteenth- and early twentieth-century settler-colonial histories and, second, in response to recent indigenous political affirmations and associated shifts in the understanding of public history in Aotearoa and Australia.[1]

In Australia, the events of Cook's visit provided historical material that, from the point of view of national narrative, might be considered unpromising. On 29 April 1770, the *Endeavour*, having sighted the Australian coast ten days earlier, entered the broad estuary that would later be called Botany Bay. There were people around the shoreline who, perplexingly, paid the ship no attention whatsoever. They were fishing, 'totaly engag'd in what they were about: the ship passd within a quarter of a mile of them and yet they scarce lifted their eyes', Joseph Banks wrote. After the vessel came to anchor a woman with a couple of children nearby on the shore looked at the ship 'but expressd neither surprize nor concern'; later, some people who had been out in canoes arrived and began to cook, 'to all appearance totaly unmoved at us'.[2] Only when the mariners approached the shore did these Gweagal people seem to react at all: two men came to the water's edge, brandished spears and shouted. Though decidedly outnumbered, these two remained defiant, even after being fired at twice with small shot, at which point one went to fetch a shield. When the Europeans landed, the two men threw spears, were fired on again and then retreated. Throughout the nine-day visit the local Aboriginal people consistently ran away, withdrew, avoided contact or signalled that they wanted the visitors to leave. Perhaps an encounter took place, but not much of a meeting.[3]

The *Endeavour* sailed north up the coast, and within the Great Barrier Reef struck coral on 11 June. Cook was lucky to save the ship, which was then beached at the entrance to what would be called the Endeavour River in the far north of Queensland. Here contacts with the local Aboriginal people, the Guugu Yimidhirr, were slightly less constrained than they had been at Botany Bay: on a couple of occasions local men sat about with the Europeans, though they would neither accept gifts nor share food, and were angered when Cook refused to give them one of the turtles his crew had caught. Rudimentary communication, however, did take place and a list of words of the local language was obtained.

Despite these limited contacts, Cook's proto-anthropological curiosity was stimulated, and he wrote an extended description of the Aboriginals encountered that ranged over physique, hair, ornament, body paint and piercing, canoes, subsistence and dwellings. He proceeded to offer more general reflections:

From what I have said of the Natives of New-Holland they may appear to some to be the most wretched people upon Earth, but in reality they are far more happy than we Europeans; being wholy unacquainted not only with the superfluous but the necessary Conveniences so much sought after in Europe, they are happy in not knowing the use of them. They live in a Tranquillity which is not disturb'd by the Inequality of Condition: the Earth and sea of their own accord furnishes them with all things necessary for life, they covet not Magnificent Houses, Houshold-stuff &c, they live in a warm and fine Climate and enjoy a very wholsome Air, so that they have very little need of Clothing and this they seem to be fully sencible of, for many to whome we gave Cloth &c to [sic], left it carelessly upon the Sea beach and in the woods as a thing they had no manner of use for. In short they seem'd to set no value on any thing we gave them, nor would they ever part with any thing of their own for any one article we could offer them; this in my opinion argues that they think themselves provided with all the necessarys of Life and that they have no superfluities.[4]

This statement seems a classic expression of the primitivist idealisation of noble savagery; Banks included similar reflections in his own journal. Yet, even though Cook's comment partakes of this familiar rhetoric, it addresses a practical issue of immediate relevance to his mission: he was under instruction to make friends with people and report on the scope for commerce. Aboriginal people had absolutely no interest in barter or traffic of any sort, and this is something that Cook felt he needed to discuss and explain. The explanation he offered, which turns on his shallow understanding of the disposition and needs of Aboriginals, might thus have been considered significant, among Cook's observations. It is therefore a little surprising that Hawkesworth – who was not unsympathetic to broadly related Enlightenment ideas – omitted these remarks altogether (or rather transposed them, in distorted form, to the discussion of the native people of Tierra del Fuego, whom Cook had denigrated, without a hint of primitivist idealisation). It is interesting that the idea of Aboriginal simplicity was aired in the course of at least one Royal Society dinner – we know, because Benjamin Franklin was there and reported on the notion in a letter – but the passage from Cook's journal was consigned to the archives. It would not enter into public perceptions of indigenous Australians until nearly 200 years after the voyage; nor, until then, would it shape or qualify public ideas about the sort of person or thinker Cook was.

Cook's contacts with Maori were far more varied and extensive than his Australian encounters, although they began very badly. Over 9–10 October 1769, parties from the *Endeavour* several times attempted to make personal contact with Maori at one end or the other of

– what would be called – Poverty Bay (later the site of the town of Gisborne). At first, one man, part of a group which approached and seemed to threaten one of the ship's boats, was fatally shot; then, just as Maori and whites began uneasily to mingle, a man who snatched a sword was killed. Later, Cook perversely thought he could convince Maori of European friendliness by kidnapping a few men in a canoe and treating them hospitably on board the *Endeavour*, before releasing them; but the seizure went wrong and 3 or 4 of the men were killed. Some days later, a few more Maori, who approached the *Endeavour* offshore and attempted to seize the Tahitian boy Taiata, were shot at and 2 or 3 of them were killed. It was not long before rather more amicable relations were established, further up the coast and subsequently at Queen Charlotte Sound, at the northern end of Te Wai Pounamu, the South Island; but the events of the first meetings – which resulted in the deaths of more native people in one week than would be killed over the subsequent nine years of Cook's voyages, up to the time of his death – prompted considerable anguish at the time. 'Thus ended the most disagreeable day My life has yet seen, black be the mark for it and heaven send that such may never return to embitter future reflection', Joseph Banks wrote.[5]

Cook himself composed and revised a troubled passage, that was further reworked in the published text. Assuming Cook's voice, Hawkesworth wrote that the Maori 'certainly did not deserve death for not chusing to confide in my promises; or not consenting to come aboard my boat . . . but the nature of my service required me to obtain a knowledge of their country, which I could no otherwise effect than by forcing my way into it in a hostile manner'. It was inevitable, Hawkesworth acknowledged, that innocent people would legitimately resist the intrusions of foreigners. It was inevitable, also, that their resistance would prompt responses that could not always be controlled. It followed from the chaotic nature of all violence that people would be killed in the course of voyages of discovery. Hawkesworth raised the question of whether those voyages could therefore be justified. His convoluted deliberations issued in the finding that, despite their particular evils, such voyages contributed to the greater good. His reasoning may or may not have convinced his readers (who were generally displeased with what was considered an immoral book), but the discussion focused attention, importantly, on the morality of encounter, which was contentious in the eighteenth century and has remained so, in changing terms, ever since.[6]

In the second half of the nineteenth century, as the populations of the Australian colonies grew, debates emerged concerning the distinctiveness of white Australasian culture and history. National landscapes

7.1 J. A. Gilfillan's *Captain Cook Taking Possession of the Australian Continent on Behalf of the British Crown AD 1770*, 1866

were painted, pioneers were romanticised, and suitable historical beginnings were identified and imaginatively refashioned. One of those who contributed to this effort was John Alexander Gilfillan, a successful painter of colonial views in New Zealand and Australia.[7] In 1866 he depicted *Captain Cook Taking Possession of the Australian Continent on Behalf of the British Crown, AD 1770*, the grand and formal scene set in Botany Bay (figure 7.1), where Cook is unlikely to have made any such formal declaration of possession. So far as can be established from the journals, he did no more than display the flag and leave a post bearing the names of the ships and the date of the visit, the purpose of which was to record 'new discovery' and tacitly rather than overtly to claim possession. Although he later staged a ceremony at Possession Island, off Cape York, when a toast was made and guns fired, even there the scene would have been nothing like this: Cook spent perhaps an hour ashore with no great number of people, and did not establish a camp of any sort. So far from being embarrassed by the dispossession implicit in Cook's declaration,

Gilfillan makes a point of it, positioning bestial and cowering Aboriginals amid dark shrubbery, manifestly horrified, as if they are fully aware that they and their savage way of life are to be permanently banished by the light of civilisation; the coloured servant at the centre of the image exhibits the subordination considered appropriate to native peoples in the future evolution of the empire.

This depiction is evidently an invention of the 1860s that had nothing to do with the 1770s' event, but it was a significant invention, because the image – which made an event out of a non-event – was widely reproduced over an extended period in the popular media, notably the *Illustrated Melbourne Post* (1865), the *Picturesque Atlas of Australasia* (1886), the *Sydney Mail* (1926), and went through a host of editions as a separately published print. A number of extant copies suggest that it was a popular scene among amateur painters; until at least the last quarter of the twentieth century it appeared intermittently on plates, jugs, biscuit tins, tea-towels, stamps and other objects. 'History', fabricated on this industrial scale, could only put the past itself out of business.

In 1901, with the federation of the Australian colonies, the Commonwealth of Australia came into being, and Emmanuel Phillips Fox, a painter of some stature at the time, produced a major historical work, *The Landing of Captain Cook at Botany Bay, 1770* (figure 7.2), which entered the collection of the National Gallery of Victoria. Unlike Gilfillan's utterly concocted scene, Fox appears to have made some study of both the location and the primary sources. He has Cook's boat landing, and the party being confronted, as they in fact were, by two Aboriginal men, defending the camp visible behind them. One marine kneels in the act of shooting at the indigenous men; two sailors are readying themselves to join him. At the centre of the painting, however, Cook's arm is outstretched in an authoritative gesture of restraint as he signals to his men to hold their fire, his intent regarding native people one of charity. The larger message, evidently, is that the colony's beginning was distinguished by this honourable imperial benevolence. This view of Cook's character was not new: in the eighteenth century the general perception was, as William Cowper put it, that 'the rights of man were sacred in [Cook's] view'.[8] Nor was this thesis entirely without justification: Cook was more concerned to avoid indigenous fatalities than most of his contemporaries and successors, but he was all too aware that 'the rights of man' were routinely transgressed when the locals resisted his intrusion. Fox borrowed the outstretched arm from Webber's imaginative painting of Cook's death, and one interpretation of that controversial event

7.2 Emmanuel Philips Fox's *Landing of Captain Cook at Botany Bay, 1770*

was that Cook had been momentarily distracted, trying (on that occasion, too) to get his men to cease firing when he should have been watching his own back. Yet Fox's incorporation of this noble propensity into the settler nation's moment of origin was both novel and entirely without justification. As any reader of Cook's journal will be aware, Cook made no such signal on the morning of Sunday, 29 April 1770: indeed, we have his own word for it that he fired the first shot and did most of the shooting that followed.

The violence of early contact was not universally effaced: a filmed re-enactment of the Poverty Bay landing, produced just a few years after Fox's painting, did represent the shooting of at least one Maori.[9] In general, however, the idealising and monumentalising pattern of Cook imagery in both Australia and New Zealand through most of the twentieth century was along the lines of Gilfillan's and Fox's representations. Over the same period, all the available texts of the voyage narratives were heavily abridged: accounts of violent incidents were abbreviated or slanted; and references to sexual contact, and the transmission of venereal disease to indigenous populations that Cook had tried, and failed, to prevent were edited out. The voyage of the *Endeavour* thus provided a dramatic and benevolent first chapter to the Australian national narrative. It was given great emphasis – for example, in primary-school history teaching – in part because the actual beginnings of the colony in the 1788 penal settlement were unavoidably brutal. New Zealand's national origins were more often located in the 1840 Treaty of Waitangi, though Cook's circumnavigation of the islands was often celebrated, and throughout the twentieth century, as in Australia, New Zealand's politicians, historians and others felt the need to regularly restate Cook's greatness. There were some dissenting voices, but only of a minority.

Over the last three decades of the twentieth century, indigenous issues and struggles became increasingly visible and were gradually acknowledged and responded to, in fits and starts, in the public sphere and through a range of official policies. In Australia, this process was barely in motion at the time of the bicentenary (1970) of Cook's visit, which despite some Aboriginal protest was celebrated essentially in the conventional manner. It was rather the bicentenary of white settlement in 1988 that occasioned a far more widespread reconsideration and debate around national history. Although Cook was occasionally, then and subsequently, the direct target of protest or satirical art, national historical preoccupations focused not on him but on the process of dispossession generally and with increasing particularity the 'stolen generations' debate.

Cook remained historically useful, however. His idealising response to north Queensland's Aboriginal people had come back into view via the 1955 edition of the explorer's *Endeavour* journal, prepared for publication by J. C. Beaglehole. The New Zealand historian drew attention to the passage I quoted earlier in his commentary, as well as in his subsequent biography of Cook. An admirer of the no-nonsense navigator, Beaglehole was dismayed that Cook should have lapsed into what he saw as Rousseau-like silliness, which could, however, be blamed on the influence of the philosophical and silly young Banks.[10] Ironically, though, Beaglehole's treatment of this blip in his hero's otherwise pragmatic intelligence prompted further discussion of the passage and made it available to others who were less inclined to dismiss it. The Aboriginal historian and curator James Miller gave the text a central place in the opening chapter of his 1985 account of indigenous resistance and survival, *Koori: A Will to Win*,[11] using the enduring national authority of Cook's name to authorise his own affirmative account of early Aboriginal society, while insisting on the possibility of a noble and respectful European response to indigenous society and culture. The history that Cook inaugurated was thus a history of betrayal and perversion: one that perhaps had begun positively but had lapsed immediately from worthy admiration to denigration and exploitation. A settler-colonial history was thus being challenged on its own ground: the pioneers who had opened up the outback were not the inheritors of Cook's indomitable spirit, but invaders who failed to preserve the integrity of his genuinely enlightened response to an indigenous population.

This was to attach a good deal of weight to a passage that was, if not entirely out of character, nevertheless highly singular within the range of Cook's reflections, and one moreover excluded from the published journals, that thus formed no part of the story and the findings of the voyage as they were received by the British and European publics from the late eighteenth century onwards. A more recent historian, in a prize-winning work on the *Endeavour* and the voyage, again makes much of that text in supporting the claim that the expedition sought 'knowledge not conquest' and that those who undertook it were 'men demonstrably inclined to compassion and fellow-feeling'. Ray Parkin draws attention to a 'rare empathy' manifest in Cook's reflections, and insists that 'this innocent beginning is not confused with subsequent events and exploitation, over a great deal of which hangs the tragic shadow of the Mark of Cain'.[12] It may be reasonable enough to argue that acts and projects need to be seen in their immediate contexts rather than judged on the basis of their medium-term ramifications, but the biblical burden that 230 or so words written by Cook could assume is arresting.

As Sydney prepared for the 2000 Olympics, this once-suppressed passage of Cook's journal would be further publicised and accorded literally monumental status. Among the many projects associated with the millenial games was the redevelopment of the airport. The most conspicuous public art commission in the new international terminals is a large work credited to the artist Fiona McDonald, known for her broadly postcolonial stance, for which Jo Holder, an art historian similarly concerned with feminist and postcolonial perspectives, did background research. The piece (figure 7.3) consists essentially of a range of silhouettes, wall-mounted, representing aspects of Aboriginal life, European voyaging, contact and subsequent history. This might be considered a hotch-potch, were the array of images not complemented by a line of elegant handwritten script across the bottom: 'They live in a Tranquillity which is not disturb'd by the Inequality of Condition – James Cook.'

What exactly those words and the work as a whole do for travellers in the departure lounge varies, needless to say, according to their

Fiona McDonald's wall-mounted sculpture, 2000, Qantas terminal, Kingsford-Smith International Airport, Sydney

predispositions, and indeed according to the extent to which they notice or reflect on the piece at all. Yet it would seem that at the very least it uses Cook to celebrate Aboriginal society, and conversely uses that respectful and appreciative construct of Aboriginal society to celebrate Cook. Cook is never just a dead man: he is an emblem of a moment in history and, for many people, still a national founder-figure. What is unavoidably celebrated, then, is not just Cook or Cook's response, but something of the nation that came after him. In this public, semi-official, situation the use of Cook's words is not the same as James Miller's. In a liberal epoch that struggles to come to terms with the violence of settler history, and in the millenial moment of the Olympic Games, the older, overtly triumphalist and colonialist understanding, which saw Australian history as an emanation and extension of Cook's adventurousness and humanity is not going to be restated, but neither is Miller's view which denounced and lamented the holocaust perpetrated by Cook's successors. If neither of these national narratives are offered, Cook remains present as a presiding spirit with an ambivalent legacy.

Cook figures in a similar way in what I regard as Australia's most impressive recent historical monument. In what is today Cooktown, in the far north of Queensland, there is a park along the southern bank of the Endeavour River, where the ship was beached for repair in 1770. This park features a host of older statues and monuments, but also a

7.4 The Milbi Wall, north Queensland, 2001

low and sinuous tiled wall that takes the form of the python whose body, in Guugu Yimidhirr myth, created the meanders of the shallow and shimmering waters of the river before one here (figure 7.4). The ceramics bear pictures and carry a script distilling local myth and oral history, and narrating the Guugu Yimidhirr experience since creation.

The story begins with creator beings – bats, water-rats and snakes – and with the qualities of pre-colonial life. The *Endeavour*'s arrival is said to have astonished locals, but 'Cook gained the confidence of the Aboriginal people without violence. Scientific recordings were made and the Gangurru was given the name Kangaroo.' Further contact was episodic and limited, until 'the next invasion, the gold rush' of the late nineteenth century, which 'was not so amicable. Greed left no room for respect': sacred places, food supplies, and water sources were overrun; and between them guns and new diseases killed whole groups of people and produced pervasive trauma among those who remained alive. Further images outline the arrival of missions, twentieth-century experiences and recent struggles for self-determination. In this narrative Cook's visit does not define what happens subsequently, either positively or negatively. His visit marks neither a beginning nor an ending but an anomaly, a respectful intrusion, an odd moment followed by more predictably violent and exploitative colonisation. The implication is that for Guugu Yimidhirr Cook is important, but *not* foundational; it is the creation that comes before him and the history that comes after him that have made and injured this group of people. Further, what matters now is not how we judge Cook, but the interplay of black and white footprints around the wall, and the partnership and reconciliation that they exemplify.

There is another contemporary perspective on Cook that exudes neither conventional reverence nor the guarded respect of those who notice and mobilise his respectful idealisation of indigenous life. On the Captain Cook Highway, on the way out of Cairns, the Endeavour Inn, a low-budget establishment, is marked by a monumental road-side statue of Cook, which has been repainted more recently than the hostel itself. The figure is arresting but is artistically without accomplishment. Cook looks like a deranged robot, playing the part of a traffic policeman: his hand is outstretched in some gesture that is certainly purposeful but pretty obscure, to passers-by and backpacking guests alike. The figure's designer, however, extracted this pose from Fox's 1902 *Landing of Captain Cook at Botany Bay, 1770*. In the painting, the gesture commands the marines and sailors to hold their fire, Fox liberally supplementing the events with a morality that was missing from the moment. The Cairns statue strips the whole story away, evoking a historical figure in the absence of historical meaning. I have no idea of the intentions of those who commissioned or produced this figure (which, despite its unofficial status, must possess the distinction of being the largest and one of the most visible Cook sculptures in Australia). Whatever they were, Cook becomes neither hero nor villain, but a kitsch concrete icon to drink beer beneath or to drive past en route to reef and rainforest.

One of the results of the last thirty years of Maori struggle has been the official redefinition of New Zealand as a bicultural nation. What exactly this means, what exactly its effects are, remain open and chronically controversial. But the general principle is that the nation must be understood as a partnership between two peoples, Maori and Pakeha, whose cultures are of equivalent worth, while the precedence of Maori is acknowledged. Several fine New Zealand historians have produced work that has both informed and reflected this understanding. Of particular relevance here is Anne Salmond's prize-winning study of early encounters, *Two Worlds*. Though built on prior anthropological and ethno-historical writings, this was the first major work organised around a rigorous and consistent attempt to accord equal attention to both parties. Both European and Maori worldviews were explicated ethnographically, and the cultural and practical rationales of each side's action in the context of contact explored. The book has been read widely and has done much to reinforce the bicultural under-standing of New Zealand history and shape perceptions, in particular, of Cook's visits.

Around Poverty Bay, there is a range of older statues of the usual sort and bearing the usual inscriptions. The text inscribed on the most recent statue, together with a bilingual plaque close to the actual meeting-site, however, emphasise the two-sided character of Cook's visit and expresses regret that Maori were killed. Their wording care-fully refrains from allocating blame, stressing that the shooting resulted from misunderstanding rather than malevolence: Cook's men, it is claimed, thought that Maori were about to attack, confusing an aggres-sive performance with hostile intent, and so opened fire. At best, this reflects a speculative interpretation of *one* out of some 5–6 deaths that took place here. The source of the account is probably Anne Salmond's suggestion that the man who rushed at and threw a spear into the yawl, soon after the first landing at Turanganui, was making a formal challenge rather than actually attacking the boat.[13] This is probably sound, even if the distinction between aggressive ritual and ritualised aggression is a fuzzy one; but the mariners might well have fired even if they realised that they faced the former rather than the latter; and this suggestion has no bearing on the subsequent shootings at the river mouth or of the people in the canoe. The cultural differences between Europeans and Maori – profound though they may have been – did not prevent those on either side from understanding intrusions, threats and aggressive gestures for what they were. There was no point at which either Cook or his men mistook a war-dance for an actual attack; nor were these performances what prompted them to open fire.

There is no getting away from the fact that the violence occurred because of a straightforward collision of wills: Cook would land, and Maori would resist him; Maori would snatch at the Europeans' weapons which they wanted and mariners would shoot to stop them being taken. Cook was committed to seizing Maori, and Maori would fight to the last to escape seizure. This was the inherently immoral conflict of interest that troubled and perplexed Hawkesworth. Its contradictory quality now seems to be suppressed in the public packaging of history, because the bicultural understanding of the nation wants to see the rupture between white settlers and native people as resolvable – and as prospectively resolved. The bilingual plaque just referred to advises the viewer that both sides 'began to learn about each other, exchanged gifts, and mourned the deaths which had occurred'. (In fact, no real exchanges of gifts took place between Europeans and Maori during that encounter.) It is easier to digest the notion that a moment of violence at the beginning of the nation's European history was an unfortunate accident, importantly succeeded by mutual regret and reciprocity, than it is to acknowledge that the killings may equally be seen to prefigure contradictions of interest around possession and sovereignty – contradictions that would in time result in many more deaths and which remain somewhat intractable today.

If the machinery of public history has done some violence to the events of 1769, it has also, quite unexpectedly, effaced their hero. On the edge of the hill above the site of conflict, there is now a paved area called Cook's Plaza: here is a lookout presided over by a statue, an old plaque, a tree planted by Princess Diana that now serves as a memorial to her, some graffiti and a stunning view across the moody waters of Poverty Bay. The statue was cast from a marble piece in the collection of a New Zealand businessman who formerly owned the Captain Cook Brewery in Auckland. This circumstance led to the assumption that the statue represented Cook, and to it being replicated in bronze and placed here for the bicentenary in 1969. But a recent sign produced by the local historical committee acknowledges with refreshing frankness that the uniform and facial features are entirely wrong. 'Who is he?' it asks. 'We have no idea.' A coil of rope suggests that a naval officer is represented, but otherwise the identity of the subject is anyone's guess. This usefully reminds us of a point that is obvious, yet is perhaps easily overlooked: the histories made memorable at sites such as Poverty Bay are real and have enduring ramifications in the injurious inequities and intractable conflicts of

[153]

the present. But their making-memorable involves not just the politicised process of representation that has become almost banal, so
abundant has been its academic deconstruction: making-memorable
involves also mistakes, humour and absurdity – elements that prejudice the very keeping of national memory.

At Poverty Bay, the history of what was the settler nation, and is
now the bicultural polity, is threatened in a different way. The shores
of the river entrance that provided the site of the momentous and
tragically violent meeting of 1769 are essentially obliterated, buried
beneath a huge wood-chipping plant. Here trees from massive pine
plantations are processed for export to Japan. A sort of enclave by the
entrance to this factory and dock incorporates a botanical garden, the
largest of the earlier colonial monuments and the new bilingual plaque
I quoted from earlier. If you are inclined to reflect on the past or to
mourn those who died, you'd better come here out of working hours:
you might otherwise be distracted by the whining sawmills, the
forklifts, the conveyers and the big lumber trucks, relentlessly changing gears and groaning on and off the highway. No doubt the town of
Gisborne needs the jobs.

Notes

My thanks to Annie Coombes for much discussion of the subjects covered in this
chapter, and also for her comments on a draft.

1 For a useful though no longer up to date review of the Cook cult in Australia,
see J. Robertson, *The Captain Cook Myth* (Sydney: Angus & Robertson, 1981);
for more general and more current information see www.captaincooksociety.com.
The official edition referred to in the text is J. Hawkesworth, *An Account of the
Voyages Undertaken by the Order of His Present Majesty for Making Discoveries
in the Southern Hemisphere* (London: Strahan & Cadell, 1773); citations below are
from the Dublin edition, printed for A. Leathley *et al.* (1773). For controversies
around Hawkesworth, see J. Lamb, V. Smith and N. Thomas (eds), *Exploration and
Exchange: A South Seas Anthology 1680–1900* (Chicago, IL: University of Chicago
Press, 2000), pp. 73–91.
2 J. Banks, *The Endeavour Journal of Joseph Banks*, ed. J. C. Beaglehole (Sydney:
Angus & Robertson, 1963), vol. 2, p. 54.
3 For fuller discussion, see N. Thomas, *Discoveries: The Voyages of Captain Cook*
(London: Penguin, 2003), pp. 111–30.
4 J. Cook, *The Journals of Captain James Cook*, ed. J. C. Beaglehole (Cambridge:
Hakluyt Society, 1955–67), vol. 1, p. 399; for fuller discussion, see G. Williams,
'Reactions on Cook's Voyage', in I. Donaldson and T. Donaldson (eds), *Seeing
the First Australians* (Sydney: Allen & Unwin, 1985), and Thomas, *Discoveries*,
pp. 128–30.
5 Banks, *Endeavour Journal*, vol. 1, p. 403; for the most extensive recent discussion,
see A. Salmond, *Two Worlds: First Meetings between Maori and Europeans* (Auckland: Viking, 1991), pp. 119–38.
6 Hawkesworth, *An Account*, vol. 1, pp. xix–xxii; and vol. 2, p. 321.
7 Although *Captain Cook Taking Possession of the Australian Continent* is now
Gilfillan's best-known painting – ironically only through reproduction, since the
original has been missing from the Royal Society of Victoria for more than fifty

years – the bulk of his work dealt with Maori genre scenes and views; for fuller discussion see: Leonard Bell, *Colonial Constructs: European Images of Maori 1840–1914* (Auckland: Auckland University Press, 1992), pp. 53–74; and the Gilfillan entry in J. Kerr (ed.), *The Dictionary of Australian Artists* (Melbourne: Oxford University Press, 1993).

8   *Charity*, from *The Poems of William Cowper*, ed. J. D. Baird and C. Ryskamp (Oxford: Oxford University Press, 1980), pp. 337ff.; the poem also appears in most other editions of Cowper's poetry.
9   The film itself has not survived; for the photographs and an account quoted from the *Gisborne Times*, see J. Berry and S. Robinson (eds), *Gisborne Exposed: The Photographs of William Crawford, 1874–1913* (Gisborne: Te Rau Press, 1990), pp. 132–3.
10   J. C. Beaglehole, *The Life of Captain James Cook* (London: Black, 1974), pp. 251–2.
11   J. Miller, *Koori: A Will to Win* (Sydney: Angus & Robertson, 1985), pp. 20–2.
12   R. Parkin, *H. M. Bark Endeavour* (Melbourne: Melbourne University Press, 1997), pp. x–xi.
13   Salmond, *Two Worlds*, p. 125.

CHAPTER EIGHT

Selective memory: the *British Empire Exhibition* and national histories of art

Christine Boyanoski

The *British Empire Exhibition* of 1924, held at Wembley in north London, offered the settler societies – the 'new Britains' – an opportunity to demonstrate that they had achieved a level of cultural maturity in the arts, and independence from the mother country reflective of recent developments in imperial–colonial relations. While it was not the first occasion on which representative art of the Dominions[1] was displayed in the imperial metropole, Wembley was significant for the fact that it was here, under one roof, that the art of all the Dominions was shown together alongside British art for the first time. This allowed British critics, the educated public and the participants themselves to make comparisons and evaluate how far these new societies had progressed along the road of cultural development, moving away from what critics had observed to be 'sheer materialism' of the art produced in the early years of settlement, and towards becoming *true* civilisations. Among the participating nations – Australia, Canada, India, New Zealand and South Africa – Canada alone was considered to have achieved this level of maturity because it had established a *national* school of art. The Wembley exhibition has figured as an important moment in national art history only in Canada.[2]

In this chapter I explore why that moment was identified by Canada as memorable, and as such written into the annals of national cultural history, whereas it was consigned to insignificance and erased from the collective memory by the other Dominions. I argue that where a nation was most successful in displaying a *national* school, the selection of art works for exhibition at Wembley suppressed the true heterogeneous nature of the nation, its history and people in order to create a collective national identity that countered the unifying drive of the imperial machinery. This reflected the larger task faced by the settler societies, which in their efforts to construct independent national identities while still belonging to the Empire – albeit one then referred to as a 'Commonwealth of Nations' – ironically engaged in practices every bit as homogenising as those of the advocates of imperial unity, and took liberties with national history and memory. What has also been suppressed in the name of cultural nationalism is the fact that in order for an art work to qualify as the product of an independent nation, it had to be made and evaluated within the terms of the imperial discourse, which meant that it was still bound by imperial ties.

The *British Empire Exhibition* was essentially a large trade fair, intended by its organisers to rekindle interest in the declining Empire and to encourage support for government initiatives that promoted closer imperial ties. Facing unemployment, economic problems and decimated European markets for its exports at the close of the First World War, the British Government soon realised that a solution lay in a re-orientation of its commercial policy to ensure that its Empire was economically self-sufficient. As one commentator put it, 'the obvious direction seems to be the cultivation of our own inheritance ... Britons in all parts of the world are bound together by ties of sentiment and custom which neither distance or difference of conditions can seriously weaken.'[3] The interwar years thus witnessed numerous efforts to strengthen trade ties between members of the British Commonwealth and to enhance markets abroad for British goods by populating the Dominions with British settlers. The Empire Settlement Act of 1922 sought to redistribute the white population of the Empire by moving Britons from crowded metropolitan areas to regions of 'room and opportunity', thereby opening up natural resources and creating new markets under British control.[4] This explains the renewed interest in the Dominions at the time.

Wembley was therefore a means of driving home the importance to Great Britain of the former colonies. According to the *Official Guide*, the purpose of the *Exhibition* was 'to stimulate trade, strengthen the bonds that bind the Mother Country to her Sister States and Daughter Nations, to bring all in closer touch the one with the other ... to meet on common ground and to know each other ...',[5] playing on Britannic nationalism which was based on imperial sentiment and blood ties, and which still prevailed throughout much of the Empire. Aware that their attempts to reinforce imperial ties came at a time both of rising Dominion nationalism and of widespread indifference to imperial matters within Britain itself, Wembley's organisers drew on racial theories held over from the previous century (in which there was a revived interest in the 1920s) to underscore the theme of imperial unity. They claimed that the constituent members of the Empire were essentially all of the same race, explaining differences between

them as the result of the modifying influence of the diverse environmental conditions to which the Anglo-Saxon diaspora was subjected.

In addition to racial unity, continuity of tradition was used to
reinforce imperial ties. This was reflected in the design of the main
exhibition buildings, whose modern ferro-concrete construction was
concealed by a classical veneer. Nowhere was emphasis on these
themes more evident than in the Palace of Arts, wherein the art of
the Dominions and Great Britain was shown together for the first
time. It was the preference of all the major participants to exhibit
their art in a purpose-built gallery rather than in the separate national
pavilions, not only for the practicalities of lighting and fire-proofing,
but because they welcomed the opportunity for comparison. In the
Introduction to the catalogue, Lawrence Weaver, director of the British exhibits at Wembley, remarked that the significance of the Palace
of Arts was that it made possible the assembling under one roof of
examples of the art of the whole Empire, in order to mark the relation
of United Kingdom paintings to those in the overseas galleries, and to
represent the widely divergent impulses which influenced the art of
the Dominions.[6] The *Official Guide* described the collection as demonstrating the development of British art in which 'the masterpieces
of Hogarth and his contemporaries lead up to the ultra-modernists
and the characteristic work of the Canadians and Australians'.[7]
Dominion art was clearly seen as continuing the British tradition,
and the organisers went to great lengths to include the 'Retrospective'
section in order to demonstrate 'how the Daughter nations have
developed their art from the English school',[8] or, as one journalist put
it, 'to show our kinsmen Overseas the aesthetic forbears of their own
growing schools of art'.[9]

It was in response to this unifying agenda of the imperial hosts that
the 'competitive nationalisms'[10] of the participants had to be negotiated. British critics clearly wanted to see the difference that location
made to their stock, particularly in the fine arts, and evidence of
independent national schools would be taken as signifying the possibility of regeneration and robust continuity of the race in new lands,
thus alleviating the fear of decline or even of extinction that had been
exacerbated by the First World War. Aston Webb, president of the
Royal Academy of Arts (RA) and chairman of the Arts Council which
oversaw the Palace of Arts, made this clear in his speech at the Annual
Academy Banquet in May 1924, expressing his desire that all the
countries of the Empire would develop their own art, suited to their
climates and ways of living.[11] While the Dominions were expected
to display those characteristics that distinguished them within the
imperial family, they had also to appeal to prospective settlers; and

since the whole process of national representation was overseen by Dominion officials, anything perceived to be damaging to the national image, however distinctive, was bound to be suppressed.[12]

The Dominions, for their part, had been working towards establishing national schools of art since the late nineteenth century; by 1916, however, none of them was able to claim such an institution for its country. When they were invited by Charles Holme, the editor of *Studio*, to contribute to a special issue on the current state of landscape painting in their respective countries, the South African Edward Roworth flatly denied that a national school of art existed in his country, although both Eric Brown of Canada and James Ashton of Australia were more optimistic, predicting that the birth of a national school was imminent in the work of their younger landscape painters. It was evident that the 'Art of the British Empire Overseas' – the title given to this special issue of *Studio* – was inextricably linked to *landscape* painting, for, while Holme's request had been specific, their contributions were published under the more general title in March 1917.

The identification of national schools of art with landscape painting in the Dominions at this time (a late development following nineteenth-century European precedents) coincided with two other trends. First, fresh attention was being focused on pastoral landscape painting as the embodiment of the British national character in art, for it was thought that 'the characteristic British love of nature' would prevent this genre of art from falling under undue foreign (French) influence. Second, the British Empire itself was in a state of evolution. Discussions around this time concerning a new relationship between Britain and the Dominions had been precipitated by increased pressure from Canada and South Africa for greater political independence and by the growing national pride in all the Dominions, a result of their wartime contributions.[13] The constitution of the Empire had been on the agenda of the 1917 Imperial War Conference, but it was decided to defer discussions until after the war, the matter being seen as too important and intricate to deal with at that time. The war therefore interrupted both the evolving imperial–dominion relations and the development of national art, both of which would again receive attention following the cessation of hostilities and throughout the 1920s. Increased political freedom was granted to the Dominions through the 1931 Statute of Westminster, the outcome of the 1926 Balfour Report on Inter-Imperial relations. As for Dominion art, British critics at last discovered a national school among the collections assembled at Wembley in 1924. The *British Empire Exhibition*, first proposed in 1913, but itself postponed, was the first opportunity after the First World War for the

Dominions to demonstrate how far they had progressed in their national development.

The fine arts at Wembley

The fine arts had long been associated with trade fairs, serving to bolster competing nationalisms through cultural differentiation and elevating the whole enterprise above the strictly commercial by injecting it with an element of high culture. The RA, vigilant in its role as defender of British culture, assumed a leading role in initial discussions concerning art at Wembley. The Academy Council was of the opinion that, for the sake of art in Britain, the fullest possible use should be made of the opportunities provided by the *British Empire Exhibition*, the aim of which 'should be higher than that of a trade exhibition'.[14] The advisory arts council for Wembley, comprising 116 members, was chaired by the president of the RA and included not only academicians and associates, but members from a broad range of metropolitan art associations representing a diversity of artistic practice. The aim was to be as democratic as possible, so that it was necessary for Lawrence Weaver, director of British exhibits, to dispel rumours that the RA would be the sole adjudicator of the art section. For some, however, the RA continued to represent the very height of artistic achievement. For example, the Sydney Society of Artists, organisers of an exhibition of Australian art held in London six months prior to the opening of the Wembley exhibition had chosen Burlington House, home of the RA, as their preferred venue; they considered that the *Empire Exhibition* would not be of the same value artistically to Australia because it was for trade, not art, and would not attract the same public that would be drawn to Burlington House. Sydney Ure Smith, president of the Sydney Society and promoter of Australian art, predicted that the official mechanisms involved in an official exhibition would have to include all the national art societies and would not result in a selection 'to a high enough standard required in London'. The point of the exhibition, after all, was to 'convince the English people of the highest standards of Australian Art'.[15]

The gallery, or Palace of Arts, nestled alongside the Palace of Industry, reflecting the close relationship that was being forged between art and industry in Britain at that time.[16] As we have seen, it had been decided to construct a separate building to house the art of all the nations in 1922, but promises made to the Dominions concerning space allocations were broken when the building was scaled down during the planning stages, prompting Canada and South Africa to threaten to pull out. In its final form, the gallery was dominated by

Britain, with art from Canada, Australia, India and Burma, South Africa and New Zealand tightly packed into the eastern galleries, occupying only one-fifth of the entire space.[17] The Dominions had little, if any, input to this arrangement, their space allocations depending on their monetary contribution to the *British Empire Exhibition* as a whole.[18] This severely restricted the extent to which each country could represent its artistic activity, and naturally had a direct bearing on the selection process. Although Canada had been given the lion's share of the space (250 running feet compared with Australia's 150), Eric Brown, director of the National Gallery of Canada (NGC), who strategically engineered Canada's display, made a special visit to London in September 1923 in order to rectify the 'broken promises and unfair treatment of the Overseas Dominions regarding their art exhibits' and to voice Canada's objection to the layout of the galleries. In the end, Canada gained additional hanging space by blocking off the doorways that led to the adjoining Australian gallery, a fact not recorded in the illustrated floor-plan. This last-minute alteration upset the Australian contingent, who felt that they had been blocked into a corner so that their works were even less accessible than before. South Africa gained space when it increased its overall contribution and the adjacent space became available, but New Zealand had to drastically alter its selection process due to the inadequacy of its designated space.

Their lesser importance relative to Britain's being reflected in the poetics of space, the Dominions could not hope to be nearly as comprehensive in what they showed, although they claimed to represent *nation-wide* activity, as stipulated by the organisers.[19] The responsibility for organising the national art sections fell to the Dominions themselves, each of which formed an *ad hoc* art committee as a branch of its central committee and reported to the department of the Dominion government responsible for organising national exhibitions abroad.[20] In this way, central control could be exercised over all aspects of each national presentation, including the fine arts. One reason for the exclusion of expatriate artists from the Australian, New Zealand and South African sections was the logistical complexity of adding work sight-unseen after the final selection had been made at home; but, more importantly, it would have meant the loss of official control over the final presentation. In Canada, where the selection committee enjoyed relative freedom from this level of interference, expatriate status was not an issue.

Neither New Zealand nor South Africa had a centralised body to oversee artistic activity on a national scale. Although the New Zealand Academy of Fine Arts (NZAFA) in Wellington and the South African Society of Artists (SASA) based in Cape Town had been established in the previous century to advance the arts nation-wide, both of them having a national membership, neither society could be said to exert a unifying force; indeed, on occasion, they could act in a divisive manner.[21] While initially consulted by government representatives about the *British Empire Exhibition*, they worked in partnership with the other art societies, and were not given sole responsibility over the selection process. For example, in South Africa, the central art committee, presided over by Edward Roworth – an establishment figure and member of the SASA council – consisted of one representative from each of the four regions: Western Province (Cape); the Eastern Province; Natal; and the Transvaal and Orange Free State. Because there was no representative group in the Orange Free State, a corporate body was formed solely for the occasion. In New Zealand, a similar plan was devised, the central committee being constituted by 12 delegates, 3 from each of the 4 art societies in the major centres – Wellington, Christchurch, Auckland and Dunedin. In both cases, the regional bodies would make preliminary selections which would be sent to a *central* location – Cape Town and Wellington – at which a committee consisting of representatives from all the societies would make the final selection. New Zealand went to great pains to ensure that each region/society was proportionally represented,[22] but the South African committee resolved that the final exhibit would be a purely Union one, with no allocations of space accorded to any one particular section, province or exhibitor.[23] This reflected South Africa's larger aim at Wembley, which was to demonstrate that stability and true political unity between the British and the Boer State had been secured by the relatively recent Act of Union (1910), this being a vital condition if South Africa were to attract settlers and new investors.

Australia's selection process was also intended to be as broadly representative as possible. The selection of art works for Wembley was drawn into the complex structure of committees and sub-committees that made up the large central commission for Australia, and reflected continuing state rivalries (Federation had taken place only in 1901). The central art committee was formed by the central commission, the names of its members having been supplied by the state commissions, which in turn had consulted their main art societies; it consisted of representatives from Victoria, New South Wales, Western Australia, South Australia, Queensland and Tasmania. The final selection would be made by the central committee in Melbourne, excluding an important 'core' group of paintings chosen from the 1923 *Exhibition of Australian Art* at Burlington House, mentioned earlier, so that the Wembley exhibition would be 'as representative as possible of the finest works of Australian artists'.[24] The inclusion of which was non-negotiable. That core represented one-third of the Australian section. So, in spite of the elaborate measures taken to ensure fair representation of all national art societies, the Australian section at Wembley ended up resembling the Burlington House exhibition in which Sydney and Melbourne had dominated, and which presented a very specific view of Australian art – one that reflected the past more than it did the present. Indeed, some of the works selected from the Burlington House show dated back to the 1880s and 1890s, an earlier moment of national significance in the years leading up to federation.

Of the Dominions it was Canada that had the strongest central authority in charge of its art section. The trustees of the NGC – an agency of federal government – were empowered to make the selection. This had been the advice of a British official acting on information provided early on by Eric Brown, although it was inevitable that this action would bring the gallery into conflict with the Royal Canadian Academy (RCA) which had traditionally been responsible for Canada's artistic representation abroad. This untraditional and controversial move enabled Canada to project a strong collective visual identity, one that was highly selective, without having to consult all of the numerous art societies scattered widely across the country, though concentrated in Ontario and Québec.[25] Brown had many reasons for wanting to prevent the RCA from taking charge of Canada's exhibits: he was at the time engaged in a struggle with the RCA for control over the recently re-opened (1921) NGC; more importantly, he wanted wider exposure and recognition for a younger group of artists whose work he was championing through acquisitions for the national collection, in the face of opposition from academic quarters, which was considered to constitute a *national* school. The works of these younger artists would be the focus of the Canadian section, which would not have been the case had the RCA been at the helm.

I have indicated how space restrictions imposed by the British organisers and the selection mechanisms put in place by the Dominions themselves affected their artistic representation at Wembley. It is important also to consider the official guidelines and the extent to which they were followed by Dominion participants, because they demonstrate the dialogic relationship characteristic of inter-imperial relations, which varied according to their historical connection within the British Empire. The guidelines were quite loose, suggesting that 'old pictures and modern pictures of historical events in the development of the Empire', notable more for their subject matter than for their inherent aesthetic merit, be shown in the various overseas pavilions rather than in the Palace of Arts; and advising each Dominion selection committee to choose paintings, sculptures, engravings and drawings by modern and preferably living artists.[26] It is evident from this that the British were interested primarily in seeing current aesthetic developments in the Dominions, as mentioned earlier. It was the Dominion art committees that imposed additional conditions to further narrow the range of acceptable work.

For example, the South African committee, determined that its exhibition be 'a distinctively South African one', stipulated that the works be as far as possible confined to scenery and other subjects that were typically South African. The governor-general himself had suggested examples, including 'some very fine native types peculiar to this continent', old Dutch homesteads whose architecture was unique in the world, and the Rand goldfields which supplied 'an industrial landscape of surpassing grandeur'.[27] Similarly, in New Zealand, the central art committee resolved that 'as far as possible, works of typical New Zealand subjects by living New Zealand Artists should be selected',[28] a resolution reinforced both by the chair of the committee in his correspondence with individual artists[29] and by a staunchly imperialist group based in Christchurch calling itself the Society for Imperial Culture. As for Australia, one of the conditions for entry was that the works were *produced in Australia* by Australian artists. South Australia went even further, advising that the subjects be specifically South Australian. This naturally met with protestations from expatriate artists, living in London and Paris, who consequently organised their own exhibition at the Faculty of Arts in June 1924 so as to coincide with Wembley and to demonstrate that Australian art was not simply the art produced in Australia. Australian artists, they argued, were 'Australians by upbringing' but, 'by right of spiritual inheritance, Europeans too'.[30] The importance the Australian committee placed on the domicile of the artist and origin of the work, ensured that the concept of 'nation' would be expressed through an emphasis on those features that were unique to the local environment and set them apart from Britain and the other Dominions, and that landscape painting would dominate. Perhaps with a clear agenda in mind, Canada imposed no such limitations with regard to subject matter. In order to participate, artists had only to be considered 'Canadian'; that is, 'born in Canada or a Canadian citizen or resident in Canada for not less than three years'.[31]

Focusing on those features that most distinguished them within the imperial family, or identifying a *typical* landscape, meant engaging in a process of selection that could not possibly represent the entire nation, since conditions varied widely across these vast territories, and demonstrates how, for the settler societies, the imperial context was part of identity formation. In the larger context of the *Exhibition*, each positioned itself in relation to Britain: New Zealand as 'Great Britain of the Pacific', claiming to have escaped the worst difficulties that beset the mother country and some of the older Dominions; South Africa as the 'Riviera of the Empire'; Canada, 'the New Homeland'; and Australia as 'John Bull's Vineyard' or 'the Land of Sunshine and Opportunity'.[32] Anne-Marie Willis, writing about Australian art, has pointed out how the intense light and the implied heat depicted in Heidelberg School pictures, like those of Arthur Streeton, which were recognised as being distinctively Australian, were in fact *not* unique to Australia, and signified Australia only when put in a binary relation to the less intense English or North European light.[33] And although there were heated debates in the Canadian legislature about the advisability of sending winter landscapes abroad, these indeed became the typical view, being representative of the country's most distinctive, albeit inhospitable, season.[34]

New Zealand perhaps had the greatest difficulty in presenting the distinctiveness of its geographical features: not only was its selection process designed to represent regional differences, but its climate was considered to most closely resemble that of Britain. The atmospheric effects in which most of the views were rendered reflected an outdated aesthetic – an observation made by British critics. Variety of scene was also the keynote of the South African section, which seemed to respond to the governor-general's suggestions, referred to earlier, although impressionistic paintings of Cape Province and the Transvaal dominated, reflecting the concerns of many of the English-trained artists and members of SASA. Not only the native landscape, but the indigenous peoples – Maori and Bushman, rendered in both two- and three-dimensional form – stood to represent these nations, because current domestic debates allowed for their inclusion in the construction of a national cultural identity, which was not the case for the two larger Dominions.

Canada and Australia were rivals for predominance among the Dominions exhibiting at Wembley, particularly in the fine arts. As noted earlier, Australia took a retrospective approach in including works of the Heidelberg School that had become icons by the 1920s, namely: Streeton's *Purple Noon's Transparent Might* (1898) and Tom Roberts's *The Golden Fleece* (1894). These pictures, and those of their successors Hans Heysen and Elioth Gruner (the latter's 1921 *Valley of the Tweed* was also shown at Wembley), served to link the 1890s' struggle for national identity in the lead-up to federation with Australia's desire for recognition of its national individuality and achievement in the years immediately following the First World War. The collection of Australian art at Wembley testifies to what Bernard Smith and Ian Burn have referred as a 'nostalgic desire to return to the past glories of the Heidelberg School'[35] and the start of a 'selective revaluing of the Heidelberg School'[36] during that period. This meant that the eastern states dominated (artists had gathered in camps around Sydney and Melbourne, which provided their subject matter), represented by pictures that typically depicted a pastoral utopia, rendered in an impressionistic style, in a high key and full sunlight. It is not surprising that British critics found the Australian collection 'twenty years out of date', demonstrating a 'liquidation of the English character',[37] and 'lacking distinction in form'.[38] Selectivity went further in the suppression of any suggestion of drought and in the complete omission of Aboriginals, as noted above, even though they had been included in earlier exhibitions (the *Colonial and Indian*, in 1886, for example) and their portraits, notably by Tom Roberts in the early 1890s,[39] were in the public domain. Those aspects of Australian life were seen as detrimental to the country's efforts to attract British immigrants.

The Canadian collection, too, was tightly focused. The spotlight was trained on a group of younger painters who called themselves the 'Group of Seven' and other affiliated non-academic artists, whose works were hung in the larger space. Their paintings can be described as boldly decorative landscapes, devoid of human content, depicting *wilderness* scenes located to the north of the largest urban centres, Toronto, Ottawa and Montreal, many in winter. In the Foreword to the Canadian special catalogue, seemingly intended to prime the British press, Eric Brown now promised that Canada would be shown to possess 'an indigenous and vigorous school of painting and sculpture, moulded by the tremendously intense character of her country and colour of her seasons'.[40] This movement came to stand for the entire country, even though it was representative of specific regional concerns, as noted by contemporary francophone critics in Montreal who had no stake in the imperial debate and for whom the Group of Seven was simply the 'Toronto school', and not a 'national' school at all.[41]

It was not that more traditional work went unrepresented; this was shown in the smaller of the two spaces allocated, prompting one critic to comment that here was evidence that Dominion art typically passed very quickly through all phases of development, when in truth it reflected merely the concurrence of artistic styles.[42] Rather, it was quietly ignored – as indicated both by its positioning in a lesser space and by the silence of the organisers who were busy promoting the work of the younger artists – and was considerably pared back or eliminated in subsequent versions of the show.[43] At Wembley, it had served to appease those who wanted a broad representation, filling out the show numerically and providing a foil against which the newer work shone.

Because landscape painting, particularly that devoid of human content, had become *the* lingua franca of imperial art[44] – the signifier of dominion independence – figural work was also thrust into the background. Scattered among the landscapes were paintings and sculptures representing a broad range of the Canadian populus, including eminent persons (Fred Varley's portrait *Vincent Massey, Esq.*), immigrants (Regina Seiden's *Old Woman*, also known as *Old Immigrant Woman*, and Stanley Turner's *Immigrants*), fishermen, munitions workers, French Canadian 'types', and native peoples in historicised depictions (Emanuel Hahn's *The Indian Scout*), to name a few.[45] British critics looking for signs of cultural independence in these new lands paid little attention to the figural work, believing them to be present in landscape painting. This knowledge, shared by Dominion organisers and metropolitan critics alike, prompted certain decisions to be made and aroused specific reactions. The figures, while not actually inhabiting the pictorial space of the landscapes, are nonetheless conceptually connected to those places, which, in the absence of human/ narrative content, take on a timeless quality. If the Australians sought to conjure up the past, the Canadians suppressed it, intent on revealing eternal truths about the land itself. Executed in a style that the critics could consider *modern*, that is, one in which the emphasis on form did not compromise Britannic national character, the Canadian work was proclaimed to constitute a national school – an expression of national individuality.

Had the Canadian collection failed to impress British critics at Wembley in 1924, it is unlikely that this moment would have been marked as significant in the national history of Canadian art. It has certainly not figured as such in Australia, New Zealand and South Africa. The work of the Group of Seven had been promoted as constituting a national school in North America prior to 1924, but recognition of its independence by the mother culture at the *British Empire Exhibition* was essential to establish the claim and, what is more, to guarantee its acceptance by domestic audiences. Wembley's significance was first signalled in F. B. Housser's mythologising account entitled *A Canadian Art Movement: The Story of the Group of Seven*, published in 1926; by 1933 it had been marked as 'a red-letter day in the history of Canada's status among the nations of the world'.[46]

Looking again at the *British Empire Exhibition* is instructive for two reasons. While the exclusionary tactics employed in the name of national representation at Wembley may be considered legitimate in the context of the time, justified by the need to create a collective identity and driven by dominion nationalism, the perpetuation of these myths into the present, with the attendant neglect of other traditions, is no longer an appropriate model, and is in need of serious revision. It demonstrates also a characteristic typical of the settler societies: that the struggle for national cultural identity in the visual arts took place within the bounds of imperial discourse, and that these nations could hold a position of independence while still being part of a transforming Empire.

Notes

1 'Dominion' is the technical term for the self-governing colonies.
2 This must be qualified as English-speaking Canada. The 'national school' was considered by French Canada to be a regional phenomenon centred on Ontario; this is explored later in the chapter.
3 E. Geddes, GCB, 'General Introduction', in S. J. Duly (ed.), *A Businessman's Survey of the Empire's Resources prepared by the Federation of British Industries*, Resources of Empire Series (London: Ernest Benn, 1924), p. 10.
4 *Guide to the Pavilion of His Majesty's Government, British Empire Exhibition 1924* (London: Fleetway Press, 1924), p. 51.
5 G. C. Lawrence (ed.), *British Empire Exhibition 1924 Official Guide* (London: Fleetway Press, 1924).
6 L. Weaver, 'Introduction', *Illustrated Souvenir of the Palace of Arts: British Empire Exhibition 1924* (London: Fleetway Press, 1924), p. 10.
7 *British Empire Exhibition 1924 Official Guide*, p. 62.
8 L. Weaver, 'Introduction', *Catalogue of Palace of Arts British Empire Exhibition (1924)* (London: Fleetway Press, 1924), p. 8.
9 'Art of the Empire', *Morning Post*, 31 December 1923.
10 A term used in J. E. Findling and K. O. Pelle, *Historical Dictionary of World's Fairs* (New York: Greenwood Press, 1990), p. 29.
11 'The Academy Banquet', *The Times*, 5 May 1924.
12 Australia suppressed any signs of drought and its Aboriginal peoples; Canada was less censorious; and while snow was not considered a drawing card, its purpose in signalling its northernness was not disputed.
13 A number of articles appeared in *The Times* in 1916 which speculated on a 'new way of Empire', including 'A New Way of Empire: The Part of the Dominions: Task of a British Convention' (4 May); 'The Vision of the Commonwealth' (24 May); and 'A New Way of Empire: The Part of the Dominions: Constitutional Reform' (24 May).
14 Royal Academy of Arts (RA) Archives, Memorandum on the British Empire Exhibition, 1924, February 1922, 3 pp.
15 S. U. Smith, 'Australian Art for London/The Proposed Exhibition', *Forum*, 14 (February 1923), 21.
16 Two of the executive members of the British Institute of Industrial Art were seconded to sit on the art section of the board of the exhibition and were charged with administering the Palace of Arts.
17 I do not discuss the Indian section here – India held a distinct place within the Empire – except to say that the art section was chosen by the British heads of the major art schools in the three principal 'modern centres' – Bengal, Bombay and the Punjab.
18 Contributions to the national pavilions were as follows: Canada and Australia – £200,000, entitling them to 150,000 sq. ft each; India – £167,000, allowing 100,000

sq. ft; New Zealand – £60,000 and 45,000 sq. ft; and South Africa – £50,000 and 25,000 sq. ft.

19   The British wanted an assurance from the Dominions that where a central body representing all of a nation's artists was lacking, a selection committee would be set up to ensure that no single group or region was favoured: see State Library of Victoria, La Trobe Australian Manuscripts Collection, MacGeorge Papers, MS 8236, Letter from E. A. Belcher, Assistant General Manager of the British Empire Exhibition, to Norman MacGeorge, 7 July 1922. Belcher seems to have offered advice to the Dominions on how to go about setting up their committees, since they appear to have followed a similar formula.

20   Most of these were attached to Ministries of Trade, Industry and Commerce, though Canada was the exception: its Government Exhibition Commission was a branch of Immigration and Colonisation until 1927 when it was transferred to Trade and Commerce.

21   A case in point occurred when Leo Francois, president of the Natal Society of Artists proposed setting up a unifying body called the South African Academy. The proposal met with strong opposition from SASA, fearful that its role would be usurped by a new national union of artists dominated by Natal.

22   In fact, space was allocated on the basis of the relative levels of activity of the societies: the NZAFA (Wellington) and the Canterbury Society of Arts (Christchurch) were each given 200 sq. ft, while the two smaller societies – the Otago Society of Artists (Dunedin), and the Auckland Society of Arts, each had 150 sq. ft.

23   National Archives of South Africa, Pretoria, Industries Committee Papers, MNW 596 3/29/21, Minutes of the first meeting of the Central Art Committee, South African Section: British Empire Exhibition, 12 November 1923, p. 14.

24   National Archives of Australia, Department of Trade and Customs, CP 374/2/1 16, Part 1, Art, Letter from Secretary to the Commission to C. H. Read, Organising Secretary, Burlington House Art Exhibition Committee, Sydney, 15 March 1923.

25   Brown, born and educated in England, immigrated to Canada in 1909. He had written to the Wembley authorities to warn them of the divisions between academic and non-academic in the Canadian art world, and it was he who suggested that the trustees be recommended as responsible for the selection. The selection of the actual committee was made by Brown in consultation with the Board.

26   National Archives of Australia (ACT), Prime Minister's Department, A458/1, A104/1, 'British Empire Exhibition, Erection of Palace of Arts, British Empire Exhibition: Note on the Participation of India, the Dominions and the Colonies, in the Main British Art Palace', memorandum enclosed with letter from Lawrence Weaver to the Official Secretary, Commonwealth of Australia, Australia House, 20 November 1922, in letter dated 28 November. Presumably each Dominion received a similar letter. Very little material concerning the Wembley exhibition has survived in British archives, so dominion archives have been extremely useful in providing crucial information.

27   Prince Arthur of Connaught had acted briefly as chair of the central art committee. He was quoted at the opening of the 22nd Annual Exhibition of SASA on 8 February 1923 at which he enthused about South Africa's potential art exhibition at Wembley: *Cape Times* 9 February 1923.

28   National Art Gallery and Museum of New Zealand Archives, MU 1,26, 28/1/4, Letters to the Secretaries of the four art societies from James McDonald, 8 May 1923.

29   McDonald advised one artist that all works should be typically representative of New Zealand life and conditions, suggesting she submit 'something striking of Mt. Egmont': ibid., undated and 21 June 1923.

30   C. Davies, Foreword, *Australian Artists in Europe: Exhibition of Paintings and Sculpture* (London: Faculty of Arts Gallery, 1924).

31   National Gallery of Canada Archives, 5.4B, British Empire Exhibition, Regulations for the guidance of intending exhibitors, British Empire Exhibition 1924 Canadian Section of Fine Arts, issued by the National Gallery of Canada, 1 May 1923.

32   *British Empire Exhibition 1925 Official Guide* (London: Fleetway Press, 1925).

33 The 'Heidelberg School' refers to a group of impressionist landscape painters in Australia which sprung up between 1885 and 1890, and included Streeton, Tom Roberts, and others. Willis and others have argued that from a Eurocentric point of view, everything European is taken as the 'norm': Anne-Marie Willis, *Illusions of Identity: The Art of Nation* (Sydney: Hale & Ironmonger Pty, Ltd, 1993), p. 82. Australia and the other Dominions measured themselves against both Europe and each other.

34 Canadian critic Newton MacTavish wrote an article for *Studio* in which he acknowledged that for decades Canada's snow was not something about which they would ever boast: 'in its advertising propaganda abroad the Government kept the winter season in the background, taking it for granted that most persons abroad already looked to Canada as to a country icebound during more than half of every year . . . To permit a picture of a stretch of country delightfully mantled with snow was regarded as unpatriotic, untactful, and unwise': 'Some Canadian Painters of the Snow', *Studio*, 75 (1918), 78–82. This had changed by 1925 when one critic praised Canadian artists for their enthusiasm for snow subjects, as demonstrated in the two Wembley exhibitions: 'Snow in Canadian Art', *Ottawa Citizen*, 30 May 1925.

35 B. Smith and T. Smith, *Australian Painting 1788–1990*, 3rd edn (Melbourne: Oxford University Press, 1991), p. 187.

36 I. Burn, *National Life and Landscapes: Australian Painting 1900–1940* (Sydney and London: Bay Books, 1991), pp. 72–4.

37 P. G. Konody writing on the Burlington House exhibition, 'The Australian Exhibition in London', *Art in Australia*, 3 (1924), n.p.

38 'Empire Art at Wembley: Dominion Contrasts', *The Times*, 28 May 1924.

39 One of these portraits, *Aboriginal Head (Charlie Turner)*, was purchased by the Art Gallery of New South Wales in 1892.

40 E. Brown, *Canadian Section of Fine Arts Catalogue: British Empire Exhibition London 1924* (Toronto: Rous & Mann, 1924), p. 3.

41 See Esther Trépanier, 'Nationalisme et Modernité: La réception critique du groupe des sept dans la presse montréalaise francophone des années vingt', *Journal of Canadian Art History/Annales d'histoire de l'art canadien*, 17:2 (1996); the negative view of European influence on Canadian art was not shared by francophone artists and critics.

42 Metropolitan misconceptions of Dominion art are reflected in the following passage from a review: 'as the way is with the younger communities of the new world, they go through their phase at a rate impossible among the more slowly moving people of Europe. We have on the walls of the palace of arts in Wembley, Canadian pictures representing everything from early French impressionism to the last developments of the last decade': from the *Daily News*, 13 June 1924, quoted in *Press Comments on the Canadian Section of Fine Arts British Empire Exhibition 1924–1925* (Ottawa: National Gallery of Canada, 1925), p. 9.

43 The traditionalist critic Hector Charlesworth, who opposed the Group of Seven, lamented that it had come to represent all artistic activity in Canada: 'What some of us feared has come to pass . . . that the group of painters which elects to present in exaggerated terms the crudest, most sinister aspects of the Canadian wilds . . . would be accepted by British critics as the exclusive authentic interpreters of Canadian landscape . . .': 'Canadian Pictures at Wembley', *Saturday Night*, 17 May 1924. In the exhibitions of Canadian art that took place in the immediate aftermath of Wembley, that is, a provincial tour of the Canadian section organised by the Art Exhibitions Bureau, a selection of twenty-five works included as part of the British section at the *Exposition Triennale de Gand*, in Ghent in 1925, and the *Exposition d'art canadien* at the Musée de Paume, Paris, in 1927, where the academic work was eliminated altogether.

44 See Mitchell's 'Imperial Landscape', in W. J. T. Mitchell (ed.), *Landscape and Power* (Chicago, IL, and London: University of Chicago Press, 1994).

45 My thanks to Dr Shulamith Behr for encouraging me to look more closely at the figurative work in the *Exhibition*.

46 T. Morris Longstreth, 'When Canadian Art "Arrived" in Europe', *Saturday Night*, 48:22 (1933), 15.

PART III

Engagement and resistance

CHAPTER NINE

Challenging the myth of indigenous peoples' 'last stand' in Canada and Australia: public discourse and the conditions of silence

Elizabeth Furniss

In this chapter I explore discussions between indigenous and non-indigenous peoples engaged in public debates about the history of colonisation in settler-colonial societies. In advocating for recognition of Aboriginal title and rights in their attempt to secure a more favourable position *vis-à-vis* the dominant settler society, what are the strategies used by indigenous peoples to challenge the foundational settler histories that pervade popular understandings of history? What forms of representation–engagement do they employ and, more specifically, what narrative strategies do they use? What conditions favour, or constrain, their choices? And what factors condition the silences that surrounds public discourse? In what follows I present an overview of work I have carried out in rural Canada and Australia in an attempt to understand these questions. I focus on some of the methodological problems that arise in the study of public discourse in different settler societies and, by implication, on the utility of a comparative perspective in understanding commonalities in indigenous–settler relations and the forces shaping public debates about history in settler-colonial societies as they approach the postcolonial era.

In order to examine public discourse in rural settings in Canada and Australia I have selected two sites: the forestry city of Williams Lake in the central interior of British Columbia; and the mining city of Mount Isa in north-western Queensland. The two cities share a number of features. Both are sites in which European (British) colonisation, becoming significant in the mid-1800s, resulted in indigenous people's territorial dislocation (albeit to different degrees in Canada and Australia), subordination to colonial governments and marginalisation in the structure of labour and class relations that developed through the colonial economies. Today both are prosperous industrial centres in which the regional economy is based on the activity of transnational corporations extracting natural resources on land theoretically owned by the Crown but now under Aboriginal claim. Both cities have populations of 10,000–20,000, with a significant Aboriginal component (about 10 per cent). Both are sites in which Aboriginal rights are being actively asserted and publicly debated. In each city industry representatives, government officials and non-Aboriginal area-residents in general perceive Aboriginal claims to pose a serious threat to the region's economic stability and the survival of local settler communities.

There is another common thread: each town's public identity and history, as represented in tourism venues, popular books, museums and newspaper–magazine accounts of local history, is founded on frontier symbolism and narratives which highlight the heroic acts of the first pioneers and explorers in *discovering* and settling the region. There is a readily identifiable narrative structure to these frontier histories.[1] The past is presented as the heroic struggle between the forces of good and evil in which conflict and violence are naturalised and seen as the very motor that drives history-as-progress. Second, the complex interplay of diverse individuals and groups in the newly settled regions is condensed into a simple binary narrative structure of the protagonist's struggle with opposing forces: it is a story of man v. nature, civilization v. savagery, the European settler v. hostile natives and even, at times, the heroic pioneer v. tyrannical urban government. Third, the past is represented through a series of 'epitomizing events',[2] dramatic incidents that serve as convenient, easily grasped, condensed symbols that represent (just as they draw attention away from) the more complex historical processes. Finally, the frontier narrative is tremendously flexible: it consists of a set of images, symbols and metaphors that can be drawn on to create histories that may, alternately, affirm or contest existing structures of power and celebrate or condemn past actions of colonial expansion. Critical frontier narratives, for example, typically romanticise indigenous peoples and lament their destruction by the forces of European expansion. In so doing, they project ideal images of the past (whether onto native cultures or the romantic ideal of the settlers' early agricultural communities) which they contrast with the current moral–social decline of contemporary industrial society. The standard narrative structure, a frontier encounter of binary opposites and an outcome of absolute conquest, remains the same, with only the moral weighting of the agents and the outcome being reversed.

Frontier histories dominate public consciousness in both Canada and Australia, and undoubtedly other settler-colonial societies as well.

What is striking, however, is just how similar some frontier histories are. An outstanding example is provided by the histories that circulate in the cities of Williams Lake and Mount Isa. Despite their wide geographical separation and their different colonial histories, in both cities there is a pervasive frontier narrative of the final desperate efforts of local Aboriginal tribes to resist European invaders: in Williams Lake this is the story of the Chilcotin War of 1864; in Mount Isa, the 'last stand' of the Kalkadoon in 1884. In both, the 'last stand' is presented as an event which epitomises a watershed moment, distinguishing a past in which settlers struggled against indigenous peoples to establish a tenuous hold in the new land, from a present – and a future – in which colonial authority is established, unproblematical and unchallenged. In reality, however, this is not the case. In both cities indigenous leaders are now actively challenging the legitimacy of these settler histories, seeking to draw attention to the persistence of indigenous title and rights into the present.

These two settings provide an ideal opportunity to examine a series of questions:

- Under what historical conditions have these last-stand narratives emerged?
- How, over the decades, have these narratives been revised in relation to the changing socio-political contexts and broader regional and national shifts in representations of the national identity and history?
- How are indigenous leaders in Williams Lake and Mount Isa engaging with, challenging and/or subverting these settler narratives in their own political struggles to assert Aboriginal title and rights?

After a brief historical overview, followed by a discussion of the historical shifts in the Kalkadoon last-stand narrative, I focus on the third question, which gives rise to methodological issues concerning the analysis of indigenous discourse in comparative settings.

Queensland's colonial history

As the pastoral industry expanded in north-west Queensland from the 1860s to the 1880s, incoming settlers and local Aboriginal tribes, including the Kalkadoon, the Mitakoodi, the Pitta-Pitta and others, were brought into increasingly violent contact. With cattle displacing other game animals and polluting water sources, Aboriginal hunters turned their attention to cattle, which they speared, as an alternative food source; to protect their lands and water sources, and in response to the violence perpetrated on their kin Aboriginal people launched murderous attacks against settlers.[3] Colonial administrators and settlers retaliated with violence to clear Aboriginal people from the pastoral runs and to protect settler interests and property. The Mounted Native Police (MNP) – essentially a government-sanctioned death-squad – became the sole arm of government authority on the frontier, engaging in a regime of terror in which Aboriginal people were shot down and driven off lands desired by settlers.[4] Where the MNP were unavailable, settlers were expected to protect themselves and their property as they saw fit, and violence, killings and other depredations against Aborigines became common.

In the Mount Isa–Cloncurry region, the killing of four white settlers in 1878 set off several years of back-and-forth reprisals and punitive expeditions in which a number of Aboriginal and settler lives were lost. In 1883 Sub-Inspector Beresford of the Cloncurry Native Police detachment was attacked and killed; the following year another prominent settler was killed. Determined to break Aboriginal resistance, in 1884 Sub-Inspector Urquart and native troopers from the Cloncurry station, assisted by several groups of armed settlers, engaged in a nine-week campaign to 'clear up' the district.[5] The final and best-known conflict occurred in September 1884, when Urquhart, native troopers and area settlers pursued a group of Kalkadoons into the hilly region later known as Battle Mountain. The ensuing conflict resulted in the deaths of many Kalkadoons and marked the end of that era of direct Aboriginal resistance.

The passage of Queensland's Aborigines Protection and Restriction of the Sale of Opium Act in 1897 signalled an important shift in colonial policy towards the goal of the protection, segregation and regulation of the Aboriginal population.[6] The 1897 Act assigned 'protectors of Aborigines' in certain districts and gave those officials sweeping controls. Aboriginal people were to be removed from the vicinity of towns and settlements to reserves run by superintendents responsible for providing food, shelter, clothing and medical aid. By this time, however, pastoralists had begun the practice of 'letting in' Aboriginal people to stations, where, working as labourers, stockmen and domestics in exchange for the bare necessities of life, their labour was an essential resource.[7] Under the Act, Aboriginal people's freedom of movement was denied, and they could take up employment outside of reserves only with the permission of the protector, who then controlled their wages. The Act also empowered a protector to regulate Aboriginal marriages. Other legislation allowed government officials to remove any child from an Aboriginal mother, and to remove neglected children into service as labourers or domestics on pastoral stations.[8] Individuals who resisted these controls were labelled troublesome, and they could be summarily removed to mission settlements or government reserves many hundreds of miles from their home country. Palm Island, frequently the destination for removed Aboriginals, it is still known by older indigenous people in the Mount Isa area as the 'punishment island'.

In the 1960s this system of authoritarian repression began to shift in significant ways. Technological changes in the cattle industry that lowered labour requirements, legislation requiring that Aboriginal stockmen receive pay equal to that of white labourers and the emergence of new employment opportunities saw a move by Aboriginal workers away from regional cattle stations.[9] Around Mount Isa, Aboriginal fringe camps began to swell to accommodate a growing urban Aboriginal population. Today there is a diverse Aboriginal and Torres Straits Islander population comprising about 10 per cent of the city of Mount Isa's residents. Aboriginal people in the city experience profound socio-economic marginalisation in terms of health, poverty, unemployment, living conditions and educational level; they are subjected to a blatantly disproportionate police scrutiny and are grossly overrepresented in the criminal justice system. The historical roots of these disadvantages remain invisible and ill-understood by the general population. Overall, relations between indigenous and non-indigenous peoples are fraught. With the rise of the native title debate, and with the Mabo and Wik court decisions, recognising the existence of native title and suggesting that it may persist (and co-exist) on pastoral and mining lease-land, tensions between Aboriginal and non-Aboriginal people in north-western Queensland have only intensified.

Codification, circulation and revision of the Kalkadoon's 'last-stand' narrative

The story of the Kalkadoon's last stand at Battle Mountain is sporadically mentioned only in a few archival sources.[10] It was first codified in a written narrative in Hudson Fysh's *Taming the North* in 1933. The work was written during Australia's depression years and was overtly intended to boost the morale of Australians by celebrating the accomplishments of the early pioneers. This narrative, typical of frontier histories generally, celebrates colonialism as an economic, social and moral triumph by focusing on the lives of ordinary pioneers and settlers who encountered overwhelming obstacles, primarily 'primitive' and 'bloodthirsty' indigenous peoples and a harsh, forbidding environment. By drawing on their own stubborn determination, courage and strength, and by engaging in protracted struggle, conflict and occasional violence these pioneers manage to rise above such obstacles to establish civilisation in the wilderness. The flavour of this narrative is captured in the following passage:

> The race of western Queensland pioneers is well-nigh extinct, and already the present generation but dimly realizes their battle against the primitive wilderness, peopled by a savage and uncivilized race, or their grim fortitude in struggling against drought and flood, that the wild lands might be tamed ... a few pages of pioneering anecdotes should provide a good tonic [for the young generation of Australians] and make them realize that they have a definite tradition to live up to.[11]

Taming the North is largely a biography of Queensland settler Alexander Kennedy.[12] Kennedy arrived in Queensland from Scotland in the 1860s, and over the next few decades established a series of pastoral stations in various Queensland locales. In 1877 he took up land in Kalkadoon territory, and over the next decade instigated or participated in a number of violent and murderous attacks against the Kalkadoon, including the conflict at Battle Mountain in 1884. The depiction of Kennedy's struggles with the Kalkadoon are secondary to the main biographical narrative; nevertheless certain key components of the story are presented that later formed the core of the last-stand myth: the depiction of the Kalkadoon as 'savage and warlike' tribe; the fact that the Kalkadoon, displaying a kind of 'primitive' military intelligence, could avoid reprisals by strategically retreating into the mountainous regions of their territory; the belief that the Battle Mountain (or Battle Hill) incident was 'one of the few cases where the natives stood up to an attack by whites and native troopers with fire-arms, and fought it out', attesting to the fact that 'the Kalkadoons were a tribe above the average in savagery and bravery'; and the idea that after the Battle Mountain massacre the Kalkadoons were a broken and vanishing people.[13] They are portrayed as formidable opponents whose ultimate defeat and disappearance only enhances the tradition of Kennedy's heroism, bravery and ultimate moral (and economic) triumph.

The story of the Battle Mountain incident underwent some significant shifts in subsequent decades. Among the most comprehensive versions, in chronological order (most of which draw heavily on Fysh's or each others' accounts), are Pearson's 'In the Kalkadoon Country' (1949), Holthouse's *Up Rode the Squatter* (1970), Armstrong's *The Kalkadoons* (1980), Pike's *Campfire Tales* (1981), Grassby and Hill's *Six Australian Battlefields* (1988) and Lowe's *Forgotten Rebels* (1994).[14] There is a consistent pattern to these narratives:

- There is a narrowing of narrative focus to highlight the Battle Mountain conflict, so that it became the singular epitomising event in Kalkadoon–settler history, and is now repeatedly described as the Kalkadoon's 'last stand'.

- More importantly, the conflict at Battle Mountain is now presented as a military engagement, and the Kalkadoon are imbued with a quasi-European military intelligence and valour: Kalkadoon resistance is now 'guerilla warfare'; the Kalkadoon are described as 'the bravest and best organized fighting men of all the Aboriginal tribes'; their hilly retreats were 'regular fortresses, well-stocked with weapons', their chief 'planned his raids like a general', their 'final defeat' at Battle Mountain was 'their finest hour'.
- There is a simultaneous militarisation of the process of colonial expansion in general (an 'Australian Hundred Years' War' in Grassby and Hill) and the actions of the MNP and settler vigilantes in particular. Through this process, the bloody and at times genocidal violence between Aboriginal people and incoming settlers in Queensland is transformed into, and justified and rationalised as, a fair fight that followed established rules of European military engagements.

These narrative shifts reflect the assimilation of the Kalkadoon story into a broader and more pervasive narrative of Australian national identity and history, one that highlights Australian military history and has, as its own epitomising event, the tragic deaths and defeat of Australian (and New Zealand) troops at Gallipoli in 1915 during the First World War. Coming shortly after Australia's formation as a nation state in 1901, and widely seen as one of the new nation's first major engagements on the global stage, Australian participation in the First World War and the Gallipoli massacre in particular became transformed into a story – the Anzac legend – that symbolises what are purported to be key Australian national values: courage, valour and heroic suffering, where war becomes the proving ground of national character and death in war the ultimate patriotic sacrifice.[15] The pervasiveness of the Anzac legend is immediately evident not only in Australia's national holiday (Anzac Day) but in the numerous war memorials and monuments found in state capitals and small country towns alike.

Not all of the Kalkadoon's last-stand narratives promote and justify colonisation and Aboriginal dispossession. The post-1960s narratives of the Kalkadoon's last stand also reflect shifting public attitudes in Australia concerning questions of civil rights, racism, poverty and Aboriginal land rights. After the 1960s an immense amount of public attention became focused on the question of Australia's past treatment of Aboriginal peoples, and the prevailing myth of Australia's national foundation – that Australia had been peacefully settled, that colonisation had proceeded without bloodshed or violence and that Australia in fact had been empty and unoccupied at the time of European 'discovery' – came under strong criticism. Revisionist histories sought to redress the invisibility of Aboriginal people in earlier histories by highlighting their resistance to colonisation. In this vein, a number of historians rewrote the Kalkadoon's last-stand narrative, presenting the Kalkadoon in a sympathetic light both as victims of brutal colonialism (i.e., the 'good guys') and as metaphorical Anzacs who died in an attempt to protect their homeland from invasion. In short, the Kalkadoon's last-stand narrative exists in both conservative and critical forms while retaining a standard narrative structure and being closely interconnected with shifting historiographical trends and narrative genres over the last half-century.

British Columbia's colonial history and the Chilcotin War narrative

By the turn of the 1800s the European land-based fur trade had expanded westwards into British Columbia. For the first half of the century, relations between Europeans and Aboriginal peoples, while certainly not free from coercion, force and occasional violence, for the most part were manageable within the framework of continued Aboriginal ownership of lands and resources. The discovery of gold in the Cariboo region in the late 1850s, however, brought about a radical disruption of these relationships. Thousands of miners and, later, settlers and entrepreneurs were drawn to the goldfields; after them came missionaries and government officials, the latter desperately attempting to impose law and order and to mediate escalating Aboriginal–settler conflicts. The Tsilhqot'in's territory, in the western interior plateau of British Columbia, was believed to have little gold potential, and was relatively untouched by that invasion. However, access to the goldfields remained a problem, and in 1862 a private entrepreneur launched a plan to build a new road from the southern BC coast up through Tsilhqot'in territory to facilitate the flow of miners, settlers and goods to the goldfields. It is in this context of several years of intensifying conflict between Tsilhqot'in and incoming settlers that the Chilcotin War incident occurred. At this point I focus on one of the popular narratives that purports to recount the specific events:

> In the early morning of April 30th, 1864, a work party charged with constructing a new road to the Barkerville goldfields slept in tents by the Homathko River near the rugged B.C. Coast. A small band of Chilcotin warriors, fearing a recurrence of smallpox, and theft of their

land by the Europeans, descended on the sleeping camp and killed 13 whites. To the Chilcotin, it was not murder, but an act of war. Led by their great warchief, Klatassine, they fled homeward, soon to be pursued by two colonial expeditions in a classic example of early guerrilla warfare. It was the last, desperate attempt by native people of the colony to halt the inexorable advance of European civilization onto their land.[16]

Ultimately, 6 Tsilhqot'in men were taken into custody and tried in a colonial court, following which 5 of them were convicted and hanged in what most colonial officials and settlers generally viewed as appropriate punishment for acts of murder.

In the following decades non-Aboriginal settlement in the Chilcotin plateau overall remained sparse. The south-eastern region of the plateau, which contained natural grasslands ideal for cattle-ranching, gradually were pre-empted by settlers, and by 1900 reserves had been established for the Tsilhqot'in by federal government. The Tsilhqot'in, however, remained largely in control of their territories. The remoteness of the plateau, the lack of sufficient settler or government interest in its lands and resources, and the will of the Tsilhqot'in to maintain their culture in the face of the destabilising influences of colonialism resulted ultimately in a period of tenuous accommodation and co-existence between the Tsilhqot'in and regional settler culture. For the most part, the Tsilhqot'in were able to avoid bureaucratic interference in their lives and maintain the integrity of their communities and culture, sustaining themselves through a combination of hunting, fishing, trapping and small-scale stock-raising and farming.

The expansion of the forest industry to the Chilcotin plateau in the post-Second World War period began a new era of relations between the Tsilhqot'in and dominant settler society. As hunting- and trapping-grounds were increasingly threatened by the clear-cutting practices of multinational corporations, Tsilhqot'in leaders launched a new political struggle. Like most other Aboriginal groups in the province, and in contrast to governmental practice elsewhere in southern Canada, the Tsilhqot'in had never established a treaty with federal government to address the question of Aboriginal title. Riding the wave of increasing public attention to questions of land claims and Aboriginal rights, and using a variety of strategies from logging-road blockades to court actions, Tsilhqot'in leaders by the 1990s had begun to articulate forcefully a position of continued ownership of traditional lands and sovereignty independent of the Canadian state. In this context, Tsilhqot'in leaders began to publicly assert different interpretations of the Chilcotin War that, until then, had pervaded public tellings. During the Cariboo–Chilcotin Justice Inquiry of 1992, Tsilhqot'ins spoke bitterly of how those men involved in the incident had been induced to surrender and the promises of immunity made to them violated. To many Tsilhqot'ins, the hanging of these men over 130 years ago represents a fundamental miscarriage of justice and a betrayal of trust that continues to haunt Tsilhqot'in relations with the dominant settler society.[17] For the most part, these reinterpretations of the Chilcotin War induce little sympathy in non-Aboriginal residents of rural BC towns whose economic base is dependent on dwindling forestry resources and whose inhabitants see Aboriginal land claims as a threat to what little security remains amid the economic decline that the province now faces.

In raising challenges to the state's authority by re-interpreting the events surrounding the Chilcotin War, Tsilhqot'in leaders are challenging a narrative that has long had great currency and symbolic weight among the general public. The events surrounding the Chilcotin War were well documented in government records, letters and newspapers pertaining to 1864's events. The story has been widely written about in dozens of popular books, magazines and newspapers ever since.[18] Exactly how this event first became codified into a distinct narrative, how that narrative has shifted over time according to the changing historical contexts and changing trends in the narration of a broader BC and Canadian national history, are important points, though they must be left aside here. Suffice it to say that despite the diversity of the story-tellers, the venues of publication and the sheer bulk of material on the event, and despite similar post-1960s' shifts towards a more sympathetic portrayal of the Tsilhqot'in as victims of colonialism, most representations of the event are consistent with the kind of frontier narratives I discussed earlier – narratives that remain the most prevalent vehicle for the telling of Canada regional and national histories. In essence, the Chilcotin War is a story of whites v. Indians, of civilisation v. savagery, with the outcome being the (rightful or unjust) success of colonial conquest.

While these last-stand narratives may take on the unique flavour of the distinct nationalist narrative traditions in Canada and Australia, the Chilcotin War and Kalkadoon last-stand stories represent similar and readily identifiable settler viewpoints on both the essential Aboriginal *other* and the colonial process. In their conservative form, these stories reassure the reading public of the righteousness of colonisation, the savagery of the indigenous and the completion of conquest. As may be seen from the current political climate, however, all of that is far from being evident: indigenous peoples continue to resist the authority of the Canadian – and the Australian – state. Kalkadoon people now must challenge how the last-stand narrative attempts to wipe out the biological existence of the Kalkadoon people from the current setting. In contrast, Tsilhqot'in leaders must challenge how the Chilcotin War story attempts to render the Tsilhqot'in people quiet, docile and subservient to the Canadian state.

Indigenous political discourse: challenging settler narratives

How are indigenous peoples attempting to project alternative perspectives on history into the public context? At this point I wish to shift away from historical and ethnographical description to some of the methodological issues that arise when analysing indigenous discourse in public settings.

First, to understand the challenge indigenous peoples face we must appreciate the resilience of these frontier narratives and how deeply interconnected they are with the cultural forms and practices of settler society more generally. I first explored this question in the course of ethnographical research in the BC interior, where my interest was the dynamics of Aboriginal–non-Aboriginal relations in the rural town of Williams Lake. In part, I was attempting to understand the racism against Aboriginal people that pervades social relations in this region. I came to understand that this 'common-sense' racism was part of a more general package of cultural attitudes and beliefs that non-Aboriginal residents and newcomers pick up through powerful processes of socialisation that are widely diffused and often explicit in their condemnation of Aboriginal peoples for their moral inferiority to whites. I made sense of this through the idea of a *frontier complex*, which I saw to be a diverse yet interrelated set of values, beliefs, attitudes, identities and understandings about society, history and Aboriginal–non-Aboriginal relations that appears repeatedly in multiple domains of Euro-Canadian everyday life, ranging from casual conversations to public history and town festivals to political discourse on contemporary issues.[19] At its heart, I believe, the frontier complex is a form of historical consciousness, a way of seeing history that provides certain sets of rules that govern how truths about the past, and the present, are to be determined and conveyed. And here I get back to narrative. This frontier historical consciousness is made manifest in narrative – specifically, through uniquely Canadian frontier narratives that tell the story of Canada's past through the heroic encounter of opposing forces – man and nature, civilisation and wilderness, whites and Indians – and of how conquest was achieved sometimes through righteous violence, but more often through Aboriginal people's willing submission to the benevolent force of missionaries, Mounties and settlers. This idea of 'conquest through benevolence' not only sustains broader narratives of Canadian national identity – the idea that we have been 'good to the Indians' – but then masks its racism in paternalistic, benevolent humour.

In short, these frontier narratives of history not only pervade public spaces in Williams Lake and many other rural settings across Canada, but are functionally interrelated with many other domains of cultural expression and deeply embedded in a Euro-Canadian settler worldview. This is to deny neither the heterogeneity of settler narratives of history nor their capacity to be mobilised for critical or counter-hegemonic purposes. But in looking at settler narratives from this broader perspective, we can understand how they are part of a much bigger cultural machinery which then gives us clues both to their resilience and to what this then means, in pragmatic terms, for indigenous peoples seeking to interject an alternative perspective on history into the public domain.

The second issue is how to locate indigenous perspectives on history. It could be argued that historical expression is to be found in everything: in subtle gestures, in quiet language, in humour, in the way indigenous peoples carry themselves in the public space of rural settler towns, or in what James Scott would call the private or 'hidden transcripts' in which indirect resistance is richly dramatised and enacted.[20] Here I am concerned not with the private and varied contexts of historical expression, but specifically with the way indigenous peoples openly engage with settler histories through public debate and discourse. What are their strategies for public engagement?

In both Williams Lake and Mount Isa, indigenous leaders seem to be using dominant settler historical narratives in order to project indigenous voices into the public domain and to advocate for Aboriginal rights and title. For example, in 1984, to mark the centenary of the Battle Mountain massacre, leaders of the Kalkadoon tribal council erected a memorial cairn in the tiny settlement of Kajabbi, 22 kilometers from Battle Mountain. The memorial plaque presents a critical, oppositional formulation of Kalkadoon history resonant with Anzac symbolism:

> This obelisk is in memorial to the Kalkatungu tribe who, during September 1884, fought one of Australia's historical battles of resistance against a para-military force of European settlers and the Queensland Native Mounted Police at a place known today as Battle Mountain ... the spirit of the Kalkatungu never died at battle, but remains intact and alive today within the Kalkadoon Tribal Council.

At the Kalkadoon Tribal Council and Memorial Keeping House, tourists encounter a historical miscellany of stone artifacts, wooden implements and modern Aboriginal paintings, and clipping from newspapers and popular magazines describing the Kalkadoon massacre on Battle Mountain. Aboriginal leaders are also re-interpreting the significance of the Battle Mountain episode. One Aboriginal leader and native title claimant, for example, said to me in an interview:

> Battle Mountain was a position where the Kalkadoon showed their resistance to the Europeans, that they would not sacrifice their land, and that it would be better to die in the cause of the counter-resistance . . . We went down in history, in Australian history, by many archaeologists and anthropologists and book writers, to be proclaimed as a great fighting tribe in the Australian counter-resistance against European invasion. And these things are the roots of survival, and an inspiration to the next generation to consider us as a great fighting tribe and to continue that in the pursuit of land rights.

Memorialisation, in this leader's view, is an important political strategy for reinforcing the visibility of the Kalkadoon in the minds of the general public, and he envisions more public memorials being erected in the future.

In short, the prominence of the stories of the Kalkadoon last stand and the Chilcotin War has created for both tribes a context, a space, for public receptivity towards contemporary indigenous peoples who are speaking out about their past. In Mount Isa, the Kalkadoon are manipulating the public's fascination with the Kalkadoon myth while revising colonial narratives to further their own goals of advancing native title, thus fostering Aboriginal people's pride in their culture and identity, to securing a more respected position for Aboriginal people in the city.

When indigenous peoples choose to use dominant settler narratives to voice alternative historical perspectives, are they not simply contributing to the hegemony of colonial culture? By using the language of the colonisers and manipulating their narrative strategies (albeit for critical purposes), are they not contributing to the saturation of the field of public discourse by colonial forms, and therefore occluding the possibility of other historical narrative forms – oral traditions, for instance – gaining public recognition and legitimacy? In contrast, I believe, we need to consider not so much the textual or narrative qualities of these public representations as their pragmatic effects in specific local contexts. From that vantage-point, academic concerns with the reproduction of hegemonic narrative genres become less pressing when we consider the intentions of indigenous speakers and the consequences – or the effects – of their narrative strategies. It may be that critical histories aimed at capturing public attention and mobilising public sympathy for indigenous concerns are more effective when couched in a historical language that is familiar and under-standable to the non-indigenous public.

In returning to my initial concern with identifying the strategies indigenous peoples are using to engage in public discourse about colonial history, there are complicating factors that become increasingly relevant when engaging in comparative work.

First, it is difficult on the basis of short term ethnographical fieldwork in indigenous communities to adequately analyse the meanings which indigenous peoples understand themselves to be conveying in using certain narrative forms to engage in public debate about history. That is, a Kalkadoon memorial can include, as part of a more general physical representation of the past, a counter-hegemonic variant of the settler last-stand narrative, resonant now with positive Anzac symbolism. But it would be a mistake to infer meaning simply from a reading of the *form* of this narrative. Here I draw on the work of David Dinwoodie, who examined the Nemiah Declaration, a formal statement that the Nemiah Valley Tsilhqot'in put out to assert Aboriginal title over their territory in the face of increasing encroachment by logging companies and tourism operators.[21] The declaration, initially drafted in collaboration with the First Nation's lawyer and supporting environmentalists, can be read as a Western legal document affirming the nationhood and sovereignty of the Nemiah First Nation. It is recognisable in its surface features, then, in terms of Western political and legal discourse, and it is undoubtedly read by many non-Aboriginal people as such. But the declaration is read quite differently by Tsilhqot'in people. Dinwoodie argues that Nemiah people strongly support the declaration as a powerful expression of their deep-seated sense of belonging, identity and separateness from Canadian society. The declaration is read by Tsilhqot'in people, he argues, not as an appropriation of Western political discourse but as representing the voice of a Tsilqhot'in culture hero central to mythic traditions that are recognised by all Tsilqhot'in people yet are present in the community in different ways for different people. It is on this basis that the Nemiah people construe the declaration as an authoritative representation. An interpretation of public discourse, then, requires it to be read against the background of the forms of discourse (and, in the case of the Kalkadoon, the physical form of the memorial in which the text is literally embedded), and the meanings associated with these forms, that occur within indigenous communities in more restricted and private settings.

Second, when thinking about the strategies indigenous peoples use to engage in public discourse about history, we need to consider the factors impinging on their freedom to choose different ways of speaking about history. How do relations of power limit the possibilities of speech? Public silences are as important to study, from an ethnographical standpoint, as are forms of public discourse. So to understand the ways in which indigenous and settler contact narratives are encountering one another in public we have also to examine public silences and their conditions.

How do we begin an ethnography of silence? First of all, that such silence was an important factor became apparent to me when, in 1998, I undertook fieldwork in rural Queensland, where racism was prevalent, and relations between whites and Aborigines were strained, and I came to the region as a complete stranger with no prior contacts. My field research was limited to three months, and during that time it became very apparent that my identity as a white person, as a 'foreigner' or Canadian, were significant factors, conditioning in different ways both the silence I encountered when talking with indigenous people and the ways in which they chose to speak to me about issues of historical representation. I concluded then that any ethnography of silence I produced would have to be reflexive, in that I would have to write myself into the account because my presence was a key factor shaping the kinds of silences I encountered.

How do we know whether silence is a relevant contributor to the quality of public discourse, particularly in situations where people are reluctant to speak? In some contexts, of course, people *do* speak about public silences. Leaders of the Tsilhqot'in nation, for example, have spoken quite openly about the strategies they have enacted to talk about the Chilcotin War in public contexts. A Tsilhqot'in spokesperson indicated during an interview in 2000 that the Tsilhqot'in leaders and elders refuse to allow their oral traditions recounting the Chilcotin War story to being made public. This is due, in part, to what occurred when the Nemiah First Nation was negotiating with the Government for the creation of Ts'ilos Provincial Park, which is within Nemiah traditional territory. The people of Nemiah agreed to make public an origin story associated with the region, only to find, in later tellings, that the meaning of the story had become distorted and perverted in ways that contributed to negative stereotypes of the Tsilhqot'in; further, and to make matters worse, the name 'Ts'ilos' was quickly appropriated, without the consent of the Nemiah people, by a local tourism outfit. In short, the Tsilhqot'in's experience has been one of their inability to control the meaning and use of oral tradition once it goes beyond the Tsilhqot'in community context; and in their effort to maintain control they choose to exclude those stories from the public domain.

A second instance of this concern to regulate public silence occurred when, in 1994, Tsilhqot'in leaders participated in a public symposium at the UBC Museum of Anthropology to discuss the Chilcotin War of 1864 and the recently released Cariboo–Chilcotin Justice Inquiry, which condemned the hanging of the five Tsilhqot'in men involved in the incident, and called on the provincial government to grant a posthumous pardon. Several representatives of the Tsilhqot'in nation provided their perspectives on the event, and in doing so made use of different narrative strategies. Some of the speeches clearly drew on the basic narrative structure of the frontier myth, but with the moral outcome inverted: the Tsilhqot'in men were 'warriors'; they did not 'lose' the Chilcotin War; and they remain 'undefeated today'. One Tsilhqot'in speaker, however, gave a memorable presentation that clearly stepped outside of the frontier narrative. Speaking from the perspective of Tsilhqot'in oral tradition, he framed the events, the individuals involved and the values motivating their behaviour in distinctive terms reflective of core features of Tsilhqot'in culture. Also notable was the fact that although the UBC Museum of Anthropology, with the speakers' prior approval, videotaped the presentations, there was to be no media coverage, and the audience was strictly prohibited from making any kind of recording of the presentations.

These kinds of deliberate silence may be contrasted with repressive silence, which I believe is more prominent in rural Australia than in Canada. When I began fieldwork in Mount Isa, for example, I remarked to two indigenous leaders that in contrast to my experience in Canada, there seemed to be little public debate about history or native title going on in the city, and I asked why indigenous people weren't speaking out? There response was simply 'No, there wouldn't be [any public challenges]', and 'No, they wouldn't [speak in public].' It was obvious that their silence was a common-sense, taken-for-granted, reality for local residents, and it was clear that mechanisms were in place here to perpetuate that silence, which I, as a newcomer, did not understand.

What evidence is there that this was a repressive silence? Silence could, alternatively, mean public agreement. One of the best indicators of repression is, of course, what transpires when indigenous peoples *do* attempt to challenge conventional settler history. Are their actions met with violence? Are they resisted? Two brief examples illustrate just how contentious indigenous expressions of history are in the current Queensland setting.

The first concerns what transpired after a public memorial to the Kalkadoon was erected in 1988, Australia's bicentennial year. A major theme of the national events was reconciliation with Aboriginal peoples. The memorial itself is located about 60 kilometers west of Mount Isa, on the Barkly Highway (the major highway to the coast) and on the purported tribal boundaries of the Kalkadoon and Mitakoodi peoples. The memorial was designed and built by a local white doctor to draw attention to Aboriginal history and ownership of the land prior to the arrival of Europeans. The texts included on the monument are highly romanticised and patronising, portraying the Kalkadoon as noble savages inevitably defeated by the 'civilising' forces of European settlement – not exactly a challenging narrative. Despite this fact, the local indigenous leaders I spoke with supported the monument as a positive expression of Aboriginal identity. Public response to the memorial has been less favourable: it has been repeatedly vandalised with spray-paint and bullet holes attest to its use as a target. Shortly after its erection it was destroyed with explosives; it was quickly rebuilt, only to be defaced again. Today the memorial is literally a site of competing visions of history: racist graffiti co-exists with a spray-painted image of the Aboriginal flag. Significantly, a memorial to the expedition of Burke and Wills, the first white explorers to cross this region of Queensland in 1861, lies untouched just a kilometer down the road.

The second example dates from the same year (1988): during Mount Isa's annual Aboriginal Awareness Days, civic officials and indigenous leaders participated in a ceremony in which the Australian Aboriginal flag was raised on the city's flagpole; by the next day it had been replaced by a hanged effigy of an Aboriginal person.

These examples illustrate that public receptivity to efforts to assert Aboriginal perspectives on history and cultural identity in public settings is at best mixed. The examples show how contentious Aboriginal challenges to Australia's foundational histories are in a Queensland context of longstanding repressive legislation restricting Aboriginal rights, in a setting where native title claims are now at the forefront, with an outback culture of pervasive anti-Aboriginal racism. In that context, speaking out – breaking the public silence about the past, about Aboriginal issues – can, in fact, be a dangerous thing to do.

A second way to situate repressive silence is to ask: what is it in the history of Aboriginal–settler relations in Queensland that has created the contemporary situation in which silence is perpetuated? Although I have hinted at the issues involved in the above examples, I wish to pursue them by considering whether the notion of a *culture of terror* is a useful way of framing these silences.

The culture of terror notion has been used in the Australian context to understand the manner in which settler societies ideologically justified the development of extreme forms of colonial violence against indigenous peoples; or, more specifically, how colonial agents – settlers, governments, missionaries, etc. – created images of indigenous peoples as savage, bloodthirsty and treacherous, and how those images were then used to validate and, indeed motivate the treacherous and brutal actions of colonial agents against indigenous peoples:[22] colonial violence was validated as a kind of pre-emptive strike. One of the consequences of a settler culture of terror is that fear of indigenous peoples becomes deeply ingrained in the settler culture. Through the savagery of colonial violence, indigenous peoples, in turn, come to experience that terror.

What indications are there that this may be a useful way of approaching an ethnography of silence? Many historians have provided evidence that indigenous people in Queensland experienced this kind of sustained violence and terror.[23] I recall reading an account by an early Queensland settler who witnessed a group of chained Aborigines being led into a white settlement – he described them as literally shaking with terror from head to foot as they were brought in. Another settler recorded in his journal how he had invited a friend for the Christmas holidays to stay at his rural Queensland pastoral station, where they would sit in the shade of the verandah shooting at passing Aborigines. This callous account, I believe, is typical of a culture of terror, one in which brutal violence becomes completely neutralised, stripped of any moral content.

What about the present? What indication is there that Australian settler culture retains a lingering terror of indigenous people? During the native title debate of the 1990s, in which the courts recognised that native rights on pastoral leases might persist, pastoralists in Queensland were reported in the major Australian newspapers to be 'taking up arms' to defend themselves against an anticipated indigenous attack.[24] This fear was evident in the rhetoric of One Nation leader Pauline Hanson, who at the same time expressed concern that indigenous corporations in Queensland were buying up pastoral properties, engaging in a kind of economic take-over of the country.[25] In short, there seems to be a lingering culture of terror in Australia – a constructed fear of indigenous reprisal – that permeates much of the public opposition to the native title movement.

What of Mount Isa? What are the mechanisms enforcing Aboriginal silence? First of all, Queensland, particularly during the notorious regime of Joh Bjelke-Petersen (1968–87), has been described as a 'police state', the standard definition of which is a totalitarian regime controlled by political police supervision of citizen's activities.[26] To what extent this is true is debatable. What is clear from recent scholarship investigating politics and government in Queensland is the degree to which the institutional structure of government in Queensland has been corrupted over the decades. Rather than operating impartially to ensure accountability and to protect the public interest, parliament, the police, the institutions of justice and the public services have been politicised to protect the ruling party: 'The police force has been used not so much to uphold the law, but as an active arm of government. Even the state's judiciary has shown itself vulnerable to political interference.'[27] By the 1980s, corruption in Queensland's police force had reached the ultimate stage of development: not only was it acting as an agent of organised crime (drugs, gambling and prostitution), it was actually franchising it.[28]

For Aboriginal people in Mount Isa, relations with the police provide one example of an ongoing system of extreme repression. As in Canada, Aboriginal people are grossly over-represented in the criminal justice system: they are over-policed and poorly represented; and they receive longer jail terms than their non-Aboriginal counterparts. What is most significant is that the typical cycle of involvement in the criminal justice system is often sparked by verbal acts of resistance. An Aboriginal person can be arrested for swearing at a police officer: the police harassment that ensues is met by a verbal protest at such treatment; his or her protestation leads to arrest and a court date; the court hearing is missed for some reason and a warrant for arrest is issued and served, and that individual is jailed. The cycle of spiralling involvement with the criminal justice system begins. Here we can trace the way power is used to enforce Aboriginal silence.

In conclusion I re-emphasise one point: in order to understand indigenous strategies for engaging in public debates about history, we need to assess not only public discourse but the conditions of silence that surround public discourse. I have suggested that there are two kinds of silence to consider: *deliberate* silence and *repressive* silence. There is, though, a third kind that may be relevant to indigenous communities: *traumatic* silence. Robin Ridington has recently suggested the usefulness of looking at narrative as an adaptive technology, which is to say that people's use of narrative to organise an understanding of the world around them is central to cultural adaptation.[29] But what happens when that narrative technology is disrupted? Here, I think it is useful to consider yet another kind of silence: the silence that emerges from experiences of terror. Clinical psychologists, for example, argue that profoundly traumatic experiences of terror – such as a sudden, life-threatening, car crash or a violent physical attack, or prolonged traumas such as those experienced by child victims of incest or by soldiers in wartime – are often blocked out from conscious memory. These experiences, psychologists argue, are so profoundly traumatic that the individual simply cannot make sense of them in a normal way. In later life, individuals may come to experience the patchy return of traumatised memory; central to the process of recovery is the individual's eventual ability to organise those memories into a narrative.[30] If this is true at the level of the individual, might it hold true for a social body? Might we consider the possibility that a third kind of silence is operating among indigenous peoples who have experienced profound terror in their relations with settler society? This kind of traumatic silence then manifests itself in the breakdown of a narrative technology: not the social collective's inability to make itself heard but the deeper still inability to speak. The task for an ethnography of silence would be to look both at the processes of narration and the conditions that create silence, and to explore the processes by which narrative technologies are destroyed and are subsequently rebuilt.

Notes

A portion of this chapter was published previously in Oceania 71(A) (June 2001) and is reproduced with permission.

1 E. Furniss, *The Burden of History: Colonialism and the Frontier Myth in a Rural Canadian Community* (Vancouver, BC: UBC Press, 1999).
2 R. Fogelson, 'The Ethnohistory of Events and Non-Events', *Ethnohistory*, 36:2 (1989), 133–47.
3 R. E. M. Armstrong, *The Kalkadoons: A Study of an Aboriginal Tribe on the Queensland Frontier* (Sydney: William Brooks, 1980), p. 124; D. S. Trigger, *Whitefella Comin': Aboriginal Responses to Colonialism in Northern Australia* (Cambridge: Cambridge University Press, 1992), pp. 20, 22.
4 C. D. Rowley, *The Destruction of Aboriginal Society* (Sydney: Penguin, 1970), pp. 157–86; N. Loos, *Invasion and Resistance: Aboriginal–European Relations on the North Queensland Frontier 1861–1897* (Canberra: Australian National University Press, 1982), pp. 25, 28–61.
5 Armstrong, *The Kalkadoons*, p. 138.
6 Rowley, *Destruction of Aboriginal Society*, pp. 183–6.
7 Trigger, *Whitefella Comin'*, p. 38.
8 R. Kidd, *The Way We Civilise* (St Lucia: University of Queensland Press, 1997), pp. 20–1.
9 D. May, *Aboriginal Labour and the Cattle Industry: Queensland from White Settlement to the Present* (Cambridge: Cambridge University Press, 1994), pp. 151–2, 168–73.
10 See Armstrong, *The Kalkadoons*.
11 H. Fysh, *Taming the North: The Story of Alexander Kennedy and Other Queensland Pathfinders* (Sydney: Angus & Robertson, 1950 [1933]), p. xiv.
12 Fysh's work is based on his close friendship with Kennedy over a thirteen-year period; interviews and conversations with Kennedy, supplemented by references to written sources, form the content of *Taming the North*.
13 Ibid., pp. 114, 184, 209.
14 S. E. Pearson, 'In the Kalkadoon Country: The Habitat and Habits of a Queensland Aboriginal Tribe', *Historical Society of Queensland Journal*, 4:2 (1949), 190–205; H. Holthouse, *Up Rode the Squatter* (Sydney: Angus & Robertson, 1970); Armstrong, *The Kalkadoons*; G. Pike, *Queensland Frontier* (Adelaide: Rigby, 1978); A. Grassby and M. Hill, *Six Australian Battlefields* (St Leonards, NSW: Allen & Unwin, 1988);

D. Lowe, *Forgotten Rebels: Black Australians Who Fought Back* (Melbourne, Vic.: Permanent Press, 1994).

15 P. J. Dennis, E. Grey and R. Prior (with J. Connor), *The Oxford Companion to Australian Military History* (Melbourne: Oxford University Press, 1995), pp. 42–9; K. S. Inglis, *Sacred Places: War Memorials in the Australian Landscape* (Carlton South, Vic.: Melbourne University Press, 1998).

16 M. Rothenburger, *The Chilcotin War* (Langley, BC: Mr Paperback, 1978), p. 1.

17 A. Sarich, *Report on the Cariboo–Chilcotin Justice Inquiry* (Victoria: Province of British Columbia, 1993).

18 Some recent examples include N. Barlee, 'The Chilcotin War of 1864', *Canadian West Magazine*, 6:4 (1976), 13–23; Rothenburger, *The Chilcotin War*; R. Blacklaws, 'Waddington's Gold Road', *Beautiful British Columbia*, 29:1 (1987), 38–45; M. Emery, *River of Tears* (Surrey, BC: Hancock House, 1992); T. Glavin, *Nemiah: The Unconquered Country* (Vancouver: New Star, 1992); and J. Williams, *High Slack: Waddington's Gold Road and the Bute Inlet Massacre of 1864* (Vancouver: New Star, 1996).

19 Furniss, *Burden of History*.

20 J. Scott, *Domination and the Arts of Resistance: Hidden Transcripts* (New Haven, CT: Yale University Press, 1990).

21 D. Dinwoodie, *Reserve Memories: ThePower of the Past in a Chilcotin Community* (Lincoln: University of Nebraska Press, 2002), pp. 82–102.

22 B. Morris, 'Frontier Colonialism as a Culture of Terror', in B. Attwood and J. Arnold (eds), *Power, Knowledge and Aborigines* (Bundoora, Vic.: La Trobe University Press, 1992), pp. 72–87.

23 Rowley, *Destruction of Aboriginal Society*; Loos, *Invasion and Resistance*; H. Reynolds, *Frontier* (St Leonards, NSW: Allen & Unwin, 1987).

24 'Whites Would Quit the North', *Sunday Times*, 7 December 1997; 'Pastoralists Taking Up Arms, Says MP', *Sydney Morning Herald*, 5 December 1997.

25 Pauline Hanson's speech at Longreach, 11 September 1998, online: www.gwb.com.au/onenation/speeches/long.html (October 1998).

26 E. Whitton, *The Hillbilly Dictator: Australia's Police State* (Crows Nest, NSW: ABC Enterprises, 1989).

27 P. Coaldrake, *Working the System: Government in Queensland* (St Lucia: University of Queensland Press, 1989), p. 55.

28 Whitton, *Hillbilly Dictator*, p. 179.

29 R. Ridington, 'Dogs, Snares, and Cartridge Belts: The Poetics of a Northern Athapaskan Narrative Technology', in M.-A. Dobres and C. R. Hoffman (eds), *The Social Dynamics of Technology: Practice, Politics, and World Views* (Washington, DC: Smithsonian Institute, 1999), pp. 167–85.

30 J. Herman, *Trauma and Recovery* (New York: Basic Books, 1997).

CHAPTER TEN

Being Indian the South African way: the development of Indian identity in 1940s' Durban

Parvathi Raman

In 1860, the first Indian indentured labourers were shipped to South Africa to work on the sugar plantations of Natal. 'Passenger' Indians,[1] traders who came to provide services and set up businesses there, soon joined them. Since then, the Indian population has become permanently settled in South Africa and from 1994 has been an uneasy part of the 'Rainbow Nation'.[2] The Indians who came to South Africa were a heterogeneous group, differentiated by region of origin, language, religion, caste and class, and the subcontinent they left in the late nineteenth and the early twentieth century was still a British colony, not yet the Indian nation. Despite these obstacles, from early on Indians began to generate a loose sense of community and a notion of *Indianness* that was partly negotiated through a continued relationship with India. In addition, early attempts to segregate Indians[3] and disenfranchise those entitled to vote also led to a loose sense of collective identity, as Indians had to foster an ethos of *self-help* – bereft, as they were, of citizenship rights and faced with discrimination in areas of employment, housing and services. The Indian community came to occupy a marginalised and ambivalent position in the political and social landscape of South Africa.

The making of community was, however, a contentious project. Indians were not transformed into a single and essentialised ethnic group; rather, the South African Indian community has been differentiated over time, its material circumstances in continual flux. At times, Indians have been deeply divided by material and ideological differences. This chapter looks at the ways in which Indians came to define themselves as *Indian South Africans* in Durban in the 1940s, and traces how a displaced and divided community came to re-configure its identity and its struggle for a reasserted social–political space under

[193]

segregation and apartheid. An exploration of the cultural and political practices that helped shape the language of being *Indian* in South Africa reveals the forms through which notions of *community* were developed and performed. *Indianness* was articulated through acts of translation, which drew on the discourse of imperial brotherhood, the developing dialogue of Indian nationalism and an idealised sense of Indian 'tradition' which was integrated with a sense of belonging in South Africa. The language of Indianness transformed from one that voiced its struggle for rights as temporary settlers to one demanding permanent citizenship in South Africa.

Although Indians were initially a primarily rural population, by the 1940s they were moving in larger numbers to urban centres where they tried to put down roots. Their presence was unwelcome and they were characterised as the 'Asiatic menace', a term which encompassed ideas of disease, economic competition and struggles over social space. In this period, political struggles were acted out against a backdrop of accelerating segregationist legislation, racial zoning and increasing attempts to exclude Indians from the political process. The growth of segregationist practices helped define the boundaries of identification between communities and also gave rise to oppositional political practices. In the 1940s, the continuing threat to the status and location of Indians created an endemic sense of anxiety and instability in their lives, leading many of them to crave places where they could 'stay put', where locality could be produced as a property of being, facilitating the setting down of roots and reproducing communal ties. Their social and political landscapes were defined by the fear of Indians expressed by racial *others'* in South Africa, a response which was shaped by ideas of them as 'coolies' – a term of abuse extended to all Indians[4] – and exploiters. Nevertheless, despite this hostility Indians wanted to maintain a foothold in Durban. Their attempts to carve a space for themselves helped to reinforce a sense of Indianness, but the notion of what a South African Indian might be varied considerably between different sections of the community.

Fuelled by experiences of continual displacement, many Indians desired to produce neighbourhoods with communal kith and kin, shared histories and 'collectively traversed places and spaces', which can be of particular importance for displaced and deterritorialised people.[5] How Indian workers understood the spaces they experienced and how they interacted with the spaces they produced, given the constant threat of dislocation, helped shape their value systems and social landscapes, and became matters of acute concern in the 1940s. The drive to put down roots encouraged some Indian workers to accept the political language of *voluntary* segregation, to facilitate the creation of social space that was settled, signifying that they had made the transition from 'routes to roots'.[6] This desire for permanent social space became a prime concern for workers in particular.[7]

Indians were anxious to build stable homes that would accommodate the extended family structures they had transplanted to South Africa. Ownership of a permanent house was, for many, the ultimate goal, what they had 'planned, worked and saved for'.[8] Building houses was one way to produce locality, reproduce neighbourhoods and stabilise social living. Also, the recreation of religious landscapes[9] and the re-inscription of religious practices were crucial in developing a language of Indianness. Religious societies were closely aligned with political organisations, creating networks which helped generate ideas of what it meant 'to be an Indian'. Unlike the migrant, mostly male, African population, Indians continually threatened to become a lasting presence in the towns, visibly putting down roots, to the horror of white colonists. The so-called 'penetration' of Indians into white areas was seen as a major problem for the Durban authorities, at a time when increasing numbers of white South Africans were also moving to Durban from small outlying towns, drawn by expanding industry, and the improving trading opportunities and service provision. More and more, white South Africans wanted exclusive control of the desirable areas of Durban, with African and Indian workers bussed in from surrounding areas to work in the factories and the industrial and service sectors.

By the 1940s, there was an intensification in the struggle for social space, through which issues of citizenship, property rights and segregationist measures became inexorably interlocked, and purportedly brought together an Indian *community* in a political sense. The social and economic insecurity that many Indians faced in the 1940s made them identify with an Indianness that drew on the growing prestige of the Indian nationalist movement and helped counter the series of dislocations that they faced in South Africa. Yet the notion of an Indian *community* was contested and fragile because variant readings of *nation, citizenship* and *democratic rights* existed in distinct sections of the community. Segregation acted on Indians in different ways, and the question of *rights'* also came to mean different things. By the 1940s, Indians fell into one of three loosely defined groups – workers, so-called colonial-born Indians and the merchant class – whose differences came to be more marked by the end of the decade.

The Indian working class

In the 1940s, the vast majority of Indians in Durban lived in relative poverty. A survey undertaken in 1941 found that 36 per cent of Indian families were in debt and a 1944 University of Natal survey showed 70.6 per cent of Indians to be living below the poverty line in comparison to 5 per cent of whites, 38 per cent of coloureds and 25 per cent of Africans;[10] 40 per cent of Indians were destitute. Unemployment figures were also high, and Indians' average income per head was one-sixth that of whites. Contrary to the popular image of them as exploitative shopkeepers, the majority of Indians in South Africa were, in fact, poor members of the working class.

This was a time of rapidly changing work patterns for many Indians. The capitalisation of agriculture diminished their prospects for work in the rural economy, and Africans continued to replace Indian workers in agricultural production. It was these circumstances that spurred the movement of Indians to South Africa's towns. In 1910, 88 per cent of the South African Indian population had been engaged in rural labour; by 1945 that figure was drastically reduced to 7 per cent.[11] Four years later there were 123,165 Indians living in Durban, constituting 32 per cent of the city's total population.[12] While the population of Durban was increasing, especially after the outbreak of the Second World War, however, the city's municipality had not developed an infrastructure adequate to the numbers 'flooding' the urban environment. Indians became prominent entrepreneurs in the informal sector that sprang up to fill the gap left by the State in such areas as petty trade, transport and housing. There, however, they came into competition with both Africans and whites, often in geographical spaces beyond the direct control of state bodies, such as the police. In those spaces, Indians developed cultures of marginality through which they became 'ambivalent parts of a social formation', leaving them side-lined by white society, though socially and politically privileged over black workers.[13] Indians, like many Jews in South Africa, were subject to the radicalising potential of marginality, leaving them 'alienated from the social order, conventions and ideological norms' of wider society.[14] In addition, the question of housing and property became crucial to Indians in this period. For the economically deprived working classes the lack of adequate social housing in town was a particularly acute burden.

The process of urbanisation in Durban at this point was heterogeneous and *ad hoc*, and urban conditions deteriorated by the middle of the 1940s. The Indian migration to towns grew, and severe overcrowding resulted from the lack of sufficient housing provision. At the same time, Indians were being ousted from their market-gardening enterprises at the margins of the city because Europeans wanted those sites, either for house-building or for the industries that were spreading along the coast.[15] Dispossessed Indians were thus driven into the market for unskilled labour, where they had to compete for jobs with Africans and poor whites. But many sons and daughters of indentured labourers, the so-called 'colonial-borns', also became white-collar workers, and a significant number of them were active in radical politics and set out to challenge the conservative platform of the 'merchant elite'.

'I am colonial-born'

'Colonial-born' South African Indians emerged as a powerful and influential force within the community by the 1940s, and they wanted in particular to mobilise workers as part of their political stance against repressive state policies. As offspring of indentured workers from Natal, they were members of the Indian lower-middle class who had managed to get a Western education and had entered the white-collar professions; they were mostly Tamil-speaking Hindus and Christians, and their livelihoods depended to a large extent on the colonial administration. Colonial-born Indians began to cohere self-consciously as a social group in the interwar period when it became more difficult for this Western-educated elite to maintain their standard of living.[16] In 1933, they formed the Colonial-Born Indian Association (later the Colonial-Born South African Indian Association) and resumed publishing their own newspaper, the *African Chronicle*,[17] the pages of which were filled with issues affecting Indians in South Africa. It also followed every twist and turn of the Indian independence movement: it is apparent that Indian national heroes loomed large in the imagination of the paper's white-collar South African Indian readership. Their political platform consisted of agitating for the rights and privileges of citizenship, on the grounds that they were South African-born Indians. But, by the 1940s, they were being squeezed even further by the State, their fundamental fear being that their standard of living would be reduced to the growing squalor of Indian workers, which many of them felt they had only recently escaped.

In the 1930s and 1940s, as India was forming its idea of an Indian *nation*, colonial-born activists in South Africa were creating a diaspora politics, fuelled by a morality and rationality of statehood which fed into the Defiance Campaign of 1952. To protect their position as young South African Indian professionals they challenged the compromising politics of the merchant class for more radical measures through which the State would protect Indian job security. They had been badly affected in the 1920s by the United Party's 'civilised labour' policy, and now their urban residential status was also being challenged. Their struggles over urban space in the 1940s began a contest over citizenship and belonging which continued until the 1960s. Colonial-born Indians constructed their Indianness in an ambivalent and 'oppositional mode', one which was represented as 'tradition' through Gandhi's formulation of *satyagraha* and an anti-colonial nationalism.[18] In the South African context, this form of politics framed the colonial-borns' political struggle to gain rights of citizenship in the South African State. Many of them were active in leftist politics and a number joined the Communist Party of South Africa,[19] developing a potent dialogue which combined notions of class and nation. Indians were mobilised through ideas of promoting Indian *national honour* and an idealisation of Gandhi, both of which stood in stark contrast to the attitude of communists in India at the time.

For Durban's Indian traders and merchants the question of land tenure was the most pressing issue of the 1940s. The fact that Indians could purchase land, despite growing restrictions, allowed them access to a form of capital accumulation denied to their African counterparts and explained, to an extent, their ability to compete so effectively with their entrepreneurial rivals; the use of family labour in Indian businesses also gave them a competitive edge. In the early 1940s these elite Indians were flourishing and increasingly investing in property in Natal and the Transvaal. Between 1927 and 1940, the rateable value of Indian property in Durban rose from £1.44 million to just below £3.45 million;[20] in the peripheral urban slum areas, where the land on which Indian workers' erected shacks was leased, some-times from Indian landlords, the rateable value went up from £1.73 million in 1934 to £2.39 million in 1940;[21] 70 per cent of these Indian land purchases were for investment purposes.[22]

In 1940, the Government set up the Indian Penetration Commis-sion under Justice F. N. Broome[23] to investigate the spread of Indians to the towns. In an attempt to protect their interests, Indian mer-chants collaborated with the commission. Durban City Council gave evidence that segregation was a 'natural communal instinct and that penetration ran counter to this.'[24] The council produced an 'expert' witness, Professor Burrows of Natal University, who argued the case for an 'ecological "invasion–succession" model', according to which their penetration of urban areas stemmed from Indians' psychological need to prove their equality to whites. Local rate-payers' associations also gave evidence, objecting to the 'slaughter of goats, fowls, filth, cooking smells, noise and danger to daughters' emanating from Indian residences in town.[25]

The Broome commission concluded that trading and property were the only two investment outlets for middle-class Indians.[26] As the licensing laws restricted the expansion of trade in the Transvaal, and further Indian occupation of land was prohibited, the Durban property market became a crucial outlet for Indian middle-class capital accumulation, and the Indian scramble for land accelerated as rumours spread that the Government was planning a new 'pegging' Bill. It could, however, be said that Indian penetration was more imagined than real, configured as it was in the language of racial otherness and undesirability.[27] By 1942, Indians made up 25 per cent of Durban's population, but owned only 4 per cent of the city's land acreage. Whites nevertheless feared their residential districts being swamped by unhygienic and money-grabbing Indians, and this fear was fuelled by the very real competition between Durban's racial populations in trade and in the workplace.

Segregation was a pressing issue at the time, and was clearly forcing major divisions between Indians. These were not always as clear-cut as a fight between accommodationist merchants and radical political activists. In the latter half of the 1930s and early 1940s, amid growing hysteria about Indian penetration and Indians' alarm at threats to their interests, the Natal Municipal Association called for 'voluntary Indian segregation' as a way of resolving plans for racial zoning. The Natal Indian Association and the Natal Indian Congress, two rival political organisations, were keen to accuse each other of collaborating with the authorities. In reality, both seemed prepared to enter a 'gentleman's agreement' according to which Indians would not buy residential property in white areas, but would vigorously defend their right to trade in non-Indian areas. Whites, after all, constituted the vast majority of the merchants' customers.[28] While the two organisation tried to outdo each other in calling for the protection of Indian national honour, they were nonetheless following a logic which required trading rights in all areas but was ambivalent about residential segregation. They argued that while enforced segregation was a slur on 'national honour', because of its implication of racial inferiority, it was 'natural' for people of the same race to live together: 'historical experiences show that the world over people of the same race find it congenial and convenient to live together and the Indians in South Africa are no exception to this rule'.[29] Indians, they claimed, moved into white areas only because of the dearth of amenities elsewhere: 'it is our belief that if suitable residential sites and other amenities are provided for all Indians, this alleged problem would be solved'.[30]

Though merchants wished to reach a compromise with the Government which would protect their businesses, the popular perception, current among South Africans of all races, was that it was a sociologically accepted fact that people preferred to live among their own, and some Indian workers also saw a form of segregation as a solution to their acute lack of civic amenities. Merchants were not always against segregation per se; they wished rather to help shape segregationist legislation in ways that protected their interests. From a different perspective, many workers saw voluntary segregation as a solution to their material problems. On the other hand, radicals, who in many ways advanced the interests of the business community, saw opposition to *enforced* segregation as a central principle of their political platform of equality, democratic rights and citizenship, even if that opposition was often expressed in terms of 'an affront to Indian honour' and a 'slur on the mother country'.

All sections of Indian political leadership looked to Indian workers for their political constituency. For Indian workers, the 1940s was a fear-inducing and uncertain time: by 1945, they had suffered defeat in their trade union struggles[31] and were on the defensive because of the possibility of being replaced by African labour. They retreated into a distinctively Indian working-class identity, mobilising to protect what they saw as specifically Indian jobs. White workers were returning from the war at this time, and the labour market consequently became even more competitive, with little room for militant trade union activity. Indians, on the whole, were uncertain of their present and fearful about their future. Both the lure of Indian nationalism and the expectation of imminent independence played a powerful role in the Indian consciousness, but with contrasting results. Pride in being Indian helped them deal with the way they were treated in South African society. However, whenever government legislation threatened Indians with repatriation, as it frequently did in this period, imaginings of India took on a less attractive aspect: a memorable picture in the *Leader*, a Natal Indian newspaper, of a windswept village hut during the Indian monsoon had the caption: 'Do you want to be sent home to this?'[32]

'A slur on the Indian nation': the 'pegging' Act of 1943

The Trading and Occupation of Land Restriction Act of 1943, or the 'ghetto Act', as it came to be known, was an extension of the Transvaal Pegging Act of 1939. The act proposed to prohibit the further sale of any fixed property, preventing Indians from future expansion by segregating them permanently in defined areas. This was, however, another temporary measure, and a second Broome commission was organised in 1943 to investigate whether Indian 'penetration' had accelerated since 1940. The Smuts Government was juggling international opposition to anti-Indian legislation with white South African demands for action to be taken against Indian encroachment and economic competition. When the second Broome commission failed to find that Indians would soon be flooding urban areas, a third Broome commission, set up the following year, had the task of negotiating a settlement with the Natal Indian Congress. The result was the Pretoria Agreement of 19 April 1944.[33]

It was the so-called conservative wing of the NIC,[34] which represented the interests of the merchant class rather than, as it claimed, those of the whole community, agreed to collaborate with the Smuts Government at the time. Its initial reaction to the 'pegging Act' had been to protest in the traditional political ways, calling for petitions, making statements to the Government and calling on the international community to aid its protest. By compromising with the Government through the third Broome Commission, the conservatives hoped to protect their commercial interests within the urban sector and to agree to some form of segregation, as long as housing and service provision met with European standards. In the terms of the Pretoria Agreement, a board of two Indians and three Europeans was established under the aegis of a European legal adviser, who would allocate property under licence to Indians. Legally, this agreement recognised the right of Indians to own and occupy land anywhere in Natal except where it 'engendered racial bickering due to juxtaposed living in residential areas'.[35] In practice, this meant that the NIC had agreed to accept voluntary segregation as long as reasonable civic amenities were provided, their intention being to ensure their future commercial interests and protect current investments, which were being threatened with confiscation.

Many sections of the Indian community came together to mount the passive resistance campaign of 1946–48, protesting at the measures directed against them. Merchants became involved primarily to protect their business interests, while colonial-born and radical Indians used it to further the struggle for democratic rights and citizenship in South Africa.[36] Ironically, in fighting the segregationist measures, radical activists promoted issues which affected principally the merchant community. The chronic housing shortage that workers faced became but one aspect of the wider need for a political struggle for democratic rights. In an article published in the *Guardian* in March 1947, Yusuf Dadoo, a leading member of the CP and the NIC wrote: 'In South Africa the situation is growing from bad to worse. The appalling and unbelievable housing shortage shows no signs of solution. Thousands of homeless people are forced to live in sacks and hessian shanties ... the important task is to pursue with greater intensity ... full democracy for all.'[37] Workers' interests were not concretely addressed, often coming lower down the agenda than property and trading rights, and the ideal of citizenship. Numerous examples of this can be found in the working committees set up within the NIC after the radical take-over. In 1948, a report given by the housing sub-committee at the NIC conference in Durban illustrated this starkly. Tenants of the Indian merchant and political activist E. M. Paruk, who were resident in Riverside, were given notice to vacate the shanties they occupied on Paruk's land. They asked the NIC to intervene on their behalf. Congress's response was to obtain a promise from Paruk that 'no-one would be evicted with undue harshness or severity'.[38] The same report advocated the defence of Indian land investments from a governmental intervention aimed at redistributing areas of Cato Manor to Africans in an attempt to improve the squalid living conditions of African tenants, most of whom had Indian 'shacklords'. In these circumstances, the creation of an overarching political identity was no easy task.

The passive resistance campaign was almost completely an affair of the Indian community. Although the campaign drew on Gandhi's example of passive resistance in South Africa in the first two decades of the twentieth century, and was inspired by the growing importance of passive resistance as a weapon against the British in India, the campaign of 1946–48 was nevertheless also an act of political and cultural translation. Gandhi's calls for 'truth' and 'conscience' were replaced with ideals of 'equality' and 'democracy', giving voice to the programme of the CPSA and its contemporary platform of the popular front.[39] While Gandhi's vision emphasised the attainment of spiritual truth through suffering, passive resistance became in 1946 a weapon in pursuit of democratic rights and citizenship. The campaign was able to draw on the networks of Indian political organisations and self-help groups that had developed in South Africa in the previous forty years, as well as its tradition of political journalism. Its leadership spoke in language which combined an Indian national identity with South African belonging, and many of the tactics of the campaign were conducted only after seeking the advice of Nehru and Gandhi. When India became independent in 1947, it was a heady day for Indian South Africans as well. However, by 1948, support for the campaign was dropping sharply, and the political fight for democratic rights was dealt a severe blow with the election of the National Party.

'Making a home': community redefined

We can perhaps get closer to an understanding of the collapse of passive resistance and the failure of wider mobilisation by looking in more detail at the campaign and the relations between groups within it. The Asiatic Land Tenure Bill affected in the main the material interests of the merchants, whose place within the alliance was always an uneasy one. They had continued to collaborate with commissions set up by the Government and to have a dialogue with Smuts. When the National Party came to power, the merchants' main political strategy was to negotiate with the new Government: they wanted to protect their material interests, and that required acceptance of some level of segregation. Despite the fact that the passive resistance campaign called for reforms that would benefit their interests, its methods were anathema to the merchants.

The passive resistance campaign seriously divided the Indian political leadership; and when merchants withdrew their political and, more importantly, their financial support from the campaign and formed the Natal Indian Organisation (NIO) in May 1947, it was gravely weakened, not least because it gave the Government an opportunity to further fracture the fragile unity of the Indian community. This was possible because the programme and tactics of the NIC did not resonate with the whole community. One example of this was the boycott of the royal tour that was called by the NIC and the African National Congress (ANC) in 1947. That decision was taken, for once, against the advice of Nehru, who was keen not to complicate negotiations at the UN on a series of Indian issues, including the South African question.[40] The proposed boycott did not enjoy popular support among Indians, and the NIO built on this. It formed the Durban Indian Royal Visit Committee, which organised a reception for the royal couple at Curries Fountain, where they were seated on a dais shaped like the Taj Mahal, some 65,000 Indians attending the celebrations.[41] Even given that the pomp and ceremony of royal visits always attracts onlookers, this number illustrates the complexity and the ambivalence of Indian identity at this time, ideas of imperial citizenship interacting with identification with Indian independence and notions of Indianness in South Africa. The success of the celebrations seriously undermined the NIC's leadership among Indians, whom it characterised as merely 'politically less advanced groups' and 'a deluded and curious crowd'.[42]

The homeland re-imagined

Working-class support for the NIC began to fall off sharply after the heady early days of the passive resistance campaign. CP members had succeeded in involving workers through their trade union networks, but workers' enthusiasm declined quickly. Although the rhetoric of 'Indian honour' did mobilise workers initially, there was a failure to consistently address the issues that affected workers in their everyday lives. As we have seen, the measures of the 'ghetto Act' did not directly affect workers in adverse ways. Many workers resented the merchants, who acted as their exploitative landlords, took their money in shops and benefited financially at their expense through extending loans and credit which were often hard to repay. Materially, Indian workers were in a class relationship with merchants, one which often over-rode the ambivalent umbrella of their Indian identity. Materially and ideologically, Indian workers had the least to gain from the passive resistance campaign. The manner in which the campaign addressed workers was also problematical in the long term: 'It is for the removal of the difficulties of the Indian community and for the upholding of the honour of Indians that we have launched this campaign . . . We consider this inhuman Act derogatory to the honour and dignity of the Indian community as a whole and to the Indian nation.'[43]

This, and the many other calls on Indians to uphold Indian dignity, have pride in the Indian nation and recognise a kinship with Indians in the homeland were ineffectual as a political programme that would address the inadequacies in the material living conditions of Indian workers. By the second half of the 1940s, Durban City Council had begun, in a small way, to provide segregated municipal housing,[44] and the 'ghetto Act' included measures for the expansion of the municipal housing programme to replace the overcrowded and squalid accommodation of poor Indians, proposals that were welcomed by a significant number of workers. As I have said, poor accommodation and lack of services directly affected large parts of the Indian population, and it is not surprising that some sections of the community chose to collaborate with the authorities in the creation of their new built environments.

The Cato Manor Ratepayers' Association provides an interesting illustration of the malleability of readings of identity. As Goolam Vahed has shown, this Indian association was willing to co-operate with the Durban municipality, but requested that Indian workers carry out the building work.[45] These Indian ratepayers wove together notions of class and nation in a particular configuration that was significantly different to that of the merchants, with their strong material ties to India. Indian workers, with their history of rural and urban dislocation, finally found in the promise of municipal housing, a place to be, settle, put down roots and 'produce the locality' so essential to social living. Ironically, the very process of segregation and apartheid in the development of capitalism in South Africa eventually did create the conditions for a 'home'.

The falling away of mass support for the passive resistance campaign also highlighted other factors. Despite its importance to the
communists and radical Indian nationalists, the issue of democratic
rights and citizenship, for example, failed to appeal to workers, who
were more concerned with issues of social space, access to jobs and
their place in the urban landscape. Within the Indian working classes
this required some acceptance of segregationist measures, because
these went some way to meeting long-term housing and service provision beyond those offered within the confines of their own community. Possibilities of more secure long-term settlement shaped different
readings of identity beyond a politics of national rights based on the
franchise. Theirs was a compromise with segregationist measures
fundamentally different from that of the merchant elite, whose object-
ive was to protect their business interests. Above all, at this time,
there was a reformulation of a sense of place and being, where *being*
came to represent the specific, the concrete, the known and familiar
sites of social practices within which they were shaped and formed,
and with which their identities were so closely bound up. Their *place*
had become urban South Africa – where they worked, lived and experienced their social relations. India may have provided a resting-place
for their imaginations, a seeming comfort and haven in times of
uncertainty about work and housing, but the landscape of South
Africa had become the *real*, so that 'home' had been relocated after
the dislocations of indenture and their experiences in South Africa.
Many Indian workers now wanted to arrest further displacement in
order to clear a space for the formation of new relational histories,
new shared codes of community:

> I remember when we moved into our new home the sense of over-
> whelming relief, of feeling that this was something long term and not
> under continuous threat. I came from a family of indentured labourers
> and our family had had to shift several times . . . we were still Indian
> but South Africa was our home and where we had our livelihoods. India
> seemed very remote. What would I do if I went there? I'd never even
> been there and nor have my children.[46]
>
> We wanted to have secure jobs and places to live, we wanted to send
> our children to school. The traders, the merchant Indians, they were happy
> to exploit us, but they couldn't offer us that. They said we were part of
> an Indian community, but I felt that this was only when it suited them.
> They kept on saying that the Government was insulting the Indian
> nation, but what I wanted was work so I could support my family.[47]
>
> [We] are just ordinary workers endeavouring to eke out a living . . . We
> favour segregation, and do not consider it a stigma, or an affront to our
> national pride. We welcome townships well laid out with amenities,
> solely for Indian Occupation.[48]

Community is both a narrative product and an organic achievement in which there is a tension between 'the representation of space' (the conceived) and the spaces of representation (the lived).[49] During this period, a community of Indian workers began to move from the former to the latter, and in doing so those workers opened up another fissure in the wider politics of Indianness. For some, the new urban-housing schemes also reinforced a class identity as they differentiated themselves from merchants, but they conceived of this identity in exclusively nationalist terms because of their antagonistic relations with other social groups. In housing and work, an identity of Indianness was becoming as important as one of class. Radical leaders had a different narrative of nation, one conceived out of India's political struggle for independence, and articulated through the project of modernity and democratic rights within a nation state. This project of modernity did not necessarily accord with what workers perceived as their material interests, as a result of their daily altercations with other groups. Notions of a common citizenship and non-racial alliances became political abstractions. For instance, the 'doctors' pact',[50] a symbolic marker of democratic and non-racial politics, meant little to Indian workers who regarded both Africans and whites as competitors for jobs and urban space.

In the 1940s, the Indian 'community' was redefined. If by the end of the decade, many workers had retreated into their own social landscapes, and developed their own thriving South African Indian cultures, the majority of the merchant class adopted a policy of keeping a low profile and consolidating their businesses. Many radical Indian activists went into the 1950s committed to multi-racial political partnerships, the struggle against social segregation and apartheid, and with an emphasis first and foremost on their African belonging. The language of Indianness began to drift from its moorings – the notion of India as the 'motherland' – and became instead increasingly inscribed with *being Indian the South African way*.

Notes

1 They became known by this name because they paid their own 'passage' for the journey to South Africa.
2 Despite the length of time for which Indians have been resident in South Africa, they are still mistrusted by many South Africans, who characterise them as exploitative shopkeepers with no real commitment to the 'new' South Africa.
3 See M. Swanson, 'The Asiatic Menace: Creating Segregation in Durban, 1870–1900', *International Journal of African Historical Studies*, 16:3 (1983), 401–21.
4 See V. Daniel and J. Bremen, 'The Making of a Coolie', in H. Bernstein, V. Daniel and T. Brass (eds), *Plantations, Proletarians and Peasants in Colonial Africa* (London: Frank Cass, 1992), for an exploration of the term, which highlights its linguistic roots in ideas of thieves and beggars, and also connotes a lack of personhood.

5 Appadurai, 'The Production of Locality', in R. Fardon (ed.), *Counterworks: Managing the Diversity of Knowledge* (London: Routledge, 1995), pp. 215–17.
6 P. Gilroy, *'There Ain't No Black in the Union Jack': The Cultural Politics of Race and Nation* (London: Hutchinson, 1987).
7 To some extent, this was also recognised by the Government from the late 1930s and 1940s, and it hoped to play on these desires in order to encourage ideas of *voluntary* segregation, 'in the case of Lichtenburg, where Indians had informed my office that, Congress, or no Congress, they were prepared to collaborate with the local authority . . . Indians can acquire their own properties and at last experience a feeling of security and permanence': see Cape Town, ANC Papers, ICS, GB 101 (ICS), ANC (RF/1/4/1–4), No. 10, Memorandum by J. H. Basin, Commissioner for Immigration and Asiatic Affairs, 27 March 1945.
8 W. Freund, *Insiders and Outsiders: The Indian Working Class of Durban* (London: James Currey, 1995), p. 35.
9 Indians built mosques and temples soon after their arrival in South Africa.
10 ANC Papers, ICS, No. 11, Memorandum Submitted by a Deputation of the South African Indian Organisation to the Honorary Minister of the Interior, August 1948; F. Ginwala, 'Class, Consciousness and Control: Indian South Africans, 1860–1946', D.Phil thesis, Oxford University, 1974, p. 303.
11 G. Vahed, 'The Making of "Indianness": Indian Politics in South Africa during the 1930s and 1940s', *Journal of Natal and Zulu History*, 17 (1997), 10.
12 Durban City Council, *The Durban Housing Survey* (Durban: DCC, 1952), p. 35.
13 J. Sherman, 'Serving the Natives: Whiteness as the Price of Hospitality in South African Jewish Literature', *Journal of Southern African Studies*, 26:3 (September 2000), 506; he is talking specifically about Jews here, but the description resonates with the experience of Indians.
14 G. Shimoni, 'Accounting for Radicals in Apartheid South Africa', in Milton Shain and Richard Mendelsohn (eds), *Memories, Realities and Dreams: Aspects of the South African Jewish Experience* (Johannesburg: Jonathan Ball, 2002).
15 Freund, *Insiders and Outsiders*, pp. 31–2.
16 M. Swan, 'Ideology in Organised Indian Politics, 1891–1948', in S. Marks and S. Trapido (eds), *The Politics of Race, Class and Nationalism in Twentieth Century South Africa* (Harlow: Longman, 1987), p. 184.
17 The Indian political press in South Africa was an important conduit for ideas of what constituted *Indianness*.
18 D. Chetty 'Identity and "Indianness": Reading and Writing Ethnic Discourse', paper presented at the 'Ethnicity, Society and Conflict' conference at the University of Natal, Pietermaritzburg, September 1992.
19 See P. Raman, 'Being an Indian Communist the South African Way: The Influence of Indians in the South African Communist Party, 1934–1952', unpublished PhD thesis, University of London, 2002.
20 Swan, 'Ideology in Organised Indian Politics', p. 191.
21 M. Swan, *Gandhi: The South African Experience* (Johannesburg: Ravan, 1985), p. 191.
22 Ibid.
23 This was called the *Report of the Indian Penetration Commission* (Pretoria: Government Printer, 1941).
24 J. Grest, 'The Durban City Council Indian Problem: Local Politics in the 1940s', paper presented at the ASSA Conference, Cape Town, July 1985.
25 D. R. Bhagwandeen, 'The Question of "Indian Penetration" in the Durban Area and Indian Politics 1940–46', PhD thesis, University of Natal, 1983, p. 96.
26 *Report of the Indian Penetration Commission*, p. 65.
27 By 1944, however, the British Government saw the question of Indian penetration in South Africa as 'no figment of the imagination' and considered that segregation was not working: see Office of the High Commission for Pretoria, DO 35, 1122, G.715/31 and G.689/1.
28 This was also recognised in a report entitled 'Indian Political Activists in the Union', produced for the British Government at the request of Atlee, which noted

that 'the Indian merchant . . . is not ready to risk his investment or trade by press-ing the whites, who purchase 95 per cent of his goods to far': Office of the High Commission for Pretoria, 19 October 1943, DO 35, 1122, G.715/10.

29   NIC Pamphlet, ANC Papers, ICS, No. 18. This was a sentiment voiced by CP members, colonial-born Indians and merchants alike, as well as the Broome com-missions and government bodies.
30   Ibid.
31   Indian workers were involved in militant trade union activity in the late 1930s and early 1940s: see University of Durban-Westville, Institute for Social and Eco-nomic Research, Report no. 20, by V. Padyachee, S. Vawda and P. Tichmann, 'Indian Workers and Trade Unions in Durban, 1930–50'.
32   *Leader*, 23 February 1949.
33   ANC Papers, ICS, No. 20, Memorandum Submitted on Behalf of the NIC to the Select Committee of the Provisional Council on the Subject of the Draft Ordinance for the Licensing Regulations and Control of Occupation of Dwellings.
34   There was a continuous struggle in this period for control of the NIC between conservative and radical sections of the Indian political community.
35   S. B. Mukherji, *The Indian Minority in South Africa* (New Delhi: People's Publish-ing House, 1959), p. 132.
36   These tactics were in part a result of the anti-fascist platform adopted by the CP in this period.
37   Y. Dadoo, *Guardian*, March 13, 1947.
38   ANC Papers, ICS, No. 26, Report of the Sub-Committee on Housing, NIC Second Provisional Conference, 29–31 May 1948.
39   See Y. Dadoo, 'Facts About the Ghetto Act', Communist Party of South Africa pamphlet, 1946.
40   *Indian Views*, 26 February 1947.
41   *Leader*, 22 March 1947.
42   ANC Papers, ICS, No. 25, Presidential Address, NIC First Biennial Conference, 31 May–1 June 1947.
43   Y. Dadoo, *Guardian*, 4 July1946.
44   By June 1946, according to official sources, the Durban City Council had built 675 Indian houses under its municipal housing scheme, and promised another 18,533: Durban City Council, 'The Indian in Natal' (1947).
45   Vahed 'The Making of "Indianness" ', p. 29; the South African Indian Organisation (SAIO) also suggested using Indian workers for specifically Indian municipal projects as a way of creating employment opportunities in Natal: ANC Papers, ICS, No. 11, SAIO Memorandum, July 1948.
46   SK in interview with the author, Durban, June 1995.
47   KD in interview with the author, Durban, July 1995.
48   *Natal Mercury*, 19 February 1946.
49   This is drawn from H. Lefebvre, *The Production of Space* (Oxford: Blackwell, 1991), pp. 68–168; see also L. Back and M. Keith, ' "Rights and Wrongs": Youth, Community and Narratives of Racial Violence', in P. Cohen (ed.), *New Ethnicities, Old Racisms* (London: Zed Books,1999).
50   This was an agreement between Drs Dadoo, Naicker and Guma to work more closely together across the racial divide.

CHAPTER ELEVEN

An 'education in white brutality': Anthony Martin Fernando and Australian Aboriginal rights in transnational context

Fiona Paisley

In January 1929, an Aboriginal man appeared before the Old Bailey in London, accused of brandishing a pistol at a white man. He defended his actions on the grounds that he had been subjected to intolerable racism, claiming to have been taunted for being black. Confident and well spoken, Anthony Martin Fernando advised the court that his early years in Australia had instilled in him little confidence either in white people or in British law. Although he had been witness to the murder of an Aborigine by two men in 1880s Australia, he said that he had been barred from giving evidence, and the murderers were set free. Despairing of a future in his own country, he left soon afterwards, destined to spend the rest of his days overseas.

This chapter investigates Fernando's life of self-imposed exile and his overseas protests concerning the failure of British justice in Australia. From his early adulthood in the 1880s until his death in 1949, Fernando sought to bring international attention to Aboriginal rights. In England and across continental Europe, he engaged in street protest, wrote for daily newspapers, approached international networks and organisations for assistance, and (as the opening lines of this chapter illustrate) used the courtroom as a site from which to disseminate information about the injustices faced by his people. His life provides significant counter-evidence to the notion that independent travel between Britain, Europe and the Australian colonies was the domain solely of the white imperialist. Moreover, his mobility and speech contradict the idea that the Aborigine historically has been the object of the European gaze, lacking the capacity to participate first hand in self-representation in Europe.

Fernando is an exceptional figure in Australian Aboriginal history because of the non-coerced travelling and political activities he first engaged in during the late nineteenth century. In contrast, since the early days of colonisation Aboriginal people had been presented for European consumption as evidence of the success of white civilisation in the Australian colonies. Only four years after the setting up of the colony, Bennelong, an Aboriginal leader from Port Jackson in Sydney, travelled to London in 1792 with Governor Phillip. He later returned to the colonies where he offered commentary on the relative merits of his own and European culture.[1] In 1846 Governor Eyre presented Queen Victoria with two South Australian Aboriginal boys as examples of the potential of their race to respond to uplift and in the hope that greater attention would be paid to Aboriginals' place within the British Empire.[2]

While such living 'specimens of English manners'[3] of the eighteenth and early nineteenth centuries were admired for their mastery of English and for their gentlemanly demeanour, by the late nineteenth century they seemed representatives of a doomed race. The rapid decrease in Aboriginal numbers, especially of the Tasmanian Aborigines (who were considered to have recently died out) appeared to confirm that these most primitive of peoples would pass inevitably into oblivion.[4] No doubt, for many of those English and Europeans who met Fernando in the late nineteenth and early twentieth centuries, Aborigines had been little more than skeletons on display in their museums or among those circus troops they saw performing in their city.[5] By living among Europeans, Fernando reversed the imperial order. Furthermore, by drawing attention to white agency in the purported demise of his race, he revealed that colonialism, not the Aborigines, was the uncivilised *other* within the British imperial world.

Recent transnational histories have shown that numbers of non-white subjects similarly travelled Europe in the nineteenth and twentieth centuries, participating in debates about their own rights.[6] They were, in Antoinette Burton's words, 'negotiating power across a variety of national–political boundaries, both imagined and real';[7] and the historian Paul Gilroy has described such negotiators of imperial and colonial geopolitics as agents in European history.[8] Until now indigenous people from Australia have not been recognised as participants in this global movement. As I will show, Fernando was perhaps first among the Aboriginal people personally engaged in this transnational critique of the Empire. As he confronted authorities with his account of life as an Aboriginal British Australian, Fernando's protest disturbed – as it continues to do – Australian settler colonialism's claim to historical insularity from overseas criticism,[9] most particularly that voiced by indigenous Australians.

According to Fernando's testimony, he was born in Woolloomooloo on 6 April 1864.[10] An important gathering place for a range of local language groups, Woolloomooloo was in the country of the Cadigal, a fishing people who lived on the southern banks of Sydney Cove. Tragically, by 1791, only a few years after first 'settlement', the devastating effects of conflict, disease and starvation had reduced their population to only three.[11] Thus Fernando's mother is likely to have been a member of the Dharuk, whose hunting and fishing grounds extended from Sydney northwards into the highly fertile Hawkesbury region. Although similarly suffering from the combination of violence, disease and loss of hunting grounds, the Dharuk survived in sufficient numbers to perpetuate their presence in the area to the present.[12]

In common with many generations of mixed-descent Aboriginal people taken from their mothers at an early age, Fernando's pride in his Aboriginal identity was linked to the maternal rather than the paternal. Much of his childhood, Fernando explained, had been spent apart from his mother, for he had been 'taken away' as a young boy.[13] It may be that he was removed by force to work for a white family as a house servant, even a companion, or that he was given over to indentured employment.[14] Many such children were educated by white people intent on 'civilising' them. Or Fernando may have been educated at the Black Town Native Institution, taken into this boarding school run by members of the local Christian Missionary Society mainly for mixed-descent children.[15] If his mother had hoped thereby to equip him for life under colonial rule, her strategy was successful. Those who met Fernando in adult life described him as educated, well-spoken and able to quote extensively from the Bible.[16] Sadly, Fernando made his way back to his community only after his mother's death, a loss that remained a source of grief, as well as of inspiration, throughout his life. His recollection of her became his 'guiding star'.[17]

Although he later referred to his people as the Aborigines of Australia, Fernando never discussed his paternal lineage. Silence concerning an absent father has been typical of many Aboriginals of mixed descent in Australia, for most white fathers abandoned any offspring they had with Aboriginal women. This gendered effect of interracial contact became a cornerstone of racial science and racial policy. Where paternity became increasingly important in determining citizenship status from the late nineteenth century onwards, in settler Australia the authorities emphasised maternity as the defining feature of Aboriginal identity. Maternal blood inheritance and the cultural and social influence of Aboriginal mothers were used to justify the removal of mixed-descent children from their communities. Following *protective'* legislation instigated by colonial governments from the 1880s on, such children were increasingly taken away by the authorities in order to be 'merged into white', usually through unpaid work.[18]

In Fernando's case, silence about paternity further complicates this history. Firstly, he asserted that 'Fernando' was not his birth surname. While working as a mechanic in Milan at the turn of the last century, he honoured the friendly Italian people (who were therefore unlike British Australians) by taking an ordinary Italian name as his surname.[19] Determining one's own name is a highly political act, especially for an Aboriginal man who had left Australia at a time when demeaning or mocking names were often given to Aboriginal workers by their white masters and mistresses.[20] Having not two but three names marked Anthony Martin Fernando apart from the majority of Aboriginal people of his own generation in colonial Australia.

Secondly, Fernando's two first two names yield a possible Caribbean connection. According to James Kohen, a historian of early New South Wales, Martin is the name of a long-standing African–Aboriginal lineage in Australia. John Martin was a Caribbean convict transported from Britain on the First Fleet in 1788. He and a number of his descendants raised children with Dharuk women over the following generations.[21] Perhaps Fernando was silent on his paternity because being both Aboriginal and African created difficulties for a young man living in late nineteenth-century Australia. Unlike Africans, the Aborigines had been found to be proto-Caucasians and thus amenable to biological absorption without throw-back (hence the removal of mixed-descent children). Yet, contradictorily, the Tasmanian Aborigines had been explained in terms of their *negroid* origins.[22] The dissonance that an Aboriginal–Caribbean racial could represent to contemporary authorities is well illustrated by the diverse approaches of Governor Eyre to the Aborigines in South Australia and the Caribbeans in Jamaica under his control in the mid–late nineteenth century: while he considered that the former should be protected, the 'excitable indolence' of the latter required violent repression.[23]

Living among Aboriginal people who had witnessed extraordinary changes in their world, Fernando no doubt learned at an early age to doubt the civilising effects of colonisation. Aboriginal people in his immediate community undoubtedly spoke of the horrifying smallpox epidemic in 1789 (estimated to have resulted in a 50–90 per cent drop in the Aboriginal population in and around Sydney[24]) or of the violence and loss they had experienced since the white sails of the European boats had first been sighted. In the face of such rupture, some Aboriginal people living in close proximity to whites re-articulated their status as civilised savages through carnivalesque or pantomime appropriations of colonial power. In the earliest years of colonisation,

Bungaree donned a soldier's uniform and welcomed ships arriving in Sydney to his land: a local landmark, and for many colonists their first personal encounter with the natives, he would board each ship demanding payment for bringing it safely to shore.[25] Several decades later, African convict Billy Blue, 'commodore' of the local ferry service, demanded similar recognition of his status.[26] In each case, *performance* anchored the negotiation of colonial rule. No doubt well aware of such legendary figures, Fernando would later apply this embodied black politics in his street protests in Europe.

Fernando did not have to wait until he travelled abroad to meet with people from around the world: sailors from Africa and the Caribbean regularly arrived in ships engaged in sugar trading. The editor of New South Wales' first newspaper, George Howe, was a Caribbean; among those in the early township on whom he reported were Chinese and Muslims conducting their religious rituals.[27] Sydney attracted also a wide array of Europeans. Accounts by French, Spanish, Russian and other residents often reflected their authors' fascination with local Aborigines.[28] What of the curiosity of Aboriginal people about this cosmopolitan array? At one level, those Europeans confirmed the larger colonial and imperial frameworks under which Aboriginal people lived in Australia; at another, they provided glimpses of cultures, languages, and places far away.

As Fernando explained, while working as a young railwayman he had witnessed the murder of an Aboriginal man and attempted to give evidence against the two white men accused of the crime.[29] In doing so he had been trying to exercise rights only recently formally extended to Aboriginal people in Australia: in 1876, the New South Wales Evidence Amendment Act made provision for witnesses to give evidence without oath, and Aboriginals, previously considered unable to comprehend the magnitude of testifying before God, could no longer be legally precluded as witnesses.[30] The double injustice of being denied his right to give evidence, resulting in the freeing of the white men accused, convinced Fernando to leave Australia and inspired his determination to speak whenever he could about the suffering of his people.

If that experience had been the impetus for Fernando's departure, how he was *able* to leave Australia remains a mystery. For white people, travel was relatively easy in the late nineteenth century as passports and other identity documents became essential only in the post-First World War era, meaning that Australian passports did not exist until after 1948;[31] even as late as the 1910s, English travellers sailing from Britain to Australia required only a certificate of identity.[32] For Aboriginal people, travel was an entirely different matter. Living under increasing legislation designed to restrict their movement within the colonies,[33] they were necessarily restricted from departing the country's shores. It was surely no coincidence that independent travel became one of Fernando's greatest pleasures and political tools, and he guarded it jealously. Fernando likely left New South Wales as an engineer on a ship.[34] Here his (possible) connection with Africans and Caribbeans working on the wharves and on ships in Port Jackson would have been useful, as Fernando could have been taken for one of them.

However it was that Fernando made his way overseas, it is clear that he was an extraordinarily mobile and active individual. Various official and personal reports testify that he had been a trader in jewellery in South-East Asia before living and working in Italy; after imprisonment in Austria, he went to England, then Switzerland, Germany, Italy again, finally being deported to England, where he was living still in 1929. During these years outside of Australia, he apparently taught himself many languages, and worked variously as a cook, a mechanic or an engineer, a toy-maker and a street-hawker.

While Fernando no doubt lacked Aboriginal compatriots in Europe, he encountered there a large diaspora of black people, mainly from the crown colonies, most of whose communities had lived – or still did – under slavery or its threat. At the end of the nineteenth century, considerable numbers of West Africans and Caribbeans were living in Europe. The majority were sailors; others were entertainers (including some African-Americans), labourers and ex-soldiers.[35] Most faced poverty, living in slum areas in port towns, particularly (by the early twentieth century) Liverpool and Cardiff, in England and Wales, where they had to contend with endemic discrimination and racial vilification. White violence against them flared in 1919 as their manpower, welcomed during the war, was now considered to threaten the post-war employment of whites.[36] It is likely that some Aboriginal soldiers also remained in London after demobilisation, and along with Fernando, became part of Britain's black population.[37] As his Old Bailey appearance attests, even ten years after those 1919 riots Fernando considered it necessary to carry a pistol for self-defence.

Fernando's battle for official recognition as an Aboriginal British Australian began in earnest during the early twentieth century, no doubt reflecting the end of his life as a trader and the beginning of his sojourn in various European cities. Since his departure, Aboriginal rights had diminished, not improved, in Australia. Although Aboriginal men had been granted the vote in various colonial states, NSW among them, prior to federation, from 1901 the Federal Constitution excluded Aborigines from citizenship as 'aliens' in the new nation.[38] Official recognition of his Aboriginal identity had become an urgent matter when war broke out, and Fernando was interned in Austria, alongside other English-speaking nationals, including North Americans (and presumably some British Africans and African-Americans). Where his fellow prisoners were able to access prison relief through their respective embassies, Fernando was without means of support. The only known documents in Fernando's own hand, the 1916 applications he made for prison relief, afford insight into his transnational project for rights.

Fernando addressed British authorities through the American consul in Vienna (there was no British representative in the city). He represented himself as a British subject of Australia forced to leave his country due to the hostile conditions native people faced there. Advising that he had appealed, unsuccessfully, for recognition of his identity since 1910, Fernando recognised the irony in his present position. He argued cogently that a further rejection while he was held as a British prisoner of war should surely lead to his release! Calling for 'fair play', he pointed out that internment had cost him his job, his health and his property, 'which is too much for any working man'.[39] (Owning property, whether land or house, was denied Aboriginal people living under increasing government control in twentieth-century Australia, and has figured historically as the subject of one of the most persistent of Aboriginal activist campaigns.[40]) In both of his 1916 letters, Fernando identified himself as A. M. Fernando (indicating that he had already made one visit to Italy where he had assumed his new name), an 'Honest Hardworking Black Man'.

Given the importance to him of his mother's people and given his silence about his father, why did not he describe himself as an Aborigine, let alone a Dharuk? One possible answer lies in the fact that such categories were the invention of colonists intent on identifying, manipulating or even inventing power groups to their own advantage. Another lies in the fact that by identifying with the wider black world Fernando aimed to occupy an identity beyond the reach of racial science and to re-articulate blackness as a resistant category. After all, Fernando had been one of the 'blacks' many thought should be exterminated if they did not die out quickly of their own accord.[41] By turning 'black' into a proper noun, as Fernando did in his second letter, he asserted his place in this community at the same time as extending its scope to include Aboriginal people. Viewed comparatively, the oppression of the Aborigines had much in common with the African experience of slavery.[42] Furthermore, by calling himself a hardworking black man, Fernando countered contemporary racist stereotypes of black men as lazy and dishonest.[43]

Official responses to his case, however, persistently described him as 'a negro who claims to have been born in Australia and who is interned as a British subject'.[44] (Was this because US officials visited him in prison and assumed his blackness to indicate his African origin? At the risk of re-inscribing their interpretation, it may be that their assumption offers some confirmation that Fernando's father was not a white man.) After making inquiries in NSW concerning this 'Fernando', the Australian Prime Minister's Department advised the US embassy in Vienna that 'his birth has not been registered' and that 'no information' was available concerning his origins. They concluded that he was 'a negro, at present interned in Austria' who was not an Australian and thus could not claim to be a British subject.[45]

Australian recognition of his indigeneity soon followed however. During his time in prison, Fernando befriended a London barrister, Mr Cranshaw, and when they were both deported to London following the war he became the man's servant. Soon afterwards, however, he rejected his new employer's offer of a stipend for life, and returned to independent travel in which he renewed his protests. Having removed himself from the reach of the NSW Government by leaving Australia years earlier, Fernando now confronted a larger adversary: Australian federal authorities overseas. He would increasingly target them as he struggled for recognition of his Aboriginal identity, and for wider public awareness of the conditions faced by Aboriginal people living under their control in Australia. His criticisms of policy on Aboriginals became of enormous concern to the federal authorities in London. If Anglo-Australian women promoting Aboriginal rights from London in the 1930s angered them,[46] an Aboriginal man doing the same a few years earlier would surely have given reason for alarm. Would this bring more Aboriginal people to London to pour doubt on the civilised status of the emerging Australian nation? Australian authorities reacted to Fernando's protests by instigating an undercover report covering his activities in post-war Europe from 1919 to 1921.

According to their findings, while in Italy in 1919 Fernando had sought to petition the Pope, perhaps assuming that the Vatican, with its connections to missions and native peoples, would be sympathetic to his cause. But as its 1924 World Missionary Exhibition would confirm, Vatican interest was limited to the ethnography of objects from heathen cultures since brought under missionary control.[47] In Geneva he contacted members of the newly formed League of Nations, an institution that accepted personal petitions from displaced persons; indigenous rights under settler colonialism were, however, largely beyond its scope.[48] While in Berne, he wrote for the German–Swiss newspaper *Der Bunde*, a socialist daily with strong internationalist leanings,[49] expressing both his claims of injustice towards the Aborigines and his views on the post-war world. The undercover report noted: 'In one of his [Der Bunde] articles, he considers it "a special injustice that Germany's colonies should have been taken from her and placed partially under the control of Australia".' Astounded by his activist career, the Australian investigators wondered at his capacity to operate independently as a political agitator, suspecting that Fernando had been employed by the Germans with the aim of attacking Australia and Britain's credibility as colonists. Australia had only recently gained the newly mandated territory of New Guinea as part of the war reparations paid by Germany to the League of Nations and, as a British nation, was concerned to align itself with the post-war regime of humane colonisers endorsed by international agreement. Drawing on, admittedly, hearsay evidence, they concluded that 'Fernando seems to be actuated less by a concern for the natives than by a desire to do England harm . . . the man appears not only anti-British but pro-German, and it is suggested that he is employed by the Germans'.[50] Believing, incorrectly, that Fernando was from South Australia, they made inquiries there concerning the early life of this worrying 'Australian native'. No evidence of him could be found.[51]

Back in Italy in 1921, Fernando spent part of his day walking the streets wearing a placard and handing out pamphlets accusing whites of murdering Aborigines in Australia, participating in a vibrant urban culture comprising sandwich-board men, pamphleteers, hawkers and performers vying for the attention of passing crowds, and making Aboriginal rights part of contemporary European street culture. The fascist Government imprisoned him for disseminating anti-British propaganda (Britain and Italy were allies); he was held without trial for several months before being deported to England.[52]

Making his way to London, Fernando joined other soap-box orators in Hyde Park propounding political and social change,[53] among them Pan-Africanists who had held their first protest meeting there in 1919.[54] Fernando's ready identification with the transnational black community they proposed can be surmised. Among Caribbeans and West Africans living in Europe and London, Harold Moody, later of the League of Coloured Peoples, was a leader among a first generation of black activists proposing an international Pan-Africanist community, with Pan-African congresses linking British, North American and European black people in a post-slavery, post-imperialist movement.[55] Fernando must have felt the irony of his situation as he spoke alongside such Pan-Africanists in a gathering-place whose colonial namesake (Hyde Park in Sydney) he had known first as a boy so long ago and so many thousands of miles away.

Published scenes of London's famous Toy Market, well established by the early 1900s, show toy-hawkers wearing placards advertising their wares.[56] Fernando seems to have adapted this combination when he began picketing the most high-profile of his targets thus far, Australia House, the London home of Australia's government representatives. Along with his placard and pamphlets, he pinned to his suit toy skeletons he had made, telling passers-by that they stood for murdered Aborigines.[57] While some members of the public were perhaps aware that he was referring to recent violence against Aboriginal people in Australia, and others were possibly sympathetic more generally to humanitarian campaigns for native peoples living within the British Empire, the Australian authorities were all too clear about his intentions. They reacted by having Fernando arrested repeatedly for loitering and disturbing the peace, but to no avail. As their confidential report of 1921 inadvertently confirms, Fernando continued to be a thorn in their sides. While the Australian authorities in the early 1920s were suspicious of Fernando's motives and hostile to his perspective, those who met him during his trial, eight years later, were in no doubt of the veracity of his claims.

As the interest of the English and Australian press in Fernando's case illustrated, where better for an Aboriginal man to criticise Australia than from London? Now, when he was in his mid-sixties, Fernando's testimony finally found its Australian public. Drawing on a report in *The Times* of the previous day, on 2 February 1929 the *Sydney Morning Herald* reported under the headline 'Aborigines' Story. In London Court. Persecution of Blacks':

> Anthony Martin Fernando, 65, an aboriginal toy hawker, born near Sydney, was remanded for a month at the Old Bailey to ascertain what could be done for him.
>
> Sir Ernest Wild, after hearing the evidence of barristers about the man's good character, declined to imprison him on a charge of presenting a revolver at Philip Limber with intent to do bodily harm. It was alleged that Fernando, who pleaded guilty to the assault, threatened Limber, who taunted him about being black . . .
>
> Addressing the Court in fluent English, he said: 'I have been boycotted everywhere. Look at my rags. I cannot make ends meet. All I hear is "Go away, black man". It is all tommy rot to say that we are savages. Whites have shot, slowly starved, and hanged us. I have pleaded the aborigines' cause since 1887'.
>
> Sir Ernest Wild said that it was very provoking of anyone to call attention to Fernando's colour. He asked two barristers who had satisfactorily employed the man to arrange to assist him.[58]

In his defence, Fernando benefited from the long-standing imperial trope of the civilised black man.[59] He offered a stinging critique of white race politics, yet was successful in appealing to the court's sense of its own elevated sensibilities on racial matters. Accordingly, the Court Recorder Ernest Wild found against a prison sentence for this man of 'good character' who could speak fluent English and who had impressed with his controlled passion.

Concerned nonetheless that Fernando's crime showed a potential for violence, Wild called for a psychological test. According to the quite specific recollection of one contemporary, far from asserting that Fernando had lost his reason, the psychologist's report effectively endorsed his account of colonisation in NSW, commending his strength of mind, given the treatment of his people. His capacity to recognise support where it was offered confirmed that the source of his anger lay in the behaviour of others: 'If this man is given consideration he responds with gratitude. He holds strong views about the manner in which his people are treated – a sign, not of insanity, but of an unusually strong mind. There is no occasion to commit him to an asylum.'[60] Discovering that he was to be held on remand for six weeks, Fernando protested loudly to the court that custody was just another attempt to keep him from promoting the Aboriginal cause. In response,

> The Recorder said that nobody objected to the defendant expressing strong views concerning the treatment of Australian aborigines. He had been kept in custody because he carried and threatened to use a revolver. A man differently coloured might have been imprisoned. 'Whatever you think of whites', he said to Fernando, 'there is justice in Britain.'[61]

This idea that justice in Britain might override injustices in the colonies was important to indigenous politics around the time of Fernando's trial. In 1926, an entourage of Maori had travelled from New Zealand to England to petition King George V.[62] Only a few years later, Australian Aboriginal activist William Ferguson, president of the Australian Aborigines' League, collected thousands of signatures for an Aboriginal rights' petition addressed to the King of England.[63] But Fernando's experience in Australia had shown that British law could not be depended on to protect indigenous rights, especially where it conflicted with those of whites. He had been turned away from giving evidence in the 1880s precisely because he was an Aboriginal man whose evidence could bring white men to British justice. Nor had such occurrences diminished with the passing of time. The murder of Aborigines, particularly by parties of colonists and police claiming to be engaged in the capture of suspects, and the failure of local judges to find against white murderers of Aboriginal people, had been headline news in Australia and abroad only two years before Fernando's appearance in court.[64] Not surprisingly, Fernando did not appeal for British justice in his own case or for that of his people (although he did have confidence in his right to speak on both matters in a British court of law in London).

Several days after Fernando's first appearance in court, the secretary of the Anti-Slavery and Aborigines' Protection Society (ASAPS) noted that the humanitarian author and educator Mary Montgomery Bennett, who was living in London at this time and was well-known to the ASAPS, had become interested in Fernando's trial. Several recent studies of Bennett's commitment to Aboriginal rights have noted her increasing inclination to join with (rather than speaking for) Aboriginal people in their rights' struggles, and it seems likely that Fernando was important in this process.[65] Bennett's interest in the benevolent guardianship of the Aborigines had been expressed in her first book, *Christisson of Lammermoor*; but, within a few years, her second book, *The Australian Aborigine as a Human Being*, became one of the most important defences of Aboriginal self-determination written prior to the Second World War. She met Fernando in 1929, a year before she completed her second book, and he appears in its pages.

Bennett had telephoned the ASAPS to say that 'she wanted to get hold of an Australian aboriginal [sic] who was brought up at the Old Bailey and would like, if possible, to bring him before [their Aborigines Sub-]Committee as a live specimen'.[66] As I have said, specimen status had marked the appearance of Aborigines in Europe in the nineteenth century. Although her description of Fernando was undoubtedly an ironic comment on the lack of Aboriginal people known by the sub-committee, it also suggests the continuing assumption that Aborigines were passive subjects. Bennett would in following years cast aside this attitude in her insistence on the agency of the Aboriginal people, one of her greatest legacies.

At first Fernando refused to appear before their 'so-called philanthropic organisation' (was this Fernando's term?).[67] Bennett was not one to be defeated. Several days later she went to his cell, neatly circumventing his refusal to meet with her, but also reasserting her imperial power as a white woman. The tension between these two impulses, her desire to learn from Fernando and her wish to appropriate him into her own telling of the Aboriginal problem, is evident in her accounts of their meeting. In a letter to another of her regular correspondents interested in the Aboriginal question in Australia, she described their exchange in glowing terms:

> I have met Fernando who is small and delicate and with a gentle gravity of demeanour which only girding and insult can rouse him from. He spoke most beautifully to his employer's old mother who had come to see him. He said to her what a proud thing it was for her to have brought up such a son, and he spoke so gratefully and affectionately of

Mr Crawshaw. 'A good father is good, but a good mother is above every other good. I was taken from my mother when I was little, but the thought of her has been the guiding star of my life.' This is what he said to her. And to me, 'If you want to help my people, you must be quick, for there are not many left.'[68]

For Bennett, Fernando was no longer a specimen, but an individual whose personal and political commitments informed her own. In *The Australian Aboriginal* she wrote of Fernando both as a 'typical' Aborigine but also as a tragic hero whose people were under immediate threat, fitting his life story into a European tradition of hope against the odds:

> [He] is a typical Aboriginal, with a childlike desire to trust people, but experience has broken his confidence, and he has become a strange mixture of trustfulness and suspicion, of faithful affection to those who treat him decently and inextinguishable fury of indignation at the wrongs of his race ... He works for his living while following his mission, and might live at ease in good service. But voices of his people call to him not to forget their sufferings and wrongs, and he starts on new travels. Age cannot dim the faith that burns in his fragile, worn-out body. If he would tell the tale of these wanderings, wider than those of Ulysses or St Paul, what a history that would be of a pilgrim following not even a memory but only an imagination about his mother for his guiding star![69]

Bennett's meeting with Fernando seems to have been pivotal in her return to Australia, marking a new intensity in her work for the Aboriginal cause. In the decades which followed, through her involvement with Aborigines living on missions and with Aboriginal activists, she represented individuals in their claims against authorities, as well as speaking out nationally and internationally for Aboriginal rights. In many ways her life of protest in Australia was to become as driven and isolated as Fernando's own.[70] One element in this commitment was land, and Bennett became involved in the Model Aboriginal State Movement, calling for large self-managed reserves, a campaign never accepted by state or federal governments as a viable response to the Aboriginal question.[71]

Land was central, too, to Fernando's politics. In their 1921 undercover report, the Australian authorities had noted that Fernando would 'advocate the creation of "Reserves" or "Refuge-Territory" for the black race in Australia similar to those allotted to Indians by the Government in the U.S.A.', a provision made necessary by 'England's brutal treatment of the Australian blacks'.[72] Perhaps Fernando had spoken to Bennett about these ideas and helped to form her views; but if he had, she wasn't telling, preferring to emphasise his heroic

suffering over his political pragmatism. Given his own expert mobilisation of this tragic narrative, Fernando perhaps would not have
minded. In 1936, Bennett expressed her disgust at whites to the ASAPS
in terms Fernando might have appreciated:

> We have a long way to go before human conditions will be obtained by
> this highly gifted race. The facts are at present that they are being
> willed to death. The majority of Australians are still poisoned with a
> strong anti-native bias – the criminal cannot forgive the victim he has
> wronged . . . But that I believe in God, I should despair, not of the Abori-
> gines who respond magnificently, but of the white people . . . Nobody
> could be more cruel, greedy, dishonourable and unjust in their dealings
> with native races than the British Australian.[73]

Several weeks later London's *Morning Post* reported Fernando's second
appearance in court following his arraignment:

> Anthony Martin Fernando, aged 65, who claimed to be an Australian
> aborigine, was placed on probation for two years . . . [From the witness
> box] Fernando made a heated outburst against the white race.
>
> Mr. F. M. Crawshaw, a barrister, yesterday told the Recorder that he
> formerly employed Fernando in his house and was willing to take him
> back. In answer to the Recorder, who asked if he was willing to return,
> Fernando said, 'If everyone was like Mr. Crawshaw I should not be
> here.' Whereupon the Recorder remarked, 'We should have reached the
> millenium.'[74]

Following his trial, the ASAPS reported that Fernando, then working
as a cook for Crawshaw, did 'not wish to see anybody'.[75] We have no
information concerning the next ten years of Fernando's life. At some
point he left Crawshaw, once again preferring his independence to a
life in service, no matter that it was kindly offered. Independence was
again to prove dangerous for an Aboriginal man living in London. In
January 1938, as Australia celebrated 150 years of white settlement,
Fernando appeared for the last time in a London court. The *Sydney
Morning Herald* reported: 'Aboriginal in Trouble. White "Brutality"
Denounced.' Then in his seventies, Fernando's arraignment mirrored
his first, ten years earlier. Charged with assaulting a fellow-lodger for
his racial taunts, Fernando used the opportunity to again speak out
against racism:

> The magistrate asked what he could do to help him.
>
> Fernando declared that nobody could help him, and added that his
> knowledge of the white man's treatment of the blacks, especially the
> Australian aborigines gave him no hope of justice.
>
> The magistrate: 'You are a self-educated man?'
>
> Fernando: 'Yes, I had a bitter education in white brutality . . .'.[76]

The case against him was dismissed. Fernando died in 1949 in a home for elderly men in Essex, England.[77]

Fernando's claims about white brutality could not have been more pertinent than in the sesquicentennial year of 1938. As part of the celebrations, a re-enactment of the 'discovery' of Australia was performed in Sydney Cove, close to Woolloomooloo, and involved Aborigines cast as figures acquiescing to colonisation. Aboriginal activists from around Australia staged a Day of Mourning in protest.[78] Leading among them was Pearl Gibbs.[79] According to the historian Heather Goodall, Gibbs collected newspaper reports of Fernando's court appearances, and filed them among her most treasured personal papers.[80] The long-term impact on Aboriginal politics in Australia of Fernando's outspoken protest can only be imagined. Gibbs went on to campaign against the alienation of Aborigines under the constitution, a campaign that proved successful through referendum in 1967.[81] As a result of their inclusion in the nation and, by the 1970s, of the granting of Australian citizenship, an increasingly radical era of Aboriginal activism commenced, one focused on international courts and First Nations' networks rather than Britain. Individual protest on English soil returned unexpectedly to the spotlight, however, in the bicentennial year of 1988. In an unknowing homage to Fernando, Aboriginal activist Burnum Burnum stood on the cliffs of Dover and claimed England for the Aboriginal people. Contrasting Aboriginal rule with British justice, he promised Aboriginal colonisers would uphold the rights of their subjects.[82]

Notes

1 T. Flannery (ed.), *The Birth of Sydney* (Melbourne: Text Publishing, 2002), pp. 141–4.
2 D. Sampson, 'Strangers in a Strange Land: The 1868 Aborigines and other Indigenous Performers in Mid-Victorian Britain', PhD Thesis, University of Technology, Sydney, 2000, p. 75.
3 The words are supposedly a sarcastic comment made by the contemporary Aboriginal man Colbee concerning Bennelong's life in England: Flannery, *The Birth of Sydney*, p. 144.
4 P. Brantlinger, 'Dying Races: Rationalizing Genocide in the Nineteenth Century', in J. N. Pieterse and B. Parekh (eds), *The Decolonisation of the Imagination: Culture, Knowledge and Power* (London: Zed Books, 1995).
5 R. Corbey, 'Ethnographic Showcases, 1870–1930', in Pieterse and Parekh, *The Decolonisation of the Imagination*; R. Poignant, 'Captive Lives: Billy, Jenny, Little Toby and Their Companions', in K. Darian-Smith (ed.), *Captive Lives: Australian Captivity Narratives* (London: Institute of Commonwealth Studies, 1993).
6 S. Mathur, 'Living Ethnological Exhibits: The Case of 1886', *Cultural Anthropology*, 15:4 (November 2000), 492–524; S. Gunning, 'Travelling with Her Mother's Tastes: The Negotiation of Gender, Race, and Location in the Wonderful Adventures of Mrs Seacole in Many Lands', *Signs*, 26:4 (summer 2001), 949–81; and J. Miller, S. D. Pennybacker and E. Rosenhaft, 'Mother Ada Wright and the International

Campaign to Free the Scotsboro Boys, 1913–1934', *American Historical Review*, 106:2 (April 2001), 387–430. Thank you to Antoinette Burton for alerting me to these references.

7 A. Burton, 'Tongues Untied: Lord Salisbury's "Black Man" and the Boundaries of Imperial Democracy', *Society for Comparative Study of Society and History*, 42:1 (January 2000), 632–61, at 634.

8 P. Gilroy, 'Route Work: The Black Atlantic and the Politics of Exile', in I. Chambers and L. Curti (eds), *The Post-Colonial Question: Common Skies, Divided Horizons* (New York: Routledge, 1996).

9 Here I paraphrase A. Burton, 'Epilogue', *At the Heart of Empire: Indians and the Colonial Encounter in Late Victorian Britain* (Berkeley: University of California Press, 1998), p. 192.

10 National Archives of Australia (NAA), Canberra, Case File: 'Fernando, A. M. – Case of', Series A11803/1, Item 14/89/475, Reported by A. Law, Commonwealth Official, to R. Munro-Ferguson, Governor General, letter dated 19 October 1916.

11 P. Turbet, *The Aborigines of the Sydney District Before 1788*, 2nd edn (East Roseville, Australia: Kangaroo Press, 2001), chapters 1–3.

12 J. Kohen, *The Parramatta Native Institution and the Black Town: A History* (Kensington: University of New South Wales Press, 1991).

13 M. Brown, 'Fernando: The Story of an Aboriginal Prophet', *Aboriginal Welfare Bulletin*, 4:1 (1964), 9.

14 P. Hetherington, *Settlers, Servants, and Slaves: Aboriginal and European Children in Nineteenth-Century Western Australia* (Crawley: University of Western Australia Press, 2002).

15 Kohen, *The Parramatta Native Institution*, pp. 264–7.

16 Brown, 'Fernando', p. 7.

17 M. Bennett, *The Australian Aboriginal as a Human Being* (London: Alston Rivers Press, 1930), p. 113.

18 A. Haebich, *Broken Circles: Fragmenting Indigenous Families 1800–2000* (Fremantle: Fremantle Arts Centre Press, 2000).

19 Brown, 'Fernando', p. 7.

20 In writing of her African–Irish–English–Aboriginal great-grandfather, the circus performer Harry Cardell, Wendy Holland has noted the importance of names to Aboriginal Australians: 'Reimagining Aboriginality in the Circus Space', *Journal of Popular Culture*, 33:1 (fall 1999), 91–104.

21 Dharuk and Darug are variant forms of the same name: J. Kohen, *The Darug and Their Neighbours: The Traditional Owners of the Sydney Region* (Blacktown, NSW: Darug Link–Blacktown and District Historical Society, 1993), pp. 104 and 140.

22 R. McGregor, *Imagined Destinies: Aboriginal Australians and the Doomed Race Theory, 1880–1939* (Melbourne: Melbourne University Press, 1997), p. 36.

23 See C. Hall, 'Imperial Man: Edward Eyre in Australasia and the West Indies 1833–66', in B. Schwarz (ed.), *The Expansion of England: Race, Ethnicity and Cultural History* (London: Routledge, 1996), pp. 130–70.

24 Turbet, *The Aborigines of the Sydney District*, p. 4.

25 A. Callaway, 'Bungaree', in S. Kleinert and M. Neale (eds), *The Oxford Companion to Aboriginal Art and Culture* (Melbourne: Oxford University Press, 2000), pp. 551–2.

26 I. Duffield, 'Billy Blue: Power, Popular Culture and Mimicry in Early Sydney', *Journal of Popular Culture*, 33:1 (summer 1999), 7–22; see also C. Pybus, 'A Touch of the Tar: African Settlers in Colonial Australia and the Implications for Issues of Aboriginality', *London Papers in Australian Studies*, 3 (2001), 1–24.

27 Flannery, *The Birth of Sydney*, pp. 182, 200 and 203.

28 See ibid.

29 'Aborigine's Story', *Sydney Morning Herald*, 2 February 1929, p. 17.

30 N. E. Wright, 'The Problem of Aboriginal Evidence in Early Colonial New South Wales', in D. Kirby and C. Coleborne (eds), *Law, History, Colonialism* (Manchester: Manchester University Press, 2001).

31 J. Chesterman and B. Galligan, 'Introduction', in J. Chesterman and B. Galligan (eds), *Citizens Without Rights: Aborigines and Australian Citizenship* (Cambridge: Cambridge University Press, 1997).
32 For an example, see Lord and Lady Apsley, *The Amateur Settler* (London: Hodder & Stoughton, c.1930), np.
33 H. Goodall, *From Invasion to Embassy: Land in Aboriginal Politics in New South Wales from 1780 to 1972* (St Leonards: Allen & Unwin, 1996), p. 28.
34 Brown, 'Fernando', p. 7.
35 J. Green, *Black Edwardians: Black People in Britain 1901–1914* (London: Frank Cass, 1998).
36 P. Fryer, *Staying Power: Black People in Britain since 1805* (London: Pluto Press, 1984); N. Myers, *Reconstructing the Black Past: Blacks in Britain 1780–1830* (London and Portland, OR: Frank Cass, 1996); L. Tabili, *'We Ask for British Justice': Workers and Racial Difference in Late Imperial Britain* (Ithaca, NY: Cornell University Press, 1994); J. Walvin, *Black and White: The Negro and English Society 1555–1945* (London: Allen Lane–Penguin Press, 1973), chapter 13.
37 A. Woollacott, *To Try Her Fortune in London: Australian Women, Colonialism, and Modernity* (New York: Oxford University Press, 2001), p. 13.
38 N. Peterson and W. Sanders, 'Introduction', in N. Peterson and W. Sanders (eds), *Citizenship and Indigenous Rights: Changing Conceptions and Possibilities* (Cambridge: Cambridge University Press, 1998), pp. 6–9.
39 Commonwealth of Australia, Case File: A11803/1, 14/89/475, A. M. Fernando to the British Consul, 8 and 29 June 1916.
40 B. Attwood and A. Markus, *The Struggle for Aboriginal Rights: A Documentary History* (Crows Nest, Sydney: Allen & Unwin, 1999).
41 B. Attwood and S. G. Foster (eds), *Frontier Conflict: The Australian Experience* (Canberra: National Museum of Australia, 2003).
42 Fryer, *Staying Power*, pp. 320ff.; for the influence of Garvey on Aboriginal activism in Australia in the 1910s, see J. Maynard, 'Fred Maynard and the Australian Aboriginal Progressive Association (AAPA): One God, One aim, One destiny', *Aboriginal History*, 27 (1997), 1–13.
43 D. Hiro, *Black British, White British: A History of Race Relations in Britain* (London: Grafton Books, 1991), p. 36.
44 For example, Commonwealth of Australia, Case File: A11803/1, 14/89/475, Memorandum from American Embassy to Australian Foreign Affairs, London, 2 August 1916.
45 Ibid., N. L. Shepherd, Official Secretary, Prime Minister's Department, to the Governor General, 22 December 1916.
46 F. Paisley, *Loving Protection? Australian Feminism and Aboriginal Women's Rights, 1919–1939* (Melbourne: Melbourne University Press, 2000).
47 Corbey, 'Ethnographics', p. 70.
48 Geneva, Switzerland, League of Nations Archives, File Catalogue, 'Personal Petitions'.
49 A brief survey of *Der Bunde* shows that its readership was interested in the League of Nations and the post-war reformation of Europe. The newspaper employed a group of international reporters, and those with English surnames contributed numbers of 'letters to the editor': National Library of Switzerland, Berne, Switzerland, Microfilm Collection, 'Der Bunde'.
50 NAA, Canberra, Australia, Case File: 'Fernando, Anthony Martin', Series D1915/0, Item SA 608, Inspector H. E. Jones, Attorney General's Investigation Branch, to Inspector R. J. L. Connard, Adelaide, 18 October 1921.
51 Ibid., Memorandum, Director, Investigation Branch, Attorney-General's Department, Melbourne, 3 November 1921.
52 Ibid., Jones to Connard.
53 Ibid.
54 Fryer, *Staying Power*, p. 315.
55 Ibid., p. 320.

56 'London's Street Toy Fair', *Graphic*, 22 December 1906, p. 851. Thanks to Georgine Clarsen for this reference.
57 Brown, 'Fernando', p. 9.
58 *Sydney Morning Herald*, 2 February 1929, p. 17.
59 On the mobilisation of this trope in the 1890s, see Burton, 'Tongues Untied'.
60 As this extract appears in an interview Bennett gave several decades after meeting with Fernando in London, it is unlikely to be verbatim; and see Brown, 'Fernando', p. 9. Thanks to Alison Holland for discussion on this point. See A. Holland and F. Paisley, 'Anthony Martin Fernando', Supplementary Volume, *Australian Dictionary of Biography*, forthcoming.
61 *Sydney Morning Herald*, 21 March 1929, p. 11; and *Argus* (Melbourne), 22 March 1929, p. 7.
62 J. Belich, *Paradise Reforged: A History of the New Zealanders from the 1880s to the Year 2000* (Honolulu: University of Hawai'i Press, 2001), p. 197.
63 Unfortunately, although presented to the Federal Parliament in Australia, it was never forwarded to London. See A. Markus (ed.), *Blood from a Stone: William Cooper and the Australian Aborigines' League* (Clayton, Vic.: Monash University, 1986).
64 A. Markus, *Governing Savages* (Sydney: Allen & Unwin, 1990).
65 A. Holland, 'Feminism, Colonialism and Aboriginal Workers: An Antislavery Crusade', *Labour History*, 69 (November 1995), 52–64; M. Lake, *Getting Equal: The History of Australian Feminism* (Sydney: Allen & Unwin, 1999), chapter 5; Paisley, *Loving Protection?*
66 Rhodes House, Oxford, Anti-Slavery Society Papers (ASSP), s. 22, G 374, Travers Buxton, Secretary, Anti-Slavery and Aborigines' Protection Society, to Rev. Lefroy, 8 February 1929.
67 Ibid., Buxton to Lefroy, 26 February 1929.
68 State Archives of South Australia, Adelaide, Cooke Papers, SA GRG 52/32/25, Bennett to Cooke, 26 March 1929.
69 Bennett, *The Australian Aboriginal*, pp. 112–13.
70 Paisley, *Loving Protection?*
71 K. Blackburn, 'White Agitation for an Aboriginal State in Australia (1925–1929)', *Australian Journal of Politics and History*, 45:2 (June 1999), 157–80.
72 NAA, Case File: D1915/0, SA 608, Jones to Connard.
73 Anti-Slavery Society Papers, Rhodes House, Oxford, s. 22, G378, Bennett to Buxton, 22 August 1936.
74 *The Morning Post*, 20 March 1929, p. 5.
75 ASSP, Buxton to Bennett, 22 April 1929.
76 *Sydney Morning Herald*, 7 February 1938, p. 8.
77 H. Goodall, 'Aboriginal Calls for Justice: Learning from History', *Aboriginal Law Bulletin*, 2:33 (1988), 4–6. His death certificate, dated 9 January 1949, describes Fernando as an 84-year-old former trader who had suffered from various diseases of old age: General Register Office, Iford North, Essex, Certificate Number DXZ 896615. My thanks to Chris Cuneen, Australian Dictionary of Biography, for this information.
78 J. Horner and M. Langton, 'The Day of Mourning', in B. Gammage and P. Spearitt (eds), *Australians 1938* (Broadway, Sydney: Fairfax, Syme & Weldon, 1987), pp. 29–35.
79 'Three Tributes to Pearl Gibbs (1901–1983)', *Aboriginal History*, 7:1 (1983), 4–22.
80 Goodall, 'Aboriginal Calls', p. 5.
81 B. Attwood and A. Markus, *The 1967 Referendum, or When the Aborigines Didn't Get the Vote* (Canberra: Australian Institute of Aboriginal and Torres Strait Islander Studies, 1997).
82 M. J. Norst, *Burnum Burnum: A Warrior for Peace* (Sydney: Kangaroo Press, 1999).

PART IV

New subjectivities
and the politics of reconciliation

CHAPTER TWELVE

New world poetics of place: along the Oregon Trail and in the National Museum of Australia

Deborah Bird Rose

In this period of the global warping of time–space topologies and of increasing awareness of disorganisation and catastrophe, it is a matter of urgency to ask how we 'new world' settler peoples come to imagine that we belong to our beloved homelands. We cannot help but know that we are here through dispossession and death. What are some of the stories we tell to help us inscribe a moral presence in places we have come to through violence?

I approach this question through an analysis of landscape stories presented in three cultural interpretive centres along the Oregon Trail in the state of Oregon (USA) and of narratives of settlers and place presented in Canberra's National Museum of Australia (NMA).[1] The abrasive edges of my own wandering identities and histories lead me to contribute to emerging practices whereby we may more effectively inscribe a decolonising and reparative presence for ourselves in the new world places that have become our homes. Whether in Australia or in the Pacific north-west, one treads terrains of moral conflict and mythic failure, of densely conflicted transects of love and violence, commitment and crisis. There is no shortage of triumphal narratives of nation-building. My questions seek out spaces where we reveal glimpses of the knowledge of how we are implicated in the disasters of our histories, our homes and our own lives.

In examining public cultural interpretations of settlement as they are represented in museums and historical centres, I examine contemporary stories about settler pasts in relation to place. Comparisons between the US sites and the Australian site reveal strong articulations of national landscape mythology and national unease. The narrative of situating settlers in their new world homes is given both substance and subversion by sustaining gaps between representations of geography, ecology, narrative and the embodied presence of the visitor. Comparison enables the representations, narratives and gaps to be back-lit by one another, thus throwing each into unexpected relief. It begins to illuminate epistemic and metaphysical disaster-zones, as well as the more familiar regions of environmental crisis.

Cultural alchemy

The great American jurist Oliver Wendell Holmes wrote in 1872: 'We Americans are all cuckoos, we make our homes in the nests of other birds.'[2] The statement articulates a primary new-world exclusion: Native Americans are not included in the category of 'we Americans', who are all cuckoos. Like much great cultural and mythic work, this statement addresses a relation of power and positions it beyond human control. Here a massive historical exercise of power – dispossession, violence, conquest, wars of extermination and policies of eradication through assimilation, as well as the radical alteration of continental landscapes, including deliberate attempts to exterminate whole species – is reduced to a simple natural fact: we *are* that kind of bird. Some birds build nests, others steal them – we are the latter kind: cuckoos.

Narratives of God also exempt settler-descended Americans from moral confrontation of our own violence. The Exodus story is deeply foundational: we settler Americans are the people who escaped tyranny, were purified through hardship, entered into a covenant with God and are delivered into the promised land. In this account, we are not so much nature's cuckoos as God's own chosen cuckoos. These two deployments of narrative converge in the idea of nature's God; cultural alchemy turns scripture into landscape.

I do not claim that Exodus is the only American story, but in tracing its origins and examining its contemporary expressions I see a continuity in which I know myself to be deeply implicated. As an American it seems I have always known that to be delivered into the Promised Land you have to hit the road. My forebears who came west in their covered wagons knew this too. One of the many books and pamphlets extolling the beauties and seductions of the Willamette Valley in Oregon described it as a 'Garden of Eden where the clover grows wild and when you wade through it, it reaches your chin'.[3]

The idea of deliverance into a 'promised land' goes back to the Puritan founders of New England. As Bercovitch discusses in his brilliant study *The American Jeremiad*, Puritans consciously linked their own project to biblical events and prophesies through the intellectual structure of typology, and thus understood themselves to be the latter-day realisations of biblical events and persons.[4] Puritans claimed a total identification, literal and spiritual, of Old Israel with New Israel, Canaan with America.[5] By the end of the seventeenth century many of the tenets of Puritanism had been brought into broader religious thinking, and the view of America as promised land took hold in ever-expanding terms. The American Revolution, for example, was claimed as confirmation not only of biblical prophecy but of laws of nature and laws of history.[6] Conrad Cherry refers to this thinking as America's governing mythology; in his words: 'The history of American civil religion is a history of the conviction that the American people are God's New Israel, his newly chosen people.'[7]

The implications of this thinking, from the perspective of landscape poetics, offer a compelling and enduring vision: from the Puritans through to the present, America *is* destiny and *is* fulfilment. Isaiah foretold that God would make the wilderness to be like a new Garden of Eden, and would make the desert bloom like a rose. According to Cotton Mather, in a sermon from 1710, 'America is legible in these promises'.[8] That is, the America of 1710 (or, as I argue, America today) is legible in the words of Isaiah. In the landscape we see our own future, and we see the flourishing of the landscape as the evidence of God's blessing.[9] Time is thus stretched between two moments: prophecy and fulfilment. America is legible in the prophesies, fulfilment is legible in the land.[10] Past and future, text and landscape, are connected and mutually confirming.[11]

Jeremiah's prophecy of a new covenant carries special pertinence in the American west. Jeremiah foretold a new covenant that would be inscribed in the hearts of men, making of the covenanted person a new Adam. This, I believe, is the mythic scaffolding to the claim to innocence, analysed so vividly by Patricia Limerick.[12] Michael Walzer shows that with this new Adam, 'it is but a short and obvious step to bring him home, to make the goal of the second Exodus [the American Exodus] not Canaan but Eden'.[13] The westward push to Oregon brought this thinking to a pinnacle: Oregon itself was variously referred to as a land of milk and honey, Eden, Beulah Land, Promised Land, Paradise and Heaven.

The idea of Beulah Land achieves the convergence of action and destiny, prophecy and place, that underwrites America's geography and time concepts. Emigrants sang the hymn as they travelled, 'keeping before them the promise of Oregon'.[14] The words tell of people's longing for a land which is already theirs and in which they themselves will become legible:

I've reached the land of corn and wine
And all its riches freely mine;
Here shines undimmed one blissful day
For all my night has passed away.
Oh Beulah Land, Sweet Beulah Land,
As on the highest mount I stand,
I look away across the sea,
Where mansions are prepared for me,
And view the shining glory shore,
My heaven, my home forever more.[15]

This beautiful old hymn does not distinguish between heaven as a spiritual home and heaven as a worldly home. As people sang it on their westward way, they sang Isaiah's prophecies, American geography and their own legibility as agents in destiny.

Trails

From 1841 Americans started migrating from the United States into the western territories: first a handful, then a few hundred and, by 1849, with the California gold rush, tens of thousands. At this time the US extended as far west as (roughly) the Mississippi River. Those who travelled beyond were called 'emigrants', and it is estimated that half a million people travelled the Oregon, California and Mormon Trails (the latter terminating near Salt Lake City, Utah) in the period 1843–60.[16] The Oregon Trail took people into the Willamette Valley and to a site that came be called Oregon City. From there people fanned out north and south within the well-watered coastal zone of the Pacific north-west.[17]

A century-and-a-half later, the trail has become big business. The Oregon National Historic Trail, designated by Congress in 1978, is managed by the National Park Service, the Bureau of Land Management, the Forest Service, state and local governmental units and citizen organisations. Today's trail, 2,170 miles from the National Historic Trails Centre in Independence, Missouri, to the End of the Trail Centre in Oregon City, is traversed by highway. There are 300 miles of discernible trail ruts, 125 historic sites, and seven cross-country hiking segments.[18] There are more books than one could imagine written by people who have travelled the trail in recent years. Whole convoys of recreational vehicles filled with trail enthusiasts, known as 'rut nuts', annually make the pilgrimage.

Beginning in 1987 citizen and government groups in Oregon began to plan the construction of a series of linked interpretive centres dedicated to various aspects of the Oregon Trail and the State of Oregon; an undated brochure I picked up in 1999 describes the centres as 'Five Different Perspectives. One Big Story'.[19] I discuss only the three centres that deal most directly with landscape issues, and I emphasise that a vast amount of information has been omitted in order to present a few clear themes which are consistently presented as central to the story.

Flagstaff Hill

The National Historic Oregon Trail Interpretive Centre at Flagstaff Hill opened in 1992. It is adjacent to well-preserved ruts and is 'set atop the summit of Flagstaff Hill, where pioneers caught their first glimpse of the Promised Land'.[20] Standing there, you think of Beulah Land ('As on the highest mount I stand'). According to the pamphlet, 'They walked for 2,000 miles, men, women and children by the tens of thousands . . . With each step they drew closer to a dream called Oregon.'[21] When you enter the display area of the centre you see a map showing the trail from Independence to Oregon City and Portland, and you are told: 'They displaced the Indians, and wrested a new territory and several states from what they perceived as wilderness. Despite some tragic consequences, the story of the Oregon Trail is an epic of human endurance, and reminds us of those who came as Empire builders.'[22] The explanation continues: 'The stories told here at Flagstaff Hill recall the days when the U.S. was young, the trail was new, and people moved ever westward in search of the promised land.'

Flagstaff introduces one of the main mythic themes of the American west: the country's *agency*. Initially, according to the interpretive material, America had called Europeans to it: the country 'beckoned with meadows, forests, Mountains, rivers, fish, tobacco, gold, and freedom from kings and queens'. Later, 'the western frontier called to an entire generation. "On to Oregon!" echoed in their hearts and minds.' The Oregon Trail itself 'led' settlers to the 'promised land'; the response was all or nothing: 'Oregon or bust'.[23]

In summing up what it all meant, Flagstaff's interpretive materials state: 'The lure of the west was powerful, and emigrants kept coming.' It suggests that 'all of us are kin to these strong people'. So, like Oliver Wendell Holmes's cuckoos, it seems that 'all of us' is a category that does not readily include Native Americans. Furthermore, we learn that the country itself called, lured or gripped us, made us feverish, and demanded action: our desire for the Promised Land was brought into being by the land itself. The interpretation continues: 'We can feel the pull of the west that the pioneers experienced by looking at the wilderness and its vast adventure and beauty that still surround us.' In asserting that we can feel the country's agency (the pull of the west) by looking at its wilderness, I hear rich reverberations of Cotton Mather's assertion that our destiny is legible in these landscapes. Nature and God come together in the beauty of the wilderness; if we expose ourselves to it, it will still call to us. The innocence that Patricia Limerick posits as the defining American self-delusion in the west is here affirmed and potently mingled with an affirmation of our incomparable desirability. The continuing pull of country not only links us to our pioneer kin, but insinuates that the story continues: as long as the west pulls, the story of destiny remains unfulfilled, and we who are here today have a continuing mission.

End of the Oregon Trail Interpretive Centre
Established in 1995 on a site where many of the emigrants ended their trek, this centre is dominated by three huge covered-wagon-shaped buildings housing two mixed-media theatres and an exhibits hall. The truly unique contribution of this centre is the 'mixed-media dramatisation of the Oregon Trail experience'. The show, entitled 'The Spirit Lives On!', mingles commercially flavoured music and voices with traditional music, sounds of wind and storms, angelic choirs, flashing lights, ghostly voices, brief diary narratives and rapidly changing pictures of landscapes and pioneers. As we listen again and again to the chorus 'The spirit lives on, in Oregon', we hear also ghostly voices calling 'Oregon'. The country itself seems to be calling to us in the form of beauty and in the voices of heavenly choirs. Although we are here at the end of the trail, this truly bizarre exhibition tells us that this is not the end of the story. A man's voice sings to us:

> It's the end of the trail,
> And sisters and brothers, daughters and sons,
> we're all on our own journey too.

Here country's agency and our response are presented as a dialogical journey. Because we are the country's desire, our responsibility is to take the journey, to meet the country, to fill its desiring landscapes with our presence. This extraordinary show seems to want to tell us that because we still journey, we are ourselves destiny in the process of fulfilment. Like Flagstaff Hill, this centre assures us that the story is not yet over.

Columbia Gorge Discovery Centre
This centre takes the natural world as its main focus. It thus carries a critical burden in negotiating issues around country's agency, its

desire for us, and our actions in it. It is located on the Columbia River in the town called The Dalles, and is set between two major dams with hydroelectric plants. Quest and conquest jostle each other in the narratives here: this centre cannot conceal the shattered face of the land.

The displays take you through geological history, weather, wild flowers and invasions of people, plants and animals. We have to press through sections on naturalists and natural history, and numerous other exhibits, before we reach the displays in which the collision of the wild and the industrial, alluded to throughout, is actually disclosed. The theme of the war against nature is exemplified in displays concerning the Bonneville Dam. According to a 1930s promotional film, 'At Bonneville Oregon man picked up the battle against the frontier . . . America's conquest of the Columbia has begun'. One of the casualties of the war, a subsequent video acknowledges, is the salmon: 'The dams really narrow the window of opportunity for the salmon in the Columbia River.' The remainder of the display concerns citizens' efforts to revegetate, to improve conditions for salmon, to organise parks for the protection of scenic areas and to reduce individual human impacts on the gorge.

Visions of warfare and of restoration rest oddly with the centre's presentation of the gorge as a wilderness area. You are told: 'When you leave the theatre and find yourself in the midst of giant cliffs and peaks, nothing's left you but silent awe and delight.' I found that I could not look upstream or downstream in awe and delight because my vision was dominated by severe human interventions. Promises of Eden and Beulah Land, and the forceful representation of the country's longing for us, its people, all require us not to see the decay and death that surround us. In spite of all our conditioning in how to frame our landscape vision, as discussed so elegantly by Anne Hyde,[24] the fact is that we need to step inside and look at the man-made replica of the river in order to appreciate the qualities this centre attributes to it. There the floor of the main hall is designed with an inset of shiny liquid-like marble that is an icon of the river; it is set within dull marble, and it leads your eyes to a wall of windows which offer one of the few views dominated by neither industry nor settlement.

This centre offers some of the most destabilising moments in the narrative of the Promised Land. If nature and God come together in wilderness, the gorge shows us that we are killing both. If both are being killed, what becomes of us? How can we be God's chosen ones when it seems that not only our ancestors, but we ourselves, have been, as Cormac McCarthy says, 'patched Argonauts . . . bleeding westward like some heliotropic plague'.[25]

Both feet on the ground

American's sense of being on a mission from God, its conflicted yearning for Paradise, its sense of being always on the threshold and its claim actually to be the Promised Land constitute a war of narratives with no resolution other than to keep travelling. The cultural centres emphasise a present-world focus of threshold, positioning us always on the edge of deliverance. As the Beulah Land hymn puts it: 'For this is heaven's borderland'. Being a good American you hit the road. You travel the trail and visit the centres; you see the ruts, and you see the performances. Over and over you are told that you *are* this history; this history *is* you. The narrative entrenches national mythology in this crisis moment of imminent arrival – the trail has ended, but the Promised Land has not quite been occupied. Here all depends on that one step: the people will go into the land of milk and honey, and God will bless. You are desire and destiny, threshold and promise. One foot is firmly on the trail, the other is poised mid-air, just ready to step into Eden.

These interpretive centres offer a form of pilgrimage: one puts one's body into motion to experience a cosmogonic event – to cross that threshold once again, and to be delivered, again and again, into the promise of God's blessing without ever having to arrive completely. Trail travel becomes a cosmogonic treadmill that displaces moral anguish. We re-take that one step, re-live that moment of crossing, as if by doing it all again and again we can hold on to that moment wherein the future is as yet unsoiled. Our eyes remain fixed on that shining glory shore. Anything more than that is terrifying.

We see how selective our seeing must be at the Columbia Gorge Centre. There is an outdoor display of log cabins, covered wagons, long-house frame, salmon-drying frame and other items. You wander up to the first wagon and you see at once that there is an artfulness to the display: this wagon points toward Mount Hood, and thus to the Barlowe route to Oregon City. Looking through, you see the mountain framed by the hoop of the wagon. Once you are aware of the non-random placement of this wagon you start to wonder about the way in which the other wagon points back upstream toward The Dalles. What you see from this second wagon are power pylons, dams, smokestacks, storage tanks, smoke, smudge, bridges, highways and wires. The wagon stands beside the skeleton of a native long house, and it seems to say that the long trek leads directly to this: skeletons and ruins overlooking a zone of industrial mayhem.[26]

Standing on this bluff, I want to propose that this covered wagon, the one facing despoliation, opens a fissure wherein we might explore a more provocative configuring of time and space, one that acknowledges violence and filth. The landscape problem in the sacred–secular narrative of America is clear: if the Promised Land is our destiny and our future, and if the Promised Land is violently despoiled, then our future and our destiny is vile, degraded, broken and pitted with death.

And so we have to ask: is this the destiny that we imagined calling to us, or is this some nightmare of deluded misdirection, some metaphysical and geographical wrong turn? The cosmogonic treadmill may not be that final step towards Paradise. Perhaps it is a motion machine that transforms desire into disaster. Is that our story – wrest and trash? Do we consume our longing and expel it as filth?

It seems that a first step away from this treadmill would be to propose that we are not the fulfilment of history. Having taken this step, it follows that any reparative action we might undertake would have to be embedded in a reclamation of our own agency. We would have to claim the history of everything we have damaged in our efforts to locate Paradise for ourselves in this 'new' world.

Tangled Destinies

The landscape section of the NMA poses similar questions of agency and damage, and answers them very differently – some of its more disturbing questions being hinted at only obliquely by the Oregon Trail centres. The section implies the beginnings of a response to disturbance that, if not an answer, is a significant engagement that goes beyond the American treadmill. Different histories, timelines and cultures produce museums telling different stories. My intention here is to juxtapose them, to push their rough edges against each other and thus to continue the disturbance that each offers.

The NMA in Canberra was opened to the public on 11 March 2001 after more than a decade of wrangling over government support and finance. Set on a peninsula that juts into Lake Burley Griffin, and oriented across the lake towards Parliament House, the building is both imposing and playful. Within it, the displays as a whole vigorously avoid conventional timelines, thereby undermining the possibility of single narratives.

The NMA has been subjected to strong criticism, as well as receiving much praise. Triumphal narratives are counterbalanced by those of loss, damage and regret. The two types of narrative constitute much of Australia's national debate about settler identity and the meaning of history. This combat is ongoing and may fairly be thought of as Australia's equivalent to the American treadmill.

The displays are organised into several sections, of which I discuss only a portion of one – *Tangled Destinies: Land and People in Australia.*[27] This section addresses issues of settler Australians and their relationships to nature and place. According to Libby Robin, one of the curators, the

> key narrative line ... is the shift from settler views of Australia as a strange place to a familiar one – the story of 'settling in' and feeling at home, accepting the landscape, even belonging ... The first object in our National Museum must capture that shock, the mystery and the 'otherness' of the unsettling nature of Australia for eyes from elsewhere, and even convey these to those for whom eucalypts and marsupials are familiar and normal.[28]

The shocking differences between the Australian continent and Great Britain, and the effects of those differences on the imaginations and sensibilities of settlers, have long received considerable scholarly attention. *Tangled Destinies* takes up these themes and brings a scientific aesthetic into the story.[29]

Here scientific inquiry displays a dual role both in defining Australian nature as exceptional and in familiarising it by coming to understand it. One of the introductory panels offers a statement by J. Martin (c. 1803): 'Trees retained their leaves and shed their bark instead, the swans were black, the eagles white, the bees were stingless, some mammals had pockets, others laid eggs, it was warmest on the hills and coolest in the valleys, even the blackberries were red.' While the purpose of *Tangled Destinies* is to demonstrate people's growing feeling of being at home, the overall effect is to enhance their sense of exceptionalism. The people and their sense of national identity become implicated as part of Gondwanaland exotica. The narrative discloses a growing sense of belonging, articulated through science and through people's own actions in learning directly to know, love and defend Australia's unique landscapes and biota.

Unlike the American narrative in which settlers imagined the west as home before even getting there, *Tangled Destinies* articulates belonging as a process that develops dialogically between land and people. One of the introductory signs asserts: 'How we think about Australia decides what we do with it. Yet the land is a force in itself, changing our ideas of it and of ourselves, and changing us even as we change the land ...'.

The comparison with American concepts of time in relationship to place, as presented in the Oregon Trail sites, is powerful: the overarching American concept, it will be recalled, stretched time between two conceptual points, promise and fulfilment, and positioned *now* as an ever-shifting moment at the edge of fulfilment. It thus seems to construct a treadmill of imminent encounter, an arrival perpetually deferred. In contrast, *Tangled Destinies'* overarching concept of time in relationship to place suggests that time is an unfolding: the destinies of people and place are mutually implicated orders such that causality works in feedback loops between people and place, place and people. *Tangled Destinies* posits a concept of ecological time, while the Oregon Trail centres posit a concept most closely aligned to messianic time.[30]

The Australian storyline has a progression from the strange to the familiar; it can accommodate error and some degree of disaster far more readily than can the American story of deliverance. One of the first explanations asserts:

> Islands are known for their distinctive and vulnerable species. Australia's plants and animals were isolated for 50 million years. These species were utterly strange to European colonists. They set out to re-make a land that lacked 'useful' animals and plants by importing species that were either practical or ornamental. The result was biological invasion on an unmatched scale and the extinction of many native animals and plants.

In its openness to the representation of error, *Tangled Destinies'* thus speaks to some of the darker qualities of settler societies: their violence, their ambivalent relations with nature, their scornful assertions of their own superiority.

Let us walk into the NMA from the car park. As you get out of your car you see Parliament House across the lake, and before you the dark metallic structure of the NMA dominates your vision. Going into the main entrance you walk through a huge and magnificent hall. If you follow the footprints on the floor, you go through glass doors, past the circular theatre and straight to *Tangled Destinies.* You do not have to enter here: you could turn off to the right towards the beckoning sounds and lights of other exhibits. If you choose to enter, you might go down the left side of the exhibition or take the right side. At the centre are free-standing exhibits. If you take the left side, as the display seems to encourage you to do, you are immediately in amongst the platypus stories. This creature is the chosen medium of encounter, in which European expectations are perturbed by Australian exceptionalism: the object is a burrow with replica eggs. You see a small stuffed platypus; you learn about scientists' efforts to uncover the mysterious processes of platypus reproduction. The main headline here is a statement by eminent environmental historian Eric Rolls: 'More a new planet than a new continent.' There is a circular tape playing, and it frequently returns to Australia's most emblematic sound of exceptional nature – the laughter of the kookaburra.

You walk past numerous collections of bottled specimens. These rectangular glass jars hold in fluid a set of the life-stages of the platypus, from nestlings one day after hatching through to the final youngster, squashed into a bottle at fourteen weeks. Other jars contain the dissected limbs and the young of diverse species. A history of scientific methods of inquiry is here displayed in vivid amber fluid. The domestic use of native species is shown here, in the form of a rug made, in the early 1900s, of the skins of forty-two platypuses. We learn things we never wanted to know: 'The shock wave from a bullet fired into the water near a platypus was enough to kill it.'

At the end of this small section, the display area angles abruptly so that you are forced to turn sharply to your right. When you do that, you see a large metallic structure. Apparently square, the sides slope inward, so the top is larger than the base. From where you stand, the shiny silver metal gleams in the light, and words are faintly etched in its sides. The door is made of a pale gleaming wood. The angles all seem even more powerful than the surfaces, and the thing seems to be pressing into the floor. This structure seems to repel; its surface is shiny, almost glittery, and almost all of the writing is obscure. If you get close enough to read the etching, the wall looms ominously above you. Following the structure around its corners, you see in large black script the word 'Extinct'. You find that there are two doors; there are lights within, and so you step inside.

Here the walls are the same harsh metal. The kookaburra laughter echoes disturbingly. Spread out on a shelf, carpet-like, but at the height of a body in a coffin laid out for viewing, is the skin of a thylacine – the extinct 'Tasmanian Tiger'. 'Extinct' is written again on the wall above the case. Above the case the sign reads: 'Species depart the biota, not with a bang but a whimper ... [the] Tasmanian tiger ... is one ... where that whimper has a precise date ... 7 September 1936, when the last known specimen died in captivity in the Beaumaris Zoo, Hobart'.[31] We learn that Tasmanian settlers believed the thylacines to be killers of livestock, and that from 1886 to 1909 the Government paid £1 for every thylacine killed. There is a photograph of a hunter, a sombre-looking fellow, sitting on an overturned drum and facing a dead beast strung up by the hind legs.

Behind you is a transparent case containing the body of an adult thylacine from around 1930, preserved in 'Wentworth fluid'. When I visited the NMA, at its opening in March 2001, the thylacine had been darkly apparent, a faint presence floating in a turbid substance. By February 2002 the thylacine was no longer visible in the gloom of the tank, though I was assured that it was still there. Somehow the process of becoming invisible added to a general sense of complicity in this creature's extinction, as if the gaze of hundreds of thousands of visitors continued to break it down. According to the signage, these hated animals were hunted to extinction not long ago, and it seemed that yet another act of violence was being perpetrated on the remains of this now unbearably defenceless body.

On a side wall as you exit via the structure's door is a small sign saying that a woman named Rose Hurst had acquired the thylacine skin at a church auction, because she 'felt sorry for it'. The sign asserts that values are changing – from vermin to icon. The display finishes with notes on the Cascade Brewery. The image of a thylacine appears on all its products: 'Now the Tasmanian Tiger is an emblem that says Tasmania'.

From there it is hard to know what to do next, and your real desire is to go outside for some fresh air. You may be sickened by bottles of dead things in all stages of growth and decay, and exasperated by the recorded kookaburra yodelling away to no purpose; you may be weary of contemplating extinction, and of contemplating other people's efforts to understand life by killing and bottling it. It is not just that all this is nauseating: it is rather that it is recent, it is brutal, it is our culture and our violence. It induced in me feelings of shame, and sparked an anger that had nowhere to go.

If you were to walk out now, with those feelings of vertiginous shame still coursing through your body, your mind turning around Rose Hurst's statement that she bought the skin because she 'felt sorry for it', you might be in a condition similar to that which I experienced at the Columbia Gorge Centre. There, one looks upriver through the hoop of the covered wagon and gazes past the ruins of a long house, unable to see anything but pylons, dams and other structures of power. There, too, one feels uncertain of where to go next and what to do with the information yielded by one's senses. When you leave the NMA, however, one final word may await you. Stepping out into the fresh air, you observe the lake, and you can see the distant flag above Parliament House. The museum's walls loom above you. All along those walls, at various levels, are raised bumps. They look like gigantic Braille, and that is what they are. The letters that cover this huge surface spell out 'Sorry'.

Conclusions

The significance of biblical stories in the foundational rhetoric of Australia is currently the subject of lively discussion.[32] I have argued elsewhere that while Australia refuses any single founding myth, it is founded more on the myth of expulsion than on any other. In the first decades of British colonisation, the majority of the people who settled there did so involuntarily and as the recipients of severe punishment: Henry Parkes spoke of the original settlers as 'a despairing group of outcast persons of British origin'.[33] Expulsion is not the only story in Australia, and Ann Curthoys, in particular, has produced an inspiring analysis based on the Exodus myth.[34]

In Australian foundation narratives, Eden was home in England, the monarch was God and the convicts were cast out into a life of toil and sweat amid thorns and thistles. In my view, settlers reworked the basic parameters of that myth, eventually claiming the thorns and thistles as a brash new-world Paradise, and claiming for themselves a new kind of settler identity founded in an antipodean assertion that the thorns and thistles, the flies, dust and salt lakes are indeed 'God's own'. They thus embraced the difficulties of Australian terrains and in good pagan fashion transformed the oppressive meanings of biblical expulsion into a sensuous love of the bush.

Tangled Destinies asserts a (sometimes tentative) claim to belonging. The exceptionalism, the awareness of being a stranger in a very strange place, continues to underwrite the sense that this place is somehow outside your everyday knowledge. And at the same time, the sensuous love for and identification with this place is also asserted, so that you yourself become exceptional and, in comparison with Europe, transgressive.

Whether cast as a pagan version of sensuous love or as a scientific version of better understanding, or some combination of these factors, contemporary Australian poetics of place are not shy of expressing commitment to specific places. These poetics hold the spark of desires that to Americans might be almost unthinkable – the desires to fail in conquest and to belong by being overpowered by the place.

An Australian perspective on desire and place reveals a harsh but compelling story. To encounter that which is strange, and to learn to live with and love it, is to articulate a particular and vulnerable existential space. That space, with its violence and error along with its love and belonging, speaks powerfully to me about the American dilemma. In that space we can begin to recuperate the moral presence we abandoned when we went searching for another world, a better world, a world other than the one we actually live in.

Within this existential space it is possible to express sorrow along with triumph. In Aboriginal English the word 'sorry' has a more powerful meaning than it does in standard English: it means grief; it signals loss; and it calls for either compassion or revenge. It thus speaks not only to an inner state but to a condition of lost relationship: a statement of loss as well as of grief. Aboriginal people's relationships with animals as well as with other humans are based on the capacity to experience 'sorry'.[35] Those connotations have been brought into public discourse, focusing attention on the prime minister's refusal to offer apology for the abusive practices labelled 'assimilation'. Most broadly, 'sorry' calls for relationship to be restored, and it allows for the intensive expressions of grief and anger known as 'sorry business'.

I find myself profoundly moved towards the idea that 'sorry' is a magnificently dense place in which to position the work of decolonisation.

Notes

My research trips to the USA were funded by the North Australia Research Unit (1998) and the Research School of Pacific and Asian Studies (1999), both of the Australian National University. This chapter was written in my position as senior fellow of the Centre for Resource and Environmental Studies, ANU.

1 The issue of relations between settlers and Indigenous people is critical in both the USA and Australia, but is so complex and significant in its own right that it will be the focus of another paper.
2 Quoted in G. Marcus, *Invisible Republic: Bob Dylan's Basement Tapes* (New York: Henry Holt, 1997), p. 118.
3 Quoted in S. Butruille, *Women's Voices from the Oregon Trail: The Times that Tried Women's Souls; and A Guide to Women's History Along the Oregon Trail* (Boise, IO: Tamarack Books, 1993), p. 15.
4 S. Bercovitch, *The American Jeremiad* (Maddison: University of Wisconsin Press, 1978), p. 95.
5 Ibid., p. 76 and elsewhere.
6 Ibid., p. 134.
7 C. Cherry, *God's New Israel: Religious Interpretations of American Destiny* (Chapel Hill: University of North Carolina Press, 1998), pp. 19f.
8 Cotton Mather, Theopolis Americana, Boston, 1710, 43–44.
9 Bercovitch, *American Jeremiad*, pp. 79–80.
10 In both denominational and civic religion the gap between the ideal and the real is a source of moral and social energy; American mythology fuels itself in its own sense of crisis, Bercovitch reminds us: ibid., p. 190 and elsewhere.
11 As I write, George W. Bush is promoting his vision of an axis of evil. Here scripture is turned into place and politics, in rough accordance with the Book of Revelations. How far, one often wonders in dread, will Americans go to fulfil their sense of prophecy and destiny?
12 P. Limerick, *The Legacy of Conquest: The Unbroken Past of the American West* (New York: Norton, 1987).
13 M. Walzer, *Exodus and Revolution* (New York: Basic Books, 1985), pp. 118–19; see also C. Merchant, 'Eve: Nature and Narrative', in her *Earthcare: Women and the Environment* (London, Routledge, 1996), pp. 27–57.
14 Butruille, *Women's Voices*, p. 205.
15 E. Page and J. Sweeney, *Beulah Land*, in *A Treasury of Hymns*, ed. M. Leiper and H. Simon (New York: Simon & Schuster, 1953), p. 311.
16 J. Evans, *Powerful Rockey: The Blue Mountains and the Oregon Trail 1811–1883* (La Grande: Eastern Oregon State College, 1990).

17 Our knowledge of the people who traversed the Oregon Trail builds on contemporary diaries and bundles of letters which themselves testify to people's sense of making history or fulfilling destiny. In addition to these informal writings, the trail was the subject of numerous travel guides and some serious contemporary literature. It was painted and sketched, and thus brought into Americans' visual imagination, by amateurs and by popular artists such as Bierstadt. The continuing interest in trails is not only part of popular culture, but is integral to the 'New Western History'; see, e.g., P. Limerick, C. Milner and C. Rankin (eds), *Trails: Toward a New Western History* (Lawrence: University Press of Kansas, 1991).

18 'Oregon Trail: Oregon National Historic Trail/Missouri to Oregon', a 1993 brochure published by the National Park Service (Department of the Interior), Bureau of Land Management (Department of the Interior) and Forest Service (Department of Agriculture).

19 The Four Rivers Cultural Centre in Ontario (OR), the most easterly of the centres, is dedicated to a multicultural vision of the state of Oregon. Travelling west, the Flagstaff Hill Centre is next. After Flagstaff is the Tamastslikt Cultural Institute on the Umatilla Indian Reservation near Pendleton, Oregon. According to the brochure, 'Tamastslikt Cultural Institute' is the only Indian-owned interpretive facility on the Oregon National Historic Trail and the only one that tells the story from the Indigenous point of view – 'in the words of the Cayuse, Umatilla and Walla Walla people'. Next is the Columbia Gorge Discovery Centre at The Dalles on the Columbia River. The final centre is the End of the Oregon Trail Interpretive Centre in Oregon City on the Willamette River. This centre recapitulates the journey and attempts to summarise its meanings.

20 Oregon Trail Marketing Coalition, 'Five Different Perspectives. One Big Story. The Oregon Trail Centers', undated tourist brochure.

21 Ibid.

22 This and subsequent quoted statements are taken from my field notes, unless otherwise stated.

23 L. Fisher, *The Oregon Trail* (New York: Holiday House, 1990), p. 26.

24 A. Hyde, *An American Vision: Far Western Landscape and National Culture, 1820–1920* (New York: New York University Press, 1990); see also J. Dorst, *Looking West* (Philadelphia: University of Pennsylvania Press, 1999).

25 C. McCarthy, *Blood Meridian, or the Evening Redness in the West* (London: Picador–Pan Books, 1989 [1985]), p. 78.

26 The environmental issues I raise are not new. They are one of the major messages of the New Western History. The radical deconstruction of Frederick Jackson Turner's frontier thesis sought to disentangle scholarly history from myth. In doing so, however, it may miss the power of sounding the depths of the nightmares of history.

27 The other sections are: *Horizons: The People of Australia since 1788; First Australians: The Gallery of Aboriginal and Torres Strait Islander Peoples; Nation: Symbols of Australia;* and *Eternity: Stories from the Emotional Heart of Australia.*

28 L. Robin, 'The Strangeness of Australian Nature: Nature and National Identity', paper presented at the conference 'Taking Nature Seriously', Eugene, Oregon, February 2001.

29 L. Robin, 'A Scientific Aesthetic: Biological Diversity and a New Sense of Place', paper presented at the conference 'Taking Nature Seriously', Eugene, Oregon, February 2001.

30 The NMA and the Oregon Trail Centres contain other time concepts embedded within the overarching frame. Thus, for example, relative and absolute chronologies are presented, and geological time, or deep time, is discussed.

31 The statement is attributed to Paddle, 1993.

32 See e.g. R. Boer, 'Home Is Always Elsewhere: Exodus, Exile and the Howling Wilderness Waste' in his *Last Stop Before Antarctica: The Bible and Postcolonialism in Australia* (Sheffield: Sheffield Academic Press, 2001); Ann Curthoys, 'Expulsion,

Exodus, and Exile in White Australian Historical Mythology' in R. Nile and M. Williams (eds), *Imaginary Homelands: The Dubious Cartographies of Australian Identity* (St Lucia: University of Queensland Press, 1999); J. Docker, 'Spinoza and Mr Bloom Interpret Exodus', in his *1492: The Poetics of Diaspora* (London: Continum, 2001); D. Rose, 'Rupture and the Ethics of Care in Colonised Space', in T. Bonyhady and T. Griffith (eds), *Prehistory to Politics: John Mulvaney, the Humanities and the Public Intellectual* (Melbourne: Melbourne University Press, 1996).

33 H. Parkes, *The Federal Government of Australasia: Speeches Delivered on Various Occasions* (Sydney: Turner & Henderson, 1890), p. 74.
34 Curthoys, 'Expulsion, Exodus, and Exile'.
35 See, e.g., D. Rose, *Dingo Makes Us Human* (Cambridge: Cambridge University Press, 2000), pp. 83–4.

CHAPTER THIRTEEN

Subjectivities of whiteness

Sarah Nuttall

This chapter focuses on contemporary constructions of whiteness in South African autobiographies and other narratives of the self. It is a study of ways in which people who are referred to as white, and who understand themselves as such, account for this in narrative; in a specific set of texts. Most of the texts I look at are autobiographical, mostly from the 1980s and 1990s; a number of them draw simultaneously on different forms of self-narrative. In discussing these texts I hope to further an understanding of how the category *whiteness* – racial, social, political and economic – is given meaning within a more general economy of signs.

I aim to show the extent to which whiteness, far from being normative or consistent, emerges in these texts within a range of formations or constellations, including those which have to do with masking, concealment, transfiguration and secrecy on the one hand, and with the politics and practice of visibility (not least through writing itself) on the other. I track a number of trajectories, beginning with notions of watching the self, and watching others watch the self, of looking and being looked at, in the drama of blackness and whiteness in South Africa. More broadly, I seek to set *whiteness* and the ways in which it figures in South Africa within the parameters of an inquiry into the meanings and limits of the term 'settler' in such a context.

It is most often in terms of the 'settler' that white identity in postcolonial African contexts has been given context and meaning.[1] The notion of the settler, which always also implies a native, carries with it in its originary sense a master–slave dialectic based on land: a relationship based on conquest and ownership on the one hand and on dispossession and subjugation on the other, in which one party acts and the other is acted upon; a relationship of response rather than co-invention. The meaning of the term 'settler' shifts, however, as the move is made from the politics of conquest and subjugation to the politics of negotiation and belonging. As such, South Africa's Truth and Reconciliation Commission (TRC), marked the potential transformation of the figure of the settler into the figure of the citizen. It confronted whites with the awareness that, in the new context, *belonging* could not be assumed; rather, a process of mutual negation had to be replaced by one of mutual *recognition*, one which could *lead* to belonging. Deprived of the archaic identity of the settler, whites were also conceivably deprived of citizenship in the present. The TRC presented the spectre of privilege without belonging, and hence the task of inventing or negotiating new forms of whiteness. That many whites have yet to face this new context, and continue to claim belonging and assume responsibility and citizenship on only the most spurious of terms, does not detract from the potential and ongoing challenge that the Commission presents in the public sphere.

The texts I have chosen to discuss here are not a representative selection of writings by whites from the last several decades, although they have been selected to illuminate aspects of the representation of whiteness with which I am concerned. I discuss texts largely from the 1980s and 1990s, a period that, in my view, marks a major shift in the ways whiteness began to be looked at as the embeddedness of race in the legal and political fabric of South Africa began to crack.[2] At the same time, the texts by whites I look at here stand in intimate relationship to changing registers of how blacks see whites – and of blackness itself. Near the beginning of her well-known *Country of My Skull*, Antjie Krog, drawing on tropes of picturing and perception, looking and watching, writes: 'Nadine Gordimer once asked a black writer: "Why do you always picture a white woman lounging next to a swimming pool? We are not all like that!" He replied "Because we perceive you like that!" Gordimer admits that she has to take cognisance of that truth.'[3] This, as I show, has strong political resonance for Krog herself.

A number of the texts were written by whites who were involved in the struggle against apartheid, in some cases the military dimensions of that struggle. Clearly, such whites are demographically unrepresentative of the white population generally, although they are representative of a certain historical tension within that population – in the history of its relationships with black people. Moreover, it is these whites, in the main, who have written autobiographies and memoirs. It is they, moreover, who enable us to ask: in what ways does involvement in the nationalist and military anti-apartheid struggle situate, at least potentially, the production of whiteness differently? Does the notion of the 'settler' shift and break down, and if so, when and how? Certainly, in considering the lives and texts of

Ruth First, Joe Slovo, Mary Benson, Bram Fischer and others, we are dealing with the most publicly visible white people who believed powerfully in, and acted on, a political credo in which race would be erased.

It is my argument at present, then, and a guiding assumption of this chapter, that texts by whites involved in the anti-apartheid struggle, or by whites who have written from an oppositional stance, will be those most invested in changing the registers of whiteness. Such texts are of particular interest in the post-apartheid context, which itself situates the production of whiteness in new registers. At the same time, these texts have yet to be read for what they tell us about whiteness as such, subscribing as they do to a concept of non-racialism.

Moreover, there has been a tendency not to attend to those amplifications of whiteness which may have been at odds with official and critical orthodoxies. In most studies, the issue of racial identity has been conflated with that of racism, which is rightly cast in a language of moral condemnation. The emphasis has been less on race as such (though, clearly, in the case of whiteness, this often – if not always – involves forms of racism) than on a fully complex investigation of how race works.

In South Africa, as elsewhere, visual metaphors have come to hold a potent influence over consciousness and memory. The privileging of the image has been ubiquitous for a number of reasons. First, cultural debates in South Africa have frequently been tied to an identity politics based on visibility, a visibility largely reliant on the markers of race. Thus they have been intricately connected to the question of who speaks, and *who speaks* is defined by the visible signs of race or gender, privilege or poverty. Second, the experience of being the object of the look – one of the most extraordinary aspects of visuality – must necessarily permeate a context of racial scopophilia where the visible and the invisible have been racially coded. An important aspect of what follows, then, is the analysis of the visual metaphors which structure whiteness in this context, producing a rich and revealing set of meanings which take us closer to the making of racialised identity in South Africa.

Watching

Ruth First, one of South Africa's best-known anti-apartheid activists and intellectuals, published her prison memoir *117 Days* in 1965. It precedes the other texts I discuss here by 20–30 years, though I begin with it because of the powerful insights it yields about First's construction of her political and racial identity. The book is an account of her solitary confinement as a political activist at the time of South Africa's Treason Trial. The reader is immediately struck by the many qualifying clauses that First uses in referring to herself, and the ways in which she shows herself watching herself as well as watching others watching her (emphases added):

> *I, a prisoner* held under top security conditions, was forbidden books, visitors, contact with any other prisoner; but like any other white South African madam I sat in bed each morning, and Africans did the cleaning for the *'missus'*.[4]
>
> Every morning as the cha-cha cleaners were on their way out, the warddress on duty would thrust a large aluminium bucket at one and order him to bring hot water for the 'missus'. *That was me.*[5]
>
> [They are] men ... whose complacency, *I told myself*, was a clear complicity.[6]
>
> I minced in my high heels and thrust my bosom out firmly in my charcoal suit, free to impress them, *I thought*, while I was still outside my cell.[7]

The phrases emphasised – 'I, a prisoner', 'That was me', 'I told myself', 'I thought' – enable us to begin to decipher Ruth First's sense of her whiteness, her politics and her views of herself as a 'political white',[8] a phrase she uses towards the end of the book. In the first extract we see that even as a prisoner she cannot escape being a white 'missus' with black prison workers–servants: she cannot escape an awareness of whiteness, that is, as *being served*. In the second extract, we see her watching herself being a 'missus' – 'That was me' – a watching which functions both as an acknowledgement and as a disassociation. In the third, she watches men at a city restaurant across the road from the prison in which she is incarcerated and tells herself of their complicity. Here she captures her own yearning for freedom and good living, but also the constructedness of her political identity in the face of a whiteness which signified precisely the privileges of good living. She reasserts and exposes to the reader (by the phrase 'I told myself') the deliberateness of the process of distancing herself from a culture of whiteness in apartheid South Africa.

Elsewhere, First comments on living a 'more and more schizo-phrenic existence':

> [T]here was the good living that white privilege brought, but simultan-eously complete absorption in revolutionary politics and defiance of all the values of our own racial group. As the struggle grew sharper, the privileges of membership in the white group were overwhelmed by the penalties of political participation.[9]

Privilege is undercut by punishment, power by penalty. In the final extract above, First both gently disparages herself ('free to impress them, I thought') for her feminine strutting and reveals her complex disassociation of 'taste' and 'privilege' through the construction of her political identity. Well known for her sense of style and 'expensive tastes', First nevertheless managed to separate those aspects of her persona from the structural dimensions of white privilege per se.

First's text reveals the *watching* which her version of whiteness brings: the watching of herself and her watching of others, black and white, watching her. It brings also a *splitting*, the schizophrenia of a political whiteness which, as I have said, scrambles privilege and punishment, power and penalty. *Watching* implies, as I have argued, an identity constructed around distance – or at least a dialectic of distance and proximity; and it contains within it an active element of work – the work of 'watching you watching me'. This work of watching takes place in a context which is necessarily one of concealment, in a couple of senses. Her whiteness, particularly at the historical juncture at which she writes, makes her visible: that is, it accords her the social, political and personal power of being seen in a context where those who are marginalised labour under a certain pall of invisibility (here we may recall the title, *Invisible Man*, of Ralph Ellison's novel of black America). I also mean by her *visibility* that she is seen by others, by black people by virtue of her whiteness, as a symbol of that which is cruel and oppressive. One of her intentions – though they are not brought to the text's surface as such – may be to make herself, the self of her whiteness, less visible, to separate herself from a wider culture of repressive whiteness.

What is it to watch in this context? Implicit in watching is the fear of being caught watching. What penalty would one pay for being caught watching in a context of concealment? To be caught watching is to be caught enacting what one is trying to conceal – in this case one's whiteness as a master signifier. It is within this trope of watching, then, that we begin to see the workings of colour and the attributes it carries with it, in this text at least. In the very acts of watching, looking and seeing, that which the subject attempts to conceal is in fact reproduced – as First attempts to erase her whiteness, she marks herself as white even more strongly.

I have emphasised watching here – and in particular watching the self as a white self within a conscious political attempt to become someone else – in order to distinguish it from Fanon's analysis of 'being looked at', specifically for a black person, in a context of both violence and power. For First, this process of self-consciously watching

[249]

the self is one which in part emerges through the self-aware process of a certain mode of autobiographical writing itself. It is also one which raises the question of how crucially whiteness is gendered in this narrative of the self. Are race and gender inextricable from one another, especially as formulated in writing reflecting on the self? How much is this a psychical and political vocabulary of racial looking and how much does it have in common with John Berger's formulation: 'Women watch themselves being looked at . . . [the woman] turns herself into an object – and most particularly an object of vision: a sight'?[10] These issues take further shape in what follows.

Thirty-seven years later, in 1997, Ruth First's daughter Gillian Slovo published her memoir *Every Secret Thing: My Family, My Country*. The text tells in part the story of Gillian's parents (her father was Joe Slovo, the famous South African communist anti-apartheid activist and head of the ANC's armed wing, Umkonto we Siswe) and in part the story of Gillian herself as the daughter of her two famous and politically committed parents. Gillian's text, when dealing with the fashioning of her own white identity in relation to that of her parents, adds a further layer to the configurations of whiteness to be found in a single family.

Her childhood is marked by a sense of exclusion. One of her fears is that she will be 'found out', that she will reveal the secret of who she is – to other whites: the secret that she is not 'white like them' or in the sense that they are, that she is, as she writes at one point in the text, 'passing for white', an imposter.[11] In Gillian Slovo's use of the term, it is not skin colour that is in question but her membership of a 'culture of whiteness'. The only other white child she identifies with is the daughter of Hilda Bernstein, also an anti-apartheid activist, as she sees the fear on the young girl's face when a white man asks her what her (notorious) name is. In the world Gillian inhabited the colour of her skin should have been a passport to belonging, but it was not; nor did she belong to her parents' world of political community: her deepest memory of her white childhood is of exclusion. Years later, when she returns to South Africa for a short stay from exile, now technically as 'a member of the new ruling elite' she feels herself suddenly, at one point, to be 'a Jewish interloper from the ghetto'.[12] Slovo's experience of her whiteness is of a fake identity – one imposed by others without them knowing who she is. Once an imposter in political terms, she now, in the post-apartheid moment when political priorities have changed, gestures towards another layer of her identity – her Jewishness. Both place her at an angle to conventions of whiteness. Her whiteness in each of these contexts has to do with distancing and masking, and the keeping of secrets.

In Ruth First's case, then, white identity is defined in terms of a watching and a splitting; in Gillian's, a masking or, even stronger, the guarding of secrets. Both sets of identities work within the register of a distancing of the self from the self. Interestingly, these tropes of watching and looking, of visibility and invisibility, seem virtually non-existent in Joe Slovo's own autobiographical memoir. His *Unfinished Autobiography*[13] is a collection of largely anecdotal and often humorous fragments which he had started writing before his untimely death of cancer in 1995 (less than a year after he had taken up office as the minister of Housing in the new ANC Government). It reveals Slovo's background as a working-class Lithuanian Jewish refugee who came to Johannesburg at the age of 10, worked as a clerk and lived with his father, a fruitseller, in various boarding-houses after his mother's early death. Slovo joined the Communist Party at the age of 19, a white worker living in poor circumstances in one of the low-income areas of the city ('the suburb of Doornfontein, which was one of the lowest rungs of the Jewish residential ladder'[14]). Slovo, we are told in both his own and his daughter Gillian's book, was seen by black South Africans as a black man. This was a powerful invocation within the specific racial dynamics of apartheid. It was the signification of a rupture in a system in which one's racial origins signified everything, based on the espousal of a political cause in which people's ontologies were embedded. It was an important act of disassociation in a context in which one would normally *belong* because of one's skin colour.

Gillian Slovo records that her parents were among the very few white people buried in their respective cemeteries (Ruth in Maputo and Joe in Soweto). The circumstances of their burials seem to represent a final act of transgression in a symbolically charged site, an erasure of race in terms of a recognition by the *other*. The symbolic charge of death and burial revealed here is a potent one. Ruth First herself, we might note with equal interest, was never accorded the status of black woman. Thus we see in the figures of Ruth First and Joe Slovo at the very least diverse manoeuvres in relation to their political whiteness, based in part on different class backgrounds, and with differing results. Joe Slovo, the 'black man', Jew and white man who had never owned property in South African until he was married to Ruth First, achieves a transfiguration of white identity which was different (and seldom as self-consciously articulated, at least in writing) from First's. One of the ways in which this difference manifests itself is in relation to specific tropic economies of the white look.

In Joe Slovo's narrative of the self, what one finds is a certain blinding of the scopic economy of race and identity; the staging of a choice not to enter into regimes of watching and looking. Politics – the struggle for liberation – emerges as a space which is both sacrificial and transcendental, in which anything other than this struggle remains somewhat abstract, and one in which at some level the contradictions of Slovo's own whiteness could be subsumed within other forms of identity which had to do with the work of liberation. Because of this overarching theological commitment to the political struggle there is a sense in which Slovo, at least, appears to abolish the question of the white self and regimes of selfhood embedded in looking and watching. This would have been informed in part by the fact that much of Slovo's political life was spent hiding the self: as the most wanted white man in South Africa for his military activities, he existed in a context of profound political surveillance. First, too, engaged in a process of hiding the self, but while this led to a self-consciousness in, and also perhaps through, her writing, for Slovo it meant abolishing certain forms of self-consciousness in a way which must have been related to gendered predispositions as much as specific political and class histories.

We have, then, seen the different versions of whiteness that emerge from the histories of a single family. The difference is interesting since, as a family, they must have shared many similar experiences, though they narrated those expereriences in very different ways; or perhaps the strikingly different versions point to the very dispersed nature of this family, added to by the enclosures that a political culture they all inhabited came to maintain; or perhaps it is that the solitariness, the contrariness, of experience in a single family, any family, emerges most visibily in writing?

Whatever might be the case, I have used the striking examples of texts by First and by Gillian and Joe Slovo to open up some of the questions which seem to be among the most suggestive for an analysis of subjectivities of whiteness. The lines of enquiry and the constellations of racialised identity that the First and Slovo texts reveal bear strong relation to configurations found in other South African self-narratives. Thus, they suggest a wider set of tropic specificities which have regulated the production of certain whitenesses in this context. Mary Benson, for instance, shows herself to lead a 'strange double-life' between the worlds of her political work and writing and the 'old familiar' South Africa of white friends who condone injustice by their inactivity; she secretly aids high-profile anti-apartheid activist Bram Fischer, at the same time listening to those friends' 'idle speculation' about Fischer's disappearance underground.[15] Her whiteness, then, is marked by a duplicity, one which is in part a complicity – now with her old friends, now with politically committed South Africans.

In this section I have focused strongly on the tropes of visibility and invisibility that seem to me to structure aspects of whiteness in the texts under consideration. In the next section, I follow that trajectory, and I pick up another which has much to do with the intimacy of whiteness with violence, as explored by the writer as white Afrikaner.

Intimacies

One of the most important texts to have emerged from the post-apartheid context in South Africa is Antjie Krog's by best-selling *Country of My Skull*. Published in 1997, the text is many genres in one: a biography of others, through the recording of testimony given at South Africa's TRC, it is also Krog's autobiography – a sometimes fiction-alised one; in places, it is written in the style of personal journalism; at certain moments, it moves into poetry, Krog's 'first medium'. The book is dedicated to 'every victim who had an Afrikaner surname on her lips'. She knows that her language 'carries violence as a voice'.[16] It is also to Afrikaans that she turns as a kind of litany when she faces the greatest trauma: '*mispel, maroela, tarentaal*',[17] she chants after the testimony of a man whose family had been burnt to death.

Krog introduces an ethnic specificity into her engagement with her whiteness. It is used in the text as a marker of a set of intimacies, intimacies which take on different valencies. The first of these is language – her intimacy with a language which is indigenous, which captures the cadences of the local and which has shaped the syllables of the country's darkest acts. It is in the context of her Afrikaner identity that Krog's text introduces a difference from and a specificity in relation to the texts I have discussed above.

The second intimacy which Krog's Afrikaner identity holds for her is an intimacy with the perpetrators, the 'men of my race' who appear before the TRC. Rather than use a language of political conversion to mark her separation from these men, Krog both resists and yet insists on this intimacy. The text plays self-consciously with the paradox of the visibility of her opposition and the apparent invisibility of her intimacy, her closeness to them: 'They are as familiar as my brothers, cousins and school friends. Between us all distance is erased', she writes; and she asks too: 'Was there perhaps never a distance except the one I have built up with great effort within myself over the years?'[18] and 'What do I have in common with the men I hate most?'[19] Looking deeply into herself, Krog finds that she 'abhors and cares' for these men.[20] She is not, however, the only one watching: an 'English-speaking' colleague tells her 'your whole body language changes when you are with these men. I couldn't hear what you were talking about, but there was a definite intimacy'.[21]

Partly because of the added intensity and sense of complicity which her Afrikanerdom brings, but partly too because of the changed political moment she writes within and the kinds of narratives it makes possible, and even insists on – *and* partly because other people can see what she sees (Krog, too, is engaged in acts of looking at herself and at other people looking at her) – Krog, then, writes a text which takes us much closer to a psychological and political crisis of whiteness. While she sees clearly the 'evil' of the men of her race, she also expresses a certain familiarity on the basis of what Geschiere has called in another context 'primary patriotisms'[22] – proximity, neighbourhood, family, ethnicity, language. Yet it is her intimacies – with Afrikaners, with apartheid – that are also her terms of belonging, as long as 'repentence' (in the terms of the TRC) has taken place. Thus while the crisis of whiteness she examines is enabled by the new context, it is also her condition of belonging, precisely in this context. Speaking for Afrikaners, in the absence, as she sees it, of leaders who will do so, she writes: 'We are so utterly sorry. We are deeply ashamed and gripped with remorse. But hear us, we are from here. We will live it right – here – with you, for you'.[22]

Strikingly, though, despite the fact that I refer above to a crisis of whiteness which finds expression in Krog's text, it is sometimes as if whiteness for Krog hardly exists. It is her Afrikaner ethnicity that shapes her most profound reactions. This is an important point in a context where the process of living certain identities turns not only around self-identification but around the continual identification of the self by others. Krog knows this. For black people whiteness is, on the one hand, the key signifier of racial power and difference. At the same time, there has been in South Africa since the 1980s a public discourse by blacks to the effect that they would rather deal politically with Afrikaners than with the brand of liberalism said to characterise English-speaking South Africans. Krog herself expresses strong animosity towards what she perceives to be some of the dominant traits of white English-speaking South Africa. Whiteness as a general category carries what she perceives to be a European inflection that she rejects. She frequently distances herself in the text from Europeans and Americans, thus reinstating a sense of ethnic difference and history into 'whiteness'.

It is interesting, then, that one of the rare moments in which she refers to herself in terms of her whiteness is one which is most *dangerous* for her sense of future belonging. Krog has the following thoughts while watching the testimony of Winnie Mandela before the TRC:

This hearing is about my country, I am thinking. And whether there is space for all of us. And the conditions for this space. I also have a distinct feeling that for now this hearing has nothing to do with me, with whites. Blacks are deciding amongst themselves what they regard as right and wrong. They are making that decision here, today. Either a black person may kill because of apartheid – or none of us may kill, no matter the reason. This hearing has little to do with the past. It has everything to do with the future.[23]

Krog names South Africa as 'my country' but sees herself at that moment to be outside of the ambit of a natural belonging. In watching black people 'deciding amongst themselves' she also knows that her own belonging will have to be given by others. Until it is given, she faces the possibility of privilege without belonging.

The energies of Krog's book, and the directions it takes in relation to her working through of her own identity, are, however, frequently generated and animated by the realm of the psychoanalytic and the working through of traumas which take on highly personal dimensions. The TRC and all that it represents about the past shakes her to the foundations of her identity and leads her to try to answer the question 'Who am I?' in a highly traumatic way. The psychic intimacy of her involvement in the process of the TRC and all that it represents manifests itself in the form of a breakdown, skin rashes and her hair falling out, played out in part, too, through the violence she sometimes 'perpetrates' on those close to her.[23]

Krog responds in a highly personal way to a narrative that is always also *collective*. Yet her text scrambles those registers in ways which enable us, too, to re-read earlier texts of political commitment or conversion in the South African oeuvre. The constructing of identity is always a public political, but also a private, act. If this process of identity-making resulted in a commitment to a cause or to a new nation, it had also been about breaking from the collective conformity of whiteness itself.

At the end of the book, Krog takes stock of her *privilege* in the following terms: 'whereas this privilege used to upset me in the past, now I can hold it against a truth that we are all aware of. No longer an unaware privilege, but one that we know the price and mortality of.'[24] Privilege is something that has to be paid for, and is also something, in its form as structural white privilege, which will end. It is in fact in the working towards, the final embracing of, a collective identity – for Krog this also represents an engagement with patriotism itself – that she finds possibilities for self-reconstruction. In one of the final scenes, Krog is asked by her brother if she would die for her country. She replies that she would not, since 'no one, no country, no politician, has the right to ask anyone to die for them. They can make claims on my life, I'll make sacrifices in that, but my death is my own'.[25] At the book's end, however, standing on a wall on Robben Island doing a question-and-answer session for a local radio station, Krog looks back at the continent of Africa:

> It is mine. I belong to that continent. My gaze, my eyes are one with the thousands of others that have looked back over the centuries towards Africa. Ours. Mine. Yes, I would die for this. It slips out like a smooth, holy sound. And I realise that it is the Commission alone that has brought me to these moments of fierce belonging.[26]

Belonging carries with it a pledging of one's life, one's death, if necessary. Krog has travelled a path which becomes something akin to the sensibility of Mandela's famous statement from the dock in 1987: 'It is an ideal [for a democratic and free society] which I hope to live for and achieve. But if needs be it is an ideal for which I am prepared to die.' At the same time it remains marked by her history of or in whiteness. Despite the assertiveness of the statement above, the act of claiming it performs into being, the text always also marks the instability of her position, because it is a claim that always has to be a question or even a plea, as essential vulnerability. Writing in her first medium, Krog ends her book with a poem:

> You whom I have wronged, please
> take me
> with you.[27]

Krog's registers of writing mark a changed political moment from that of Ruth First. Yet they both – in the one case through the added urgency of the context of solitary confinement and in the other the crises and confessionality of a post-apartheid reckoning with the truth – attempt to change the terms of who they are, to extricate themselves from a racialised order of power and visuality while accounting for the difficulty of doing so – a process out of which both their writing and their political praxis emerge.

Narcissism

In 1997, J. M. Coetzee, South Africa's best-known novelist, unexpectedly produced a memoir. The book is called *Boyhood* and is written in the voice of John, the third-person narrator. In it, we move from the political subjectivities of the texts I have discussed above to what I would call the *politics of narcissism*. To the notion of narcissism I would immediately add Foucault's idea of 'caring for the self', characteristic of his later work, which he seeks to install in place of the more traditional epistemology of 'knowing the self'. He relates 'caring for the self' to three processes: the first has to do with pleasure, its anxieties and its uses, the second with an insistence on attention to the self and the third with an individualism in which a retreat is made into private space. In Foucault's argument, caring for the self is also a public act, one of the main principles of social and political life–conduct.[28] It seems to me crucial to discuss Coetzee's text alongside those already considered here, since one cannot understand whiteness in South Africa without also understanding the powerful forms of the private and the singular that such an identity has sometimes taken on. Moreover, it is through the articulation of the private, and of *privacy*, that forms of visibility and invisibility, intimacy and violence, play themselves out in his text.[29]

The narrator in Coetzee's text is a child 'set apart',[30] a term Coetzee returns to in its full ambiguity many times in the text. John is set apart, or sets himself apart, in the first instance, from a culture of conformity. Born into a family of mixed, English and Afrikaans, descent, he is alienated from Afrikanerdom, from Afrikaner nationalism, which relies on just such notions of collective conformity. It is an alienation which is marked at the level of the body and which almost always carries the threat of violation – what he terms 'a lack of privacy'. As Shaun Irlam has remarked,[31] this is part of a poetics of setting apart at a broader level: the child is segregated from a culture of segregation. He occupies an ambivalent space of privacy and shame. Fearful of 'being like everyone else', his setting apart of himself, his privacy, his 'separate development', protects him, saves him – and endows him with a sense of his own specialness; a specialness which prefigures his vocation as writer but also constitutes a shuddering away from community as such in any version.

Here, then, is the register of individualism and retreat. Space is given to the private as a way of shielding the self from the polity, from the collective. A withdrawal from the polis, from civic and political life, a valorisation of private life and the search for personal forms of enjoyment all find expression here. Coetzee's narrative, unlike Krog's, is marked by a refusal of belonging itself. The only place to which John 'belongs' is the Karoo farm of his grandfather ('the secret and sacred word that binds him to the farm is belong'[32]), Voelfontein, which is passing out of the family. Yet the farm exists from 'eternity to eternity',[33] so far beyond him and his desire to belong to it that it belies the only claim of belonging he is able to make. 'I belong to the farm',[34] John says, knowing that he should not and cannot say 'the farm belongs to me'.[35]

The narrator is torn between enjoyment, or pleasure, and austerity, to both of which the body is central. His uncertainty about his body, his responses to his emergent sexuality, are also about his concupiscence in relation to the body of the racial other. Prominent in the story are a number of his interactions with young coloured boys (that these are isolated incidents in a culture of segregation is made clear when Coetzee writes of John: 'Josiah was the fourth native he had known in his life'). In one of these, he sees a young coloured boy 'wearing pants so short that they sit tightly across his neat buttocks and leave his slim clay-brown thighs almost naked'. He is 'disturbed by the feelings that the legs of these boys . . . create in him. What is there that can be done with legs beyond devouring them with one's eyes?'[35] In other such interactions, John has wrestling matches with Eddie, who has come to work for his parents: 'the smell of Eddie's body stays with him from these bouts, and the feel of his head, the high bullet-shaped skull and the close, coarse hair'.[36] 'There is a moment when the two of them wrestle when his lips and nose are pressed against Eddie's hair. He breathes in the smell, the taste: the smell, the taste, of smoke'.[37] When Eddie is arrested by the police, after he had tried to run away, he 'spoils' John's Saturday morning. We are shown the white child's forms of looking at the body of the racial other which 'devour' their subject; here is desire in looking, the consuming of the image and the body of the other. The racial eye is devouring as the child narrator asks his child's question: 'what is desire for?'

The body of the racial other pleases and repulses him (as a body 'not taken care' of as it should be). It is the site of a 'feast', or it is that which 'spoils'. His uncertainty about his own body is also his uncertainty about pleasure. His anxiety is avoided through a regime of austerity. The tension between austerity and pleasure is part of a wider insistence on the attention one has to pay to the self and the amplitude of the vigilance that is required to do so. In all of this we see the intensity of the relationship to the self – of the forms in which, in Foucault's terms, the self is called upon to take itself as an object of knowledge, a domain of action, to transform, correct, purify and save itself.

In Antjie Krog's book, and for the most part in the other texts I have considered, the activity of self-disclosure takes place in terms of another, in relation to others, even the Other. This could be called an epistemic technology of the self. By disclosing the self in dialogue, the self is constituted. Coetzee's text emphasises the discernment, or deciphering, of what the self already is. This could be referred to as an ontic technology of the self: each reveals different forms in which public definitions of the self are provided; each reveals the genealogical modes of discourse within which whiteness in this context has operated.

If Krog's book operates within a paradigm of truth, with its attendant ambiguities (the truth about the past, about history, about the self), Coetzee's story deals in secrets, with their ambiguities ('Whatever he wants, whatever he likes, has sooner or later to be turned into a secret'). The narrator, John, craves concealment, invisibility, in order, not least, to cover the spoor of his singularity. Thus he writes the autobiography of a liar ('his difference from other boys . . . is bound up with his lying too').[38] Coetzee, then, in a context which is concerned with revealing the truth about apartheid, in the form of the TRC most obviously, leads us to a different ontological question: what is the truth of a liar? Secrets, lying and the powers and distresses of privacy, of setting the self apart, become the major tropes of identity, which is also a white identity, shot through with a complex brand of privilege and despair. Configurations of visibility and invisibility in this text take on the shapes of truth and lying, or hiding.

I said earlier that we can understand whiteness in South Africa only by understanding the forms of the private and the singular which such identities also take on. The exaltation of the self's singularity is, in Coetzee's book, in part a form of shielding from a collective culture of conformity, a 'culture of whiteness' as I have referred to it earlier in this chapter. It is also a shielding of the white from the *other*, from a wider community which includes black people. We may thus see – beyond Coetzee's text itself, which, it is important to remember, is written within the register of childhood – that such modes of privacy and singularity can account for why so many whites say they had nothing to do with apartheid, and how some can shield themselves so effectively from post-apartheid South African society.

In all the acts of *self*-disclosure I have discussed here I have tried to draw out the signs, codes and literary strategies that have shaped representations of a whiteness which has aimed to move beyond a condition, a culture and a politics that white people themselves built. I have intended to move towards a conversation about how whiteness works, nothwithstanding a long history of white racism, and in particular what tropes of watching and looking, visibility and invisibility, can tell us about how race works in the imaginations and practices of these white people. As such, the texts above dramatise the dilemmas of selfhood in the specific context of racial identity. They tell us a great deal about the process of becoming someone who you were not at the beginning: of becoming someone else. They reveal histories of how individuals in this context act on themselves and the technologies of selfhood that they respond to and employ.

Conclusion

Studying whiteness, as I have attempted to do here, can contribute to a project of desegregating our understanding of South African culture. A focus on the texts selected has helped us to unpack whiteness by drawing on the stories of those who have wanted to get 'out of white-ness'.[39] While it is useful to focus on regimes of the visual, too great a preoccupation with the visual (especially the visual lense of differ-ence) is dangerous to an understanding of culture and race. A key contention of those texts – and this chapter – has in fact been that how you look should not largely determine how you see.

The grounds on which we can continue to use Manichean terms to describe the chaos of racialised order that exists today are in any case unclear. Melissa Steyn, author of the first book on 'whiteness' to appear in South Africa, has argued that most whites still adhere to an ideology based 'outside the country, wherever European whiteness is seen to be secure and politically and socially upheld'. In a letter to the editor of the *Cape Times*, a young University of Cape Town student finds this absurd for the members of his generation, facing as they do everyday issues 'in a contemporary and fast-paced African society'.[40] He argues that insofar as there is an ideological epicentre elsewhere, it has to do with the relationship of consumers ('black, white, African, Asian, male, female') to Western popular consumer culture. That is an issue that relates less to whites than it does to South Africans, and to 'the majority of the non-Western world'. Finally, the student eschews an understanding of white identity which is 'static and therefore self-defeating', being 'typical of a generation that has its roots in the heart of the deepest darkest era of this country's history and who are riddled with guilt and confusion as to where they stand in our society today'.

The tropes and sensibilities of the texts I have examined remain crucial to the culture at large, as they stage and speak to forms of whiteness which are about confronting apartheid and attempting to find a way through to being ethical, 'non-racial', South Africans. Yet the terms of their reference are also beginning to be contested by a younger generation in *its* habits, sensibilities and trajectories, which exist irrevocably within the post-apartheid realm. Thus the texts dis-cussed here remain vivid traces in a slipstream of whitenesses, ones to which, I hope to have shown, we can usefully keep returning in reflections on race, but which increasingly need to be juxtaposed with other forms and expressions of identities lodged both with and beyond race, in this case whiteness, and the paradigms within which these generations of writers have come to explore it.[41]

The voice of a younger generation and a contemporary public sphere, at least as it is taking shape in South Africa now, would also suggest the limits of a paradigm of 'settler' societies, in which Australia, New Zealand, Canada and South Africa still speak from and to the systems of colonialism that have gone before. While these colonial histories still have force and impact on contemporary imaginaries, we need also to trace their limits as interpretative frames. In this project, South Africa could well offer a leading vision.

Notes

I wish to thank Brenda Cooper, Achille Mbembe and Stephanie Newell for their comments on the texts of this chapter.

1 See M. Chege, 'Africans of European Descent', *Transition*, 73, special issue: 'The White Issue' (1986), 74–86.
2 Due to the growing success of the anti-apartheid movement in South Africa, the retreat by the Nationalist government from major legislative cornerstones of the apartheid system, the power of international economic sanctions, the first democratic elections of 1994 and the subsequent Truth and Reconciliation Commission.
3 A. Krog, *Country of My Skull* (Johannesburg: Random House, 1998), p. 15.
4 R. First, *117 Days: An Account of Confinement and Interrogation Under the South African Ninety-Day Detention Law* (London: Penguin, 1965), p. 35.
5 Ibid., p. 37.
6 Ibid., p. 38.
7 Ibid., p. 59.
8 Ibid., p. 142.
9 Ibid., p. 114.
10 J. Berger, *Ways of Seeing* (London: Penguin, 1972), p. 47.
11 'Passing for white' is a colloquialism of the apartheid period which referred to coloured people who tried to have themselves re-classified as white and thereby gain entry to the privileges of whiteness as endowed by the apartheid State.
12 G. Slovo, *Every Secret Thing: My Family, My Country* (London: Little, Brown, 1997), p. 176.
13 J. Slovo, *The Unfinished Autobiography* (Randburg: Ravan Press, 1995).
14 Ibid., p. 14.
15 See D. Driver, 'Imagined Selves, (Un)imagined Marginalities', *Journal of Southern African Studies*, 17:2 (1991), 337–54.
16 Krog, *Country of My Skull*, p. 216.
17 Ibid., p. 48.
18 Ibid., p. 96.
19 Ibid., p. 92.
20 Ibid., p. 97.
21 Ibid., p. 92.
22 P. Geschiere, *The Modernity of Witchcraft: Politics and the Occult in Postcolonial Africa* (Charlottesville and London: University Press of Virginia, 1997), p. 99.
23 Krog, *Country of My Skull*, p. 258.
24 Ibid., p. 272.
25 Ibid., p. 274.
26 Ibid., p. 277.
27 Ibid., p. 229.
28 L. Martin, H. Gutman and P. Hutton (eds), *Technologies of the Self: A Seminar with Michel Foucault* (London: Tavistock, 1988).

29 Coetzee has never been involved in political struggle per se, although he has always made his oppositional stance clear.
30 J. M. Coetzee, *Boyhood: A Memoir* (London: Vintage, 1998), p. 15.
31 S. Irlam, 'Feral and Loathing in South Africa: J. M. Coetzee's Boyhood', unpublished paper (2000).
32 Ibid., p. 95.
33 Ibid., p. 96.
34 Ibid.
35 Ibid., p. 56.
36 Ibid., p. 75.
37 Ibid., p. 76.
38 Irlam, 'Feral and Loathing'.
39 I take this phrase from the title of the important book by V. Ware and L. Back, *Out of Whiteness: Color, Politics, and Culture* (Chicago: University of Chicago Press, 2002).
40 *Cape Times*, 28 November 2002.
41 As Achille Mbembe points out, although the category of whiteness is not so fluid as to detach it from power, privilege and oppression, it is a contingent and situated identity, and no longer carries the same meanings as it did under colonialism and apartheid: see A. Mbembe, 'African Modes of Self-Writing', *Public Culture*, 14:1 (2002), 239–74.

SELECT BIBLIOGRAPHY

Ames, M., *Cannibal Tours and Glass Boxes: The Anthropology of Museums* (Vancouver: University of British Columbia Press, 1993).

Armitage, A., *Comparing the Policy of Aboriginal Assimilation: Australia, Canada and New Zealand* (Vancouver: University of British Columbia Press, 1995).

Attwood, B. and S. G. Foster (eds), *Frontier Conflict: The Australian Experience* (Canberra: National Museum of Australia, 2003).

Attwood, B. and F. Magowan (eds), *Telling Stories: Indigenous History and Memory in Australia and New Zealand* (Crow's Nest, NSW: Allen & Unwin, 2001).

Bank, A. 'Evolution and Racial Theory: The Hidden Side of Wilhelm Bleek', *South African Historical Journal*, 43 (November 2000), 163–78.

Bercovitch, S., *The American Jeremiad* (Madison: University of Wisconsin Press, 1978).

Bhabha, H. K., 'Art and National Identity: A Critics' Symposium', *Art in America*, 79:9 (September 1991), 80–4.

Bhana, S., *Gandhi's Legacy: The Natal Indian Congress 1894–1994* (Pietermaritzburg: University of Natal Press, 1997).

Bhana, S. and B. Pachai (eds), *A Documentary History of Indian South Africans, 1860–1982* (Cape Town: D. Philip, 1984).

Bell, L., 'John Logan Campbell (1870–1912): A Career in Images', *Art New Zealand*, 67 (1993), 88–92, 106.

Biko, S., *I Write What I Like* (London: Heinemann, 1978).

Boer, R., 'Home Is Always Elsewhere: Exodus, Exile and the Howling Wilderness Waste', *Last Stop Before Antarctica: The Bible and Postcolonialism in Australia* (Sheffield: Sheffield Academic Press, 2001).

British Empire Exhibition 1924, *Canadian Section of the Fine Arts* (Toronto: Rous & Man, 1924).

British Empire Exhibition 1924, *Catalogue of the Palace of Arts* (London: Fleetway Press, 1924).

British Empire Exhibition 1924, *Official Guide* (London: Fleetway Press, 1924).

Brown, J., 'The Making of a Critical Outsider', in J. Brown and M. Prozesky (eds), *Gandhi and South Africa: Principles and Politics* (Pietermartitzburg: University of Natal Press, 1996).

Chege, M., 'Africans of European Descent', *Transition*, 73, special issue: 'The White Issue' (1998), 74–86.

Chesterman, J. and B. Galligan (eds), *Citizens Without rights: Aborigines and Australian Citizenship* (Cambridge: Cambridge University Press, 1997).

Coetzee, J. M., *White Writing: On The Culture of Letters in South Africa* (New Haven, CT, and London: Yale University Press, 1998).

Coombes, A. E., *Reinventing Africa: Museums, Material Culture and Popular Imagination in Late Victorian and Edwardian England* (New Haven, CT, and London: Yale University Press, 1994).

Coombes, A. E., *History After Apartheid: Visual Culture and Public Memory in a Democratic South Africa* (Durham: Duke University Press, 2003).

Curthoys, A., 'Expulsion, Exodus, and Exile in White Australian Historical Mythology', in R. Nile and M. Williams (eds), *Imaginary Homelands: The Dubious Cartographies of Australian Identity* (St Lucia: University of Queensland Press, 1999).

Denoon, D., *Settler Colonialism: The Dynamics of Dependent Development in the Southern Hemisphere* (Oxford and New York: Oxford University Press, 1983).

Dinwoodie, D., *Reserve Memories: The Power of the Past in a Chilcotin Community* (Lincoln: University of Nebraska Press, 2002).

Dhupelia-Mesthrie, U., *From Cane Fields to Freedom: A Chronicle of Indian South African Life* (Cape Town: Kwela, 2000).

Driver, D., 'Imagined Selves, (Un)imagined Marginalities', *Journal of Southern African Studies*, 17:2 (1991), 337–54.

Farini, G. *Through the Kalahari Desert: A Narrative of a Journey With Gun, Camera and Notebook to Lanke Ngami and Back* (London: Sampson Low, 1886).

First, R., *117 Days: An Account of Confinement and Interrogation under the South African Ninety-Day Detention Law* (London: Penguin, 1965).

Frankenberg, R., *White Women, Race Matters: The Social Construction of Whiteness* (Minneapolis: University of Minnesota Press, 1993).

Freund, W., *Insiders and Outsiders: The Indian Working Class of Durban 1910–1990* (London: James Currey, 1995).

Furniss, E., *The Burden of History: Colonialism and the Frontier Myth in a Rural Canadian Community* (Vancouver: University of British Columbia Press, 1999).

Fysh, H., *Taming the North: The Story of Alexander Kennedy and Other Queensland Pathfinders*, 2nd edn, rev. (Sydney: Angus & Robertson, 1950 [1933]).

Gamboni, D., *The Destruction of Art: Iconoclasm and Vandalism since the French Revolution* (New Haven, CT, and London: Yale University Press, 1997).

Goodall, H., *Invasion to Embassy: Land in Aboriginal Politics in New South Wales from 1780 to 1972* (St Leonards: Allen & Unwin, 1996).

Gordon, R. J., *The Bushman Myth: The Making of a Namibian Underclass* (Boulder, CO: Westview Press, 1992).

Gordon, R. J., 'Saving the Last South African Bushman: A Spectacular Failure', *Critical Arts*, 9:2 (1995).

Grundlingh, A. and H. Sapire, 'From Feverish Festival to Repetitive Ritual? The Changing Fortunes of Great Trek Mythology in an Industrializing South Africa, 1938–1988', *South African Historical Journal*, 21 (1989), 19–37.

Haebich, A., *Broken Circles: Fragmenting Indigenous Families 1800–2000* (Fremantle: Fremantle Arts Centre Press, 2000).

Havermann, P. (ed.), *Indigenous People's Rights in Australia, Canada and New Zealand* (Auckland: Oxford University Press, 1999).

[264]

Hetherington, P., *Settlers, Servants, and Slaves: Aboriginal and European Children in Nineteenth-Century Western Australia* (Crawley: University of Western Australia Press, 2002).

Holmes, C. (ed.), *Art of the British Empire Overseas* (London: Studio, 1917).

Hoy, H., *How Should I Read These? Native Women Writers in Canada* (Toronto: University of Toronto Press, 2001).

Hyslop, J., 'White Working-Class Women and the Invention of Apartheid: "Purified" Afrikaner Nationalist Agitation for Legislation Against "Mixed" Marriages, 1934–1939', *Journal of African History*, 36 (1995), 57–81.

Kawharu, I. H., 'Mana and the Crown: A Marae at Orakei', in I. H. Kawharu (ed.), *Waitangi: Maori and Pakeha Perspectives of the Treaty of Waitang* (Auckland: Oxford University Press, 1989).

Kawharu, M. W. (ed.), *Whenua: Managing Our Resources* (Auckland: Reed, 2002).

Knight, D. and A. D. Sabey, *The Lion Roars at Wembley: The British Empire Exhibition 60th Anniversary 1924–1925* (London: Barnard & Westwood, 1984).

Legassick, M. and C. Rassool, *Skeletons in the Cupboard: South African Museums and the Trade in Human Remains* (Cape Town: South African Museum, 2000).

Limerick, P., *The Legacy of Conquest: The Unbroken Past of the American West* (New York: Norton & Co., 1987).

Lindford, B., *Africans on Stage: Studies in Ethnological Show Business* (Cape Town: D. Philip, 1999).

McClintock, A., *Imperial Leather* (New York: Routledge, 1995).

McGregor, R., *Imagined Destinies: Aboriginal Australians and the Doomed Race Theory, 1880–1939* (Melbourne: Melbourne University Press, 1997).

McMaster, G. and L.-A. Martin, *Indigena: Contemporary Native Perspectives* (Vancouver: Douglas & McIntyre, 1992).

Manuel, G. and M. Posluns, *The Fourth World: An Indian Reality* (New York: Free Press, 1974).

Mbembe, A., 'African Modes of Self-Writing', *Public Culture*, 14:1 (2002), 239–74.

Mead, S. M., *Magnificent Te Maori: Te Maori Whakahirahira* (Auckland: Heinemann, 1986).

Michalski, S., *Public Monuments: Art in Political Bondage 1870–1997* (London: Reaktion, 1998).

Miller, J., *Koori: A Will to Win* (Sydney: Angus & Robertson, 1985).

Morris, B., 'Frontier Colonialism as a Culture of Terror', in B. Attwood and J. Arnold (eds), *Power, Knowledge and Aborigines* (Bundoora, Vic.: La Trobe University Press, 1992).

Nemiroff, D., R. Houle and C. Townshend-Gault, *Land, Spirit, Power: First Nations at the National Gallery of Canada* (Ottawa: National Gallery of Canada, 1992).

Nicks, T., 'Partnerships in Developing Cultural Resources: Lessons from the Task Force on Museums and First Peoples', *Culture*, 12:1 (1992), 87–94.

[265]

Peacock, S., *The Great Farini: The High-Wire Life of William Hunt* (Toronto: Penguin, 1995).

Posel, D., *The Making of Apartheid, 1948–1961: Conflict and Compromise* (Oxford: Oxford University Press, 1991).

Rassool, R. and L. Witz, 'The 1952 Jan van Riebeeck Tercentenary Festival: Constructing and Contesting Public National History in South Africa', *Journal of African History*, 34 (1993), 447–68.

Riegl, A., 'The Modern Cult of Monuments: Its Character and Origins' (translated by K. Foster and D. Ghirardo), *Oppositions*, 25 (fall, 1982), 21–51.

Robertson, J., *The Captain Cook Myth* (Sydney: Angus & Robertson, 1981).

Rose, D., 'Rupture and the Ethics of Care in Colonised Space', in T. Bonyhady and T. Griffiths (eds), *Prehistory to Politics: John Mulvaney, the Humanities and the Public Intellectual* (Melbourne: Melbourne University Press, 1996).

Rothenburger, M., *The Chilcotin War* (Langley, BC: Mr Paperback, 1978).

Russell, L. (ed.), *Colonial Frontiers, Indigenous-European Encounters in Settler Societies* (Manchester: Manchester University Press, 2001).

Salmon, E. and A. A. Longden, *The Literature and Art of the Empire*, British Empire series, general editor H. Gunn (London: W. Collins Sons & Co., 1924).

Salmond, A., *Two Worlds: First Meetings Between Maori and Europeans* (Auckland: Viking, 1991).

Sanders, M., *Complicities: The Intellectual and Apartheid* (Durham, NC: Duke University Press, 2002).

Skotnes, P., *Miscast: Negotiating the Presence of the Bushmen* (Cape Town: University of Cape Town Press, 1996).

Stasiulis, D. and N. Yuval-Davis (eds), *Unsettling Settler Societies: Articulations of Gender, Race, Ethnicity and Class* (London, Thousand Oaks, CA, and New Delhi: Sage, 1995).

Stone, R. J. C., *The Father and His Gift: John Logan Campbell's Later Years* (Auckland: Auckland University Press, 1987).

Tapsell, P., *Pukaki: A Comet Returns* (Auckland: Reed, 2000).

Tapsell, P., 'The Flight of Pareraututu', *Journal of the Polynesian Society*, 106:4 (December 1997), 323–74.

Thomas, N., *Discoveries: The Voyages of Captain Cook* (London: Penguin, 2003).

Thomas, N. and D. Losche (eds), *Double Vision: Art Histories and Colonial Histories in the Pacific* (Cambridge: Cambridge University Press, 1999).

Vahed, G., 'Uprooting and Rerooting: Culture, Religion and Community among Indentured Muslim Migrants in Colonial Natal, 1860–1911', *South African Historical Journal*, 45 (November 2001), 191–222.

Walzer, M., *Exodus and Revolution* (New York: Basic Books, 1985).

Warnke, M., *Political Landscapes: The Art History of Nature* (London: Reaktion, 1994).

Wilmsen, E. N., *Land Filled with Flies: A Political Economy of the Kalahari* (Chicago and London: University of Chicago Press, 1989).

Witz, L., *Apartheid's Festival* (Bloomington: Indiana University Press, 2003).

INDEX

Note: Literary and art works are found under the authors'/artists' names. Page numbers relating to illustrations appear in italics and those to definitions of Maori words in bold.

EU authorised representative for GPSR:
Easy Access System Europe, Mustamäe tee 50,
10621 Tallinn, Estonia
gpsr.requests@easproject.com

www.ingramcontent.com/pod-product-compliance
Lightning Source LLC
Chambersburg PA
CBHW060449290526
45791CB00001B/45